The baby names almanac

2011

Emily Larson

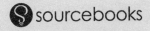

sourcebooks

Published by Sourcebooks, Inc.
P.O. Box 4410, Naperville, Illinois 60567-4410
(630) 961-3900
Fax: (630) 961-2168
www.sourcebooks.com

Library of Congress Cataloging-in-Publication Data

Larson, Emily.
  The 2011 baby names almanac / by Emily Larson.
    p. cm.
  1. Names, Personal—Dictionaries. I. Title.
CS2377.L38 2010
929.4'4--dc22

                          2010039345

          Printed and bound in Canada.
            WC 10 9 8 7 6 5 4 3 2 1

Contents

Introduction   v

Inside the Popularity Charts   1

What's Hot (or Not) Today
(And What Will—and Won't!—Be Tomorrow)   27

Girls' Names   59

Boys' Names   211

So, you've got a baby to name.

As if preparing for the arrival of the baby isn't enough, you're dealing with all the pressure of figuring out what, exactly, to call the little bundle of joy. It can be stressful to find a name that will do justice to the hope you have for your child.

After all, names influence first impressions. They can trigger great—or unpleasant—nicknames. They can affect your child's self-esteem. They can be a tangible, lasting link to a family legacy.

But let's not forget that they can be fun. And that's what this book is all about.

Remember *The Old Farmer's Almanac*, which comes out annually as a guide to each year's trends, forecasts, and hot spots? Aimed at farmers, of course, the book provides a way to put the year into context, to navigate the shifting seasons, and to understand all the factors swirling in the atmosphere.

The 2011 Baby Names Almanac aims to be a similar lifeline for parents. With a finger on the pulse of pop culture and an ear to the ground of what's hip, new, and relevant, this book offers you an instant, idiosyncratic snapshot of how the world today is shaping what you may want to name your child tomorrow.

Jam-packed with information and ideas, plus thousands of names to browse, this book analyzes the most recent trends and fads in baby naming, offering up forecasts and predictions. You'll find our take on questions like these (and much more!):

- Which cutting-edge names are on the rise?
- Which popular names are on the decline?
- What influence do celebrities have on names?

- *Names in music:* Has **Miley** peaked? Is **Taylor** now exclusively a girl's name?
- *Names in movies:* Could you name a kid **Pandora**?
- *Names in sports:* Is **Peyton** over? Will **Rooney** surge? And what's so great about **Jacoby**?

- How many babies get the most popular name, anyway?
- Which letter do most girls' names start with? How about boys' names?
- What are the most popular "gender-neutral" names today—and which gender uses each name more often? (If you name your daughter **Harley**, will she find herself playing with lots of other little girls named Harley—or little boys instead?)
- How can you take a trend and turn it into a name you love?

We understand that sometimes this information on trends and popularity is hard to digest, so we've created some easy-to-visualize graphics. Turn to page 4, for example, to see a map of the United States showing where **Isabella** reigns and where little **Jayden** is king.

And what baby name book would be complete without the names? Flip to page 59 to begin browsing through more than 20,000 names, including entries for the most popular names for girls and boys as reported by the Social Security Administration (www.ssa.gov/OACT/babynames).

A little bit of a mishmash and a screenshot of the world today, *The 2011 Baby Names Almanac* is like no other book out there. Stuffed with ideas on what's hip and hot and how you can take a trend and turn it into a name you love, this book is your all-in-one guide to baby names now.

The Top 10

Let's start with the most popular names in the country. Ranked by the Social Security Administration (SSA), these names are released around Mother's Day each year. (The top 10 names get the most attention, but you may also hear about the top 100. The total number of names widely reported is 1,000.) In 2009 the top 10 names were similar—but not identical to—the top 10 for 2008. **Emma** slid from first to second, unseated by the mighty **Isabella**. (We're pretty sure that has more than a little bit to do with the *Twilight* series!) And you know **Jayden** hasn't peaked yet, because it climbed into the top 10 for the first time in 2009 (in 2000, it was way down at 194). Here's a quick comparison of 2009 and 2008.

2009 Girls	2008 Girls	2009 Boys	2008 Boys
1. Isabella	1. Emma	1. Jacob	1. Jacob
2. Emma	2. Isabella	2. Ethan	2. Michael
3. Olivia	3. Emily	3. Michael	3. Ethan
4. Sophia	4. Madison	4. Alexander	4. Joshua
5. Ava	5. Ava	5. William	5. Daniel
6. Emily	6. Olivia	6. Joshua	6. Alexander
7. Madison	7. Sophia	7. Daniel	7. Anthony
8. Abigail	8. Abigail	8. Jayden	8. William
9. Chloe	9. Elizabeth	9. Noah	9. Christopher
10. Mia	10. Chloe	10. Anthony	10. Matthew

Just How Many Isabellas Are There, Anyway?

Sure, these names are popular, but what does that mean? Well, it seems that new parents are increasingly looking for off-the-beaten-path names for their little ones, and it shows. According to the SSA, the top 1,000 names represent 73.09 percent of all babies born and named in the United States in 2009—a significant drop from the 77.84 percent recorded in 2000.

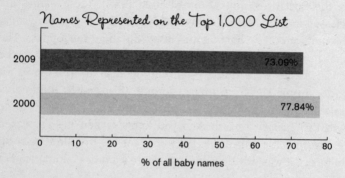

Names Represented on the Top 1,000 List

Although parents of either gender have always been looking beyond the top 1,000, parents of boys are more likely to pick a name in that mix—79.03 percent of boys' names are represented on the top 1,000 list, while only 66.86 percent of girls' names are.

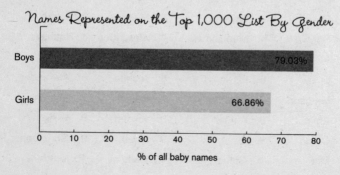

Names Represented on the Top 1,000 List By Gender

Plus, although it may seem like you know a zillion people with daughters named **Madison** or **Ava**, the most popular names are actually bestowed upon a relatively small number of babies each year. For example, in 2009 only 1 percent of all male babies born in the United States (that's 20,858 little guys total) got the most popular name, **Jacob**. There are slightly more girls (22,067 total) with the most popular name, **Isabella**, but even that's only 1.12 percent of all girls born. Only a fifth of the Jacob total—4,134 babies—were given the 100th most popular name, **Kyle**. The number of babies with the number 1 name is dropping swiftly—back in 1999, the first year Jacob hit number 1, more than 35,000 boys got that name, which is more than 15,000 additional babies compared to 2009. And back in 1965, 4.28 percent of all male babies (a staggering 81,041 tots) were named **Michael**, the most popular name of that year. So if you've got your heart set on naming your son **Ethan** but you're worried that he'll be surrounded by Ethans wherever he goes, take heart!

> *Mary, Mary Quite Contrary*
>
> **Mary** has been the most frequent number 1 girls' name over the past 100 years, appearing in the top spot 46 times. For boys? It's **Michael**, topping the charts 44 times.

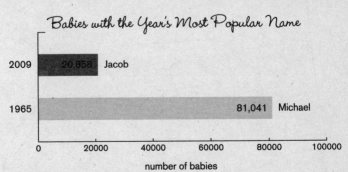

Babies with the Year's Most Popular Name

Year	Number of babies	Name
2009	20,858	Jacob
1965	81,041	Michael

number of babies

What's Popular in My State?

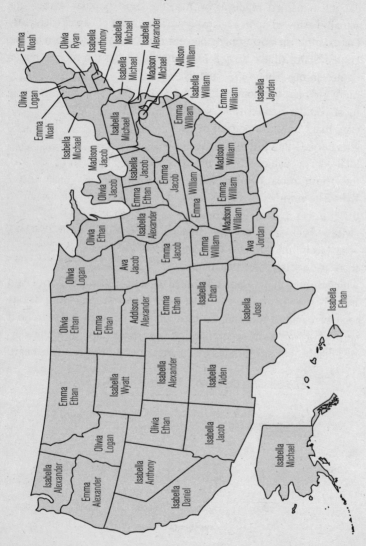

It's interesting to see how some names are more popular in certain states than in others. For example, **Landon** ranks 36th nationally for boys, but in Louisiana it's the third most popular name. Likewise, **Angel** ranks third among California's baby boys, but only 37th in the nation.

The following chart lists the top five names for girls and boys for each of the 50 states, and it also shows the actual number of births for each of those names in each state. Check out how many girl babies got the number 1 name in Wyoming (**Isabella**, 36) compared to the number of girl babies with the same name in California (3,127)

Top Five Names by State

State	Girl	Births	Boy	Births
Alabama	Emma	336	William	507
	Madison	312	James	341
	Isabella	270	Jacob	320
	Ava	252	Jackson	305
	Anna	231	John	304
Alaska	Isabella	57	Michael	58
	Sophia	46	Ethan	56
	Olivia	44	Logan	49
	Abigail	43	Samuel	49
	Ava	41	Elijah	47
Arizona	Isabella	536	Jacob	490
	Sophia	411	Alexander	478
	Emma	365	Daniel	478
	Mia	360	Angel	471
	Emily	302	Anthony	455

State	Girl	Births	Boy	Births
Arkansas	Emma	181	William	217
	Madison	177	Jacob	197
	Addison	176	Ethan	186
	Isabella	162	Joshua	173
	Ava	141	Jayden	163
California	Isabella	3,127	Daniel	3,375
	Sophia	2,639	Anthony	3,068
	Emily	2,523	Angel	2,990
	Mia	2,098	Jacob	2,933
	Samantha	1,821	Alexander	2,861
Colorado	Isabella	347	Alexander	339
	Olivia	318	Jacob	317
	Sophia	258	Noah	308
	Abigail	249	William	299
	Emma	239	Benjamin	281
Connecticut	Isabella	274	Michael	256
	Olivia	236	Ryan	252
	Sophia	224	Alexander	240
	Ava	219	Matthew	230
	Emma	189	Jayden	229
Delaware	Isabella	70	Alexander	69
	Olivia	58	Michael	66
	Sophia	58	James	63
	Abigail	51	Jayden	63
	Ava	50	Ethan	60
District of Columbia	Allison	41	William	83
	Sophia	40	Michael	69
	Ashley	35	James	67
	Katherine	34	Alexander	64
	Abigail	33	Daniel	58

State	Girl	Births	Boy	Births
Florida	Isabella	1,698	Jayden	1,323
	Sophia	1,142	Michael	1,157
	Emma	864	Joshua	1,138
	Emily	822	Jacob	1,086
	Olivia	822	Anthony	1,080
Georgia	Madison	646	William	882
	Isabella	550	Christopher	703
	Emma	521	Joshua	699
	Olivia	487	James	639
	Ava	477	Jayden	635
Hawaii	Isabella	81	Ethan	85
	Sophia	65	Noah	76
	Mia	50	Jayden	64
	Ava	48	Joshua	63
	Chloe	45	Elijah	61
Idaho	Olivia	117	Logan	110
	Emma	110	Jacob	104
	Isabella	91	Ethan	102
	Sophia	89	William	98
	Addison	86	Wyatt	94
Illinois	Isabella	904	Alexander	994
	Olivia	793	Daniel	835
	Sophia	718	Jacob	831
	Emma	685	Michael	767
	Emily	649	Anthony	744
Indiana	Emma	490	Ethan	493
	Olivia	463	Noah	435
	Isabella	450	Jacob	419
	Ava	437	Logan	398
	Addison	379	Elijah	395

State	Girl	Births	Boy	Births
Iowa	Ava	214	Jacob	206
	Olivia	210	Ethan	202
	Emma	204	Carter	197
	Isabella	185	Noah	192
	Addison	170	William	178
Kansas	Emma	216	Ethan	202
	Isabella	184	William	189
	Ava	181	Jacob	184
	Olivia	172	Alexander	174
	Abigail	164	Noah	173
Kentucky	Emma	328	Jacob	425
	Isabella	299	William	403
	Madison	279	James	329
	Olivia	277	Ethan	312
	Abigail	271	Noah	298
Louisiana	Ava	310	Jayden	289
	Emma	292	Ethan	285
	Isabella	275	Landon	266
	Madison	261	Joshua	264
	Olivia	236	Noah	247
Maine	Emma	103	Noah	98
	Olivia	99	Logan	88
	Isabella	84	Jacob	79
	Abigail	79	Owen	78
	Madison	78	Aiden	73
Maryland	Madison	334	Michael	388
	Olivia	331	Jayden	346
	Ava	287	Joshua	342
	Isabella	283	Ethan	335
	Emma	267	William	334

State	Girl	Births	Boy	Births
Massachusetts	Olivia	512	Ryan	484
	Isabella	511	Jacob	468
	Sophia	424	William	460
	Ava	418	Michael	455
	Emma	398	Matthew	420
Michigan	Olivia	654	Jacob	706
	Isabella	634	Ethan	594
	Ava	617	Logan	539
	Emma	587	Noah	532
	Madison	498	Aiden	521
Minnesota	Olivia	403	Logan	390
	Ava	363	Benjamin	369
	Emma	340	William	355
	Sophia	337	Ethan	350
	Isabella	328	Jacob	342
Mississippi	Madison	235	William	248
	Emma	181	Jayden	232
	Addison	160	James	227
	Ava	142	Christopher	220
	Anna	129	Joshua	184
Missouri	Emma	428	Jacob	391
	Olivia	423	Ethan	389
	Isabella	409	William	381
	Ava	351	Jackson	372
	Madison	349	Logan	361
Montana	Emma	69	Ethan	60
	Isabella	61	Wyatt	55
	Olivia	54	Logan	53
	Ava	51	Landon	49
	Madison	48	James	48

State	Girl	Births	Boy	Births
Nebraska	Addison	126	Alexander	141
	Isabella	117	Carter	127
	Ava	115	Noah	127
	Olivia	114	William	121
	Emma	108	Jacob	119
Nevada	Isabella	236	Anthony	219
	Sophia	154	Jacob	180
	Emma	132	Daniel	174
	Olivia	130	Michael	172
	Emily	122	Alexander	169
New Hampshire	Olivia	100	Logan	102
	Isabella	88	Jacob	93
	Ava	87	Liam	86
	Emma	86	Aiden	80
	Abigail	77	Ryan	78
New Jersey	Isabella	743	Michael	803
	Olivia	562	Matthew	708
	Sophia	542	Anthony	665
	Ava	515	Jayden	648
	Emily	486	Ryan	647
New Mexico	Isabella	160	Aiden	138
	Olivia	89	Noah	131
	Mia	88	Joshua	129
	Nevaeh	82	Jacob	127
	Sophia	82	Gabriel	125
New York	Isabella	1,390	Michael	1,697
	Sophia	1,183	Jayden	1,463
	Olivia	1,182	Matthew	1,438
	Emma	1,064	Ethan	1,356
	Emily	1,049	Daniel	1,345

State	Girl	Births	Boy	Births
North Carolina	Emma	583	William	784
	Madison	571	Jacob	665
	Isabella	567	Christopher	635
	Ava	533	Noah	621
	Abigail	469	Joshua	617
North Dakota	Olivia	63	Ethan	60
	Ava	61	Logan	59
	Emma	59	Jack	48
	Ella	50	Carter	47
	Isabella	47	Jacob	46
Ohio	Isabella	823	Jacob	825
	Emma	802	Noah	765
	Olivia	789	Ethan	756
	Ava	776	Logan	718
	Madison	673	William	683
Oklahoma	Isabella	243	Ethan	240
	Emma	238	Jacob	216
	Addison	214	Noah	216
	Madison	195	William	204
	Abigail	191	Joshua	197
Oregon	Emma	236	Alexander	242
	Isabella	228	Logan	205
	Olivia	227	Jacob	198
	Emily	203	Daniel	194
	Sophia	190	Ethan	190
Pennsylvania	Isabella	882	Michael	803
	Olivia	798	Jacob	800
	Ava	782	Ethan	732
	Emma	761	Logan	725
	Sophia	723	Matthew	703

State	Girl	Births	Boy	Births
Rhode Island	Isabella	89	Anthony	80
	Olivia	82	Jayden	79
	Sophia	78	Logan	76
	Ava	74	Jacob	73
	Emma	72	Michael	73
South Carolina	Emma	280	William	413
	Madison	266	Jayden	292
	Isabella	243	Christopher	286
	Olivia	224	James	284
	Abigail	200	Jacob	281
South Dakota	Emma	59	Ethan	72
	Ava	58	Noah	71
	Isabella	51	Gavin	55
	Sophia	51	Logan	55
	Alexis	49	Jackson	54
Tennessee	Emma	457	William	639
	Madison	436	Jacob	450
	Isabella	395	Joshua	432
	Olivia	373	Noah	432
	Abigail	359	Ethan	431
Texas	Isabella	2,076	Jose	2,257
	Emily	1,712	Daniel	1,986
	Mia	1,611	Jacob	1,983
	Emma	1,460	Angel	1,858
	Sophia	1,443	Christopher	1,855
Utah	Olivia	260	Ethan	287
	Emma	222	William	284
	Abigail	217	Jacob	235
	Brooklyn	202	Isaac	228
	Lily	187	James	208

State	Girl	Births	Boy	Births
Vermont	Emma	38	Noah	46
	Ava	32	William	43
	Isabella	32	Owen	40
	Madison	31	Logan	37
	Sophia	31	Aiden	34
Virginia	Isabella	473	William	598
	Madison	459	Jacob	529
	Emma	444	Michael	493
	Olivia	441	Noah	493
	Abigail	422	Ethan	492
Washington	Isabella	451	Alexander	443
	Olivia	423	Jacob	419
	Sophia	423	Ethan	415
	Emma	386	William	413
	Abigail	325	Daniel	386
West Virginia	Madison	147	Jacob	156
	Isabella	146	Hunter	139
	Emma	136	Ethan	129
	Alexis	121	Noah	127
	Emily	109	Aiden	122
Wisconsin	Olivia	362	Ethan	370
	Isabella	357	Jacob	364
	Emma	346	Noah	362
	Ava	337	Logan	358
	Sophia	311	Mason	346
Wyoming	Isabella	36	Wyatt	42
	Madison	35	William	34
	Ava	31	Aiden	33
	Emma	30	Jacob	33
	Alexis	28	Mason	31

What Joined—and Dropped Off—the Hot 100 in 2009?

One of the easiest ways to spot name trends is to watch what joins the hot 100 and what drops off. For the (young) ladies, several new names joined in 2009: **Serenity**, **Mya**, **Molly**, **Khloe** (Kardashian, we bet! This name jumped the most places in 2008 and has now cracked the hot 100), **Eva**, and **Bella** (of course, *Twilight*!).

Another bunch dropped off the list: **Sara**, **Megan**, **Mary** (the girls' name that has been number 1 more often than any other name in the past 100 years, a total of 46 times!), **Jennifer** (another hugely popular name from yesteryear), **Isabel** (so close to **Isabella**, this year's number 1!), and **Gracie**. For the boys, **Parker**, **Oliver**, **Miguel**, and **Levi** joined the list, and here's a real shocker: the very similar-sounding names **Kaden**, **Jaden**, and **Caden**, plus **Brady**, fell off. Perhaps those "-aden" names got a little bit *too* popular for some people in 2009?

New to the Hot 100

Serenity	Parker
Mya	Oliver
Molly	Miguel
Khloe	Levi
Eva	
Bella	

Off the Hot 100

Sara	Kaden
Megan	Jaden
Mary	Caden
Jennifer	Brady
Isabel	
Gracie	

New to the Top 1,000 This Year

These names are fresh faces in the top 1,000 list this year. Some of them have appeared on the list

The boys' name Eden has appeared at number 902 for two years in a row.

in years past, but after falling off the charts, they're making a comeback. Odds are they'll keep moving up.

Girls

Vivienne:	532	Taraji:	881	River:	960
Bristol:	666	Ember:	885	Ivanna:	965
Leighton:	669	Evelynn:	899	Ayleen:	968
Milan:	775	Harlow:	902	Marleigh:	976
Brinley:	778	Alaya:	903	Kayleen:	981
Maliah:	800	Caydence:	905	Azariah:	985
Lylah:	828	Raelyn:	922	Reece:	987
Calleigh:	832	Aiyanna:	948	Cambria:	993
Adelynn:	843	Kamya:	956	Samiyah:	994
Rylan:	859	Charley:	949	Kloe:	998
Millie:	868	Kaelynn:	955	Lilyanna:	999

Boys

Archer:	679	Casen:	905	Mack:	975
Knox:	706	Westin:	934	Remy:	976
Sylas:	847	Hayes:	949	Maddux:	983
Kayson:	852	Maxx:	958	Zavion:	986
Jaxton:	855	Jaycob:	970	Cain:	987
Dilan:	875	Juelz:	972		
Camilo:	898	Kalel:	973		

Biggest Jumper: Analia

Perhaps due in part to the Telemundo show *El Rostro de Analia*, Analia zoomed onto the list this year. Not even on the top 1,000 in the last 20 years, it leaped at least 67 percent and more than 675 places to debut at 329.

How Do You Spell Aydin?

When you take into account that the name **Jayden** has ten spelling variations in the top 1,000 (see the list that follows), that means that this one name actually shows up on the list ten different times! We broke down the top 1,000 names for boys and girls this way, counting all the different spelling variations as one name, and we got some surprising results. Looking from that perspective, there aren't 1,000 unique names at all! We counted roughly 639 unique girls' names, and approximately 747 unique boys' names. The girls have fewer unique names, spelled in more ways, whereas parents of boys reach into a bigger pool of names. Let's take a look at some of the names with the most (or most interesting!) variations in the top 1,000.

Note: some of these names could be pronounced slightly differently from one another, but if they could also be pronounced the same as the main name on the list, we included them.

Boys

It's no surprise that the "-ayden" names (such as **Aiden**, **Jayden**, **Brayden**, and **Kaden**) offer lots of spelling variety, but the changes in **Tristan** and **Kason** struck us as a little more unusual.

Aiden	Jayden	Kaden	Brayden
1. Aiden	1. Jayden	1. Kaden	1. Brayden
2. Aidan	2. Jaden	2. Caden	2. Braden
3. Ayden	3. Jaiden	3. Kayden	3. Braydon
4. Aden	4. Jaydon	4. Cayden	4. Braeden
5. Aaden	5. Jadon	5. Kaiden	5. Braiden
6. Adan	6. Jaeden	6. Caiden	6. Bradyn
7. Aydan	7. Jaydin	7. Kaeden	7. Braedon
8. Aydin	8. Jadyn	8. Kadyn	
9. Aidyn	9. Jaidyn	9. Kadin	
10. Aedan	10. Jaydan		

Cameron
1. Cameron
2. Kameron
3. Camron
4. Camren
5. Camryn
6. Kamron
7. Kamryn

Tristan
1. Tristan
2. Tristen
3. Triston
4. Tristin
5. Tristian
6. Trystan

Giovanni
1. Giovanni
2. Giovani
3. Giovanny
4. Jovanni
5. Jovanny
6. Geovanni

Devin
1. Devin
2. Devon
3. Davin
4. Deven
5. Devan
6. Devyn

Kason
1. Kason
2. Cason
3. Kasen
4. Kayson
5. Casen

Jackson
1. Jackson
2. Jaxon
3. Jaxson
4. Jaxton
5. Jaxen

Connor
1. Connor
2. Conner
3. Conor
4. Konner
5. Konnor

Top 643 Names, Not Top 1,000

Only 64 percent of the top 1,000 girls' names are unique names.
Only 75 percent of the top 1,000 boys' names are unique names.
The rest of the names are spelling variations of those names.
Here are the three names with the most spelling variations:

Boys
1. Aiden
2. Jayden
3. Kaden

Girls
1. Kaylee
2. Carly
3. Kaelyn, Hailey, Madelyn

Girls

Some of these seemed more obvious—**Kaitlyn**, for one—but others, like **Carly**, surprised us with their robust variety.

Kaylee
1. Kaylee
2. Kayleigh
3. Caylee
4. Kailey
5. Kaylie
6. Kaleigh
7. Kailee
8. Calleigh
9. Caleigh
10. Kayley

Carly
1. Carly
2. Carlee
3. Karlee
4. Carlie
5. Carley
6. Karly
7. Karley
8. Karlie
9. Karli

Kaelyn
1. Kaelyn
2. Kaylin
3. Kailyn
4. Kaylynn
5. Kaylen
6. Kaylyn
7. Cailyn
8. Kaelynn

Hailey
1. Hailey
2. Haley
3. Haylee
4. Hayley
5. Hailee
6. Haleigh
7. Haylie
8. Hayleigh

Madelyn
1. Madelyn
2. Madeline
3. Madilyn
4. Madeleine
5. Madalyn
6. Madelynn
7. Madalynn
8. Madilynn

Abigail
1. Abigail
2. Abby
3. Abbigail
4. Abbie
5. Abbey
6. Abagail
7. Abigale

Kaitlyn
1. Kaitlyn
2. Katelyn
3. Caitlyn
4. Caitlin
5. Katelynn
6. Kaitlin
7. Kaitlynn

Lilyana
1. Liliana
2. Lilliana
3. Lilyana
4. Lilianna
5. Lillianna
6. Lilyanna

Adeline
1. Adeline
2. Adalyn
3. Adelyn
4. Adalynn
5. Adelynn

Aaliyah
1. Aaliyah
2. Aliyah
3. Aleah
4. Aliya
5. Alia

Eliana
1. Eliana
2. Elliana
3. Iliana
4. Elianna
5. Aliana

Jaelyn
1. Jaelyn
2. Jaylynn
3. Jaylin
4. Jaylyn
5. Jaylen

Jasmine
1. Jasmine
2. Jazmin
3. Jazmine
4. Jasmin
5. Jazmyn

Allison
1. Allison
2. Alison
3. Allyson
4. Alyson
5. Allisson

Emily
1. Emily
2. Emely
3. Emilee
4. Emilie
5. Emmalee

Laila
1. Layla
2. Laila
3. Leyla
4. Lailah
5. Laylah

Makayla
1. Makayla
2. Mikayla
3. Michaela
4. Mikaela
5. Mckayla

Natalie
1. Natalie
2. Nataly
3. Nathalie
4. Natalee
5. Nathaly

What Do the Most Popular Names Start With?

You may find it surprising, but only three of the names in the top 1,000 girl baby names for 2009 start with a *W*: **Wendy**, **Whitney**, and **Willow**. At the same time, you probably won't find it surprising that the most popular letter that girls' names start with is *A* (162 of the top 1,000), with *M* as a close second with 106 names. Among the boys' names, 118 start with *J*, and *A* names comprise 90 of the total 1,000 names. In 2008 there were no *U* names for girls in the top 1,000 (sorry, **Uma**). What a difference a year makes—in 2009 every single letter in the alphabet has at least one popular boy and girl name, as **Unique** hopped back onto the chart (at 929) for the first time in four years.

Gender-Neutral Options

Lots of names are popular for both boys and girls, but they're generally more popular for one gender than the other. Here's a list of names that appeared on both the boys' top 1,000 and the girls' top 1,000, plus how they ranked in 2009 for each gender. Some interesting trends here—despite the popularity of NFL quarterback Peyton Manning, **Payton/Peyton** are both more popular for girls! And two names are roughly given to equal numbers of boys and girls: **Hayden** and **Dakota**.

Spelling Matters!

If you're going to choose...

Skyler/Skylar: Skylar is the more popular choice for girls, Skyler for boys

Jayden, etc: Jayden is the most popular choice for boys. Jaden, Jadyn, Jaiden, and Jaidyn are all more popular for girls.

Casey/Kasey: Casey is the winner for boys, Kasey for girls

Reese/Reece: Reese is more popular for girls, Reece for boys

Nearly Equal

Name	Girl Rank	Boy Rank
Dakota	276	251
Hayden	131	91

More Popular for Girls

Name	Girl Rank	Boy Rank
Addison	12	866
Alexis	13	186
Ariel	206	556
Avery	32	223

Name	Girl Rank	Boy Rank
Bailey	85	941
Camryn	246	778
Eden	205	902
Emerson	321	437

Name	Girl Rank	Boy Rank
Emery	336	779
Finley	526	772
Harper	174	734
Jaden	101	538
Jadyn	452	804
Jaiden	171	562
Jaidyn	640	807
Jamie	308	669
Jordyn	124	712
Kamryn	291	946
Kasey	799	965
Kendall	133	600
London	121	517
Lyric	408	880

Name	Girl Rank	Boy Rank
Marley	149	790
Morgan	56	457
Payton	84	330
Peyton	43	147
Reagan	128	963
Reese	144	475
Riley	38	107
Rylee	116	796
Sage	396	761
Sidney	529	846
Skylar	185	497
Taylor	22	298
Teagan	274	648

More Popular for Boys

Name	Girl Rank	Boy Rank
Amari	484	300
Angel	176	37
Armani	766	552
Cameron	356	59
Casey	528	366
Charlie	616	274
Dylan	556	29
Devyn	969	868
Jayden	188	8
Jaylen	886	175

Name	Girl Rank	Boy Rank
Jaylin	618	175
Jessie	695	573
Jordan	150	45
Justice	557	428
Kamari	932	532
Kayden	441	138
Logan	453	17
Micah	818	118
Parker	502	96
Phoenix	720	367

Name	Girl Rank	Boy Rank
Quinn	486	258
Reece	987	431
River	960	448
Rory	937	756
Rowan	496	336

Name	Girl Rank	Boy Rank
Ryan	581	19
Rylan	859	195
Skyler	419	261
Zion	732	240

Which Names are Moving Up—and Falling Down—the Fastest?

The SSA compiles a list of names that have made the biggest moves when compared to their rank the previous year (assuming the name has made the top 500 at least once in the last two years). Some of these jumpers have obvious triggers, while the reasons for other jumps and declines are more open to interpretation. Take a look and see what you think.

40 Girls' Names Heating Up

Name	Number of Spots It Moved Up	Name	Number of Spots It Moved Up
Maliyah	342	Londyn	140
Isla	273	Kinsley	135
Caylee	251	Juliet	134
Kinley	214	Norah	132
Arabella	209	Emery	131
Adelyn	180	Annabella	130
Fernanda	165	Paisley	129
Adalyn	162	Addisyn	125
Malia	153	Harper	122

Name	Number of Spots It Moved Up	Name	Number of Spots It Moved Up
Yaretzi	119	Kennedi	89
Juliette	112	Braelyn	82
Penelope	106	Zariah	76
Brylee	103	Luna	75
Sasha	101	Lyla	72
Khloe	101	Izabella	71
Nathalie	99	Aurora	71
Journey	97	Presley	69
Mila	94	Alice	69
Willow	93	Amiyah	67
Brielle	93	Bella	64

40 Girls' Names Cooling Down

Name	Number of Spots It Moved Down	Name	Number of Spots It Moved Down
Marely	517	Cheyanne	104
Mylee	420	Kaitlin	104
Jaslene	294	Amari	96
Allisson	197	Cindy	95
Haylie	145	Asia	92
Lindsay	143	Nancy	90
Rachael	132	Taryn	86
Kimora	118	Denise	85
Kathleen	113	Shannon	83

Name	Number of Spots It Moved Down	Name	Number of Spots It Moved Down
Yasmin	81	Dana	64
Rihanna	76	Miley	61
Kiana	75	Karina	56
Hanna	74	Hailee	55
Heather	73	Diamond	53
Sandra	73	Erica	53
Gloria	67	Karla	53
Jaden	67	Kiley	53
Alessandra	66	Lesly	53
Claudia	66	Cynthia	52
Tori	65	Kayden	49

40 Boys' Names Heating Up

Name	Number of Spots It Moved Up	Name	Number of Spots It Moved Up
Cullen	297	Jasper	112
Jax	266	Brooks	109
King	248	Matteo	101
Emmett	215	Paxton	93
Colt	164	Zayden	89
Braylen	162	Ahmad	80
Jett	143	Mohamed	75
Kason	113	Aaden	71

Name	Number of Spots It Moved Up	Name	Number of Spots It Moved Up
Gunner	69	Silas	56
Waylon	67	Abram	56
Judah	66	Weston	54
Beckett	66	Romeo	54
Ryker	65	Bennett	53
Maximiliano	64	Byron	50
Jaxson	64	Warren	49
Everett	62	Easton	48
Jameson	60	August	45
Ryder	59	Emiliano	44
Leland	59	Terrance	43
Leon	58	Jaylin	43

40 Boys' Names Cooling Down

Name	Number of Spots It Moved Down	Name	Number of Spots It Moved Down
Alvin	133	Kane	66
Marc	106	Jermaine	65
Jonas	105	Quinton	65
Isiah	91	Shaun	65
Brett	80	Roy	63
Terry	77	Franklin	62
Brodie	69	Chad	56
Dorian	69	Payton	54

Name	Number of Spots It Moved Down
Jerry	52
Ricky	51
Triston	51
Ernesto	50
Javon	48
Alberto	47
Rodrigo	47
Nickolas	46
Damon	45
Issac	45
Jalen	45
Marvin	44

Name	Number of Spots It Moved Down
Lance	43
Taylor	42
Cory	41
Douglas	41
Joe	41
Morgan	41
Clayton	39
Maurice	38
Alfredo	36
Philip	36
Dayton	35
Jadon	35

What's Hot (or Not) Today (And What Will—and Won't!—Be Tomorrow)

Now that we've seen the state of baby names today, let's take a look at a snapshot of some interesting trends we've spotted, as well as some predictions as to what might play out on the playground sometime soon.

You'll notice that within some fads, certain names are on the rise, and certain names are on the decline, showing how trends are morphing over time (how Mary is fading as a popular religious name, for instance, but Nevaeh is skyrocketing.) We've also included some offbeat and unique ways to take each of these trends and find a name that really fits you and your family.

Trends Today

THE RISE OF SULLIVAN

The name **Sully** was on the lips of many in 2009, starting in January and ending with a bang in December.

On January 15, 2009, US Airways pilot Chesley "Sully" Sullenberger became a hero and a part of history by guiding the completely disabled jet he was flying to a safe landing in the Hudson River. All 155 passengers and crew members escaped the jet safely, and Sully was credited with saving those lives.

In December of the same year, the movie *Avatar* debuted and broke all existing box office records. The main character's name was already very popular (**Jake**), but his last name was...Sully! Another hero and another source of inspiration for baby names!

Now, not everyone wants to name their kid Sully, of course (in fact, it isn't even on the top 1,000 list), but Sullivan debuted on the list for the first time in 2002 at 991, and it's moved steadily, and sharply, upward ever since. Check out this brief history of a name poised to break out:

SULLY	
Year	Rank
2002	991
2003	955
2004	952
2005	927
2006	927
2007	732
2008	705
2009	652

NEW SUPERSTARS INSPIRING NAMES

An unexpected young superstar was launched in 2009—and for once, this one didn't come from the Disney machine. **Justin** Bieber, a Canadian teenager, started out by teaching himself to play many instruments, including the guitar and piano. His mom, seeing his great potential, uploaded some videos of his performances to YouTube, and before his sixteenth birthday, he became a major star. The name Justin has been on a downward slide since the beginning of the twenty-first century (from 19 down to 46), but we believe Bieber's popularity will result in a renewed interest in the name.

Another young star is poised to inspire lots of newborns' names in 2011—look out for the rise of **Kesha**. The singer, a Nashville native, has quickly established herself on the music scene after her first album debuted on the charts in 2010 at number 1. Expect to see her name debut on the 2010 top 1,000 as well! Kesha is a variation of **Keisha**, which was quite popular in the 1980s, ranking at 332 in 1986 but then dropping off the chart in 1999. There are many other popular variations of the name, such as **Keysha**, **Kesia**, **Keshia** (last ranked at 813 in 1991), **Keyshia**, and **Keesha**.

GIMME A V!

There's a really hot trend with the *v* sound in names, particularly for girls. **Ava** (number 5 in 2009), **Eve**, **Vivian**, and **Nevaeh** are trending upward for girls. And **Vivienne**, due no doubt to Angelina Jolie's daughter, debuted on the list at 532. Among the boys, it's more of a split, with **Vaughn**, **Giovanni**, and **Sullivan** trending up, and **Javon**, **Davian**, and **Kevin** trending a bit down. Here's a look at a sampling of names with that powerful *v* sound and how they've risen since 2000.

Girls' Names	2000 Rank	2009 Rank
Ava	180	5
Avery	176	32
Nevaeh*	–	34
Evelyn	150	39
Heaven	340	275
Genevieve	507	288
Vivienne	–	532
Evie	–	723
Maeve	777	591

*Heaven spelled backward

A dash means that the name did not make the list that year.

Ways to Make This Trend Your Own

Options still off the radar: Viveca, Lavinia, Divine, Vandie

Boys' Names	2010 Rank	2009 Rank
Giovanni	201	132
Devon	133	277
Everett	585	320
Oliver	305	98
Javion	949	606
Ivan	153	136
Davian	–	707
Maverick	865	543

Ways to Make This Trend Your Own
Options still off the radar: Vin, Vinson, Shavon, Daven

RELIGIOUS NAMES

Religious names have become quite a bit more popular in recent years, and the trend is reflected in the different kinds of religious names that are popular now versus years ago (prime example: Sarah is slightly down, but Heaven is up). Here's a look at some religious names and how they've changed in popularity over the past 15 years.

Girls' Names	1995 Rank	2009 Rank
Sarah	5	21
Nevaeh*	–	34
Trinity	662	74
Mary	40	102
Rebecca	28	132
Heaven	558	275
Eve	–	582

Girls' Names	1995 Rank	2009 Rank
Aisha	556	742

*Heaven spelled backward

Ways to Make This Trend Your Own
Options still off the radar: Khadija, Dinah, Seraphina

Boys' Names	1995 Rank	2009 Rank
Joshua	5	6
Daniel	9	7
Noah	100	9
Benjamin	31	20
Isaac	98	40
Adam	38	74
Moses	598	504
Muhammad	779	603
Messiah	–	663

Ways to Make This Trend Your Own
Options still off the radar: Aasif, Cain

DESTINATION NAMES

Ten years ago, naming a child after a location was quite unusual. But that was before celebrities started naming their kids **Brooklyn**, **Dakota**...you get the idea. Some location names were more popular ten years ago—**Chandler**, for example, was 151 in 1999 and ranks at 469 in 2009, which probably has less to do with the town in Arizona and more to do with a little show called *Friends* that was popular in the 1990s—but for the most part, naming tots after places is still a hot idea these days. Here are some place-names on the rise:

Girls' Names	1999 Rank	2009 Rank
Madison (Wisconsin)	7	7
Brooklyn (New York)	182	37
Savannah (Georgia)	42	40
Charlotte (North Carolina)	307	68
London (England)	919	121
Aurora (Illinois)	503	217
Paris (France)	465	412
Adelaide (Australia)	–	567
Ireland	–	821

Ways to Make This Trend Your Own

Options still off the radar: Orleans (New Orleans, Louisiana), Helena (Montana), Olympia (Washington), Juneau (Alaska), Valletta (Malta)

Boys' Names	1999 Rank	2009 Rank
Jackson (Mississippi)	83	25
Santiago (Chile)	403	130
Lincoln (Nebraska)	748	188
Phoenix (Arizona)	913	367
London (England)	–	517
Boston (Massachusetts)	–	540
Memphis	–	605

Ways to Make This Trend Your Own

Options still off the radar: Richmond (Virginia), Salem (Oregon), Montgomery (Alabama), Wellington (New Zealand), Dakar (Senegal)

NAMES FROM GREEK AND ROMAN MYTHOLOGY AND LITERATURE

When we say these names are old, we're not kidding. These names have been around for a long, long time...and while many girls' names are becoming more popular, the boys' names are surprisingly less popular (and perfect for someone looking for the cutting edge).

Girls' Names	1998 Rank	2009 Rank
Chloe	87	9
Phoebe	606	325
Paris	457	412
Daphne	757	476
Diana	83	165
Helen	349	389

Ways to Make This Trend Your Own

Options still off the radar: Artemis, Antigone, Aphrodite, Ariadne, Athena, Calliope, Cassandra, Circe, Cleopatra, Echo, Electra, Eurydice, Euterpe, Gaia, Halcyone, Ione, Iris, Juno, Lavinia, Maia, Medea, Minerva, Persephone, Psyche, Rhea, Selene, Thalia, Venus

Boys' Names	1998 Rank	2009 Rank
Alexander	22	4
Cassius	–	998
Jason	40	66
Marcus	96	123
Hector	185	204
Antony	832	984

Ways to Make This Trend Your Own

Options still off the radar: Achilles, Aeneas, Apollo, Cadmus, Dionysus, Endymion, Hercules, Hermes, Hyperion, Icarus, Janus, Mercury, Midas, Minos, Morpheus, Odysseus, Orion, Orpheus, Pegasus, Perseus, Prometheus, Ptolemy, Theseus, Vulcan, Zeus

A CORNUCOPIA OF PURITAN NAMES

Many names have remained popular for hundreds of years, such as **Emily**, **Olivia**, **Michael**, and **Matthew**. However, in recent years, names with a Puritan bent in particular have been all the rage. You probably know at least one **Ethan** or **Emma**—names that would be equally at home in 1700s Salem, Massachusetts, and on today's playgrounds. Here's a look at trends in Puritan names from this decade and the last.

Girls' Names	1995 Rank	2009 Rank
Abigail	36	8
Leah	103	28
Faith	172	80
Hope	193	233
Martha	305	682
Charity	496	876
Constance	748	–

Ways to Make This Trend Your Own

Options still off the radar: Honor, Mercy, Providence

Boys' Names	1995 Rank	2009 Rank
Caleb	54	31
Levi	158	88
Asher	929	165

Boys' Names	1995 Rank	2009 Rank
Silas	755	254
Tobias	722	506
Asa	799	553
Frederick	316	536
Hugh	806	988

Ways to Make This Trend Your Own

Options still off the radar: Ebenezer, Abner, Enoch, Sylas

NAMES ENDING WITH AN *N* SOUND

For years, parents have selected names ending with an *n* sound. It's not hard to see the appeal—they go well with both usual and unusual last names. Many have noted how many hot 100 boys' names rhyme with **Aiden (Jayden, Brayden, Caden)**, but there are countless other common names that end with that familiar, last-name-friendly consonant ending.

Girls' Names	2000 Rank	2009 Rank
Madison	3	7
Brooklyn	177	37
Evelyn	150	39
Peyton	168	43
Madelyn	126	59
Jocelyn	122	70
Payton	163	84
Vivian	272	164
Quinn	311	258
Kaylen	–	681

Ways to Make This Trend Your Own

Options still off the radar: Raelin, Avan, Jessamyn, Jean (while this name seems traditional, it hasn't appeared in the top 1,000 since 1994)

Boys' Names	2000 Rank	2009 Rank
Ethan	25	2
Jayden	194	8
Aiden	324	12
Logan	40	17
Nathan	30	24
Jackson	72	25
Landon	200	36
Brayden	199	47
Grayson	313	172
Jaylen	224	175
Anderson	781	288

Ways to Make This Trend Your Own

Options still off the radar: Runyan, Jameson, Ryman, Wilson

SHE'S NO LADY…SHE'S A PALINDROME

A number of fairly common girls' names are palindromes—words that are spelled the same backward and forward—but only one palindrome pops up in the boys' top 1,000: **Asa**. Of course, one of the most popular boys' names has a nickname that fits the bill: **Bob**, for **Robert**. Note that a popular twin combination, **Aidan** and **Nadia**, is a palindrome.

Name	2009 Rank
Ava	5
Hannah	23
Anna	29
Elle	442
Eve	582

Ways to Make This Trend Your Own
Options still off the radar: Aviva, Emme, Aja

LAST NAMES FIRST

We've already looked at gender-neutral names on page 20, and the surname as first name fad is a deeper twist on that. It's interesting that the top 10 names for both genders in 2009 were all "traditional" first names, considering last names as first names is perhaps one of the biggest trends of the past 10 years. Take a look at some of the more popular choices for boys and girls.

Girls' Names	2009 Rank
Peyton	43
Morgan	56
Mackenzie	77
Kennedy	114
Reagan	128
Kendall	133
Shelby	167
Macy	286
Ansley	658

Ways to Make This Trend Your Own

Options still off the radar: Golden, Kingsley, Sheridan, Easton, Curtis, Banfield, Robinson

Boys' Names	2009 Rank
Carter	50
Chase	61
Cooper	84
Maddox	180
Graham	262
Paxton	327
Beckett	413
Reed	422
Chandler	469
Nelson	522
Sullivan	652
Jensen	832

Ways to Make This Trend Your Own

Options still off the radar: Foster, Ford, Albee, Burroughs, Pelham, Wilder, Barnes

ERIN GO BRAGH!

Irish names have become very, very popular for boys, but interestingly enough, traditional Irish girls' names are dropping in popularity. Poor **Colleen**, which consistently ranked in the top 200 names from 1948 to 1993, has dropped like a stone since then (from 207 in 1994 to falling off the top 1,000 list entirely in 2007). The counterpoint to this is **Malachi**, a name that first appeared on the top 1,000 in 1987 ranked at 992. Since then, it's taken off in popularity, ranked at 167 in 2009.

Girls' Names	2000 Rank	2009 Rank
Erin	60	194
Kelly	111	260
Bridget	273	424
Kathleen	204	564
Eileen	627	810
Colleen	455	–

Ways to Make This Trend Your Own

Options still off the radar: Deirdre, Saoirse, Siobhan, Nuala

Boys' Names	2000 Rank	2009 Rank
Riley	109	107
Liam	140	49
Malachi	351	167
Declan	545	308
Finn	834	343
Seamus	827	813

Ways to Make This Trend Your Own

Options still off the radar: Conan, Daire, Lorcan

Despite Nicole Kidman and Keith Urban naming their little one **Sunday**, the name hasn't yet popped up on the top 1,000 (no days of the week are represented). In fact, names of seasons (**Autumn**, **Summer**) and months (**April**) are trending down or not even on the radar (although Mad Men's January Jones may provoke a spike soon!). The big exceptions are **June**, which debuted on the list at 867 in 2008 and zoomed to 662 in 2009, and **August**, which jumped from 613 in 2000 to 433 in 2009.

TRADITIONAL VS. MODERN

It's really something when a modern interpretation of a name overtakes the traditional version. Here's a great example: in 2009 the modern **Makayla** was the 44th most popular name for girls, while the name's traditional spelling, **Michaela**, was 370th. You'll see that the girl names lean toward this trend, whereas parents of boys often prefer the traditional spelling. Here's a look at the rising popularity of some new takes on the names of yesteryear. (The 2009 rankings are listed next to each variation.)

Girls' Names	
Traditional Spelling	**Modern Spelling**
Michaela (370)	Makayla (44)
Madeline (64)	Madelyn (59)
Caitlin (266)	Kaitlyn (67)
Layla (45)	Laila (135)

Ways to Make This Trend Your Own
Options still off the radar: Katheryn/Catheryn (Katherine/Catherine), Cathrina (Katrina), Avah (Ava), Emalee (Emily)

Boys' Names	
Traditional Spelling	**Modern Spelling**
Aiden (12)	Ayden (85)
Jackson (25)	Jaxon (126)
Jonathan (30)	Johnathan (205)
Cameron (59)	Kameron (275)

Ways to Make This Trend Your Own
Options still off the radar: Etan (Ethan), Noa (Noah), Rian (Ryan), Cayleb (Caleb)

PRESIDENTIAL PEDIGREES

One of the hottest trends in names these days is presidential surnames, at least the ones that differ from already popular names (**Madison**, **Taylor**). Other presidential options are popping up everywhere—even **Lincoln** has had a meteoric rise from 710th place in 2000 to 188th in 2009. Some probably won't ever catch on, however—it's hard to imagine a playdate with little **Coolidge** and her brother **Nixon**, isn't it?

You might also want to consider changing up the spelling to create your own spin on this trend. For example, if you don't want to name your darling **Reagan** because your politics are more to the left, consider **Regan** (2009 rank: 685) or even **Teagan** (2009 rank: 321).

Girls' Names	2000 Rank	2009 Rank
Madison (James)	3	7
Taylor (Zachary)	10	22
Kennedy (John F.)	139	114
Reagan (Ronald)	286	128

Ways to Make This Trend Your Own
Options still off the radar: McKinley (William), Monroe (James), Carter (Jimmy)

Boys' Names	2000 Rank	2009 Rank
Jackson (Andrew)	72	25
Tyler (John)	10	28
Grant (Ulysses)	123	144
Lincoln (Honest Abe)	710	188
Harrison (Benjamin)	184	242
Pierce (Franklin)	498	481

Boys' Names	2000 Rank	2009 Rank
Jefferson (Thomas)	716	587
Wilson (Woodrow)	526	539

Ways to Make This Trend Your Own

Options still off the radar: Roosevelt (pick your fave!), Harding (Warren), Cleveland (Grover)

Options trending down: Clinton (William)

Sarah Palin Names

The former governor of Alaska has used some pretty unusual names for her children (and her daughter Bristol continued this with her own son, Tripp), and those names have steadily moved upward on the charts:

- Bristol (entered the baby girl charts this year at 666)
- Piper (jumped 71 percent since 2000 to a high of 147 this year)
- Willow (jumped 59 percent since 2000 to a high of 315 this year)
- Tripp (entered baby boy charts at 930 in 2008, stands at 671 this year)

Levi, the father of Bristol's son, Tripp, is also on the rise. The other unusual boys' names associated with Palin's family (Trigg and Track) haven't cracked the top 1,000 yet...but expect to see them soon.

NATURE NAMES

Are you a nature lover? Are you planning to make your little one a part of your outdoorsy lifestyle? Despite perhaps a rise in eco-consciousness, many of these nature names are in free fall. Does that mean they're ripe for the picking?

Girls' Names	2000 Rank	2009 Rank
Daisy	141	153
Violet	738	141
Summer	145	175
Sierra	53	198
Rose	299	352

Ways to Make This Trend Your Own

Options still off the radar: Blossom, Evergreen, Lake, Everest, Skye, Azalea

Boys' Names	2000 Rank	2009 Rank
Hunter	35	56
River	612	448
Fisher	–	841
Stone	722	994

Ways to Make This Trend Your Own

Options still off the radar: Ranger, Trail, Trek, Forest, Cliff, Scout

WHAT'S GOING ON WITH MACKENZIE?

The girls' name **Mackenzie** suddenly debuted on the top 1,000 in 1976, which isn't all that surprising considering that Mackenzie Phillips was one of the stars of *One Day at a Time*, a longtime TV hit that debuted in December of 1975. What's interesting, though, is that after 15 years of languishing in the lower to middle part of the list, Mackenzie began to take off in popularity in 1990, going from 247 in that year to its present ranking of 77. It's been solidly in the hot 100 since 1995, and several of its variants are incredibly popular today as well. Take a look at how they stack up:

Name	2009 Rank
Mackenzie/MacKenzie	77
Mckenzie/McKenzie	155
Makenzie	172
Mckenna/McKenna	213
Makenna	243
Kinsley	428
Kinley	451
Kenley	659
Mckinley/McKinley	760
Makena	950

ENDS WITH AN -O

Many boys' names with Spanish or Italian heritage end in an -o suffix, which can go beautifully with countless last names. Plus, they're O-so-romantic! Imagine calling for little **Francisco** or **Romeo** across the playground—all the other moms will swoon! Madonna's young son **Rocco** (2009 rank: 389, a steady climber since 2001) is an example of this trend.

It's an interesting twist that there aren't many popular girls' names ending in -o, and the ones that are fairly common might be nicknames for another name (**Coco**, **Cleo**, or **Margo**, for example).

Here's another tip: they make fantastic middle names too.

Name	2009 Rank
Alejandro	121
Eduardo	128
Santiago	130

Name	2009 Rank
Leonardo	164
Ricardo	168
Fernando	178
Francisco	181
Mario	198
Sergio	224
Mateo	229
Marco	241
Julio	304
Emilio	311
Pablo	344
Gustavo	362
Rodrigo	373
Mauricio	383
Rocco	389
Hugo	409
Orlando	410
Romeo	411
Alfredo	423
Milo	451
Ernesto	461
Guillermo	501

Ways to Make This Trend Your Own

Options still off the radar: Carmelo, Cosmo (remember Kramer from Seinfeld?), Dario, Stasio, Viggo

Predictions: Hot Names

Okay, so you've read about the trends. But what other names might be taking off in the near future? Here's some of what we think could be gaining ground.

GIRLS

It's tempting to think that **Miley** is over, and the name did slide some sixty places this year, from 128 to 189. But it's not going away anytime soon. The name wasn't even on the chart before 2007, when it debuted at 278 (the same year Miley Cyrus's first solo album was released). It more than doubled in popularity the next year, coming in at 128 in 2008. Despite the name's slip in 2009, Miley's got legs to carry it for a long time.

First Children

Presidential children are always a big inspiration for names (**Chelsea**, anyone?), and this year is no different: we think **Sasha** will be a serious player in 2011. Often a nickname for **Alexandra** or **Natasha** among girls, in Russia Sasha is a nickname for boys named **Alexander**. Sasha is already popular in the United States (at 261 in 2009 and moving steadily upward on the list for the past 10 years), and we think young Sasha Obama is increasing its cred for 2011. Sasha's sister led the name **Malia** to leap in popularity 44 percent to number 192 in 2009. Perhaps even more notable is Malia's variant **Maliyah**, which soared in popularity 53 percent in 2009 to 296, up from 638 in 2008. Look for Malia and Maliyah to continue their ascent in 2011 as well.

Variants of Sasha: Natasha, Alexandra, Sascha, Saskia, Sasheen
Variants of Malia: Maliyah, Malea, Maleah, Maleia, Melia

Pandora

It's never been on the chart before, but we see **Pandora** as a breakout star for 2011 thanks to the amazing popularity of *Avatar*. Pandora, a Greek name meaning "all gifts," is the name of the faraway moon in *Avatar*, but it's got a rich history in Greek mythology as well. Pandora was a mortal woman created by the gods, each of whom gave her a unique gift. She was charged by the gods to protect a box (in the original story, it was a jar), but they would not tell her what was inside. Overwhelmed by her curiosity, she opened it. To her horror, out into the world poured many evils of mankind, such as plagues and diseases. Only hope remained inside after Pandora closed the box. While it's a rather loaded name, Pandora is on everyone's lips these days—and we think that's enough for it to find its way onto the chart in 2011.

Variants: Dora, Pandorah, Panndora, Pandorra, Pandoura, Doura

Zoe

Avatar is also behind the popularity of **Zoe**, as in the film's star Zoe Saldana. Zoe, a Greek name meaning "life," has moved up in the rankings from 58 in 2008 to 47 in 2009. It's a great alternative to the much more popular **Chloe**. The actress **Zooey** Deschanel has also increased the popularity of her alternate spelling.

Variants: Zoee, Zoelie, Zooey, Zoya, Zoelle, Zoie, Zoey

Gemma

We think 2011 is going to be a big year for **Gemma**. It debuted on the list at 888 in 2008 and shot up to 568 in 2009. The popularity of Bond girl-starlet Gemma Arterton is behind this surge in popularity, but it's an evergreen name in Britain (253 on the 2008 girls' list in the UK). A Latin name meaning "jewel," Gemma is girly, pretty, and suggests a bygone time: perfect for baby naming in an economic downturn. It's also a great alternative to the superhot **Emma**, which many folks feel is a bit *too* popular.

Variants: Jemma, Jemsa, Jemima, Gem, Gemmalyn, Gemmalynn

More 2011 Forecasts: Getting Hotter

Adelaide, Ada: New names for fans of **Ava**

Arabella, Annabella: Twists on the uber-popular **Isabella** and rising **Bella**

Juliet/Juliette: A more romantic take on the ever-popular **Julia**

Adelyn/Adalyn: A modern twist on **Adeline**, perhaps a natural evolution of the popularity of **Addison** and **Madelyn**

Bella, Alice: Spurred by *Twilight* fans?

Harper, Harley, Hayden, Harlow: Six-letter gender-neutral names that start with *H* are skyrocketing on the girls' side of the list.

Names ending in -*ley*: **Finley** (up 47 percent in 4 years), **Brynlee** (898 last year, 676 this year, with its counterpart **Brinley** debuting on the list this year at 778), **Kenley** (994 in 2008, 659 in 2009), **Paisley** (318), and **Brylee** (425)

Old-fashioned girls: **Millie** (unranked in 2008, 868 in 2009), **Hazel** (343 in 2008, 294 in 2009), **Ruby** (113 in 2008, 108 in 2009), **Matilda** (825 in 2008; 762 in 2009), **June** (867 in 2008, 662 in 2009), and **Lucille** (607 in 2008, 570 in 2009)

Em: In addition to the 5 variations of **Emily** in the top 1,000, folks are gravitating toward other girls' names beginning with *Em*: **Ember, Emelia, Emilia, Emerson, Emery, Emmy**

Lil: When you add in the 7 variations of **Liliana**, there are a total of 13 *Lil* names in the top 1,000, and the trend isn't showing any signs of stopping. Others include **Lily, Lilly, Lillie, Lilian, Lillian, Lilia**

Aniya: Parents are adding this popular collection of letters to a wide variety of consonants for 9 different popular names: **Zaniyah, Aniya, Aniyah, Janiah, Janiyah, Saniya, Saniyah, Taniya, Taniyah**

BOYS

Twilight Stars

Look out, top 10—here comes **Cullen.** It rose a stunning 297 percent in 2009, accelerating from 782 in 2008 to 485 in 2009. It's a no-brainer why: the ladies get all swoony from *Twilight* vampire Edward Cullen (not surprisingly, the Gaelic name means "good-looking boy"). If you like Cullen, you could also consider **Kellan**—yet another *Twilight* connection! Hot actor Kellan Lutz plays Emmett Cullen in the *Twilight* series, and his name has leaped back onto the chart in 2009 at 632 (after being a total no-show in 2008). Oh, and after years on a downward trend, **Edward** was also up 8 percent in 2009...it's not old fashioned anymore! What's perhaps more surprising is **Emmett**—this dowdyish name ranked at 740 in 2000, but is now 332, up 39 percent over 2008.

We can't ignore Jacob, of course, but the fact is that Jacob has been the number 1 boys' name for 11 years, long before the *Twilight* books. What's more, Jacob is actually *declining*, even though it's still number 1. As we mentioned earlier, more than 35,000 babies were named Jacob when it hit number 1 in 1999. Today, a mere 20,858 babies received the name.

Variants for Cullen: Cullan, Cullin, Cullinan, Collen, Callan, Collin, Colin

Variants for Kellan: Kellen, Keelan, Kelan, Keillan, Keilan, Kellin

Variants for Edward: Edwards, Ed, Eddie, Eddy, Edison, Eduard, Edouard, Eduardo, Edvard, Ted, Teddie, Teddy, Ned, Neddie, Neddy

Variants for Emmett: Emmitt, Emet, Ahmet, Emerson, Emery

Jacoby

Jacoby is a modern spin on **Jacob**, a Hebrew name meaning "he who supplants," and we think its incredible rise in popularity—despite being nearly off the chart in 2006 at 913, it ranked at 444 in 2009—is only going to accelerate in 2011. The fame of Houston Texans wide receiver Jacoby Jones and Boston Red Sox outfielder Jacoby Ellsbury certainly isn't hurting its ascent.

Variants: Jakobe, Jacob, Jacobi, Jacobus, Giacomo, Hamish, Iago, Jago, Jaime, Jake, Jakob, Jakov

Trace

We see 2011 as a big year for **Trace**, a much more boyish version of the name **Tracy**. It's also popular for girls, but we like Trace as a breakout name for boys next year. Trace came in at 533 in 2009. Country star Trace Adkins has been a star for a long time, but it's Trace Cyrus, older brother of Miley Cyrus, who's really behind the surge in popularity. Trace and his band, Metro Station, are on the rise.

Variants: Traye, Drake, True, Tre, Trey, Brice, Bryce, Trai, Tracy

Liam

Liam is all the rage, and it's going to be even stronger in 2011. This name, which ranked at 49 in 2009 (up from 75 in 2008), is an old German word for "protection" and is also an Irish diminutive of **William**. Liam has almost tripled in popularity over the last 10 years. Lots of celebrities have named their little ones Liam (Tori Spelling, for example), and it's also the moniker of one of the young and gorgeous characters on *90210*.

Variants: William, Len

More 2011 Forecasts: Getting Hotter

Cash, Gamble, Keno, and Chance: In these tough economic times, people are gravitating toward casino-friendly names.

Jax, Jaxson: Spinning the popular **Jack** in a more futuristic way

Casen/Kasen: We've already seen the wide variety of variations in this name, but it's worth noting that the whole pack is relatively new to the list, and likely to gain.

Tristan/Trystan: This name also brings in quite a few variants, but the increase in both popularity and variety makes us think we'll see more **Tristan**s around soon.

Beckett, Bennett, Beckham: This surname trio springs from the popularity of David Beckham, no doubt, but all three are on the rise.

Easton, Weston, Westin: These direction names are moving up.

Urijah, Alijah: New twists on the popular **Elijah**

Hidden Climbers

These names aren't necessarily the biggest jumpers in popularity, and they don't quite fit into some of the other trends we've discussed, but we wanted to bring them to your attention because over the last few years they have steadily climbed the charts. Look for them to gain even more ground in 2011.

Girls	Boys
Naomi	Bentley
Sherlyn	Nash
Myla	Bridger
Karma	Cannon
Olive	Atticus
Gracelyn	Ace
Giselle	Madden
Rowan	Gideon
Raelynn	Maverick
Skyla	Izayah
Karsyn	Johan
	Remington
	Cruz
	Holden
	Zander
	Jadiel
	Lucian

Predictions: The Coldest Baby Names

We think these names are over with a capital *O*. In some cases, they became really hot really fast, and now they're oh-so-out-of-style. Others are surprisingly low in popularity considering their perceived "commonality." Perhaps you might want to consider some of these options if you want your baby to stand out in a crowd? See if you agree.

BOYS

Brayden: Are the Bray- names (Brayden, Brayan, Braeden, Braydon, Braden, Braylen, Braylon) losing their luster? Ten spelling variations in the top 1,000 alone is a sure sign of oversaturation.

Jonas: Are the Bros losing some of their fans?

Marc, Isiah, Nickolas: Alternate spellings are sliding down the list as parents return to tradition.

Taylor: Taylor Swift's superstardom has pushed this unisex name onto the girl side of the list.

GIRLS

The many forms of Kaitlyn. It's been a good ride, Kaitlyn, but you may be on your way out. After more than 20 strong years, Kaitlyn is beginning to slip a bit in popularity. In order of common usage, the primary variants are Katelyn, Caitlyn, Caitlin, Kaitlin, and Kaitlynn—and the popularity of each has decreased in last three years.

Marely: This name fell the farthest in 2009.

Jaslene: America's Next Top Model Jaslene Gonzalez broke onto the scene in 2007, and this name first appeared on the 2007 charts at 598, zooming to 396 in 2008, and falling to 670 in 2009 (still at least 330 places above where it had been for the last 20 years, out of the top 1,000).

Mylee: This alternate spelling of **Miley** is falling fast.

Bridget: The uber-popularity of *Bridget Jones's Diary* has faded.

Julie: This sturdy name has given way to **Juliet** and **Juliana**.

Mining the NFL for Your Child's Name

Stumped for a name? Look no further than the NFL's quarter-backs. A growing number of parents are finding inspiration there. In particular, lots of moms and dads are choosing the fun name **Colt**, after Cleveland Browns' QB Colt McCoy. Colt wasn't even ranked in 2003, but it has rocketed up the list to 370 in the years since, and it's risen in popularity 164 percent just between 2008 and 2009. Of course, many parents are choosing the longer name **Colton** (ranked 98 and 93 in 2008 and 2009, respectively) and still calling their young'uns Colt.

Just look at the following list of somewhat unusual names of current NFL quarterbacks. In most cases, the names are growing in popularity.

Boy's Name	Player	Team	2003 Rank	2009 Rank
Colt	McCoy	Cleveland Browns	–	370
Peyton	Manning	Indianapolis Colts	207	147
Carson	Palmer	Cincinnati Bengals	89	86
Byron	Leftwich	Pittsburgh Steelers	491	401
Eli	Manning	New York Giants	191	90
Brady	Quinn	Denver Broncos	142	109
Kyle	Orton	Denver Broncos	53	100
Donovan	McNabb	Washington Redskins	176	215
Drew*	Brees	New Orleans Saints	222	272

*Drew Brees has a son named **Baylen**, a name that hits all the same notes as today's most popular names, but one that has yet to crack the top 1,000.

That Other Sport Called Football

The 2010 World Cup brought a month-long focus to the game of soccer, and the names of the world's best may spark some World Cup babies whose names will hit the charts next year.

Worldly Names We Think Will Rise
Cristiano (Ronaldo), Portugal
Ronaldo *(don't be surprised to see Cristiano's last name get a bump also!)*
Lionel (Messi), Argentina
Rooney* (Wayne Rooney), England
Fernando (Torres), Spain
Franck (Ribéry), France
Fabio (Cannavaro), Italy
Wesley (Sneijder), Netherlands
Arjen (Robben), Netherlands
Steven (Gerrard), England
Gianluigi (Buffon), Italy
Thierry (Henry), France

U.S. Names We Think Will Rise
Donovan (Landon Donovan)
Landon (Landon Donovan)
Clint (Dempsey)
Bradley (Michael Bradley)
Tim (Howard)

*An interesting note: England star Wayne Rooney's son is named **Kai**–a name that has jumped nearly 200 places in popularity since 2000, up to 214 today, and a name that sits right next to (U.S. star Landon) **Donovan** (215) on the top 1,000 list.

Celebrity-Inspired Names on the Rise

Audrina (Patridge): Entered the list at 706 in 2007, now stands at 355

Chace (Crawford): Entered the list at 658 in 2008, now stands at 527

Leighton (Meester): Debuted at 669 this year

Khloe (Kardashian): Khloe was ranked 961 in 2006, and now stands at 95. Kloe entered the list this year at 998.

Taraji (P. Henson): Entered the list at 881 this year

Giada (de Laurentiis): 845 in 2007, 830 in 2008, 754 this year

Evangeline (Lilly): 598 in 2006, 429 in 2009

Dane (Cook): 424 in 2000, 368 this year

Recent Celebrity Babies

Here's a quick overview of what the celebustork has dropped off.

Harper Renn (Tiffani Thiessen)
Cosima Violet (Claudia Schiffer and Matthew Vaughn)
Sundance Thomas (Kerri Walsh and Casey Jennings)
Aviana Olea (Amy Adams and Darren Le Gallo)
Louis Bardo (Sandra Bullock)
Axel (Will Farrell and Viveca Paulin)
Bandit Lee (Lyn-Z and Gerard Way)
Bardot Vita (David Boreanaz and Jaime Bergman)
Blaise Ray (Amanda Beard and Sacha Brown)
Billie Beatrice (Eric Dane and Rebecca Gayheart)
Nancy Leigh (Katherine Heigl and Josh Kelley)
Charlotte Grace (Sarah Michelle Prinze and Freddie Prinze, Jr.)
Goldie Priya (Ben Lee and Ione Skye)
Hartley Grace (Mark McGrath and Carin Kingsland)
Jasper Warren (Kimberly Williams and Brad Paisley)
Julian Fuego (Robin Thicke and Paula Patton)

Lou Sulola (Heidi Klum and Seal)
Lydon Edward (Mark McGrath and Carin Kingsland)
Lyla Rose (Lisa Loeb and Roey Hershkovitz)
Mason Dash (Kourtney Kardashian and Scott Disick)
Sparrow James Midnight (Joel Madden and Nicole Ritchie)
Stella Luna (Ellen Pompeo and Chris Ivery)
Vida (Matthew McConaughey and Camila Alves)
Walker Nathaniel (Taye Diggs and Idina Menzel)
Easton Quinn Monroe (Jenna Elfman and Bodhi Elfman)
Liberty Grace (Joey Lawrence and Chandie Yawn-Nelson)
Seraphina Rose Elizabeth (Ben Affleck and Jennifer Garner)
Atlas (Anne Heche and James Tupper)
Levi James (Sheryl Crow)
Daniel Hiram (Keyshia Cole and Daniel Gibson)
Amadeus Benedict Edley Luis (Boris Becker)
Grace Margaret (Mark Wahlberg and Rhea Durham)
Kloey Alexandra (Joey Fatone)
Rhys Edward (Joey McIntyre)
Lucia (Mel Gibson)
Isaiah Timothy (Elizabeth and Tim Hasselbeck)

Girls

Aadi (Hindi) Child of the beginning
Aadie, Aady, Aadey, Aadee, Aadea, Aadeah, Aadye

*Aaliyah (Arabic) An ascender, one having the highest social standing
Aaleyah, Aaliya, Aliyah, Aliyah, Alliyah, Alieya, Aliyiah, Alliyia, Aleeya, Alee, Aleiya, Alia, Aleah, Alea, Aliya

Aaralyn (American) Woman with song
Aaralynn, Aaralin, Aaralinn, Aaralinne, Aralyn, Aralynn

Aba (African) Born on a Thursday
Abah, Abba, Abbah

Abarrane (Hebrew) Feminine form of Abraham; mother of a multitude; mother of nations
Abarrayne, Abarraine, Abarane, Abarayne, Abaraine, Abame, Abrahana

Abena (African) Born on a Tuesday
Abenah, Abeena, Abyna, Abina, Abeenah, Abynah, Abinah

Abiela (Hebrew) My father is Lord
Abielah, Abiella, Abiellah, Abyela, Abyelah, Abyella, Abyellah

*ᵀAbigail (Hebrew) The source of a father's joy
Abagail, Abbigail, Abigael, Abigale, Abbygail, Abygail, Abygayle, Abbygayle, Abbegale, Abby, Abbagail, Abbey, Abbie, Abbi, Abigayle

Abijah (Hebrew) My father is Lord
Abija, Abisha, Abishah, Abiah, Abia, Aviah, Avia

Abila (Spanish) One who is beautiful
Abilah, Abyla, Abylah

Abilene (American / Hebrew) From a town in Texas / resembling grass
Abalene, Abalina, Abilena, Abiline, Abileene, Abileen, Abileena, Abilyn

Abir (Arabic) Having a fragrant scent
Abeer, Abyr, Abire, Abeere, Abbir, Abhir

Abira (Hebrew) A source of strength; one who is strong
Abera, Abyra, Abyrah, Abirah, Abbira, Abeerah

Abra (Hebrew / Arabic)
Feminine form of Abraham;
mother of a multitude;
mother of nations / lesson;
example
Abri, Abrah, Abree, Abria,
Abbra, Abrah, Abbrah

Abril (Spanish / Portuguese)
Form of April, meaning
opening buds of spring

Academia (Latin) From a com-
munity of higher learning
Akademia, Academiah,
Akademiah

Acantha (Greek) Thorny; in
mythology, a nymph who was
loved by Apollo
Akantha, Ackantha, Acanthah,
Akanthah, Ackanthah

Accalia (Latin) In mythology,
the foster mother of Romulus
and Remus
Accaliah, Acalia, Accalya,
Acalya, Acca, Ackaliah, Ackalia

Adah (Hebrew) Ornament;
beautiful addition to the
family
Adda, Adaya, Ada

Adanna (African) Her father's
daughter; a father's pride
Adana, Adanah, Adannah,
Adanya, Adanyah

Adanne (African) Her
mother's daughter; a
mother's pride
Adane, Adayne, Adaine,
Adayn, Adain, Adaen, Adaene

Adara (Greek / Arabic)
Beautiful girl / chaste one;
virgin
Adair, Adare, Adaire, Adayre,
Adarah, Adarra, Adaora, Adar

Addin (Hebrew) One who is
adorned; voluptuous
Addine, Addyn, Addyne

^*T**Addison** (English) Daughter
of Adam
Addeson, Addyson, Adison,
*Adisson, **Addisyn**, Adyson*

Adeen (Irish) Little fire shin-
ing brightly
Adeene, Adean, Adeane, Adein,
Adeine, Adeyn, Adeyne

Adela (German) Of the nobil-
ity; serene; of good humor
Adele, Adelia, Adella, Adelle,
Adelie, Adelina, Adali

Adelaide (German) Of the
nobility; serene; of good
humor
Adelaid

^**Adeline** (German) Form of
Adela, meaning of the nobility
***Adalyn**, Adalynn, **Adelyn**,*
Adelynn

Adianca (Native American) One who brings peace
Adianka, Adyanca, Adyanka

Adira (Hebrew / Arabic) Powerful, noble woman / having great strength
Adirah, Adeera, Adyra, Adeerah, Adyrah, Adeira, Adeirah, Adiera

Admina (Hebrew) Daughter of the red earth
Adminah, Admeena, Admyna, Admeenah, Admynah, Admeina

Adoración (Spanish) Having the adoration of all

Adra (Arabic) One who is chaste; a virgin

ᵀAdriana (Greek) Feminine form of Adrian; from the Adriatic Sea region; woman with dark features
Adria, Adriah, Adrea, Adreana, Adreanna, Adrienna, Adriane, Adriene, Adrie, Adrienne, Adrianna, Adrianne, Adriel

Adrina (Italian) Having great happiness
Adrinna, Adreena, Adrinah, Adryna, Adreenah, Adrynah

Aegea (Latin / Greek) From the Aegean Sea / in mythology, a daughter of the sun who was known for her beauty

Aegina (Greek) In mythology, a sea nymph
Aeginae, Aegyna, Aegynah

Aelwen (Welsh) Woman with a fair brow
Aelwenn, Aelwenne, Aelwin, Aelwinn, Aelwinne, Aelwyn, Aelwynn, Aelwynne

Aerwyna (English) A friend of the ocean

Afra (Hebrew / Arabic) Young doe / white; an earth color
Affra, Affrah, Afrah, Afrya, Afryah, Afria, Affery, Affrie

Afrodille (French) Daffodil; showy and vivid
Afrodill, Afrodil, Afrodile, Afrodilla, Afrodila

Afton (English) From the Afton river

Agave (Greek) In mythology, a queen of Thebes

Agnes (Greek) One who is pure; chaste
Agneis, Agnese, Agness, Agnies, Agnus, Agna, Agne, Agnesa, Nessa, Oona

Agraciana (Spanish) One who forgives
Agracianna, Agracyanna, Agracyana, Agraciann, Agraciane, Agracyann, Agracyane, Agracianne

Agrona (Celtic) In mythology, the goddess of war and death
Agronna, Agronia, Agrone

Ahelia (Hebrew) Breath; a source of life
Ahelie, Ahelya, Aheli, Ahelee, Aheleigh, Ahelea, Aheleah, Ahely

Ahellona (Greek) Woman who has masculine qualities
Ahelona, Ahellonna, Ahelonna

Ahinoam (Hebrew) In the Bible, one of David's wives

Ahuva (Hebrew) One who is dearly loved
Ahuvah, Ahuda, Ahudah

Aida (English / French / Arabic) One who is wealthy; prosperous / one who is helpful / a returning visitor
Ayda, Aydah, Aidah, Aidee, Aidia, Aieeda, Aaida

Aidan (Gaelic) One who is fiery; little fire
Aiden, Adeen, Aden, Aideen, Adan, Aithne, Aithnea, Ajthne

Aiko (Japanese) Little one who is dearly loved

Ailbhe (Irish) Of noble character; one who is bright

Aileen (Irish / Scottish) Light bearer / from the green meadow
Ailean, Ailein, Ailene, Ailin, Aillen, Ailyn, Alean, Aleane

Ailis (Irish) One who is noble and kind
Ailish, Ailyse, Ailesh, Ailisa, Ailise

Ailna (German) One who is sweet and pleasant; of the nobility
Ailne

Ain (Irish / Arabic) In mythology, a woman who wrote laws to protect the rights of women / precious eye

Aine (Celtic) One who brings brightness and joy

Aingeal (Irish) Heaven's messenger; angel
Aingealag

Ainsley (Scottish) One's own meadow
Ainslie, Ainslee, Ainsly, Ainslei, Aynslie, Aynslee, Aynslie, Ansley

Aionia (Greek) Everlasting life
Aioniah, Aionea, Aioneah, Ayonia, Ayoniah, Ayonea, Ayoneah

Airic (Celtic) One who is pleasant and agreeable
Airick, Airik, Aeric, Aerick, Aerik

Aisha (Arabic, African) lively; womanly
Aiesha, Ayisha, Myisha

Aisling (Irish) A dream or vision; an inspiration
Aislin, Ayslin, Ayslinn, Ayslyn, Ayslynn, Aislyn, Aisylnn, Aislinn, Isleen

Aitheria (Greek) Of the wind
Aitheriah, Aitherea, Aithereah, Aytheria, Aytheriah, Aytherea, Aythereah

Ajaya (Hindi) One who is invincible; having the power of a god
Ajay

Aka (Maori / Turkish) Affectionate one / in mythology, a mother goddess
Akah, Akka, Akkah

Akili (Tanzanian) Having great wisdom
Akilea, Akilee, Akilie, Akylee, Akylie, Akyli, Akileah

Akilina (Latin) Resembling an eagle
Akilinah, Akileena, Akilyna, Akilinna, Ackilina, Acilina, Akylina, Akylyna

Akira (Scottish) One who acts as an anchor
Akera, Akerra, Akiera, Akirah, Akiria, Akyra, Akirrah, Akeri, Akeira, Akeara

Aksana (Russian) Form of Oksana, meaning "hospitality"
Aksanna, Aksanah, Aksannah

Alaia (Arabic / Basque) One who is majestic, of high worth joy
Alaya, Alayah, Alaiah

Alaina (French) Beautiful and fair woman; dear child.
Alayna, Alaine, Alayne, Alainah, Alana, Alanah, Alanna, Alannah, Alanis, Alyn, Alani, Alanni, Alaney, Alanney, Alanie

Alair (French) One who has a cheerful disposition
Alaire, Allaire, Allair, Aulaire, Alayr, Alayre, Alaer

Alanza (Spanish) Feminine form of Alonzo; noble and ready for battle

Alarice (German) Feminine form of Alaric; ruler of all
Alarise, Allaryce, Alarica, Alarisa, Alaricia, Alrica

Alcina (Greek) One who is strong-willed and opinionated
Alceena, Alcyna, Alsina, Alsyna, Alzina, Alcine, Alcinia, Alcyne

Alda (German / Spanish) Long-lived, old / wise; an elder
Aldah, Aldine, Aldina, Aldinah, Aldene, Aldona

Aldis (English) From the ancient house
Aldys, Aldiss, Aldisse, Aldyss, Aldysse

Aldonsa (Spanish) One who is kind and gracious
Aldonza, Aldonsia, Aldonzia

Aleah (Arabic) Exalted
Alea, Alia, Aliah, Aliana, Aleana

Aleen (Celtic) Form of Helen, meaning "the shining light"
Aleena, Aleenia, Alene, Alyne, Alena, Alenka, Alynah, Aleine

Alegria (Spanish) One who is cheerful and brings happiness to others
Alegra, Aleggra, Allegra, Alleffra, Allecra

Alera (Latin) Resembling an eagle
Alerra, Aleria, Alerya, Alerah, Alerrah

Alethea (Greek) One who is truthful
Altheia, Lathea, Lathey, Olethea

*Alexa (Greek) Form of Alexandra, meaning "helper and defender of mankind"
Aleka, Alexia

*ᵀAlexandra (Greek) Feminine form of Alexander; a helper and defender of mankind
Alexandria, Alexandrea, Alixandra, Alessandra, Alexis, Alondra, Aleksandra, Alejandra, Sandra, Sandrine, Sasha

*Alexis (Greek) Form of Alexandra, meaning "helper and defender of mankind"
Alexus, Alexys, Alexia

Ali (English) Form of Allison or Alice, meaning "woman of the nobility"
Allie, Alie, Alli, Ally

Aliana (English) Form of Eliana, meaning "the Lord answers our prayers"
Alianna

^Alice (German) Woman of the nobility; truthful; having high moral character
Ally, Allie, Alyce, Alesia, Aleece

Alicia (Spanish) Form of Alice, meaning "woman of the nobility"
Alecia, Aleecia, Aliza, Aleesha, Alesha, Alisha, Alisa

Alika (Hawaiian) One who is honest
Alicka, Alicca, Alyka, Alycka, Alycca

Alina (Arabic / Polish) One who is noble / one who is beautiful and bright
Aline, Aleena, Alena, Alyna

Alivia (Spanish) Form of Olivia, meaning of the olive tree

***ᵀAllison** (English) Form of Alice, meaning "woman of the nobility, truthful; having high moral character"
Alisanne, Alison, Alicen, Alisen, Alisyn, Allyson, Alyson, Allisson

Alma (Latin / Italian) One who is nurturing and kind / refers to the soul
Almah

Almira (English) A princess; daughter born to royalty
Almeera, Almeira, Almiera, Almyra, Almirah, Almeerah, Almeirah

Aloma (Spanish) Form of Paloma, meaning "dove-like"
Alomah, Alomma, Alommah

Alondra (Spanish) Form of Alexandra, meaning "helper and defender of mankind"

Alpha (Greek) The firstborn child; the first letter of the Greek alphabet

Alphonsine (French) Feminine form of Alphonse; one who is ready for battle
Alphonsina, Alphonsyne, Alphonsyna, Alphonseene, Alphonseena, Alphonseane, Alphonseana, Alphonsiene

Alura (English) A divine counselor
Allura, Alurea, Alhraed

Alvera (Spanish) Feminine of Alvaro; guardian of all; speaker of the truth
Alveria, Alvara, Alverna, Alvernia, Alvira, Alvyra, Alvarita, Alverra

***Alyssa** (German) Form of Alice, meaning "woman of the nobility, truthful; having high moral character"
Alisa, Alissya, Alyssaya, Alishya, Alisia, Alissa, Allisa, Allyssa, Alysa, Alysse, Alyssia

Amada (Spanish) One who is loved by all
Amadia, Amadea, Amadita, Amadah

Amadea (Latin) Feminine form of Amedeo; loved by God
Amadya, Amadia, Amadine, Amadina, Amadika, Amadis

Amadi (African) One who rejoices
Amadie, Amady, Amadey, Amadye, Amadee, Amadea, Amadeah

Amalia (German) One who is industrious and hardworking
Amelia, Amalya, Amalie, Amalea, Amylia, Amyleah, Amilia, Neneca

Amalthea (Greek) One who soothes; in mythology, the foster mother of Zeus
Amaltheah, Amalthia, Amalthya

Amanda (Latin) One who is much loved
Amandi, Amandah, Amandea, Amandee, Amandey, Amande, Amandie, Amandy, Mandy

Amani (African / Arabic) One who is peaceful / one with wishes and dreams
Amanie, Amany, Amaney, Amanee, Amanye, Amanea, Amaneah

Amara (Greek) One who will be forever beautiful
Amarah, Amarya, Amaira, Amaria, Amar

Amina (Arabic) Truthful, trustworthy

Amari (African) Having great strength, a builder
Amaree, Amarie

Amaya (Japanese) Of the night rain
Amayah, Amaia, Amaiah

Amber (French) Resembling the jewel; a warm honey color
Ambur, Ambar, Amberly, Amberlyn, Amberli, Amberlee, Ambyr, Ambyre

Ambrosia (Greek) Immortal; in mythology, the food of the gods
Ambrosa, Ambrosiah, Ambrosyna, Ambrosina, Ambrosyn, Ambrosine, Ambrozin, Ambrozyn, Ambrozyna, Ambrozyne, Ambrozine, Ambrose, Ambrotosa, Ambruslne, Amhrosine

*Amelia (German) Form of Amalia or (Latin) form of Emily, meaning "one who is industrious and hardworking"
Amelie, Amelita, Amylia, Amely

America (Latin) A powerful ruler
Americus, Amerika, Amerikus

Amina (Arabic) A princess;
one who commands
*Amirah, Ameera, Amyra,
Ameerah, Amyrah, Ameira,
Ameirah, Amiera*

Amissa (Hebrew) One who is
honest; a friend
*Amisa, Amise, Amisia, Amiza,
Amysa, Amysia, Amysya, Amyza*

^**Amiyah** (American) Form of
Amy, meaning "beloved."
Amiah, Amiya, Amya

Amrita (Hindi) Having immor-
tality; full of ambrosia
*Amritah, Amritta, Amryta,
Amrytta, Amrytte, Amritte,
Amryte, Amreeta*

Amser (Welsh) A period of
time

Amy (Latin) Dearly loved
*Aimee, Aimie, Aimi, Aimy,
Aimya, Aimey, Amice, Amicia*

Anaba (Native American) A
woman returning from battle
Anabah, Annaba, Annabah

Anabal (Gaelic) One who is
joyful
Anaball, Annabal, Annaball

Anahi (Latin) Immortal

Analia (Spanish) Combination
of Ana and Lea or Lucia
*Annalee, Annali, Annalie,
Annaleigh, Annalea, Analeigh,
Anali, Analie, Annalina,
Anneli, Annaleah, Annaliese,
Annalise, Annalisa, Analise,
Analiese, Analisa*

Anarosa (Spanish) A graceful
rose
Annarosa, Anarose, Annarose

Anastasia (Greek) One who
shall rise again
*Anastase, Anastascia,
Anastasha, Anastasie, Stacia,
Stasia, Stacy, Stacey*

Ancina (Latin) Form of Ann,
meaning "a woman graced
with God's favor"
*Ancyna, Anncina, Anncyna,
Anceina, Annceina, Anciena,
Annciena, Anceena*

★**Andrea** (Greek / Latin)
Courageous and strong /
feminine form of Andrew;
womanly
*Andria, Andrianna, Andreia,
Andreina, Andreya, Andriana,
Andreana, Andera*

Angel (Greek) A heavenly messenger

Angela (Greek) A heavenly
messenger; an angel
*Angelica, **Angelina**, Angelique,
Anjela, Anjelika, Angella,
Angelita, Angeline, Angie, Angy*

*Angelina (Greek) Form of
Angela, meaning "a heavenly
messenger, an angel"
*Angeline, Angelyn, Angelene,
Angelin*

Ani (Hawaiian) One who is
very beautiful
*Aneesa, Aney, Anie, Any, Aany,
Aanye, Anea, Aneah*

Aniceta (French) One who is
unconquerable
Anicetta, Anniceta, Annicetta

Aniya (American) Form of
Anna, meaning "a woman
graced with God's favor"
Aniyah, Anaya

*ᵀAnna (Latin) A woman
graced with God's favor
*Annah, Ana, Ann, Anne, Anya,
Ane, Annika, Anouche, Annchen,
Ancina, Annie, Anika*

^Annabel (Italian) Graceful
and beautiful woman
*Annabelle, Annabell,
Annabella, Annabele, Anabel,
Anabell, Anabelle, Anabella*

Annabeth (English) Graced
with God's bounty
*Anabeth, Annabethe, Annebeth,
Anebeth, Anabethe*

Annalynn (English) From the
graceful lake
*Analynn, Annalyn, Annaline,
Annalin, Annalinn, Analyn,
Analine, Analin*

Annmarie (English) Filled with
bitter grace
*Annemarie, Annmaria,
Annemaria, Annamarie,
Annamaria, Anamarie,
Anamaria, Anamari*

Annora (Latin) Having great
honor
*Anora, Annorah, Anorah,
Anoria, Annore, Annorya,
Anorya, Annoria*

Anouhea (Hawaiian) Having a
soft, cool fragrance

Ansley (English) From the
noble's pastureland
*Ansly, Anslie, Ansli, Anslee,
Ansleigh, Anslea, Ansleah,
Anslye, Ainsley*

Antalya (Russian) Born with
the morning's first light
*Antaliya, Antalyah, Antaliyah,
Antalia, Antaliah*

Antea (Greek) In mythology, a woman who was scorned and committed suicide
Anteia, Anteah

Antje (German) A graceful woman

Antoinette (French) Praiseworthy
Toinette

Anwen (Welsh) A famed beauty
Anwin, Anwenne, Anwinne, Anwyn, Anwynn, Anwynne, Anwenn, Anwinn

Anya (Russian) Form of Anna, meaning "a woman graced with God's favor"

Aphrah (Hebrew) From the house of dust
Aphra

Aphrodite (Greek) Love; in mythology, the goddess of love and beauty
Afrodite, Afrodita, Aphrodita, Aphrodyte, Aphhrodyta, Aphrodytah

Aponi (Native American) Resembling a butterfly
Aponni, Apponni, Apponi

Apphia (Hebrew) One who is productive
Apphiah

Apple (American) Sweet fruit; one who is cherished
Appel, Aple, Apel

April (English) Opening buds of spring, born in the month of April
Avril, Averel, Averill, Avrill, Apryl, Apryle, Aprylle, Aprel, Aprele, Aprila, Aprile, Aprili, Aprilla, Aprille, Aprielle, Aprial, Abrielle, Avrielle, Avrial, Abrienda, Avriel, Averyl, Averil, Avryl, Apryll

Aquene (Native American) One who is peaceful
Aqueena, Aqueene, Aqueen

Arabella (Latin) An answered prayer; beautiful altar
Arabela, Arabel, Arabell

Araceli (Spanish) From the altar of heaven
Aracely, Aracelie, Areli, Arely

Aranka (Hungarian) The golden child

Ararinda (German) One who is tenacious
Ararindah, Ararynda, Araryndah

Arava (Hebrew) Resembling a willow; of an arid land
Aravah, Aravva, Aravvah

Arcadia (Greek / Spanish)
Feminine form of Arkadios;
woman from Arcadia / one
who is adventurous
*Arcadiah, Arkadia, Arcadya,
Arkadya, Arckadia, Arckadya*

Ardara (Gaelic) From the
stronghold on the hill
*Ardarah, Ardarra, Ardaria,
Ardarrah, Ardariah*

Ardel (Latin) Feminine form of
Ardos; industrious and eager
*Ardelle, Ardella, Ardele,
Ardelia, Ardelis, Ardela, Ardell*

Arden (Latin / English) One
who is passionate and enthusiastic / from the valley of the
eagles
*Ardin, Ardeen, Ardena, Ardene,
Ardan, Ardean, Ardine, Ardun*

Ardra (Celtic / Hindi) One
who is noble / the goddess of
bad luck and misfortune

Argea (Greek) In mythology,
the wife of Polynices
Argeia

Aria (English) A beautiful
melody
Ariah

*Ariana (Welsh / Greek)
Resembling silver / one who
is holy
*Ariane, Arian, **Arianna**, Arianne,
Aerian, Aerion, Arianie, Arieon,
Aryana, Aryanna*

Ariel (Hebrew) A lionness of
God
*Arielle, Ariele, Airial, Ariela,
Ariella, Aryela, Arial, Ari,
Ariely, Arely, Arieli, Areli*

Arietta (Italian) A short but
beautiful melody
*Arieta, Ariete, Ariet, Ariett,
Aryet, Aryeta, Aryetta, Aryette*

Arin (English) Form of Erin,
meaning "woman of Ireland"
Aryn

Arisje (Danish) One who is
superior

Arissa (Greek) One who is
superior
Arisa, Aris, Aryssa, Arysa, Arys

Arizona (Native American)
From the little spring / from
the state of Arizona

Armani (Persian) One who is
desired
*Armanee, Armahni, Armaney,
Armanie, Armaney*

Arnette (English) A little eagle
*Arnett, Arnetta, Arnete, Arneta,
Arnet*

Aroha (Maori) One who loves and is loved

Arona (Maori) One who is colorful and vivacious
Aronah, Aronnah, Aronna

Arrosa (Basque) Sprinkled with dew from heaven; resembling a rose
Arrose

Artis (Irish / English / Icelandic) Lofy hill; noble / rock / follower of Thor
Artisa, Artise, Artys, Artysa, Artyse, Artiss, Arti, Artina

Arusi (African) A girl born during the time of a wedding
Arusie, Arusy, Arusey, Arusee, Arusea, Aruseah, Arusye

Arwa (Arabic) A female mountain goat

Arya (Indian) One who is noble and honored
Aryah, Aryana, Aryanna, Aryia

Ascención (Spanish) Refers to the Ascension

Ashby (English) Home of the ash tree
Ashbea, Ashbie, Ashbeah, Ashbey, Ashbi, Ashbee

Asherat (Syrian) In mythology, goddess of the sea

Ashima (Hebrew) In the Bible, a deity worshipped at Hamath
Ashimah, Ashyma, Asheema, Ashimia, Ashymah, Asheemah, Asheima, Asheimah

Ashira (Hebrew) One who is wealthy; prosperous
Ashyra, Ashyrah, Ashirah, Asheera, Asheerah, Ashiera, Ashierah, Asheira

*T**Ashley** (English) From the meadow of ash trees
Ashlie, Ashlee, Ashleigh, Ashly, Ashleye, Ashlya, Ashala, Ashleay

Ashlyn (American) Combination of Ashley and Lynn
Ashlynn, Ashlynne

Asia (Greek / English) Resurrection / the rising sun; in the Koran, the woman who raised Moses; a woman from the east
Aysia, Asya, Asyah, Azia, Asianne

Asis (African) Of the sun
Asiss, Assis, Assiss

Asli (Turkish) One who is genuine and original
Aslie, Asly, Asley, Aslee, Asleigh, Aslea, Asleah, Alsye

Asma (Arabic) One of high status

Aspen (English) From the aspen tree
Aspin, Aspine, Aspina, Aspyn, Aspyna, Aspyne

Assana (Irish) From the water-fall
Assane, Assania, Assanna, Asanna, Asana

Astra (Latin) Of the stars; as bright as a star
Astera, Astrea, Asteria, Astrey, Astara, Astraea, Astrah, Astree

Astrid (Scandinavian / German) One with divine strength
Astryd, Estrid

Asunción (Spanish) Refers to the Virgin Mary's assumption into heaven

Athena (Greek) One who is wise; in mythology, the goddess of war and wisdom
Athina, Atheena, Athene

*Aubrey (English) One who rules with elf-wisdom
Aubree, Aubrie, Aubry, Aubri, Aubriana

*Audrey (English) Woman with noble strength
*Audree, Audry, Audra, Audrea, Adrey, Audre, Audray, Audrin, **Audrina***

Augusta (Latin) Feminine form of Augustus; venerable, majestic
Augustina, Agustina, Augustine, Agostina, Agostine, Augusteen, Augustyna, Agusta

Aulis (Greek) In mythology, a princess of Attica
Auliss, Aulisse, Aulys, Aulyss, Aulysse

^Aurora (Latin) Morning's first light; in mythology, the goddess of the dawn
Aurore, Aurea, Aurorette

*ᵀAutumn (English) Born in the fall
Autum

*ᵀAva (German / Iranian) A birdlike woman / from the water
Avah, Avalee, Avaleigh, Avali, Avalie, Avaley, Avelaine, Avelina

Avasa (Indian) One who is independent
Avasah, Avassa, Avasia, Avassah, Avasiah, Avasea, Avaseah

Avena (English) From the oat field
Avenah, Aviena, Avyna, Avina, Avinah, Avynah, Avienah, Aveinah

Avera (Hebrew) One who transgresses
Averah, Avyra, Avira

*ᵀ**Avery** (English) One who is a wise ruler; of the nobility
Avrie, Averey, Averie, Averi, Averee, Averea, Avereah

Aviana (Latin) Blessed with a gracious life
Avianah, Avianna, Aviannah, Aviane, Avianne, Avyana, Avyanna, Avyane

Aviva (Hebrew) One who is innocent and joyful; resembling springtime
Avivi, Avivah, Aviv, Avivie, Avivice, Avni, Avri, Avyva

Awel (Welsh) One who is as refreshing as a breeze
Awell, Awele, Awela, Awella

Awen (Welsh) A fluid essence; a muse; a flowing spirit
Awenn, Awenne, Awin, Awinn, Awinne, Awyn, Awynn, Awynne

Axelle (German / Latin / Hebrew) Source of life; small oak / axe / peace
Axella, Axell, Axele, Axl, Axela, Axelia, Axellia

Ayala (Hebrew) Resembling a gazelle
Ayalah, Ayalla, Ayallah, Aylin, Ayleen, Ayline, Aileen

Ayanna (Hindi / African) One who is innocent / resembling a beautiful flower
Ayana, Ayania, Ahyana, Ayna, Anyaniah, Ayannah, Aiyanna, Aiyana

Ayla (Hebrew) From the oak tree
Aylah, Aylana, Aylanna, Aylee, Aylea, Aylene, Ayleena, Aylena, Aylin, Ayleen, Ayline, Aileen

Aza (Arabic / African) One who provides comfort / powerful
Azia, Aiza, Aizia, Aizha

Azana (African) One who is superior
Azanah, Azanna, Azannah

Azar (Persian) One who is fiery; scarlet
Azara, Azaria, Azarah, Azarra, Azarrah, Azarr

Aznii (Chechen) A famed beauty
Azni, Aznie, Azny, Azney, Aznee, Aznea, Azneah

Azriel (Hebrew) God is my
helper
*Azrael, Azriell, Azrielle,
Azriela, Azriella, Azraela*

Azul (Spanish) Blue

B

Badia (Arabic) An elegant lady;
one who is unique
*Badiah, Badi'a, Badiya, Badea,
Badya, Badeah*

Bahija (Arabic) A cheerful
woman
*Bahijah, Bahiga, Bahigah,
Bahyja, Bahyjah, Bahyga,
Bahygah*

***Bailey** (English) From the
courtyard within castle walls;
a public official
*Bailee, Bayley, Baylee, Baylie,
Baili, Bailie, Baileigh, Bayleigh*

Baka (Indian) Resembling a
crane
Bakah, Bakka, Backa, Bacca

Baligha (Arabic) One who is
forever eloquent
*Balighah, Baleegha, Balygha,
Baliegha, Baleagha, Baleigha*

Banba (Irish) In mythology, a
patron goddess of Ireland

Bansuri (Indian) One who is
musical
*Bansurie, Bansari, Banseri,
Bansurri, Bansury, Bansurey,
Bansuree*

Bara (Hebrew) One who is
chosen
Barah, Barra, Barrah

Barbara (Latin) A traveler from
a foreign land; a stranger
*Barbra, Barbarella, Barbarita,
Baibin, Babette, Bairbre,
Barbary, Barb*

Barika (African) A flourishing
woman; one who is success-
ful
*Barikah, Baryka, Barikka,
Barykka, Baricka, Barycka,
Baricca, Barycca*

Barr (English) A lawyer
Barre, Bar

Barras (English) From among
the trees

Beatrice (Latin) One who
blesses others
*Beatrix, Beatriz, Beatriss,
Beatrisse, Bea, Beatrize,
Beatricia, Beatrisa*

Becky (English) Form of Rebecca, meaning "one who is bound to God"
Beckey, Becki, Beckie, Becca, Becka, Bekka, Beckee, Beckea

Bel (Indian) From the sacred wood

Belen (Spanish) Woman from Bethlehem

Belinda (English) A beautiful and tender woman
Belindah, Belynda, Balynda, Belienda, Bleiendah, Balyndah, Belyndah

Belisama (Celtic) In mythology, a goddess of rivers and lakes
Belisamah, Belisamma, Belysama, Belisma, Belysma, Belesama

^**Bella** (Italian) A woman famed for her beauty
Belle, Bela, Bell, Belita, Bellissa, Belia, Bellanca, Bellany

Bena (Native American) Resembling a pheasant
Benah, Benna, Bennah

Benigna (Spanish) Feminine form of Benigno; one who is kind; friendly

Bernice (Greek) One who brings victory
Berenisa, Berenise, Berenice, Bernicia, Bernisha, Berniss, Bernyce, Bernys

Bertha (German) One who is famously bright and beautiful
Berta, Berthe, Berth, Bertina, Bertyna, Bertine, Bertyne, Birte

Bertilda (English) A luminous battle maiden
Bertilde, Bertild

Beryl (English) Resembling the pale-green precious stone
Beryll, Berylle, Beril, Berill, Berille

Bess (English) Form of Elizabeth, meaning "my God is bountiful; God's promise"
Besse, Bessi, Bessie, Bessy, Bessey, Bessee, Bessea

Beth (English) Form of Elizabeth, meaning "my God is bountiful; God's promise"
Bethe

Bethany (Hebrew) From the house of figs
Bethan, Bethani, Bethanie, Bethanee, Bethaney, Bethane, Bethann, Bethanne

Beyonce (American) One who surpasses others
Beyoncay, Beyonsay, Beyonsai, Beyonsae, Beyonci, Beyoncie, Beyoncee, Beyoncea

Bianca (Italian) A shining, fair-skinned woman
Bianka, Byanca, Byanka

Bibiana (Italian) Form of Vivian, meaning "lively woman"
Bibiane, Bibianna

Bijou (French) As precious as a jewel

Billie (English) Feminine form of William; having a desire to protect
Billi, Billy, Billey, Billee, Billeigh, Billea, Billeah

Blaine (Scottish / Irish) A saint's servant / a thin woman
Blayne, Blane, Blain, Blayn, Blaen, Blaene

Blair (Scottish) From the field of battle
Blaire, Blare, Blayre, Blaer, Blaere, Blayr

Blake (English) A dark beauty
Blayk, Blayke, Blaik, Blaike, Blaek, Blaeke

Blythe (English) Filled with happiness
Blyth, Blithe, Blith

Bo-bae (Korean) A treasured child

Bonamy (French) A very good friend
Bonamey, Bonami, Bonamie, Bonamee, Bonamei, Bonamea, Bonameah

Bonnie (English) Pretty face
Boni, Bona, Bonea, Boneah, Bonee

Brady (Irish) A large-chested woman
Bradey, Bradee, Bradi, Bradie, Bradea, Bradeah

^**Braelyn** (American) Combination of Braden and Lynn
Braylin, Braelin, Braylyn, Braelen, Braylen

Braima (African) Mother of multitudes
Braimah, Brayma, Braema, Braymah, Braemah

Brandy (English) A woman wielding a sword; an alcoholic drink
Brandey, Brandi, Brandie, Brandee, Branda, Brande, Brandelyn, Brandilyn

Braulia (Spanish) One who is glowing
Brauliah, Braulea, Brauleah, Brauliya, Brauliyah

Brazil (Spanish) Of the ancient tree
Brasil, Brazile, Brazille, Brasille, Bresil, Brezil, Bresille, Brezille

Brencis (Slavic) Crowned with laurel

Brenda (Irish) Feminine form of Brendan; a princess; wielding a sword
Brynda, Brinda, Breandan, Brendalynn, Brendolyn, Brend, Brienda

Brenna (Welsh) A raven-like woman
Brinna, Brenn, Bren, Brennah, Brina, Brena, Brenah

*⊤**Brianna** (Irish) Feminine form of Brian; from the high hill; one who ascends
Breanna, Breanne, Breana, Breann, Breeana, Breeanna, Breona, Breonna, Bryana, Bryanna, Briana

Brice (Welsh) One who is alert; ambitious
Bryce

Bridget (Irish) A strong and protective woman; in mythology, goddess of fire, wisdom, and poetry
Bridgett, Bridgette, Briget, Brigette, Bridgit, Bridgitte, Birgit, Birgitte

Brie (French) Type of cheese
Bree, Breeyah, Bria, Briya, Briah, Briyah, Brya

^**Brielle** (French) Form of Brie, meaning "type of cheese"

Brilliant (American) A dazzling and sparkling woman

Briseis (Greek) In mythology, the Trojan widow abducted by Achilles
Brisys, Brisa, Brisia, Brisha, Brissa, Briza, Bryssa, Brysa

Bristol (English) From the city in England Brystol, Bristow, Brystow

Brittany (English) A woman from Great Britain
Britany, Brittanie, Brittaney, Brittani, Brittanee, Britney, Britnee, Britny

*****Brook** (English) From the running stream
***Brooke**, Brookie*

***Brooklyn** (American) Borough of New York City
Brooklin, Brooklynn, Brooklynne

^**Brylee** (American) Variation of Riley
Brilee, Brylie, Briley, Bryli

Brynley (English) From the burnt meadow
Brynlee, Brynly, Brinley, Brinli, Brynlie

Brynn (Welsh) Hill
Brin, Brinn, Bryn, Brynlee, Brynly, Brinley, Brinli, Brynlie

Bryony (English) Of the healing place
Briony, Brionee

C

Cabrina (American) Form of Sabrina, meaning "a legendary princess"
Cabrinah, Cabrinna

Cabriole (French) An adorable girl
Cabriolle, Cabrioll, Cabriol, Cabryole, Cabryolle, Cabryoll, Cabryol, Cabriola

Cacalia (Latin) Resembling the flowering plant
Cacaliah, Cacalea, Cacaleah

Caden (English) A battle maiden
Cadan, Cadin, Cadon

Cadence (Latin) Rhythmic and melodious; a musical woman
Cadena, Cadenza, Cadian, Cadienne, Cadianne, Cadiene, Caydence, Cadencia, Kadence, Kaydence

Caia (Latin) One who rejoices
Cai, Cais

Cailyn (Gaelic) A young woman
Cailin

Cainwen (Welsh) A beautiful treasure
Cainwenn, Cainwenne, Cainwin, Cainwinn, Cainwinne, Cainwyn, Cainwynn, Cainwynne

Cairo (African) From the city in Egypt

Caitlin (English) Form of Catherine, meaning one who is pure, virginal
Caitlyn, Catlin, Catline, Catlyn, Caitlan, Caitlinn, Caitlynn

Calais (French) From the city in France

Cale (Latin) A respected
woman
*Cayl, Cayle, Cael, Caele, Cail,
Caile*

Caledonia (Latin) Woman of
Scotland
*Caledoniah, Caledoniya,
Caledona, Caledonya, Calydona*

California (Spanish) From
paradise; from the state of
California
Califia

Calise (Greek) A gorgeous
woman
Calyse, Calice, Calyce

Calista (Greek) Most beautiful; in mythology, a nymph
who changed into a bear
and then into the Great Bear
constellation
*Calissa, Calisto, Callista, Calyssa,
Calysta, Calixte, Colista, Collista*

Calla (Greek) Resembling a
lily; a beautiful woman
Callah

Callie (Greek) A beautiful girl
Cali, Callee, Kali, Kallie

Calypso (Greek) A woman
with secrets; in mythology,
a nymph who captivated
Odysseus for seven years

Camassia (American) One
who is aloof
*Camassiah, Camasia,
Camasiah, Camassea,
Camasseah, Camasea,
Camaseah*

Cambay (English) From the
town in India
Cambaye, Cambai, Cambae

Cambria (Latin) A woman of
Wales
*Cambriah, Cambrea, Cambree,
Cambre, Cambry, Cambrey,
Cambri, Cambrie, Cambreah*

Camdyn (English) Of the
enclosed valley
*Camden, Camdan, Camdon,
Camdin*

Cameron (Scottish) Having a
crooked nose
*Cameryn, Camryn, Camerin,
Camren, Camrin, Camron*

*Camila (Italian) Feminine
form of Camillus; a ceremo-
nial attendant; a noble virgin
*Camile, Camille, Camilla,
Camillia, Caimile, Camillei,
Cam, Camelai*

Campbell (Scottish) Having a
crooked mouth
Campbel, Campbelle, Campbele

Candace (Ethiopian / Greek) A queen / one who is white and glowing
Candice, Candiss, Candyce, Candance, Candys, Candyss, Candy

Candida (Latin) White-skinned

Candra (Latin) One who is glowing

Candy (English) A sweet girl; form of Candida, meaning "white-skinned"; form of Candace, meaning "a queen / one who is white and glowing"
Candey, Candi, Candie, Candee, Candea, Candeah

Caneadea (Native American) From the horizon
Caneadeah, Caneadia, Caneadiah

Canika (American) A woman shining with grace
Canikah, Caneeka, Canicka, Canyka, Canycka, Caneekah, Canickah, Canykah

Canisa (Greek) One who is very much loved
Canisah, Canissa, Canysa, Caneesa, Canyssa

Cannes (French) A woman from Cannes

Cantabria (Latin) From the mountains
Cantabriah, Cantebria, Cantabrea, Cantebrea

Caprina (Italian) Woman of the island Capri
Caprinah, Caprinna, Capryna, Capreena, Caprena, Capreenah, Caprynah, Capriena

Cara (Italian / Gaelic) One who is dearly loved / a good friend
Carah, Caralee, Caralie, Caralyn, Caralynn, Carrah, Carra, Chara

Carina (Latin) Little darling
Carinna, Cariana, Carine, Cariena, Caryna, Carinna, Carynna

Carissa (Greek) A woman of grace
Carisa, Carrisa, Carrissa, Carissima

Carla (Latin) Feminine form of Carl; a free woman
Carlah, Carlana, Carleen, Carlena, Carlene, Carletta

Carlessa (American) One who is restless
Carlessah, Carlesa, Carlesah

Carly (American) Form of Carla, meaning "a free woman
Carlee, Carleigh, Carli, Carlie, Carley

Carmel (Hebrew) Of the fruitful orchid
Carmela, Carmella, Karmel

Carmen (Latin) A beautiful song
Carma, Carmelita, Carmencita, Carmia, Carmie, Carmina, Carmine, Carmita

Carna (Latin) In mythology, a goddess who ruled the heart

Carni (Latin) One who is vocal
Carnie, Carny, Carney, Carnee, Carnea, Carneah, Carnia, Carniah

Carol (English) Form of Caroline, meaning "joyous song"; feminine form of Charles; a small, strong woman
Carola, Carole, Carolle, Carolla, Caroly, Caroli, Carolie, Carolee

*Caroline (Latin) Joyous song; feminine form of Charles; a small, strong woman
Carol, Carolina, Carolyn, Carolann, Carolanne, Carolena, Carolene, Carolena, Caroliana

Carrington (English) A beautiful woman; a woman of Carrington
Carington, Carryngton, Caryngton

Carson (Scottish) Son of the marshland
Carsan, Carsen, Carsin, Carsyn

Carys (Welsh) One who loves and is loved
Caryss, Carysse, Caris, Cariss, Carisse, Cerys, Ceryss, Cerysse

Casey (Greek, Irish) A vigilant woman
Casie, Casy, Caysie, Kasey

Cason (Greek) A seer
Cayson, Caison, Caeson

Cassandra (Greek) An unheeded prophetess; in mythology, King Priam's daughter who foretold the fall of Troy
Casandra, Cassandrea, Cassaundra, Cassondra, Cass, Cassy, Cassey, Cassi, Cassie

Cassidy (Irish) Curly-haired girl
Cassady, Cassidey, Cassidi, Cassidie, Cassidee, Cassadi, Cassadie, Cassadee, Casidhe, Cassidea, Cassadea

Casta (Spanish) One who is pure; chaste
Castah, Castalina, Castaleena, Castaleina, Castaliena, Castaleana, Castalyna, Castara

Catherine (English) One who is pure; virginal
Catharine, Cathrine, Cathryn, Catherin, Catheryn, Catheryna, Cathi, Cathy, Katherine, Catalina

Catrice (Greek) A wholesome woman
Catrise, Catryce, Catryse, Catreece, Catreese, Catriece

Cayenne (French) Resembling the hot and spicy pepper

Cayla (American) Form of Kaila, meaning "crowned with laurel"
Caila, Caylah, Cailah

^Caylee (American) form of Kayla, meaning "crowned with laurel"
Caleigh, Caley, Cayley, Cailey, Caili, Cayli

Cecilia (Latin) Feminine form of Cecil; one who is blind; patron saint of music
Cecelia, Cecile, Cecilee, Cicely, Cecily, Cecille, Cecilie, Cicilia, Sheila, Silka, Sissy, Celia

Celand (Latin) One who is meant for heaven
Celanda, Celande, Celandia, Celandea

Celandine (English) Resembling a swallow
Celandyne, Celandina, Celandyna, Celandeena, Celandena, Celandia

Celeste (Latin) A heavenly daughter
Celesta, Celestia, Celisse, Celestina, Celestyna, Celestine

Celia (Latin) Form of Cecelia, meaning patron saint of music

Celina (Latin) In mythology, one of the daughters of Atlas who was turned into a star of the Pleiades constellation; of the heavens; form of Selena, meaning "of the moon"
Celena, Celinna, Celene, Celenia, Celenne, Celicia

Celosia (Greek) A fiery woman; burning; aflame
Celosiah, Celosea, Celoseah

Cera (French) A colorful woman
Cerah, Cerrah, Cerra

Cerina (Latin) Form of Serena, meaning "having a peaceful disposition"
Cerinah, Ceryna, Cerynah, Cerena, Cerenah, Ceriena

Cerise (French) Resembling the cherry
Cerisa

Chadee (French) A divine woman; a goddess
Chadea, Chadeah, Chady, Chadey, Chadi, Chadie

Chai (Hebrew) One who gives life
Chae, Chaili, Chailie, Chailee, Chaileigh, Chaily, Chailey, Chailea

Chailyn (American) Resembling a waterfall
Chailynn, Chailynne, Chaelyn, Chaelynn, Chaelynne, Chaylyn

Chakra (Arabic) A center of spiritual energy

Chalette (American) Having good taste
Chalett, Chalet, Chalete, Chaletta, Chaleta

Chalina (Spanish) Form of Rosalina, meaning "resembling a gentle horse / resembling the beautiful and meaningful flower"
Chalinah, Chalyna, Chaleena, Chalena, Charo, Chaliena, Chaleina, Chaleana

Chameli (Hindi) Resembling jasmine
Chamelie, Chamely, Chameley, Chamelee

Chan (Sanskrit) A shining woman

Chana (Hebrew) Form of Hannah, meaning "having favor and grace"
Chanah, Channa, Chaanach, Chaanah, Chanach, Channah

Chance (American) One who takes risks
Chanci, Chancie, Chancee, Chancea, Chanceah, Chancy, Chancey

Chanda (Sanskrit) An enemy of evil
Chandy, Chaand, Chand, Chandey, Chandee, Chandi, Chandie, Chandea

Chandra (Hindi) Of the moon; another name for the goddess Devi
Chandara, Chandria, Chaundra, Chandrea, Chandreah

Chanel (French) From the canal; a channel
Chanell, Chanelle, Channelle, Chenelle, Chenel, Chenell

Channary (Cambodian) Of the full moon
Channarie, Channari, Channarey, Channaree, Chantrea, Chantria

Chantrice (French) A singer
Chantryce, Chantrise, Chantryse

Charisma (Greek) Blessed with charm
Charismah, Charizma, Charysma, Karisma

Charity (Latin) A woman of generous love
Charitey, Chariti, Charitie, Charitee

Charlesia (American) Feminine form of Charles; small, strong woman
Charlesiah, Charlesea, Charleseah, Charlsie, Charlsi

Charlie (English) Form of Charles, meaning "one who is strong"
Charlee, Charli, Charley, Charlize, Charlene, Charlyn, Charlaine, Charlisa, Charlena

*Charlotte (French) Form of Charles, meaning "a small, strong woman"
Charlize, Charlot, Charlotta

Charlshea (American) Filled with happiness
Charlsheah, Charlshia, Charlshiah

Charnee (American) Filled with joy
Charny, Charney, Charnea, Charneah, Charni, Charnie

Charnesa (American) One who gets attention
Charnessa, Charnessah

Charsetta (American) An emotional woman
Charsett, Charsette, Charset, Charsete, Charseta

Chartra (American) A classy lady
Chartrah

Charu (Hindi) One who is gorgeous
Charoo, Charou

Chasia (Hebrew) One who is protected; sheltered
Chasiah, Chasea, Chaseah, Chasya, Chasyah

Chasidah (Hebrew) A religious woman; pious
Chasida, Chasyda, Chasydah

Chavi (Egyptian) A precious daughter
Chavie, Chavy, Chavey, Chavee, Chavea, Chaveah

Chaya (Hebrew) Life
Chaia

Chedra (Hebrew) Filled with happiness
Chedrah

Cheer (American) Filled with joy
Cheere

Chekia (American) A saucy woman
Cheekie, Checki, Checkie, Checky, Checkey, Checkee, Checkea, Checkeah

Chelone (English) Resembling a flowering plant

Chelsea (English) From the landing place for chalk
Chelcie, Chelsa, Chelsee, Chelseigh, Chelsey, Chelsi, Chelsie, Chelsy

Chemarin (French) A dark beauty
Chemarine, Chemaryn, Chemareen, Chemarein, Chemarien

Chemda (Hebrew) A charismatic woman
Chemdah

Chenille (American) A soft-skinned woman
Chenill, Chenil, Chenile, Chenilla, Chenila

Cherika (French) One who is dear
Chericka, Cheryka, Cherycka, Cherieka, Cheriecka, Chereika, Chereicka, Cheryka

Cherish (English) To be held dear, valued

Cherry (English) Resembling a fruit-bearing tree
Cherrie, Cherri, Cherrey, Cherree, Cherrea, Cherreah

Chesney (English) One who promotes peace
Chesny, Chesni, Chesnie, Chesnea, Chesneah, Chesnee

Cheyenne (Native American) Unintelligible speaker
Chayanne, Cheyane, Cheyene, Shayan, Shyann

Chiante (Italian) Resembling the wine
Chianti, Chiantie, Chiantee, Chianty, Chiantey, Chiantea

Chiara (Italian) Daughter of the light
Chiarah, Chiarra, Chiarrah

Chiba (Hebrew) One who loves and is loved
Chibah, Cheeba, Cheebah, Cheiba, Cheibah, Chieba, Chiebah, Cheaba

Chidi (Spanish) One who is cheerful
Chidie, Chidy, Chidey, Chidee, Chidea, Chideah

Chidori (Japanese) Resembling a shorebird
Chidorie, Chidory, Chidorey, Chidorea, Chidoreah, Chidoree

Chikira (Spanish) A talented dancer
Chikirah, Chikiera, Chikierah, Chikeira, Chikeirah, Chikeera, Chikeerah, Chikyra

Chiku (African) A talkative girl

Chinara (African) God receives
Chinarah, Chinarra, Chinarrah

Chinue (African) God's own blessing
Chinoo, Chynue, Chynoo

Chiriga (African) One who is triumphant
Chyriga, Chyryga, Chiryga

Chislaine (French) A faithful woman
Chislain, Chislayn, Chislayne, Chislaen, Chislaene, Chyslaine, Chyslain, Chyslayn

Chitsa (Native American) One who is fair
Chitsah, Chytsa, Chytsah

Chizoba (African) One who is well-protected
Chizobah, Chyzoba, Chyzobah

*ᵀChloe (Greek) A flourishing woman; blooming
Clo, Cloe, Cloey, Chloë

Christina (English) Follower of Christ
Christinah, Cairistiona, Christine, Christin, Christian, Christiana, Christiane, Christianna, Kristina, Cristine, Christal, Crystal, Chrystal, Cristal

Chula (Native American) Resembling a colorful flower
Chulah, Chulla, Chullah

Chulda (Hebrew) One who can tell fortunes
Chuldah

Chun (Chinese) Born during the spring

Chyou (Chinese) Born during autumn

Ciara (Irish) A dark beauty
Ceara, Ciaran, Ciarra, Ciera, Cierra, Ciere, Ciar, Ciarda

Cidrah (American) One who is unlike others
Cidra, Cydrah, Cydra

Cinnamon (American)
Resembling the reddish-
brown spice
Cinnia, Cinnie

Ciona (American) One who is
steadfast
Cionah, Cyona, Cyonah

Claennis (Anglo-Saxon) One
who is pure
*Claenis, Claennys, Claenys,
Claynnis, Claynnys, Claynys,
Claynyss*

*Claire (French) Form of Clara,
meaning "famously bright"
Clare, Clair

Clancey (American) A light-
hearted woman
*Clancy, Clanci, Clancie,
Clancee, Clancea, Clanceah*

*Clara (Latin) One who is
famously bright
*Clarie, Clarinda, Clarine,
Clarita, Claritza, Clarrie,
Clarry, Clarabelle, **Claire**,
Clarice*

Clarice (French) A famous
woman; also a form of Clara,
meaning "one who is famously bright"
*Claressa, Claris, Clarisa,
Clarise, Clarisse, Claryce,
Clerissa, Clerisse, Clarissa*

Claudia (Latin / German /
Italian) One who is lame
Claudelle, Gladys

Clelia (Latin) A glorious
woman
*Cloelia, Cleliah, Clelea, Cleleah,
Cloeliah, Cloelea, Cloeleah*

Clementine (French) Feminine
form of Clement; one who is
merciful
*Clem, Clemence, Clemency,
Clementia, Clementina,
Clementya, Clementyna,
Clementyn*

Cleodal (Latin) A glorious
woman
*Cleodall, Cleodale, Cleodel,
Cleodell, Cleodelle*

Cleopatra (Greek) A father's
glory; of the royal family
*Clea, Cleo, Cleona, Cleone,
Cleonie, Cleora, Cleta, Cleoni*

Clever (American) One who is
quick-witted and smart

Cloris (Greek) A flourishing
woman; in mythology, the
goddess of flowers
*Clores, Clorys, Cloriss, Clorisse,
Cloryss, Clorysse*

Cloud (American) A light-hearted woman
Cloude, Cloudy, Cloudey, Cloudee, Cloudea, Cloudeah, Cloudi, Cloudie

Clydette (American) Feminine form of Clyde, meaning "from the river"
Clydett, Clydet, Clydete, Clydetta, Clydeta

Clymene (Greek) In mythology, the mother of Atlas and Prometheus
Clymena, Clymyne, Clymyn, Clymyna, Clymeena, Clymeina, Clymiena, Clymeana

Clytie (Greek) The lovely one; in mythology, a nymph who was changed into a sunflower
Clyti, Clytee, Clyty, Clytey, Clyte, Clytea, Clyteah

Coby (Hebrew) Feminine form of Jacob; the supplanter
Cobey, Cobi, Cobie, Cobee, Cobea, Cobeah

Coffey (American) A lovely woman
Coffy, Coffe, Coffee, Coffea, Coffeah, Coffi, Coffie

Coira (Scottish) Of the churning waters
Coirah, Coyra, Coyrah

Colanda (American) Form of Yolanda, meaning "resembling the violet flower; modest"
Colande, Coland, Colana, Colain, Colaine, Colane, Colanna, Corlanda, Calanda, Calando, Calonda, Colantha, Colanthe, Culanda, Culonda, Coulanda, Colonda

Cole (English) A swarthy woman; having coal-black hair
Col, Coal, Coale, Coli, Colie, Coly, Coley, Colee

Colette (French) Victory of the people
Collette, Kolette

Coligny (French) Woman from Cologne
Coligney, Colignie, Coligni, Colignee, Colignea, Coligneah

Colisa (English) A delightful young woman
Colisah, Colissa, Colissah, Colysa, Colysah, Colyssa, Colyssah

Colola (American) A victorious woman
Colo, Cola

Comfort (English) One who strengthens or soothes others
Comforte, Comfortyne, Comfortyna, Comforteene, Comforteena, Comfortene, Comfortena, Comfortiene

Conary (Gaelic) A wise woman
*Conarey, Conarie, Conari,
Conaree, Conarea, Conareah*

Concordia (Latin) Peace and
harmony; in mythology, goddess of peace
*Concordiah, Concordea,
Concord, Concorde, Concordeah*

Constanza (American) One
who is strong-willed
Constanzia, Constanzea

Consuela (Spanish) One who
provides consolation
*Consuelia, Consolata,
Consolacion, Chela, Conswela,
Conswelia, Conswelea,
Consuella*

Contessa (Italian) A titled
woman; a countess
*Countess, Contesse, Countessa,
Countesa, Contesa*

Cooper (English) One who
makes barrels
Couper

Copper (American) A red-
headed woman
Coper, Coppar, Copar

Cora (English) A young maiden
Corah, Coraline, Corra

Coral (English) Resembling
the semiprecious sea growth;
from the reef
*Coralee, Coralena, Coralie,
Coraline, Corallina, Coralline,
Coraly, Coralyn*

Corazon (Spanish) Of the
heart
Corazana, Corazone, Corazona

Cordelia (Latin) A good-
hearted woman; a woman of
honesty
*Cordella, Cordelea, Cordilia,
Cordilea, Cordy, Cordie, Cordi,
Cordee*

Corey (Irish) From the hollow;
of the churning waters
*Cory, Cori, Coriann, Corianne,
Corie, Corri, Corrianna, Corrie*

Corgie (American) A humor-
ous woman
*Corgy, Corgey, Corgi, Corgee,
Corgea, Corgeah*

Coriander (Greek) A romantic
woman; resembling the spice
*Coryander, Coriender,
Coryender*

Corina (Latin) A spear-wielding
woman
*Corinne, Corine, Corinna,
Corrinne, Corryn, Corienne,
Coryn, Corynna*

Corinthia (Greek) A woman of Corinth
Corinthiah, Corinthe, Corinthea, Corintheah, Corynthia, Corynthea, Corynthe

Cornelia (Latin) Feminine form of Cornelius; referring to a horn
Cornalia, Corneelija, Cornela, Cornelija, Cornelya, Cornella, Cornelle, Cornie

Cota (Spanish) A lively woman
Cotah, Cotta, Cottah

Coty (French) From the riverbank
Cotey, Coti, Cotie, Cotee, Cotea, Coteah

Courtney (English) A courteous woman; courtly
Cordney, Cordni, Cortenay, Corteney, Cortland, Cortnee, Cortneigh, Cortney, Courteney

Covin (American) An unpredictable woman
Covan, Coven, Covyn, Covon

Coy (English) From the woods, the quiet place
Coye, Coi

Cree (Native American) A tribal name
Crei, Crey, Crea, Creigh

Cressida (Greek) The golden girl; in mythology, a woman of Troy
Cressa, Criseyde, Cressyda, Crissyda

Cristos (Greek) A dedicated and faithful woman
Crystos, Christos, Chrystos

Cwen (English) A royal woman; queenly
Cwene, Cwenn, Cwenne, Cwyn, Cwynn, Cwynne, Cwin, Cwinn

Cylee (American) A darling daughter
Cyleigh, Cyli, Cylie, Cylea, Cyleah, Cyly, Cyley

Cynthia (Greek) Moon goddess
Cinda, Cindy, Cinthia, Cindia, Cinthea

Cyrene (Greek) In mythology, a maiden-huntress loved by Apollo
Cyrina, Cyrena, Cyrine, Cyreane, Cyreana, Cyreene, Cyreena

Czigany (Hungarian) A gypsy girl; one who moves from place to place
Cziganey, Czigani, Cziganie, Cziganee

D

Dacey (Irish) Woman from the south
Daicey, Dacee, Dacia, Dacie, Dacy, Daicee, Daicy, Daci

Daffodil (French) Resembling the yellow flower
Daffodill, Daffodille, Dafodil, Dafodill, Dafodille, Daff, Daffodyl, Dafodyl

Dagmar (Scandinavian) Born on a glorious day
Dagmara, Dagmaria, Dagmarie, Dagomar, Dagomara, Dagomar, Dagomaria, Dagmarr, Dagomarr

Dahlia (Swedish) From the valley; resembling the flower
Dahlea, Dahl, Dahiana, Dayha, Daleia, Dalia

Daira (Greek) One who is well-informed
Daeira, Danira, Dayeera

Daisy (English) Of the day's eye; resembling a flower
Daisee, Daisey, Daisi, Daisie, Dasie, Daizy, Daysi, Deysi

Dakota (Native American) A friend to all
Dakotah, Dakotta, Dakoda, Dakodah

Damali (Arabic) A beautiful vision
Damalie, Damaly, Damaley, Damalee, Damaleigh, Damalea

Damani (American) Of a bright tomorrow
Damanie, Damany, Damaney, Damanee, Damanea, Damaneah

Damaris (Latin) A gentle woman
Damara, Damaress, Damariss, Damariz, Dameris, Damerys, Dameryss, Damiris

Dana (English) Woman from Denmark
Danna, Daena, Daina, Danaca, Danah, Dane, Danet, Daney, Dania

Danica (Slavic) Of the morning star
Danika

Daniela (Spanish) Form of Danielle, meaning "God is my judge"
Daniella

Danielle (Hebrew) Feminine form of Daniel; God is my judge
Daanelle, Danee, Danele, Danella, Danelle, Danelley, Danette, Daney

Daphne (Greek) Of the laurel tree; in mythology, a virtuous woman transformed into a laurel tree to protect her from Apollo
Daphna, Daphney, Daphni, Daphnie, Daffi, Daffie, Daffy, Dafna

Darby (English) Of the deer park
Darb, Darbee, Darbey, Darbie, Darrbey, Darrbie, Darrby, Derby, Larby

Daria (Greek) Feminine form of Darius; possessing good fortune; wealthy
Dari, Darian, Dariane, Darianna, Dariele, Darielle, Darien, Darienne

Daring (American) One who takes risks; a bold woman
Daryng, Derring, Dering, Deryng

Darlene (English) Our little darling
Dareen, Darla, Darleane, Darleen, Darleena, Darlena, Darlenny, Darlina

Daryn (Greek) Feminine form of Darin; a gift of God
Darynn, Darynne, Darinne, Daren, Darenn, Darene

Dawn (English) Born at daybreak; of the day's first light
Dawna, Dawne, Dawnelle, Dawnetta, Dawnette, Dawnielle, Dawnika, Dawnita

Day (American) A father's hope for tomorrow
Daye, Dai, Dae

Daya (Hebrew) Resembling a bird of prey
Dayah, Dayana, Dayanara, Dayania, Dayaniah, Dayanea, Dayaneah

Dayton (English) From the sunny town
Dayten, Daytan

Dea (Greek) Resembling a goddess
Deah, Diya, Diyah

Deborah (Hebrew) Resembling a bee; in the Bible, a prophetess
Debbera, Debbey, Debbi, Debbie, Debbra, Debby

Deidre (Gaelic) A broken-hearted or raging woman
Deadra, Dede, Dedra, Deedra, Deedre, Deidra, Deirdre, Deidrie

Deiondre (American) From
the lush valley
*Deiondra, Deiondria,
Deiondrea, Deiondriya*

Deja (French) One of remem-
brance
*Dayja, Dejah, Daejah, Daijia,
Daija, Daijah, Deijah, Deija*

Dekla (Latvian) In mythology,
a trinity goddess
*Decla, Deckla, Deklah,
Decklah, Declah*

Delaney (Irish / French) The
dark challenger / from the
elder-tree grove
*Delaina, Delaine, Delainey,
Delainy, Delane, Delanie,
Delany, Delayna*

Delaware (English) From the
state of Delaware
*Delawair, Delaweir, Delwayr,
Delawayre, Delawaire,
Delawaer, Delawaere*

Delilah (Hebrew) A seductive
woman
Delila, Delyla, Delylah

Delta (Greek) From the mouth
of the river; the fourth letter
of the Greek alphabet
Dellta, Deltah, Delltah

Delyth (Welsh) A pretty young
woman
Delythe, Delith, Delithe

Demeter (Greek) In mythology,
the goddess of the harvest
*Demetra, Demitra, Demitras,
Dimetria, Demetre, Demetria,
Dimitra, Dimitre*

Demi (Greek) A petite woman
*Demie, Demee, Demy, Demiana,
Demianne, Demianna, Demea*

Denali (Indian) A superior
woman
*Denalie, Denaly, Denally,
Denalli, Denaley, Denalee,
Denallee, Denallie*

Dendara (Egyptian) From the
town on the river
*Dendera, Dendaria, Denderia,
Dendarra*

Denise (French) Feminine
form of Dennis
*Denese, Denyse, Denice,
Deniece, Denisa, Denissa,
Denize, Denyce, Denys*

Denver (English) From the
green valley

Derora (Hebrew) As free as a
bird
*Derorah, Derorra, Derorit,
Drora, Drorah, Drorit, Drorlya,
Derorice*

Derry (Irish) From the oak
grove
*Derrey, Derri, Derrie, Derree,
Derrea, Derreah*

Deryn (Welsh) A birdlike woman
Derran, Deren, Derhyn, Deron, Derrin, Derrine, Derron, Derrynne

Desiree (French) One who is desired
Desaree, Desirae, Desarae, Desire, Desyre, Dezirae, Deziree, Desirat

*Destiny (English) Recognizing one's certain fortune; fate
Destanee, Destinee, Destiney, Destini, Destinie, Destine, Destina, Destyni

Deva (Hindi) A divine being
Devi, Daeva

Devera (Latin) In mythology, goddess of brooms
Deverah

Devon (English) From the beautiful farmland; of the divine
Devan, Deven, Devenne, Devin, Devona, Devondra, Devonna, Devonne, Devyn

Dextra (Latin) Feminine form of Dexter; one who is skillful
Dex

Dharma (Hindi) The universal law of order
Darma

Dhisana (Hindi) In Hinduism, goddess of prosperity
Dhisanna, Disana, Disanna, Dhysana

Dhyana (Hindi) One who meditates

Diamond (French) Woman of high value
Diamanta, Diamonique, Diamante

Diana (Latin) Of the divine; in mythology, goddess of the moon and the hunt
Dianna, Dayanna, Dayana, Deanna

Diane (Latin) Form of Diana, meaning "of the divine"
Dayann, Dayanne, Deana, Deane, Deandra, Deann

Diata (African) Resembling a lioness
Diatah, Dyata, Diatta, Dyatah, Dyatta, Diattah, Dyattah

Dido (Latin) In mythology, the queen of Carthage who committed suicide
Dydo

Dielle (Latin) One who worships God
Diele, Diell, Diella, Diela, Diel

Dimity (English) Resembling a sheer cotton fabric
Dimitee, Dimitey, Dimitie, Dimitea, Dimiteah, Dimiti

Dimona (Hebrew) Woman from the south
Dimonah, Dymona, Demona, Demonah, Dymonah

Disa (English) Resembling an orchid

Discordia (Latin) In mythology, goddess of strife
Dyscordia, Diskordia, Dyskordia

Diti (Hindi) In Hinduism, an earth goddess
Dyti, Ditie, Dytie, Dity, Dyty, Ditey, Dytey, Ditee

Dixie (English) Woman from the South
Dixi, Dixy, Dixey, Dixee

Dolores (Spanish) Woman of sorrow; refers to the Virgin Mary
Dalores, Delora, Delores, Deloria, Deloris, Dolorcita, Dolorcitas, Dolorita

Domina (Latin) An elegant lady
Dominah, Domyna, Domynah

Dominique (French) Feminine form of Dominic; born on the Lord's day
Domaneke, Domanique, Domenica, Domeniga, Domenique, Dominee, Domineek, Domineke

Doreen (French / Gaelic) The golden one / a brooding woman
Dorene, Doreyn, Dorine, Dorreen, Doryne, Doreena, Dore, Doirean, Doireann, Doireanne, Doireana, Doireanna

Dorothy (Greek) A gift of God
Dasha, Dasya, Dodie, Dody, Doe, Doll, Dolley, Dolli

Dove (American) Resembling a bird of peace
Duv

Drisana (Indian) Daughter of the sun
Dhrisana, Drisanna, Drysana, Drysanna, Dhrysana, Dhrisanna, Dhrysanna

Drury (French) One who is greatly loved
Drurey, Druri, Drurie, Druree, Drurea, Drureah

Duana (Irish) Feminine form of Dwayne; little, dark one
Duane, Duayna, Duna, Dwana, Dwayna, Dubhain, Dubheasa

Duena (Spanish) One who acts as a chaperone

Dulce (Latin) A very sweet woman
Dulcina, Dulcee, Dulcie

Dumia (Hebrew) One who is silent
Dumiya, Dumiah, Dumiyah, Dumea, Dumeah

Duvessa (Irish) A dark beauty
Duvessah, Duvesa, Dubheasa, Duvesah

Dylan (Welsh) Daughter of the waves
Dylana, Dylane, Dyllan, Dyllana, Dillon, Dillan, Dillen, Dillian

Dympna (Irish) Fawn; the patron saint of the insane
Dymphna, Dimpna, Dimphna

Dyre (Scandinavian) One who is dear to the heart

Dysis (Greek) Born at sunset
Dysiss, Dysisse, Dysys, Dysyss, Dysysse

E

Eadlin (Anglo-Saxon) Born into royalty
Eadlinn, Eadlinne, Eadline, Eadlyn, Eadlynn, Eadlynne, Eadlina, Eadlyna

Eadrianne (American) One who stands out
Eadrian, Eadriann, Edriane, Edriana, Edrianna

Eara (Scottish) Woman from the east
Earah, Earra, Earrah, Earia, Earea, Earie, Eari, Earee

Earla (English) A great leader
Earlah

Earna (English) Resembling an eagle
Earnah, Earnia, Earnea, Earniah, Earneah

Easter (American) Born during the religious holiday
Eastere, Eastre, Eastir, Eastar, Eastor, Eastera, Easteria, Easterea

Easton (American) A wholesome woman
Eastan, Easten, Eastun, Eastyn

Eathelin (English) Noble woman of the waterfall
Eathelyn, Eathelinn, Eathelynn, Eathelina, Eathelyna, Ethelin, Ethelyn, Eathelen

Eber (Hebrew) One who moves beyond

Ebere (African) One who shows mercy
Eberre, Ebera, Eberia, Eberea, Eberria, Eberrea, Ebiere, Ebierre

Ebony (Egyptian) A dark beauty
Eboni, Ebonee, Ebonie, Ebonique, Eboney, Ebonea, Eboneah

Ebrill (Welsh) Born in April
Ebrille, Ebril, Evril, Evrill, Evrille

Edana (Irish) Feminine form of Aidan; a fiery woman
Edanah, Edanna, Ena, Eideann, Eidana

Eden (Hebrew) Place of pleasure
Edan, Edin, Edon

Edith (English) The spoils of war; one who is joyous; a treasure
Edyth, Eda, Edee, Edie, Edita, Edelina, Edeline, Edelyne, Edelynn, Edalyn, Edalynn, Edita, Edyta, Eydie

Edna (Hebrew) One who brings pleasure; a delight
Ednah, Edena, Edenah

Edra (English) A powerful and mighty woman
Edrah, Edrea, Edreah, Edria, Edriah

Eduarda (Portugese) Feminine form of Edward; a wealthy protector
Eduardia, Eduardea, Edwarda, Edwardia, Edwardea, Eduardina, Eduardyna, Edwardina

Edurne (Basque) Feminine form of Edur; woman of the snow
Edurna, Edurnia, Edurnea, Edurniya

Egan (American) A wholesome woman
Egann, Egen, Egun, Egon

Egeria (Latin) A wise counselor; in mythology, a water nymph
Egeriah, Egerea, Egereah, Egeriya, Egeriyah

Eileen (Gaelic) Form of Evelyn, meaning "a birdlike woman"
Eila, Eileene, Eilena, Eilene, Eilin, Eilleen, Eily, Eilean

Eiluned (Welsh) An idol worshipper
Luned

Eilwen (Welsh) One with a fair brow
Eilwenne, Eilwin, Eilwinne, Eilwyn, Eilwynne

Eirene (Greek) Form of Irene, meaning "a peaceful woman"
Eireen, Eireene, Eiren, Eir, Eireine, Eirein, Eirien, Eiriene

Eires (Greek) A peaceful woman
Eiress, Eiris, Eiriss, Eirys, Eiryss

Eirian (Welsh) One who is bright and beautiful
Eiriann, Eiriane, Eiriana, Eirianne, Eirianna

Ekron (Hebrew) One who is firmly rooted
Eckron, Ecron

Elaine (French) Form of Helen, meaning "the shining light"
Ellaine, Ellayne, Elaina, Elayna, Elayne, Elaene, Elaena, Ellaina

Elana (Hebrew) From the oak tree
Elanna, Elanah, Elanie, Elani, Elany, Elaney, Elanee, Elan

Elata (Latin) A high-spirited woman
Elatah, Elatta, Elattah, Elatia, Elatea, Elatiah, Elateah

Elath (Hebrew) From the grove of trees
Elathe, Elatha, Elathia, Elathea

Eldora (Greek) A gift of the sun
Eleadora, Eldorah, Eldorra, Eldoria, Eldorea

Eldoris (Greek) Woman of the sea
Eldorise, Eldoriss, Eldorisse, Eldorys, Eldoryss, Eldorysse

Eleacie (American) One who is forthright
Eleaci, Eleacy, Eleacey, Eleacee, Eleacea

Eleanor (Greek) Form of Helen, meaning "the shining light"
Eleanora, Eleni, Eleonora, Eleonore, Elinor, Elnora, Eleanore, Elinora, Nora

Elena (Spanish) Form of Helen, meaning "the shining light"
Elenah, Eleena, Eleenah, Elyna, Elynah, Elina, Elinah, Eleni, Eliana

Eliana (Hebrew) The Lord answers our prayers
Eleana, Elia, Eliane, Elianna, Elianne, Eliann, Elyana, Elyanna, Elyann, Elyan, Elyanne

Elica (German) One who is noble
Elicah, Elicka, Elika, Elyca, Elycka, Elyka, Elsha, Elsje

Elida (English) Resembling a winged creature
Elidah, Elyda, Eleeda, Eleda, Elieda, Eleida, Eleada

Elika (Hebrew) God will judge
Elikah, Elyka, Elicka, Elycka, Elica, Elyca

Eliphal (Hebrew) Delivered by God
Eliphala, Eliphall, Eliphalla, Eliphelet, Elipheleta

Elise (English) Form of Elizabeth, meaning "my God is bountiful"
Elisha, Elle, Elice, Elishia, Elissa, Elisa, Elisia, Elisse, Elysa, Elyse, Elysha, Elysia, Elyssa, Elysse, Ilyse

Elita (Latin) The chosen one
Elitah, Elyta, Elytah, Eleta, Eletah, Elitia, Elitea, Electa

*ᵀElizabeth (Hebrew) My God is bountiful; God's promise
Liz, Elisabet, Elisabeth, Elisabetta, Elissa, Eliza, Elizabel, Elizabet, Elsa, Beth, Babette, Libby, Lisa, Itzel, Ilsabeth, Ilsabet

*ᵀElla (German) From a foreign land
Elle, Ellee, Ellesse, Elli, Ellia, Ellie, Elly, Elá

Ellan (American) A coy woman
Ellane, Ellann

Ellen (English) Form of Helen, meaning "the shining light"
Elin, Elleen, Ellena, Ellene, Ellyn, Elynn, Elen, Ellin

Ellery (English) Form of Hilary, meaning "a cheerful woman"
Ellerey, Elleri, Ellerie, Elleree, Ellerea, Ellereah

Ellie (English) Form of Eleanor, meaning "the shining light"
Elli, Elly, Elley, Elleigh

Ellyanne (American) A shining and gracious woman
Ellianne, Ellyanna, Ellianna, Ellyann, Elliann, Ellyan, Ellian

Elma (German) Having God's protection
Elmah

Eloisa (Latin) Form of Louise, meaning "a famous warrior"
Eloise, Eloiza, Eloisee, Eloize, Eloizee, Aloisa, Aloise

Elrica (German) A great ruler
Elricah, Elrika, Elrikah, Elryca, Elrycah, Elryka, Elrykah, Elrick

Elton (American) A spontaneous woman
Elten, Eltan, Eltin, Eltyn, Eltun

Elvia (Irish) A friend of the elves
Elva, Elvie, Elvina, Elvinia, Elviah, Elvea, Elveah, Elvyna

Elvira (Latin) A truthful woman; one who can be trusted
Elvera, Elvita, Elvyra

Ema (Polynesian / German) One who is greatly loved / a serious woman

Ember (English) A low-burning fire
Embar, Embir, Embyr

Emerson (German) Offspring of Emery
Emmerson, Emyrson

^**Emery** (German) Industrious
Emeri, Emerie, Emori, Emorie, Emory

*ᵀ**Emily** (Latin) An industrious and hardworking woman
Emilee, Emilie, Emilia, Emelia, Emileigh, Emeleigh, Emeli, Emelie, Emely, Emmalee

*ᵀ**Emma** (German) One who is complete; a universal woman
Emmy, Emmajean, Emmalee, Emmi, Emmie, Emmaline, Emelina, Emeline

Emmylou (American) A universal ruler
Emmilou, Emmielou, Emylou, Emilou, Emielou

Ena (Irish) A fiery and passionate woman
Enah, Enat, Eny, Enya

Encarnación (Spanish) Refers to the Incarnation festival

Engracia (Spanish) A graceful woman
Engraciah, Engracea, Engraceah

Enslie (American) An emotional woman
Ensli, Ensley, Ensly, Enslee, Enslea, Ensleigh

Eranthe (Greek) As delicate as a spring flower
Erantha, Eranth, Eranthia, Eranthea

Erasta (African) A peaceful woman

Ercilia (American) One who is frank
Erciliah, Ercilea, Ercileah, Ercilya, Ercilyah, Erciliya, Erciliyah

Erendira (Spanish) Daughter born into royalty
Erendirah, Erendiria, Erendirea, Erendyra, Erendyria, Erendyrea, Erendeera, Erendiera

Erica (Scandinavian / Latin) Feminine form of Eric; ever the ruler / resembling heather
Erika, Ericka, Erikka, Eryka, Erike, Ericca, Erics, Eiric, Rica

Erimentha (Greek) A devoted protector
Erimenthe, Erimenthia, Erimenthea

Erin (Gaelic) Woman from Ireland
Erienne, Erina, Erinn, Erinna, Erinne, Eryn, Eryna, Erynn, Arin

Ernestina (German) Feminine form of Ernest; one who is determined; serious
Ernesta, Ernestine, Ernesha

Esdey (American) A warm and caring woman
Essdey, Esdee, Esdea, Esdy, Esdey, Esdi, Esdie, Esday

Eshah (African) An exuberant woman
Esha

Eshe (African) Giver of life
Eshey, Eshay, Esh, Eshae, Eshai

Esme (French) An esteemed woman
Esmai, Esmae, Esmay, Esmaye, Esmee

Esmeralda (Spanish) Resembling a prized emerald
Esmerald, Emerald, Emeralda, Emelda, Esma

Esne (English) Filled with happiness
Esnee, Esney, Esnea, Esni, Esnie, Esny

Essence (American) A perfumed woman
Essince, Esense, Esince, Essynce, Esynce

Esthelia (Spanish) A shining woman
Estheliah, Esthelea, Estheleah, Esthelya, Esthelyah, Estheliya, Estheliyah

Esther (Persian) Resembling the myrtle leaf
Ester, Eszter, Eistir, Eszti

Estrella (Spanish) Star
Estrela

Estrid (Norse) Form of Astrid, meaning "one with divine strength"
Estread, Estreed, Estrad, Estri, Estrod, Estrud, Estryd, Estrida

Etana (Hebrew) A strong and dedicated woman
Etanah, Etanna, Etannah, Etania, Etanea, Ethana, Ethanah, Ethania

Etaney (Hebrew) One who is focused
Etany, Etanie, Etani, Etanee, Etanea

Eternity (American) Lasting forever
Eternitie, Eterniti, Eternitey, Eternitee, Eternyty, Eternyti, Eternytie, Eternytee

Ethna (Irish) A graceful woman
Ethnah, Eithne, Ethne, Eithna, Eithnah

Eudlina (Slavic) A generous woman
Eudlinah, Eudleena, Eudleenah

Eudocia (Greek) One who is esteemed
Eudociah, Eudocea, Eudoceah

Eugenia (Greek) A well-born woman
Eugenie, Gina, Zenechka

Eulanda (American) A fair woman
Eulande, Euland, Eulandia, Eulandea

Eunice (Greek) One who conquers
Eunise, Eunyce, Eunis, Euniss, Eunyss, Eunysse

Eurybia (Greek) In mythology, a sea goddess and mother of Pallas, Perses, and Astraios
Eurybiah, Eurybea, Eurybeah

Eurynome (Greek) In mythology, the mother of the Graces
Eurynomie, Eurynomi

Euvenia (American) A hardworking woman

*Eva (Hebrew) Giver of life; a lively woman
Eve, Evetta, Evette, Evia, Eviana, Evie, Evita, Eeva

Evangeline (Greek) A bringer of good news
Evangelina, Evangelyn

*Evelyn (German) A bird-like woman
Evaleen, Evalina, Evaline, Evalyn, Evelin, Evelina, Eveline, Evelyne, Eileen, Evelynn

Evline (French) One who loves nature
Evleen, Evleene, Evlean, Evleane, Evlene, Evlyn, Evlyne

F

Faillace (French) A delicate and beautiful woman
Faillase, Faillaise, Falace, Falase, Fallase, Fallace

Fairly (English) From the far meadow
Fairley, Fairlee, Fairleigh, Fairli, Fairlie, Faerly, Faerli, Faerlie

***T*Faith** (English) Having a belief and trust in God
Faythe, Faithe, Faithful, Fayana, Fayanna, Fayanne, Fayane, Fayth

Fakhira (Arabic) A magnificent woman
Fakhirah, Fakhyra, Fakhyrah, Fakheera, Fakira, Fakirah, Fakeera, Fakyra

Fala (Native American) Resembling a crow
Falah, Falla, Fallah

Fallon (Irish) A commanding woman
Fallyn, Faline, Falinne, Faleen, Faleene, Falynne, Falyn, Falina

Fantasia (Latin) From the fantasy land
Fantasiah, Fantasea, Fantasiya, Fantazia, Fantazea, Fantaziya

Farley (English) From the fern clearing
Farly, Farli, Farlie, Farlee, Farleigh, Farlea, Farleah

Fate (Greek) One's destiny
Fayte, Faite, Faete, Faet, Fait, Fayt

Fatima (Arabic) The perfect woman
Fatimah, Fahima, Fahimah

Fatinah (Arabic) A captivating woman
Fatina, Fateena, Fateenah, Fatyna, Fatynah, Fatin, Fatine, Faatinah, Fateana, Fateanah, Fatiena, Fatienah, Fateina, Fateinah

Favor (English) One who grants her approval
Faver, Favar, Favorre

Fay (English) From the fairy kingdom; a fairy or an elf
Faye, Fai, Faie, Fae, Fayette, Faylinn, Faylyn, Faylynn

Fayina (Russian) An independent woman
Fayinah, Fayena, Fayeena, Fayeana, Fayiena, Fayeina

February (American) Born in the month of February
Februari, Februarie, Februarey, Februaree, Februarea

Feechi (African) A woman who worships God
Feechie, Feechy, Feechey, Feechee, Fychi, Fychie, Fychey, Fychy

Felicity (Latin) Form of Felicia, meaning "happy"
Felicy, Felicie, Felisa

Femi (African) God loves me
Femmi, Femie, Femy, Femey, Femee, Femea, Femeah

Fenia (Scandinavian) A gold worker
Feniah, Fenea, Feneah, Feniya, Feniyah, Fenya, Fenyah, Fenja

^Fernanda (Spanish) Feminine form of Fernando; an adventurous woman

Fernilia (American) A successful woman
Ferniliah, Fernilea, Fernileah, Fernilya, Fernilyah

Fia (Portuguese / Italian / Scottish) A weaver / from the flickering fire / arising from the dark of peace
Fiah, Fea, Feah, Fya, Fiya, Fyah, Fiyah

Fianna (Irish) A warrior huntress
Fiannah, Fiana, Fianne, Fiane, Fiann, Fian

Fielda (English) From the field
Fieldah, Felda, Feldah

Fife (American) Having dancing eyes
Fyfe, Fifer, Fify, Fifey, Fifee, Fifea, Fifi, Fifie

Fifia (African) Born on a Friday
Fifiah, Fifea, Fifeah, Fifeea, Fifeeah

Filipa (Spanish) Feminine form of Phillip; a friend of horses
Filipah, Filipina, Filipeena, Filipyna, Filippa, Fillipa, Fillippa

Fina (English) Feminine form of Joseph; God will add
Finah, Feena, Fyna, Fifine, Fifna, Fifne, Fini, Feana

Finley (Gaelic) A fair-haired hero
Finlay, Finly, Finlee, Finli, Finlie, Finnley, Finnlee, Finnli, Finn, Fin

Finnea (Gaelic) From the stream of the wood
Finneah, Finnia, Fynnea, Finniah, Fynnia

Fiona (Gaelic) One who is fair; a white-shouldered woman
Fionna, Fione, Fionn, Finna, Fionavar, Fionnghuala, Fionnuala, Fynballa

Firdaus (Arabic) From the garden in paradise

Flair (English) An elegant woman of natural talent
Flaire, Flare, Flayr, Flayre, Flaer, Flaere

Flame (American) A passionate and fiery woman
Flaym, Flayme, Flaime, Flaim, Flaem, Flaeme

Flannery (Gaelic) From the flatlands
Flanery, Flanneri, Flannerie, Flannerey, Flannaree, Flannerea

Fleming (English) Woman from Belgium
Flemyng, Flemming, Flemmyng

Fleta (English) One who is swift
Fletah, Flete, Fleda, Flita, Flyta

Florence (Latin) A flourishing woman; a blooming flower
Florencia, Florentina, Florenza, Florentine, Florentyna, Florenteena, Florenteene, Florentyne

Florizel (English) A young woman in bloom
Florizell, Florizelle, Florizele, Florizel, Florizella, Florizela, Florazel, Florazell

Fola (African) Woman of honor
Folah, Folla, Follah

Fontenot (French) One who is special

Forest (English) A woodland dweller
Forrest

Forever (American) Everlasting

Francesca (Italian) Form of Frances, meaning "one who is free"
Francia, Francina, Francisca, Franchesca, Francie, Frances

Frederica (German) Peaceful ruler
Freda, Freida, Freddie, Rica

Freira (Spanish) A sister
Freirah, Freyira, Freyirah

Freya (Norse) A lady
Freyah, Freyja, Freja

Freydis (Norse) Woman born into the nobility
Freydiss, Freydisse, Freydys, Fredyss, Fraidis, Fradis, Fraydis, Fraedis

Frida (German) Peaceful
Frieda, Fryda

Fuchsia (Latin) Resembling
the flower
*Fusha, Fushia, Fushea,
Fewsha, Fewshia, Fewshea*

Fury (Greek) An enraged
woman; in mythol-
ogy, a winged goddess who
punished wrongdoers
Furey, Furi, Furie, Furee

G

*ᵀ**Gabriella** (Italian / Spanish)
Feminine form of Gabriel;
heroine of God
*Gabriela, Gabriellia, Gabrila,
Gabryela, Gabryella*

***Gabrielle** (Hebrew) Feminine
form of Gabriel; heroine of
God
*Gabriel, Gabriela, Gabriele,
Gabriell, Gabriellen, Gabriellia,
Gabrila*

Galena (Greek) Feminine
form of Galen; one who is
calm and peaceful
*Galene, Galenah, Galenia,
Galenea*

Galiana (Arabic) The name of
a Moorish princess
*Galianah, Galianna, Galianne,
Galiane, Galian, Galyana,
Galyanna, Galyann*

Galila (Hebrew) From the
rolling hills
*Galilah, Gelila, Gelilah,
Gelilia, Gelilya, Glila, Glilah,
Galyla*

Galilee (Hebrew) From the
sacred sea
*Galileigh, Galilea, Galiley,
Galily, Galili, Galilie*

Galina (Russian) Form of
Helen, meaning "the shining
light"
*Galinah, Galyna, Galynah,
Galeena, Galeenah, Galine,
Galyne, Galeene*

Garbi (Basque) One who is
pure; clean
*Garbie, Garby, Garbey, Garbee,
Garbea, Garbeah*

Gardenia (English)
Resembling the sweet-smell-
ing flower
Gardeniah, Gardenea, Gardyna

Garima (Indian) A woman of
importance
Garimah, Garyma, Gareema

Garnet (English) Resembling the dark-red gem
Garnette, Granata, Grenata, Grenatta

Gasha (Russian) One who is well-behaved
Gashah, Gashia, Gashea, Gashiah, Gasheah

Gavina (Latin) Feminine form of Gavin; resembling the white falcon; woman from Gabio

Gaza (Hebrew) Having great strength
Gazah, Gazza, Gazzah

Geila (Hebrew) One who brings joy to others
Geela, Geelah, Geelan, Geilah, Geiliya, Geiliyah, Gelisa, Gellah

Gemma (Latin) As precious as a jewel
Gemmalyn, Gemmalynn, Gem, Gema, Gemmaline, Jemma

*Genesis (Hebrew) Of the beginning; the first book of the Bible
Genesies, Genesiss, Genessa, Genisis

Genevieve (French) White wave; fair-skinned
Genavieve, Geneve, Genevie, Genivee, Genivieve, Genoveva, Gennie, Genny

Georgia (Greek) Feminine form of George; one who works the earth; a farmer; from the state of Georgia
Georgeann, Georgeanne, Georgina, Georgena, Georgene, Georgetta, Georgette, Georgiana, Jeorjia

Gerardine (English) Feminine form of Gerard; one who is mighty with a spear
Gerarda, Gerardina, Gerardyne, Gererdina, Gerardyna, Gerrardene, Gerhardina, Gerhardine

Gertrude (German) Adored warrior
Geertruide, Geltruda, Geltrudis, Gert, Gerta, Gerte, Gertie, Gertina, Trudy

Giada (Italian) Jade
Giadda

*Gianna (Italian) Feminine form of John, meaning "God is gracious"
Gia, Giana, Giovana

Gillian (Latin) One who is youthful
Gilian, Giliana, Gillianne, Ghilian

Gina (Japanese / English)
A silvery woman / form of
Eugenia, meaning "a well-
born woman"; form of Jean,
meaning "God is gracious"
*Geana, Geanndra, Geena,
Geina, Gena, Genalyn,
Geneene, Genelle*

Ginger (English) A lively
woman; resembling the spice
*Gingee, Gingie, Ginjer, Gingea,
Gingy, Gingey, Gingi*

Ginny (English) Form of
Virginia, meaning "one who
is chaste; virginal"
*Ginnee, Ginnelle, Ginnette,
Ginnie, Ginnilee, Ginna,
Ginney, Ginni*

Giona (Italian) Resembling the
bird of peace
*Gionah, Gionna, Gyona,
Gyonna, Gionnah, Gyonah,
Gyonnah*

Giovanna (Italian) Feminine
form of Giovanni; God is gra-
cious
*Geovana, Geovanna,
Giavanna, Giovana, Giovani,
Giovanni, Giovanie, Giovanee*

Giselle (French) One who
offers her pledge
Gisel, Gisela, Gisella, Jiselle

Gita (Hindi / Hebrew) A beau-
tiful song / a good woman
*Gitah, Geeta, Geetah, Gitika,
Gatha, Gayatri, Gitel, Gittel*

Gitana (Spanish) A gypsy
woman
*Gitanah, Gitanna, Gitannah,
Gitane*

Githa (Anglo-Saxon) A gift
from God
Githah, Gytha

Giulia (Italian) Form of Julia,
meaning "one who is youthful, daughter of the sky"
*Giuliana, Giulie, Giulietta,
Giuliette*

Gladys (Welsh) Form of
Claudia, meaning "one who
is lame"
*Gladdis, Gladdys, Gladi,
Gladis, Gladyss, Gwladys,
Gwyladyss, Gleda*

Glenna (Gaelic) From the val-
ley between the hills
*Gleana, Gleneen, Glenene, Glenine,
Glen, Glenn, Glenne, Glennene*

Glenys (Welsh) A holy woman
*Glenice, Glenis, Glennice,
Glennis, Glennys, Glynis*

Gloria (Latin) A renowned and
highly praised woman
*Gloriana, Glorianna, Glorya,
Glorie, Gloree, Gloriane*

Golda (English) Resembling
the precious metal
*Goldarina, Goldarine, Goldee,
Goldi, Goldie, Goldina, Goldy,
Goldia*

Gordana (Serbian / Scottish)
A proud woman / one who is
heroic
*Gordanah, Gordanna, Gordania,
Gordaniya, Gordanea, Gordannah,
Gordaniah, Gordaniyah*

T*Grace** (Latin) Having God's
favor; in mythology, the Graces
were the personification of
beauty, charm, and grace
*Gracee, Gracella, Gracelynn,
Gracelynne, Gracey, Gracia,
Graciana, Gracie, Gracelyn*

Gracie (Latin) Form of Grace,
meaning "having God's favor"
Gracee, Gracey, Graci

Granada (Spanish) From the
Moorish kingdom
Granadda, Grenada, Grenadda

Greer (Scottish) Feminine
form of Gregory; one who is
alert and watchful
Grear, Grier, Gryer

Gregoria (Latin) Feminine
form of Gregory; one who is
alert and watchful
*Gregoriana, Gregorijana,
Gregorina, Gregorine, Gregorya,
Gregoryna, Gregorea, Gregoriya*

Greta (German) Resembling
a pearl
*Greeta, Gretal, Grete, Gretel,
Gretha, Grethe, Grethel, Gretna,
Gretchen*

Guadalupe (Spanish) From
the valley of wolves
Guadelupe, Lupe, Lupita

Gudny (Swedish) One who is
unspoiled
*Gudney, Gudni, Gudnie,
Gudne, Gudnee, Gudnea,
Gudneah*

Guinevere (Welsh) One who
is fair; of the white wave; in
mythology, King Arthur's
queen
*Guenever, Guenevere, Gueniver,
Guenna, Guennola, Guinever,
Guinna, Gwen*

Guiseppina (Italian) Feminine
form of Guiseppe; the Lord
will add
*Giuseppyna, Giuseppa,
Giuseppia, Giuseppea,
Guiseppie, Guiseppia,
Guiseppa, Giuseppina*

Gulielma (German) Feminine
form of Wilhelm; determined
protector
*Guglielma, Guillelmina,
Guillielma, Gulielmina,
Guillermina*

Gulinar (Arabic) Resembling the pomegranate
Gulinare, Gulinear, Gulineir, Gulinara, Gulinaria, Gulinarea

Gwendolyn (Welsh) One who is fair; of the white ring
Guendolen, Guendolin, Guendolinn, Guendolynn, Guenna, Gwen, Gwenda, Gwendaline, Wendy

Gwyneth (Welsh) One who is blessed with happiness
Gweneth, Gwenith, Gwenyth, Gwineth, Gwinneth, Gwinyth, Gwynith, Gwynna

Gytha (English) One who is treasured
Gythah

Habbai (Arabic) One who is much loved
Habbae, Habbay, Habbaye

Habiba (Arabic) Feminine form of Habib; one who is dearly loved; sweetheart
Habibah, Habeeba, Habyba

Hachi (Native American / Japanese) From the river / having good fortune
Hachie, Hachee, Hachiko, Hachiyo, Hachy, Hachey, Hachikka

Hadara (Hebrew) A spectacular ornament; adorned with beauty
Hadarah, Hadarit, Haduraq, Hadarra, Hadarrah

Hadassah (Hebrew) From the myrtle tree
Hadassa, Hadasah, Hadasa

Hadiya (Arabic) A gift from God; a righteous woman
Hadiyah, Hadiyyah, Haadiyah, Haadiya, Hadeeya, Hadeeyah, Hadieya, Hadieyah

Hadlai (Hebrew) In a resting state; one who hinders
Hadlae, Hadlay, Hadlaye

Hadley (English) From the field of heather
Hadlea, Hadleigh, Hadly, Hedlea, Hedleigh, Hedley, Hedlie, Hadlee

Hadria (Latin) From the town in northern Italy
Hadrea, Hadriana, Hadriane, Hadrianna, Hadrien, Hadrienne, Hadriah, Hadreah

Hafthah (Arabic) One who is protected by God
Haftha

Hagab (Hebrew) Resembling a grasshopper
Hagabah, Hagaba, Hagabe

Hagai (Hebrew) One who has been abandoned
Hagae, Hagay, Hagaye, Haggai, Haggae, Hagie, Haggie, Hagi

Hagen (Irish) A youthful woman
Hagan, Haggen, Haggan

Haggith (Hebrew) One who rejoices; the dancer
Haggithe, Haggyth, Haggythe, Hagith, Hagithe, Hagyth, Hagythe

Haidee (Greek) A modest woman; one who is well-behaved
Hadee, Haydee, Haydy, Haidi, Haidie, Haydi, Haydie, Haidy

*ᵀHailey (English) from the field of hay
*Haley, Hayle, Hailee, **Haylee**, Haylie, Haleigh, Hayley, Haeleigh*

Haimati (Indian) A queen of the snow-covered mountains
Haimatie, Haimaty, Haimatey, Haimatee, Haymati, Haymatie, Haymatee, Haimatea

Haimi (Hawaiian) One who searches for the truth
Haimie, Haimy, Haimey, Haimee, Haymi, Haymie, Haymee, Haimea

Hakana (Turkish) Feminine form of Hakan; ruler of the people; an empress
Hakanah, Hakanna, Hakane, Hakann, Hakanne

Hakkoz (Hebrew) One who has the qualities of a thorn
Hakoz, Hakkoze, Hakoze, Hakkoza, Hakoza

Halak (Hebrew) One who is bald; smooth

Haleigha (Hawaiian) Born with the rising sun
Haleea, Haleya, Halya

Hall (American) One who is distinguished
Haul

Hallie (Scandinavian, Greek, English) From the hall; woman of the sea; from the field of hay
Halley, Hallie, Halle, Hallee, Hally, Halleigh, Hallea, Halleah

Halo (Latin) Having a blessed aura
Haylo, Haelo, Hailo

Halsey (American) A playful woman
Halsy, Halsee, Halsea, Halsi, Halsie, Halcie, Halcy, Halcey

Halyn (American) A unique young woman
Halynn, Halynne, Halin, Halinn, Halinne

Hammon (Hebrew) Of the warm springs

Hamula (Hebrew) Feminine form of Hamul; spared by God
Hamulah, Hamulla, Hamullah

Hana (Japanese / Arabic) Resembling a flower blossom / a blissful woman
Hanah, Hanako

Hanan (Arabic) One who shows mercy and compassion

Hang (Vietnamese) Of the moon

Hanika (Hebrew) A graceful woman
Hanikah, Haneeka, Haneekah, Hanyka, Hanykah, Haneika, Haneikah, Hanieka

Hanita (Indian) Favored with divine grace
Hanitah, Hanyta, Haneeta, Hanytah, Haneetah, Haneita, Haneitah, Hanieta

Haniyah (Arabic) One who is pleased; happy
Haniya, Haniyyah, Haniyya, Hani, Hanie, Hanee, Hany, Haney

*ᵀHannah (Hebrew) Having favor and grace; in the Bible, mother of Samuel
Hanalee, Hanalise, Hanna, Hanne, Hannele, Hannelore, Hannie, Hanny, Chana

Hanya (Aboriginal) As solid as a stone

Happy (American) A joyful woman
Happey, Happi, Happie, Happee, Happea

Hara (Hebrew) From the mountainous land
Harah, Harra, Harrah

Haradah (Hebrew) One who is filled with fear
Harada

Harika (Turkish) A superior woman
Harikah, Haryka, Hareeka, Harykah, Hareekah, Hareaka, Hareakah

Hariti (Indian) In mythology, the goddess for the protection of children
Haritie, Haryti, Harytie, Haritee, Harytee, Haritea, Harytea

Harley (English) From the meadow of the hares
Harlea, Harlee, Harleen, Harleigh, Harlene, Harlie, Harli, Harly

Harlow (American) An impetuous woman

Harmony (English / Latin) Unity; musically in tune
Harmonie, Harmoni, Harmonee

^Harper (English) One who plays or makes harps

Harriet (German) Feminine form of Henry; ruler of the house
Harriett, Hanriette, Hanrietta, Harriette, Harrietta, Harrette

Harva (English) A warrior of the army

Hasibah (Arabic) Feminine form of Hasib; one who is noble and respected
Hasiba, Hasyba, Hasybah, Haseeba, Haseebah

Hasina (African) One who is good and beautiful
Hasinah, Hasyna, Hasynah

Haurana (Hebrew) Feminine form of Hauran; woman from the caves
Hauranna, Hauranah, Haurann, Hauranne

Haven (English) One who provides a safe haven
Hayven, Havan, Hayvan, Havon, Hayvon, Havin, Hayvin, Havyn, Hayvyn, Haeven, Haevin, Haevan

Havva (Turkish) A giver of the breath of life
Havvah, Havvia, Havviah

Hayden (English) From the hedged valley
Haden, Haydan, Haydn, Haydon, Haeden, Haedyn, Hadyn

Hayud (Arabic) From the mountain
Hayuda, Hayudah, Hayood, Hayooda

Hazel (English) From the hazel tree
Hazell, Hazelle, Haesel, Hazle, Hazal, Hayzel, Haezel, Haizel

Heartha (Teutonic) A gift from Mother Earth

Heather (English) Resembling the evergreen flowering plant
Hether, Heatha, Heath, Heathe

ᵀ**Heaven** (American) From
paradise; from the sky
*Heavely, Heavenly, Hevean,
Hevan, Heavynne, Heavenli,
Heavenlie, Heavenleigh,
Heavenlee, heavenley,
Heavenlea, Heavyn*

Hecate (Greek) In mythology, a goddess of fertility and
witchcraft
Hekate

Heidi (German) Of the nobility,
serene
Heidy, Heide, Hydie

Heirnine (Greek) Form of
Helen, meaning "the shining
light"
*Heirnyne, Heirneine,
Heirniene, Heirneene,
Heirneane*

Helen (Greek) The shining
light; in mythology, Helen
was the most beautiful
woman in the world
*Helene, Halina, Helaine,
Helana, Heleena, Helena,
Helenna, Hellen, Aleen, Elaine,
Eleanor, Elena, Ellen, Galina,
Heirnine, Helice, Leanna,
Yalena*

Helia (Greek) Daughter of the
sun
*Heliah, Helea, Heleah, Heliya,
Heliyah, Heller, Hellar*

Helice (Greek) Form of Helen,
meaning "the shining light"
*Helyce, Heleece, Heliece,
Heleace*

Helike (Greek) In mythology, a
willow nymph who nurtured
Zeus
*Helica, Helyke, Helika, Helyka,
Helyca*

Helle (Greek) In mythology,
the daughter of Athamas who
escaped sacrifice on the back
of a golden ram

Helma (German) Form of
Wilhelmina, meaning "deter-
mined protector"
*Helmah, Helmia, Helmea,
Helmina, Helmyna, Helmeena,
Helmine, Helmyne*

Heloise (French) One who is
famous in battle
Helois, Heloisa, Helewidis

Hen (English) Resembling the
mothering bird

Henrietta (German) Feminine
form of Henry; ruler of the
house
*Henretta, Henrieta, Henriette,
Henrika, Henryetta, Hetta, Hette,
Hettie*

Hephzibah (Hebrew) She is
my delight
Hepsiba, Hepzibeth, Hepsey

Herdis (Scandinavian) A battle maiden
Herdiss, Herdisse, Herdys

Hermelinda (Spanish) Bearing a powerful shield
Hermelynda, Hermalinda, Hermalynda, Hermelenda

Hermia (Greek) Feminine form of Hermes; a messenger of the gods
Hermiah, Hermea, Hermila

Hermona (Hebrew) From the mountain peak
Hermonah, Hermonna

Hernanda (Spanish) One who is daring
Hernandia, Hernandea, Hernandiya

Herra (Greek) Daughter of the earth
Herrah

Hersala (Spanish) A lovely woman
Hersalah, Hersalla, Hersallah, Hersalia, Hersaliah, Hersalea, Hersaleah

Hesiena (African) The first-born of twins
Hesienna, Hesienah, Heseina

Hesione (Greek) In mythology, a Trojan princess saved by Hercules from a sea monster

Hester (Greek) A starlike woman
Hestere, Hesther, Hesta, Hestar

Heven (American) A pretty young woman
Hevin, Hevon, Hevun, Hevven, Hevvin, Hevvon, Hevvun

Hezer (Hebrew) A woman of great strength
Hezir, Hezyr, Hezire, Hezyre, Hezere

Hiah (Korean) A bright woman
Heija, Heijah, Hia

Hibiscus (Latin) Resembling the showy flower
Hibiskus, Hibyscus, Hibyskus, Hybiscus, Hybiskus, Hybyscus, Hybyskus

Hikmah (Arabic) Having great wisdom
Hikmat, Hikma

Hilan (Greek) Filled with happines
Hylan, Hilane, Hilann, Hilanne, Hylane, Hylann, Hylanne

Hilary (Latin) A cheerful woman
Hillary, Hillery, Ellery

Hina (Polynesian) In mythology, a dual goddess symbolizing day and night
Hinna, Henna, Hinaa, Hinah, Heena, Hena

Hind (Arabic) Owning a group of camels; a wife of Muhammed
Hynd, Hinde, Hynde

Hinda (Hebrew) Resembling a doe
Hindah, Hindy, Hindey, Hindee, Hindi, Hindie, Hynda, Hyndy

Hiriwa (Polynesian) A silvery woman

Hitomi (Japanese) One who has beautiful eyes
Hitomie, Hitomee, Hitomea, Hitomy, Hitomey

Holda (German) A secretive woman; one who is hidden
Holde

Hollander (Dutch) A woman from Holland
Hollynder, Hollender, Holander, Holynder, Holender, Hollande, Hollanda

Holly (English) Of the holly tree
Holli, Hollie, Hollee, Holley, Hollye, Hollyanne, Holle, Hollea

Holton (American) One who is whimsical
Holten, Holtan, Holtin, Holtyn, Holtun

Holy (American) One who is pious or sacred
Holey, Holee, Holeigh, Holi, Holie, Holye, Holea, Holeah

Hope (English) One who has high expectations through faith

Hortensia (Latin) Woman of the garden
Hartencia, Hartinsia, Hortencia, Hortense, Hortenspa, Hortenxia, Hortinzia, Hortendana

Hova (African) Born into the middle class

Hoyden (American) A spirited woman
Hoiden, Hoydan, Hoidan, Hoydyn, Hoidyn, Hoydin, Hoidin

Hudson (English) One who is adventurous; an explorer
Hudsen, Hudsan, Hudsun, Hudsyn, Hudsin

Hueline (German) An intelligent woman
Huelene, Huelyne, Hueleine, Hueliene, Hueleene, Huleane

Huhana (Maori) Form of
Susannah, meaning "white
lily"
*Huhanah, Huhanna, Huhanne,
Huhann, Huhane*

Humita (Native American)
One who shells corn
*Humitah, Humyta, Humeeta,
Humieta, Humeita, Humeata,
Humytah, Humeetah*

Hutena (Hurrian) In mythol-
ogy, the goddess of fate
*Hutenah, Hutenna, Hutyna,
Hutina*

Huwaidah (Arabic) One who
is gentle
Huwaydah, Huwaida

Huyen (Vietnamese) A woman
with jet-black hair

Hypatia (Greek) An intellectu-
ally superior woman
Hypasia, Hypacia, Hypate

Hypermnestra (Greek) In
mythology, the mother of
Amphiareos

I

Ianthe (Greek) Resembling the
violet flower; in mythology,
a sea nymph, a daughter of
Oceanus
Iantha, Ianthia, Ianthina

Ibtesam (Arabic) One who
smiles often
Ibtisam, Ibtysam

Ibtihaj (Arabic) A delight;
bringer of joy
Ibtehaj, Ibtyhaj

Ida (Greek) One who is
diligent; hardworking; in
mythology, the nymph who
cared for Zeus on Mount Ida
*Idania, Idaea, Idalee, Idaia,
Idania, Idalia, Idalie, Idana*

Idil (Latin) A pleasant woman
Idyl, Idill, Idyll

Idoia (Spanish) Refers to the
Virgin Mary
Idoea, Idurre, Iratze, Izazkun

Idona (Scandinavian) A
fresh-faced woman
Idonah, Idonna, Idonnah

Ife (African) One who loves
and is loved
Ifeh, Iffe

Ignatia (Latin) A fiery woman;
burning brightly
Igantiah, Ignacia, Ignazia

Iheoma (Hawaiian) Lifted up
by God

Ikeida (American) A spontaneous woman
Ikeidah, Ikeyda, Ikeydah

Ilamay (French) From the
island
Ilamaye, Ilamai, Ilamae

Ilandere (American) Moon
woman
*Ilander, Ilanderre, Ilandera,
Ilanderra*

Ilia (Greek) From the ancient
city
*Iliah, Ilea, Ileah, Iliya, Iliyah,
Ilya, Ilyah*

Iliana (English) Form of
Aileen, meaning, "the light-
bearer"
*Ilianna, Ilyana, Ilyanna, Ilene,
Iline, Ilyne*

Ilithyia (Greek) In mythology,
goddess of childbirth
Ilithya, Ilithiya, Ilithyiah

Ilma (German) Form of
Wilhelmina, meaning "deter-
mined protector"
Ilmah, Illma, Illmah

Ilori (African) A special child;
one who is treasured
*Illori, Ilorie, Illorie, Ilory, Illory,
Ilorey, Illorey, Iloree*

Ilta (Finnish) Born at night
Iltah, Illta

Ilyse (German / Greek) Born
into the nobility / form of
Elyse, meaning "blissful"
Ilysea, Ilysia, Ilysse, Ilysea

Imala (Native American) One
who disciplines others
*Imalah, Imalla, Imallah,
Immala, Immalla*

Iman (Arabic) Having great
faith
*Imani, Imanie, Imania,
Imaan, Imany, Imaney,
Imanee, Imanea, Imain,
Imaine, Imayn*

Imanuela (Spanish) A faithful
woman
*Imanuella, Imanuel, Imanuele,
Imanuell*

Imari (Japanese) Daughter of
today
*Imarie, Imaree, Imarea, Imary,
Imarey*

Imelda (Italian) Warrior in the universal battle
Imeldah, Imalda, Imaldah

Imperia (Latin) A majestic woman
Imperiah, Imperea, Impereah, Imperial, Imperiel, Imperielle, Imperialle

Ina (Polynesian) In mythology, a moon goddess
Inah, Inna, Innah

Inaki (Asian) Having a generous nature
Inakie, Inaky, Inakey, Inakea, Inakee

Inanna (Sumerian) A lady of the sky; in mythology, goddess of love, fertility, war, and the earth
Inannah, Inana, Inanah, Inann, Inanne, Inane

Inara (Arabic) A heaven-sent daughter; one who shines with light
Inarah, Innara, Inarra, Innarra

Inari (Finnish / Japanese) Woman from the lake / one who is successful
Inarie, Inaree, Inary, Inarey, Inarea, Inareah

Inaya (Arabic) One who cares for the well-being of others
Inayah, Inayat

Inca (Indian) An adventurer
Incah, Inka, Inkah, Incka, Inckah

India (English) From the river; woman from India
Indea, Indiah, Indeah, Indya, Indiya, Indee, Inda, Indy

Indiana (English) From the land of the Indians; from the state of Indiana
Indianna, Indyana, Indyanna

Indiece (American) A capable woman
Indeice, Indeace, Indeece, Indiese, Indeise, Indeese, Indease

Indigo (English) Resembling the plant; a purplish-blue dye
Indygo, Indeego

Ineesha (American) A sparkling woman
Ineeshah, Ineisha, Ineishah, Iniesha, Inieshah, Ineasha, Ineashah, Ineysha

Ingalls (American) A peaceful woman

Ingelise (Danish) Having the grace of the god Ing
Ingelisse, Ingeliss, Ingelyse, Ingelisa, Ingelissa, Ingelysa, Ingelyssa

Inghean (Scottish) Her father's daughter
Ingheane, Inghinn, Ingheene, Ingheen, Inghynn

Ingrid (Scandinavian) Having the beauty of the God Ing
Ingred, Ingrad, Inga, Inge, Inger, Ingmar, Ingrida, Ingria, Ingrit, Inkeri

Inis (Irish) Woman from Ennis
Iniss, Inisse, Innis, Inys, Innys, Inyss, Inysse

Intisar (Arabic) One who is victorious; triumphant
Intisara, Intisarah, Intizar, Intizara, Intizarah, Intisarr, Intysarr, Intysar

Iolanthe (Greek) Resembling a violet flower
Iolanda, Iolanta, Iolantha, Iolante, Iolande, Iolanthia, Iolanthea

Iona (Greek) Woman from the island
Ionna, Ioane, Ioann, Ioanne

Ionanna (Hebrew) Filled with grace
Ionannah, Ionana, Ionann, Ionane, Ionanne

Ionia (Greek) Of the sea and islands
Ionya, Ionija, Ioniah, Ionea, Ionessa, Ioneah, Ioniya

Iosepine (Hawaiian) Form of Josephine, meaning "God will add"
Iosephine, Iosefa, Iosefena, Iosefene, Iosefina, Iosefine, Iosepha, Iosephe

Iowa (Native American) Of the Iowa tribe; from the state of Iowa

Iphedeiah (Hebrew) One who is saved by the Lord

Iphigenia (Greek) One who is born strong; in mythology, daughter of Agamemnon
Iphigeneia, Iphigenie

Ipsa (Indian) One who is desired
Ipsita, Ipsyta, Ipseeta, Ipseata, Ipsah

Iratze (Basque) Refers to the Virgin Mary
Iratza, Iratzia, Iratzea, Iratzi, Iratzie, Iratzy, Iratzey, Iratzee

Ireland (Celtic) The country of the Irish
Irelan, Irelann

Irem (Turkish) From the heavenly gardens
Irema, Ireme, Iremia, Iremea

Irene (Greek) A peaceful woman; in mythology, the goddess of peace
Ira, Irayna, Ireen, Iren, Irena, Irenea, Irenee, Irenka, Eirene

Ireta (Greek) One who is serene
Iretah, Iretta, Irettah, Irete, Iret, Irett, Ireta

Iris (Greek) Of the rainbow; a flower; a messenger goddess
Irida, Iridiana, Iridianny, Irisa, Irisha, Irita, Iria, Irea, Iridian, Iriss, Irys, Iryss

Irma (German) A universal woman

Irta (Greek) Resembling a pearl
Irtah

Irune (Basque) Refers to the Holy Trinity
Iroon, Iroone, Iroun, Iroune

*ᵀIsabel (Spanish) Form of Elizabeth, meaning "my God is bountiful; God's promise"
Isabeau, Isabela, Isabele, Isabelita, Isabell, Isabelle, Ishbel, Ysabel

*ᵀIsabella (Italian / Spanish) Form of Isabel, meaning consecrated to God
Isabela, Isabelita, Isobella, Izabella, Isibella, Isibela

Isadore (Greek) A gift from the goddess Isis
Isadora, Isador, Isadoria, Isidor, Isidoro, Isidorus, Isidro, Isidora

Isana (German) A strong-willed woman
Isanah, Isanna, Isane, Isann

Isela (American) A giving woman
Iselah, Isella, Isellah

Isis (Egyptian) In mythology, the most powerful of all goddesses

^Isla (Gaelic) From the island
Islae, Islai, Isleta

Isleen (Gaelic) Form of Aisling, meaning "a dream or vision; an inspiration"
Isleene, Islyne, Islyn, Isline, Isleine, Isliene, Islene, Isleyne

Isolde (Celtic) A woman known for her beauty; in mythology, the lover of Tristan
Iseult, Iseut, Isold, Isolda, Isolt, Isolte, Isota, Isotta

Isra (Arabic) One who travels in the evening
Israh, Isria, Isrea, Israt

Itiah (Hebrew) One who is comforted by God
Itia, Iteah, Itea, Itiyah, Itiya, Ityah, Itya

Itidal (Arabic) One who is cautious
Itidalle, Itidall, Itidale

Itsaso (Basque) Woman of the ocean
Itasasso, Itassaso, Itassasso

Iudita (Hawaiian) An affectionate woman
Iuditah, Iudyta, Iudytah, Iudeta, Iudetah

Iuginia (Hawaiian) A high-born woman
Iuginiah, Iuginea, Iugineah, Iugynia

Ivana (Slavic) Feminine form of Ivan; God is gracious
Iva, Ivah, Ivania, Ivanka, Ivanna, Ivanya, Ivanea, Ivane, Ivanne

Ivory (English) Having a creamy-white complexion; as precious as elephant tusks
Ivorie, Ivorine, Ivoreen, Ivorey, Ivoree, Ivori, Ivoryne, Ivorea

Ivy (English) Resembling the evergreen vining plant
Ivie, Ivi, Ivea

Iwilla (American) She shall rise
Iwillah, Iwilah, Iwila, Iwylla, Iwyllah, Iwyla, Iwylah

Ixchel (Mayan) The rainbow lady; in mythology, the goddess of the earth, moon, and healing
Ixchell, Ixchelle, Ixchela, Ixchella, Ixchal, Ixchall, Ixchalle, Ixchala

Iyabo (African) The mother is home

Izanne (American) One who calms others
Izann, Izane, Izana, Izan, Izanna

Izolde (Greek) One who is philosophical
Izold, Izolda

J

Jacey (American) Form of Jacinda, meaning "resembling the hyacinth"
Jacee, Jacelyn, Jaci, Jacine, Jacy, Jaicee, Jaycee, Jacie

Jacinda (Spanish) Resembling
the hyacinth
*Jacenda, Jacenia, Jacenta,
Jacindia, Jacinna, Jacinta,
Jacinth, Jacintha, Jacinthe,
Jacinthia, Jacynth, Jacyntha,
Jacynthe, Jacynthia,*

Jakinda, Jakinta, Jaikinda,
JaekindaJacqueline (French)
Feminine form of Jacques;
the supplanter
*Jackie, Xaquelina, Jacalin,
Jacalyn, Jacalynn, Jackalin,
Jackalinne, Jackelyn, Jacquelyn*

Jade (Spanish) Resembling the
green gemstone
*Jadeana, Jadee, Jadine, Jadira,
Jadrian, Jadrienne, Jady*

Jaden (Hebrew / English) One
who is thankful to God / form
of Jade, meaning "resembling
the green gemstone"
*Jadine, Jadyn, Jadon, Jayden,
Jadyne, Jaydyn, Jaydon, Jaydine*

Jadzia (Polish) A princess;
born into royalty
Jadziah, Jadzea, Jadzeah

Jae (English) Feminine form
of Jay; resembling a jaybird
*Jai, Jaelana, Jaeleah, Jaelyn,
Jaenelle, Jaya*

Jael (Hebrew) Resembling a
mountain goat
Jaella, Jaelle, Jayel, Jaele, Jayil

Jaen (Hebrew) Resembling an
ostrich
Jaena, Jaenia, Jaenea, Jaenne

Jaffa (Hebrew) A beautiful
woman
Jaffah, Jafit, Jafita

Jalila (Arabic) An important
woman; one who is exalted
Jalilah, Jalyla, Jalylah, Jaleela

Jamaica (American) From the
island of springs
*Jamaeca, Jamaika, Jemaica,
Jamika, Jamieka*

Jamie (Hebrew) Feminine
form of James; she who sup-
plants
*Jaima, Jaime, Jaimee,
Jaimelynn, Jaimey, Jaimi,
Jaimie, Jaimy*

Janan (Arabic) Of the heart
and soul

Jane (Hebrew) Feminine form
of John; God is gracious
*Jaina, Jaine, Jainee, Janey,
Jana, Janae, Janaye, Jandy,
Sine, Janel, Janelle*

Janet (Scottish) Feminine
form of John, meaning "God
is gracious"
*Janetta, Jenetta, Janeta,
Janette, Janit*

Janis (English) Feminine form of John; God is gracious
Janice, Janeece, Janess, Janessa, Janesse, Janessia, Janicia, Janiece

Janiyah (American) Form of Jana, meaning gracious, merciful
Janiya, Janiah

Jarah (Hebrew) A sweet and kind woman

Jasher (Hebrew) One who is righteous; upright
Jashiere, Jasheria, Jasherea

Jaslene (American) Form of Jocelyn, meaning joy
Jaslin, Jaslyn, Jazlyn, Jazlynn

*Jasmine (Persian) Resembling the climbing plant with fragrant flowers
Jaslyn, Jaslynn, Jasmin, Jasmyn, Jazmin, Jazmine, Jazmyn

Javiera (Spanish) Feminine form of Xavier; one who is bright; the owner of a new home
Javierah, Javyera, Javyerah, Javeira, Javeirah

ᵀJayda (Resembling the green gemstone)
Jada, Jaydah, Jaida, Jaidah

Jayla (Arabic) One who is charitable
Jaela, Jaila, Jaylah, Jaylee, Jaylen, Jaylene, Jayleen, Jaylin, Jaylyn, Jaylynn

Jean (Hebrew) Feminine form of John; God is gracious
Jeanae, Jeanay, Jeane, Jeanee, Jeanelle, Jeanetta, Jeanette, Jeanice, Gina

Jemima (Heberw) Our little dove; in the Bible, the eldest of Job's daughters
Jemimah, Jamina, Jeminah, Jemmimah, Jemmie, Jemmy, Jem, Jemmi, Jemmey, Jemmee, Jemmea

Jemma (English) Form of Gemma, meaning "as precious as a jewel"
Jemmah, Jema, Jemah, Jemmalyn, Jemalyn

Jena (Arabic) Our little bird
Jenna, Jenah

Jendayi (Egyptian) One who is thankful
Jendayie, Jendayey, Jendayee

ᵀJennifer (Welsh) One who is fair; a beautiful girl
*Jenefer, Jeni, Jenifer, Jeniffer, Jenn, Jennee, Jenni, Jen, **Jenna**, Jenny*

Jeorjia (American) Form of Georgia, meaning "one who works the earth; a farmer"
Jeorgia, Jeorja, Jorja, Jorjette, Jorgette, Jorjeta, Jorjetta, Jorgete

Jereni (Slavic) One who is peaceful
Jerenie, Jereny, Jereney, Jerenee

Jermaine (French) Woman from Germany
Jermainaa, Jermane, Jermayne, Jermina, Jermana, Jermayna

*ᵀJessica (Hebrew) The Lord sees all
Jess, Jessa, Jessaca, Jessaka, Jessalin, Jessalyn, Jesse, Jesseca, Yessica, Jessie

Jetta (Danish) Resembling the jet-black lustrous gemstone
Jette, Jett, Jeta, Jete, Jettie, Jetty, Jetti, Jettey

Jewel (French) One who is playful; resembling a precious gem
Jewell, Jewelle, Jewelyn, Jewelene, Jewelisa, Jule, Jewella, Juelline

Jezebel (Hebrew) One who is not exalted; in the Bible, the queen of Israel punished by God
Jessabell, Jetzabel, Jezabel, Jezabella, Jezebelle, Jezibel, Jezibelle, Jezybell

Jie (Chinese) One who is pure; chaste

Jiera (Lithuanian) A lively woman
Jierah, Jyera, Jyerah, Jierra, Jyerra

ᵀJillian (English) Form of Gillian, meaning "one who is youthful"
Jilian, Jiliana, Jilllaine, Jillan, Jillana, Jillane, Jillanne, Jillayne, Jillene, Jillesa, Jilliana, Jilliane, Jilliann, Jillianna, Jill

Jimena (Spanish) One who is heard

Jinelle (Welsh) Form of Genevieve, meaning "white wave; fair-skinned"
Jinell, Jinele, Jinel, Jynelle, Jynell, Jynele, Jynel

Jiselle (American) Form of Giselle, meaning "one who offers her pledge"
Jisell, Jisele, Jisela, Jizelle, Joselle, Jisella, Jizella, Jozelle

Jo (English) Feminine form of Joseph; God will add
Jobelle, Jobeth, Jodean, Jodelle, Joetta, Joette, Jolinda, Jolisa

Joanna (French) Feminine form of John, meaning "God is Gracious"
Joana

*Jocelyn (German / Latin)
From the tribe of Gauts / one
who is cheerful, happy
*Jocelin, Jocelina, Jocelinda,
Joceline, Jocelyne, Jocelynn,
Jocelynne, Josalind, Joslyn,
Joslynn, Joselyn*

Joda (Hebrew) An ancestor of
Christ

Jolan (Greek) Resembling a
violet flower
*Jola, Jolaine, Jolande, Jolanne,
Jolanta, Jolantha, Jolandi,
Jolanka*

Jolene (English) Feminine
form of Joseph; God will add
*Joeline, Joeleen, Joeline, Jolaine,
Jolean, Joleen, Jolena, Jolina*

Jolie (French) A pretty young
woman
*Joly, Joely, Jolee, Joleigh, Joley,
Joli*

Jonina (Israeli) Resembling a
little dove
*Joninah, Jonyna, Jonynah,
Joneena, Joneenah, Jonine,
Jonyne, Joneene*

Jorah (Hebrew) Resembling an
autumn rose
Jora

Jord (Norse) In mythology,
goddess of the earth
Jorde

Jordan (Hebrew) Of the down-
flowing river; in the Bible,
the river where Jesus was
baptized
*Jardena, Johrdan, Jordain,
Jordaine, Jordana, Jordane,
Jordanka, Jordyn, Jordin*

Josephine (French) Feminine
form of Joseph; God will add
*Josefina, Josephene, Jo, Josie,
Iosepine*

^Journey (American) One who
likes to travel
Journy, Journi, Journie, Journee

Jovana (Spanish) Feminine
form of Jovian; daughter of
the sky
*Jeovana, Jeovanna, Jovanna,
Jovena, Jovianne, Jovina,
Jovita, Joviana*

Joy (Latin) A delight; one who
brings pleasure to others
*Jioia, Jioya, Joi, Joia, Joie, Joya,
Joyann, Joyanna*

Joyce (English) One who
brings joy to others
*Joice, Joyceanne, Joycelyn,
Joycelynn, Joyse, Joyceta*

Judith (Hebrew) Woman from
Judea
*Judithe, Juditha, Judeena,
Judeana, Judyth, Judit,
Judytha, Judita, Hudes*

*ᵀJulia (Latin) One who is youthful; daughter of the sky
Jiulia, Joleta, Joletta, Jolette, Julaine, Julayna, Julee, Juleen, Julie, Julianne

Juliana (Spanish) Form of Julia, meaning "one who is youthful"
Julianna

^Juliet (French) Form of Julia, meaning one who is youthful
Juliette, Julitta, Julissa

July (Latin) Form of Julia, meaning "one who is youthful; daughter of the sky"; born during the month of July
Julye

June (Latin) One who is youthful; born during the month of June
Junae, Junel, Junelle, Junette, Junita, Junia

Justice (English) One who upholds moral rightness and fairness
Justyce, Justiss, Justyss, Justis, Justus, Justise

K

Kachina (Native American) A spiritual dancer
Kachine, Kachinah, Kachineh, Kachyna, Kacheena, Kachynah, Kacheenah, Kacheana

Kadin (Arabic) A beloved companion
Kadyn, Kadan, Kaden, Kadon, Kadun, Kaedin, Kaeden, Kaydin

Kaelyn (English) A beautiful girl from the meadow
Kaelynn, Kaelynne, Kaelin, Kailyn, Kaylyn, Kaelinn, Kaelinne

Kagami (Japanese) Displaying one's true image
Kagamie, Kagamy, Kagamey, Kagamee, Kagamea

Kailasa (Indian) From the silver mountain
Kailasah, Kailassa, Kaylasa, Kaelasa, Kailas, Kailase

*Kaitlyn (Greek) Form of Katherine, meaning "one who is pure, virginal"
Kaitlin, Kaitlan, Kaitleen, Kaitlynn, Katalin, Katalina, Katalyn, Katelin, Kateline, Katelinn, Katelyn, Katelynn, Katilyn, Katlin

Kakra (Egyptian) The younger of twins
Kakrah

Kala (Arabic / Hawaiian) A moment in time / form of Sarah, meaning "a princess; lady"
Kalah, Kalla, Kallah

Kalifa (Somali) A chaste and holy woman
Kalifah, Kalyfa, Kalyfah, Kaleefa, Kaleefah, Kalipha, Kalypha, Kaleepha, Kaleafa, Kaleafah, Kaleapha

Kalinda (Indian) Of the sun
Kalindah, Kalynda, Kalinde, Kalindeh, Kalindi, Kalindie, Kalyndi, Kalyndie

Kallie (English) Form of Callie, meaning "a beautiful girl"
Kalli, Kallita, Kally, Kalley, Kallee, Kalleigh, Kallea, Kalleah

Kalma (Finnish) In mythology, goddess of the dead

Kalyan (Indian) A beautiful and auspicious woman
Kalyane, Kalyanne, Kalyann, Kaylana, Kaylanna, Kalliyan, Kaliyan, Kaliyane

Kama (Indian) One who loves and is loved
Kamah, Kamma, Kammah

Kamala (Arabic) A woman of perfection
Kamalah, Kammala, Kamalla

Kamaria (African) Of the moon
Kamariah, Kamarea, Kamareah, Kamariya, Kamariyah

Kambiri (African) Newest addition to the family
Kambirie, Kambiry, Kambyry

Kamea (Hawaiian) The one and only; precious one
Kameo

Kamyra (American) Surrounded by light
Kamira, Kamera, Kamiera, Kameira, Kameera, Kameara

Kanan (Indian) From the garden

Kanda (Native American) A magical woman
Kandah

Kanika (African) A dark, beautiful woman
Kanikah, Kanyka, Kanicka

Kantha (Indian) A delicate woman
Kanthah, Kanthe, Kantheh

Kanya (Thai) A young girl; a virgin

Kaoru (Japanese) A fragrant girl
Kaori

Kara (Greek / Italian / Gaelic) One who is pure / dearly loved / a good friend
Karah, Karalee, Karalie, Karalyn, Karalynn, Karrah, Karra, Khara

Karcsi (French) A joyful singer
Karcsie, Karcsy, Karcsey, Karcsee, Karcsea

Karen (Greek) Form of Katherine, meaning "one who is pure; virginal"
Karan, Karena, Kariana, Kariann, Karianna, Karianne, Karin, Karina

Karina (Scandinavian / Russian) One who is dear and pure
Karinah, Kareena, Karyna

Karisma (English) Form of Charisma, meaning "blessed with charm"
Kharisma, Karizma, Kharizma

Karissa (Greek) Filled with grace and kindess; very dear
Karisa, Karyssa, Karysa, Karessa, Karesa, Karis, Karise

Karla (German) Feminine form of Karl; a small strong, woman
Karly, Karli, Karlie, Karleigh, Karlee, Karley, Karlin, Karlyn, Karlina, Karleen

Karmel (Latin) Form of Carmel, meaning "of the fruitful orchard"
Karmelle, Karmell, Karmele, Karmela, Karmella

Karoline (English) A small and strong woman
Karolina, Karolinah, Karolyne, Karrie, Karie, Karri, Kari, Karry

Karsen (American) Variation of the Scottish Carson, meaning "from the swamp"
Karsyn, Karsin

Karsten (Greek) The anointed one
Karstin, Karstine, Karstyn, Karston, Karstan, Kiersten, Keirsten

Kasey (Irish) Form of Casey, meaning "a vigilant woman"
Kacie, Kaci, Kacy, KC, Kacee, Kacey, Kasie, Kasi

Kasi (Indian) From the holy city; shining

Kasmira (Slavic) A peacemaker
Kasmirah, Kasmeera

Kate (English) Form of Katherine, meaning "one who is pure, virginal"
Katie, Katey, Kati

*Katherine (Greek) Form of Catherine, meaning "one who is pure; virginal"
Katharine, Katharyn, Kathy, Kathleen, Katheryn, Kathie, Kathrine, Kathryn, Karen, Kay

Katriel (Hebrew) Crowned by God
Katriele, Katrielle, Katriell

Kaveri (Indian) From the sacred river
Kaverie, Kauveri, Kauverie, Kavery, Kaverey, Kaveree, Kaverea, Kauvery

Kavinli (American) One who is eager
Kavinlie, Kavinly, Kavinley

Kay (English / Greek) The keeper of the keys / form of Katherine, meaning "one who is pure; virginal"
Kaye, Kae, Kai, Kaie, Kaya, Kayana, Kayane, Kayanna

Kayden (American) Form of Kaden, meaning "a beloved companion"

*Kayla (Arabic / Hebrew) Crowned with laurel
Kaylah, Kalan, Kalen, Kalin, Kalyn, Kalynn, Kaylan, Kaylana, Kaylin, Kaylen, Kaylynn, Kaylyn, Kayle

*ᵀKaylee (American) Form of Kayla, meaning "crowned with laurel"
Kaleigh, Kaley, Kaelee, Kaeley, Kaeli, Kailee, Kailey, Kalee, Kayleigh, Kayley, Kayli, Kaylie

Kearney (Irish) The winner
Kearny, Kearni, Kearnie, Kearnee, Kearnea

Keaton (English) From a shed town
Keatan, Keatyn, Keatin, Keatun

Keavy (Irish) A lovely and graceful girl
Keavey, Keavi, Keavie, Keavee, Keavea

Keeya (African) Resembling a flower
Keeyah, Kieya, Keiya, Keyya

Kefira (Hebrew) Resembling a young lioness
Kefirah, Kefiera, Kefeira

Keira (Irish) Form of Kiera, meaning "little dark-haired one"
Kierra, Kyera, Kyerra, Keiranne, Kyra, Kyrie, Kira, Kiran

Keisha (American) The favorite child; form of Kezia, meaning "of the spice tree"
Keishla, Keishah, Kecia, Kesha, Keysha, Keesha, Kiesha, Keshia

Kelly (Irish) A lively and bright-headed woman
Kelley, Kelli, Kellie, Kellee, Kelliegh, Kellye, Keely, Keelie, Keeley, Keelyn

Kelsey (English) From the island of ships
Kelsie, Kelcey, Kelcie, Kelcy, Kellsie, Kelsa, Kelsea, Kelsee, Kelsi, Kelsy, Kellsey

Kendall (Welsh) From the royal valley
Kendal, Kendyl, Kendahl, Kindall, Kyndal, Kenley

Kendra (English) Feminine form of Kendrick; having royal power; from the high hill
Kendrah, Kendria, Kendrea, Kindra, Kindria

^Kennedy (Gaelic) A helmeted chief
Kennedi, Kennedie, Kennedey, Kennedee, Kenadia, Kenadie, Kenadi, Kenady, Kenadey

Kensington (English) A brash lady
Kensyngton, Kensingtyn, Kinsington, Kinsyngton, Kinsingtyn

Kenwei (Arabic) Resembling a water lily

Kenyangi (Ugandan) Resembling the white egret

Kerensa (Cornish) One who loves and is loved
Kerinsa, Keransa, Kerensia, Kerensea, Kerensya, Kerenz, Kerenza, Keranz

Kerr (Scottish) From the marshland

Keshon (American) Filled with happiness
Keyshon, Keshawn, Keyshawn, Kesean, Keysean, Keshaun, Keyshaun, Keshonna

Kevina (Gaelic) Feminine form of Kevin; a beautiful and beloved child
Kevinah, Keva, Kevia, Kevinne, Kevyn, Kevynn

Keyla (English) A wise daughter

Kezia (Hebrew) Of the spice tree
Keziah, Kesia, Kesiah, Kesi, Kessie, Ketzia, Keisha

Khai (American) Unlike the others; unusual
Khae, Khay, Khaye

Khalida (Arabic) Feminine form of Khalid; an immortal woman
Khalidah, Khaleeda, Khalyda

Khaliqa (Arabic) Feminine form of Khaliq; a creator; one who is well-behaved
Khaliqah, Khalyqa, Khaleeqa

Khayriyyah (Arabic) A charitable woman
Khayriyah, Khariyyah, Khariya, Khareeya

Khepri (Egyptian) Born of the morning sun
Kheprie, Kepri, Keprie, Khepry, Kepry, Khepree, Kepree, Kheprea

Khiana (American) One who is different
Khianna, Khiane, Khianne, Khian, Khyana, Khyanna, Kheana, Kheanna

*^**Khloe** (Greek) Form of Chloe, meaning "a flourishing woman, blooming"

Kiara (American) Form of Chiara, meaning "daughter of the light"

Kichi (Japanese) The fortunate one

Kidre (American) A loyal woman
Kidrea, Kidreah, Kidria, Kidriah, Kidri, Kidrie, Kidry, Kidrey

Kiele (Hawaiian) Resembling the gardenia
Kielle, Kiel, Kiell, Kiela, Kiella

Kikka (German) The mistress of all
Kika, Kykka, Kyka

Kiley (American) Form of Kylie, meaning "a boomerang"

Kimana (American) Girl from the meadow
Kimanah, Kimanna

Kimball (English) Chief of the warriors; possessing royal boldness
Kimbal, Kimbell, Kimbel, Kymball, Kymbal

*****Kimberly** (English) Of the royal fortress
Kimberley, Kimberli, Kimberlee, Kimberleigh, Kimberlin, Kimberlyn, Kymberlie, Kymberly

Kimeo (American) Filled with happiness
Kimeyo

Kimetha (American) Filled with joy
Kimethah, Kymetha

Kimiko (Japanese) A noble child; without equal

Kimora (American) Form of Kimberly, meaning "royal"

Kina (Hawaiian) Woman of China

^**Kinley** (American) Variation of McKinley, Scottish, meaning offspring of the fair hero

Kinsey (English) The king's victory
Kinnsee, Kinnsey, Kinnsie, Kinsee, Kinsie, Kinzee, Kinzie, Kinzey

^**Kinsley** (English) From the king's meadow
Kinsly, Kinslee, Kinsleigh, Kinsli, Kinslie, Kingsley, Kingslee, Kingslie

Kioko (Japanese) A daughter born with happiness

Kirima (Eskimo) From the hill
Kirimah, Kiryma, Kirymah, Kirema, Kiremah, Kireema, Kireemah, Kireama

Kismet (English) One's destiny; fate

Kiss (American) A caring and compassionate woman
Kyss, Kissi, Kyssi, Kissie, Kyssie, Kissy, Kyssy, Kissey

Kobi (American) Woman from California
Kobie, Koby, Kobee, Kobey, Kobea

Kolette (English) Form of Colette, meaning "victory of the people"
Kolete, Kolett, Koleta, Koletta, Kolet

Komala (Indian) A delicate and tender woman
Komalah, Komalla, Komal, Komali, Komalie, Komalee

Kona (Hawaiian) A girly woman
Konah, Konia, Koniah, Konea, Koneah, Koni, Konie, Koney

Konane (Hawaiian) Daughter of the moonlight

Kreeli (American) A charming and kind girl
Kreelie, Krieli, Krielie, Kryli, Krylie, Kreely, Kriely, Kryly

Krenie (American) A capable woman
Kreni, Kreny, Kreney, Krenee

Kristina (English) Form of Christina, meaning "follower of Christ"
Kristena, Kristine, Kristyne, Kristyna, Krystina, Krystine

Kumi (Japanese) An everlasting beauty
Kumie, Kumy, Kumey, Kumee

Kyla (English) Feminine form of Kyle; from the narrow channel
Kylah, Kylar, Kyle

*Kylie (Australian) A boomerang
Kylee, Kyleigh, Kyley, Kyli, Kyleen, Kyleen, Kyler, Kily, Kileigh, Kilee, Kilie, Kili, Kilea, Kylea

Kyra (Greek) Form of Cyrus, meaning "noble"
Kyrah, Kyria, Kyriah, Kyrra, Kyrrah

L

Lacey (French) Woman from Normandy; as delicate as lace
Lace, Lacee, Lacene, Laci, Laciann, Lacie, Lacina, Lacy

Lael (Hebrew) One who belongs to God
Laele, Laelle

*Laila (Arabic) A beauty of the night, born at nightfall
Layla, Laylah

Lainil (American) A soft-hearted woman
Lainill, Lainyl, Lainyll, Laenil, Laenill, Laenyl, Laenyll, Laynil

Lais (Greek) A legendary courtesan
Laise, Lays, Layse, Laisa, Laes, Laese

Lajita (Indian) A truthful woman
Lajyta, Lajeeta, Lajeata

Lake (American) From the still waters
Laken, Laiken, Layken, Layk, Layke, Laik, Laike, Laeken

Lala (Slavic) Resembling a tulip
Lalah, Lalla, Lallah, Laleh

Lalaine (American) A hardworking woman
Lalain, Lalaina, Lalayn, Lalayne, Lalayna, Lalaen, Lalaene, Lalaena

Lalia (Greek) One who is well-spoken
Lali, Lallia, Lalya, Lalea, Lalie, Lalee, Laly, Laley

Lalita (Indian) A playful and charming woman
Lalitah, Laleeta, Laleetah, Lalyta, Lalytah, Laleita, Laleitah, Lalieta

Lamia (Greek) In mythology, a female vampire
Lamiah, Lamiya, Lamiyah, Lamea, Lameah

Lamya (Arabic) Having lovely dark lips
Lamyah, Lamyia, Lama

Lanassa (Russian) A light-hearted woman; cheerful
Lanasa, Lanassia, Lanasia, Lanassiya, Lanasiya

Lang (Scandinavian) Woman of great height

Lani (Hawaiian) From the sky; one who is heavenly
Lanikai

Lansing (English) Filled with hope
Lanseng, Lansyng

Lanza (Italian) One who is noble and willing
Lanzah, Lanzia, Lanziah, Lanzea, Lanzeah

Lapis (Egyptian) Resembling the dark-blue gemstone
Lapiss, Lapisse, Lapys, Lapyss, Lapysse

Laquinta (American) The fifth-born child

Laramie (French) Shedding tears of love
Larami, Laramy, Laramey, Laramee, Laramea

Larby (American) Form of Darby, meaning "of the deer park"
Larbey, Larbi, Larbie, Larbee, Larbea

Larch (American) One who is full of life
Larche

Lark (English) Resembling the songbird
Larke

Larue (American) Form of Rue, meaning "a medicinal herb"
LaRue, Laroo, Larou

Lashawna (American) Filled with happiness
Lashauna, Laseana, Lashona, Lashawn, Lasean, Lashone, Lashaun

Lata (Indian) Of the lovely vine
Latah

Latanya (American) Daughter
of the fairy queen
*Latanyah, Latonya, Latania,
Latanja, Latonia, Latanea*

LaTeasa (Spanish) A flirtatious
woman
Lateasa, Lateaza

Latona (Latin) In mythology,
the Roman equivalent of Leto,
the mother of Artemis and
Apollo
*Latonah, Latonia, Latonea,
Lantoniah, Latoneah*

Latrelle (American) One who
laughs a lot
*Latrell, Latrel, Latrele, Latrella,
Latrela*

Laudonia (Italian) Praises the
house
*Laudonea, Laudoniya, Laudomia,
Laudomea, Laudomiya*

Laura (Latin) Crowned with
laurel; from the laurel tree
*Lauraine, Lauralee, Laralyn,
Laranca, Larea, Lari, Lauralee,
Lauren, Loretta*

*Lauren (French) Form of
Laura, meaning "crowned with
laurel; from the laurel tree"
*Laren, Larentia, Larentina,
Larenzina, Larren, Laryn,
Larryn, Larrynn*

*Leah (Hebrew) One who is
weary; in the Bible, Jacob's
first wife
Leia, Leigha, Lia, Liah, Leeya

Leanna (Gaelic) Form of
Helen, meaning "the shining
light"
*Leana, Leann, Leanne,
Lee-Ann, Leeann, Leeanne,
Leianne, Leyanne*

Lecia (English) Form of Alice,
meaning "woman of the
nobility; truthful; having high
moral character"
*Licia, Lecea, Licea, Lisha,
Lysha, Lesha*

Ledell (Greek) One who is
queenly
*Ledelle, Ledele, Ledella, Ledela,
Ledel*

Legend (American) One who
is memorable
Legende, Legund, Legunde

Legia (Spanish) A bright
woman
*Legiah, Legea, Legeah, Legiya,
Legiyah, Legya, Legyah*

Leila (Persian) Night, dark
beauty
Leela, Lela

Lenis (Latin) One who has soft and silky skin
Lene, Leneta, Lenice, Lenita, Lennice, Lenos, Lenys, Lenisse

Leona (Latin) Feminine form of Leon; having the strength of a lion
Leeona, Leeowna, Leoine, Leola, Leone, Leonelle, Leonia, Leonie

Lequoia (Native American) Form of Sequoia, meaning "of the giant redwood tree"
Lequoya, Lequoiya, Lekoya

Lerola (Latin) Resembling a blackbird
Lerolla, Lerolah, Lerolia, Lerolea

Leslie (Gaelic) From the holly garden; of the gray fortress
Leslea, Leslee, Lesleigh, Lesley, Lesli, Lesly, Lezlee, Lezley

Leucippe (Greek) In mythology, a nymph
Lucippe, Leucipe, Lucipe

Leucothea (Greek) In mythology, a sea nymph
Leucothia, Leucothiah, Leucotheah

Levora (American) A homebody
Levorah, Levorra, Levorrah, Levoria, Levoriah, Levorea, Levoreah, Levorya

Lewa (African) A very beautiful woman
Lewah

Lewana (Hebrew) Of the white moon
Lewanah, Lewanna, Lewannah

Lia (Italian) Form of Leah, meaning "one who is weary"

Libby (English) Form of Elizabeth, meaning "my God is bountiful; God's promise"
Libba, Libbee, Libbey, Libbie, Libet, Liby, Lilibet, Lilibeth

Liberty (English) An independent woman; having freedom
Libertey, Libertee, Libertea, Liberti, Libertie, Libertas, Libera, Liber

Libra (Latin) One who is balanced; the seventh sign of the zodiac
Leebra, Leibra, Liebra, Leabra, Leighbra, Lybra

Librada (Spanish) One who is free
Libradah, Lybrada, Lybradah

Lieu (Vietnamese) Of the willow tree

Ligia (Greek) One who is musically talented
Ligiah, Ligya, Ligiya, Lygia, Ligea, Lygea, Lygya, Lygiya

^**Lila** (Arabic / Greek) Born at night / resembling a lily
Lilah, Lyla, Lylah

Lilac (Latin) Resembling the bluish-purple flower
Lilack, Lilak, Lylac, Lylack, Lylak, Lilach

Lilette (Latin) Resembling a budding lily
Lilett, Lilete, Lilet, Lileta, Liletta, Lylette, Lylett, Lylete

Liliana (Italian, Spanish) Form of Lillian, meaning "resembling the lily"
Lilliana, Lillianna, Liliannia, Lilyana, Lilia

Lilith (Babylonian) Woman of the night
Lilyth, Lillith, Lillyth, Lylith, Lyllith, Lylyth, Lyllyth, Lilithe

*****Lillian** (Latin) Resembling the lily
Lilian, Liliane, Lilianne, Lilias, Lilas, Lillas, Lillias

Lilo (Hawaiian) One who is generous
Lylo, Leelo, Lealo, Leylo, Lielo, Leilo

*^T***Lily** (English) Resembling the flower; one who is innocent and beautiful
Leelee, Lil, Lili, Lilie, Lilla, Lilley, Lilli, Lillie, Lilly

Limor (Hebrew) Refers to myrrh
Limora, Limoria, Limorea, Leemor, Leemora, Leemoria, Leemorea

Lin (Chinese) Resembling jade; from the woodland

Linda (Spanish) One who is soft and beautiful
Lindalee, Lindee, Lindey, Lindi, Lindie, Lindira, Lindka, Lindy, Lynn

Linden (English) From the hill of lime trees
Lindenn, Lindon, Lindynn, Lynden, Lyndon, Lyndyn, Lyndin, Lindin

Lindley (English) From the pastureland
Lindly, Lindlee, Lindleigh, Lindli, Lindlie, Leland, Lindlea

Lindsay (English) From the island of linden trees; from Lincoln's wetland
Lind, Lindsea, Lindsee, Lindseigh, Lindsey, Lindsy, Linsay, Linsey

Lisa (English) Form of Elizabeth, meaning "my God is bountiful; God's promise"
Leesa, Liesa, Lisebet, Lise, Liseta, Lisette, Liszka, Lisebeth

Lishan (African) One who is
awarded a medal
*Lishana, Lishanna, Lyshan,
Lyshana, Lyshanna*

Lissie (American) Resembling
a flower
Lissi, Lissy, Lissey, Lissee, Lissea

Liv (Scandinavian / Latin) One
who protects others / from
the olive tree
*Livia, Livea, Liviya, Livija,
Livvy, Livy, Livya, Lyvia*

Liya (Hebrew) The Lord's
daughter
*Liyah, Leeya, Leeyah, Leaya,
Leayah*

Lo (American) A fiesty woman
Loe, Low, Lowe

Loicy (American) A delightful
woman
*Loicey, Loicee, Loicea, Loici,
Loicie, Loyce, Loice, Loyci*

Lokelani (Hawaiian)
Resembling a small red rose
*Lokelanie, Lokelany, Lokelaney,
Lokelanee, Lokelanea*

Loki (Norse) In mythology, a
trickster god
*Lokie, Lokee, Lokey, Loky,
Lokea, Lokeah, Lokia, Lokiah*

Lola (Spanish) Form of
Dolores, meaning "woman
of sorrow"
Lolah, Loe

^T**London** (English) From the
capital of England
Londyn

Lorelei (German) From the
rocky cliff; in mythology, a
siren who lured sailors to
their deaths
*Laurelei, Laurelie, Loralee,
Loralei, Loralie, Loralyn*

Loretta (Italian) Form of
Laura, meaning "crowned
with laurel; from the laurel
tree"
*Laretta, Larretta, Lauretta,
Laurette, Leretta, Loreta,
Lorette, Lorretta*

Lorraine (French) From the
kingdom of Lothair
*Laraine, Larayne, Laurraine,
Leraine, Lerayne, Lorain,
Loraina, Loraine*

Love (English) One who is full
of affection
*Lovey, Loveday, Lovette, Lovi,
Lovie, Lov, Luv, Luvey*

Lovely (American) An attrac-
tive and pleasant woman
*Loveli, Loveley, Lovelie, Lovelee,
Loveleigh, Lovelea*

Luana (Hawaiian) One who is content and enjoys life
Lewanna, Lou-Ann, Louann, Louanna, Louanne, Luanda, Luane, Luann

Lucretia (Latin) A bringer of light; a successful woman; in mythology, a maiden who was raped by the prince of Rome
Lacretia, Loucrecia, Loucrezia, Loucresha, Loucretia, Lucrece, Lucrecia, Lucreecia

Lucy (Latin) Feminine form of Lucius; one who is illuminated
Luce, Lucetta, Lucette, Luci, Lucia, Luciana, Lucianna, Lucida, Lucille

Lucylynn (American) A lighthearted woman
Lucylyn, Lucylynne, Lucilynn, Lucilyn, Lucilynne

Luna (Latin) Of the moon
Lunah

Lunet (English) Of the crescent moon
Lunett, Lunette, Luneta, Lunete, Lunetta

Lupita (Spanish) Form of Guadalupe, meaning "from the valley of wolves"
Lupe, Lupyta, Lupelina, Lupeeta, Lupieta, Lupeita, Lupeata

Lurissa (American) A beguiling woman
Lurisa, Luryssa, Lurysa, Luressa, Luresa

Luyu (Native American) Resembling the dove

Lydia (Greek) A beautiful woman from Lydia
Lidia, Lidie, Lidija, Lyda, Lydie, Lydea, Liddy, Lidiy

^**Lyla** (Arabic) Form of Lila, meaning "born at night, resembling a lily"
Lylah

Lynn (English) Woman of the lake; form of Linda, meaning "one who is soft and beautiful"
Linell, Linnell, Lyn, Lynae, Lyndel, Lyndell, Lynell, Lynelle

Lyric (French) Of the lyre; the words of a song
Lyrica, Lyricia, Lyrik, Lyrick, Lyrika, Lyricka

Lytanisha (American) A scintillating woman
Lytanesha, Lytaniesha, Lytaneisha, Lytanysha, Lytaneesha, Lytaneasha

M

Macanta (Gaelic) A kind and gentle woman
Macan, Macantia, Macantea, Macantah

Machi (Taiwanese) A good friend
Machie, Machy, Machey, Machee, Machea

Mackenna (Gaelic) Daughter of the handsome man
Mackendra, Mackennah, McKenna, McKendra, Makenna, Makennah

*ᵀMackenzie (Gaelic) Daughter of a wise leader; a fiery woman; one who is fair
*Mckenzie, Mackenzey, Makensie, **Makenzie**, M'Kenzie, McKenzie, Meckenzie, Mackenzee, Mackenzy*

Macy (French) One who wields a weapon
Macee, Macey, Maci, Macie, Maicey, Maicy, Macea, Maicea

Mada (Arabic) One who has reached the end of the path
Madah

Madana (Ethiopian) One who heals others
Madayna, Madaina, Madania, Madaynia, Madainia

Maddox (English) Born into wealth and prosperity
Madox, Madoxx, Maddoxx

*Madeline (Hebrew) Woman from Magdala
*Mada, Madalaina, Madaleine, Madalena, Madalene, **Madelyn**, Madalyn, Madelynn, Madilyn*

Madhavi (Indian) Feminine form of Madhav; born in the springtime
Madhavie, Madhavee, Madhavey, Madhavy, Madhavea

Madini (Swahili) As precious as a gemstone
Madinie, Madiny, Madiney, Madinee, Madyny, Madyni, Madinea, Madynie

*ᵀMadison (English) Daughter of a mighty warrior
Maddison, Madisen, Madisson, Madisyn, Madyson

Madoline (English) One who is accomplished with the stringed instrument
Mandalin, Mandalyn, Mandalynn, Mandelin, Mandellin, Mandellyn, Mandolin, Mandolyn

Madonna (Italian) My lady;
refers to the Virgin Mary
Madonnah, Madona, Madonah

Maeve (Irish) An intoxicating
woman
Mave, Meave, Medb, Meabh

Maggie (English) Form of
Margaret, meaning "resem-
bling a pearl"
Maggi

Magnolia (French) Resembling
the flower
*Magnoliya, Magnoliah,
Magnolea, Magnoleah,
Magnoliyah, Magnolya,
Magnolyah*

Mahal (Native American) A
tender and loving woman
Mahall, Mahale, Mahalle

Mahari (African) One who
offers forgiveness
Maharie, Mahary, Maharey

Mahesa (Indian) A powerful
and great lady
Maheshvari

Mahira (Arabic) A clever and
adroit woman
Mahirah, Mahir, Mahire

Maia (Latin / Maori) The great
one; in mythology, the goddess
of spring / a brave warrior
Maiah, Mya, Maja

Maida (English) A maiden; a
virgin
*Maidel, Maidie, Mayda,
Maydena, Maydey, Mady,
Maegth, Magd*

Maiki (Japanese) Resembling
the dancing flower
*Maikie, Maikei, Maikki,
Maikee*

Maimun (Arabic) One who is
lucky; fortunate
Maimoon, Maimoun

Maine (French) From the
mainland; from the state of
Maine

Maiolaine (French) As delicate
as a flower
Maiolainie, Maiolani

Maisha (African) Giver of life
*Maysha, Maishah, Mayshah,
Maesha, Maeshah*

Maisie (Scottish) Form of
Margaret, meaning "resem-
bling a pearl"
*Maisee, Maisey, Maisy, Maizie,
Mazey, Mazie, Maisi, Maizi*

Majaya (Indian) A victorious
woman
Majayah

Makala (Hawaiian)
Resembling myrtle
Makalah, Makalla, Makallah

*ᵀMakayla (Celtic / Hebrew /
English) Form of Michaela,
meaning "who is like God?"
*Macaela, MacKayla,
Mak,Mechaela, Meeskaela,
Mekea, Mekelle*

Makani (Hawaiian) Of the
wind
*Makanie, Makaney, Makany,
Makanee*

Makareta (Maori) Form of
Margaret, meaning "resem-
bling a pearl / the child of
light"
Makaretah, Makarita

Makea (Finnish) One who is
sweet
Makeah, Makia, Makiah

Makelina (Hawaiian) Form of
Madeline, meaning "woman
from Magdala"
*Makelinah, Makeleena,
Makelyna, Makeleana*

Makena (African) One who is
filled with happiness
*Makenah, Makeena, Makeenah,
Makeana, Makeanah, Makyna,
Makynah, Mackena*

Makenna (Irish) Form of
McKenna, meaning "of the
Irish one"
Makennah

Malak (Arabic) A heavenly
messenger; an angel
*Malaka, Malaika, Malayka,
Malaeka, Malake, Malayk,
Malaek, Malakia*

Malati (Indian) Resembling a
fragrant flower
*Malatie, Malaty, Malatey,
Malatee, Malatea*

Mali (Thai / Welsh)
Resembling a flower / form
of Molly, meaning "star of
the sea / from the sea of
bitterness"
*Malie, Malee, Maleigh, Maly,
Maley*

ˆMalia (Hawaiian) Form of
Mary, meaning "star of the
sea / from the sea of bitterness
*Maliah, **Maliyah**, Maleah*

Malika (Arabic) Destined to be
queen
*Malikah, Malyka, Maleeka,
Maleika, Malieka, Maliika,
Maleaka*

Malina (Hawaiian) A peaceful
woman
*Malinah, Maleena, Maleenah,
Malyna, Malynah, Maleina,
Maliena, Maleana*

Malinka (Russian) As sweet as
a little berry
*Malinkah, Malynka, Maleenka,
Malienka, Maleinka, Maleanka*

Mana (Polynesian) A charismatic and prestigious woman
Manah

Manal (Arabic) An accomplished woman
Manala, Manall, Manalle, Manalla, Manali

Mangena (Hebrew) As sweet as a melody
Mangenah, Mangenna, Mangennah

Manyara (African) A humble woman
Manyarah

Maola (Irish) A handmaiden
Maoli, Maole, Maolie, Maolia, Maoly, Maoley, Maolee, Maolea

Mapenzi (African) One who is dearly loved
Mpenzi, Mapenzie, Mapenze, Mapenzy, Mapenzee, Mapenzea

Maram (Arabic) One who is wished for
Marame, Marama, Marami, Maramie, Maramee, Maramy, Maramey, Maramea

Marcella (Latin) Dedicated to Mars, the God of war
Marcela, Marsela, Marsella, Maricela, Maricel

Marcia (Latin) Feminine form of Marcus; dedicated to Mars, the god of war
Marcena, Marcene, Marchita, Marciana, Marciane, Marcianne, Marcilyn, Marcilynn

Marely (American) form of Marley, "meaning of the marshy meadow"

Margaret (Greek / Persian) Resembling a pearl / the child of light
Maighread, Mairead, Mag, Maggi, Maggie, Maggy, Maiga, Malgorzata, Megan, Marwarid, Marjorie, Marged, Makareta

Marged (Welsh) Form of Margaret, meaning "resembling a pearl / the child of light"
Margred, Margeda, Margreda

*Maria (Spanish) Form of Mary, meaning "star of the sea / from the sea of bitterness"
Mariah, Marialena, Marialinda, Marialisa, Maaria, Mayria, Maeria, Mariabella

*Mariah (Latin) Form of Mary, meaning "star of the sea"

Mariana (Spanish / Italian) Form of Mary, meaning "star of the sea"
Marianna

Mariane (French) Blend of Mary, meaning "star of the sea / from the sea of bitterness," and Ann, meaning "a woman graced with God's favor"
Mariam, Mariana, Marian, Marion, Maryann, Maryanne, Maryanna, Maryane

Marietta (French) Form of Mary, meaning "star of the sea / from the sea of bitterness"
Mariette, Maretta, Mariet, Maryetta, Maryette, Marieta

Marika (Danish) Form of Mary, meaning "star of the sea / from the sea of bitterness"

Mariko (Japanese) Daughter of Mari; a ball or sphere
Maryko, Mareeko, Marieko, Mareiko

Marilyn (English) Form of Mary, meaning "star of the sea / from the sea of bitterness"
Maralin, Maralyn, Maralynn, Marelyn, Marilee, Marilin

Marissa (Latin) Woman of the sea
Maressa, Maricia, Marisabel, Marisha, Marisse, Maritza, Mariza, Marrissa

Marjam (Slavic) One who is merry
Marjama, Marjamah, Marjami, Marjamie, Marjamy, Marjamey, Marjamee, Marjamea

Marjani (African) Of the coral reef
Marjanie, Marjany, Marjaney, Marjanee, Marjean, Marjeani, Marjeanie, Marijani

Marjorie (English) Form of Margaret, meaning "resembling a pearl / the child of light"
Marcharie, Marge, Margeree, Margery, Margerie, Margery, Margey, Margi

Marlene (German) Blend of Mary, meaning "star of the sea / from the sea of bitterness," and Magdalene, meaning "woman from Magdala"
Marlaina, Marlana, Marlane, Marlayna

Marley (English) Of the marshy meadow
Marlee, Marleigh, Marli, Marlie, Marly

Marlis (German) Form of Mary, meaning "star of the sea / from the sea of bitterness"
Marlisa, Marliss, Marlise, Marlisse, Marlissa, Marlys, Marlyss, Marlysa

Marlo (English) One who resembles driftwood
Marloe, Marlow, Marlowe, Marlon

Malati (Indian) Resembling a fragrant flower
Malatie, Malaty, Malatey, Malatee, Malatea

Marsala (Italian) From the place of sweet wine
Marsalah, Marsalla, Marsallah

Martha (Aramaic) Mistress of the house; in the Bible, the sister of Lazarus and Mary
Maarva, Marfa, Marhta, Mariet, Marit, Mart, Marta, Marte

Mary (Latin / Hebrew) Star of the sea / from the sea of bitterness
Mair, Mal, Mallie, Manette, Manon, Manya, Mare, Maren, Maria, Marietta, Marika, Marilyn, Marlis, Maureen, May, Mindel, Miriam, Molly, Mia

Masami (African / Japanese) A commanding woman / one who is truthful
Masamie, Masamee, Masamy, Masamey, Masamea

Mashaka (African) A troublemaker; a mischievous woman
Mashakah, Mashakia

Massachusetts (Native American) From the big hill; from the state of Massachusetts
Massachusets, Massachusette, Massachusetta, Massa, Massachute, Massachusta

Matana (Hebrew) A gift from God
Matanah, Matanna, Matannah, Matai

Matangi (Hindi) In Hinduism, the patron of inner thought
Matangy, Matangie, Matangee, Matangey, Matangea

Matsuko (Japanese) Child of the pine tree

Maureen (Irish) Form of Mary, meaning "star of the sea / from the sea of bitterness"
Maura, Maurene, Maurianne, Maurine, Maurya, Mavra, Maure, Mo

Mauve (French) Of the mallow plant
Mawve

Maven (English) Having great knowledge
Mavin, Mavyn

Maverick (American) One who is wild and free
Maverik, Maveryck, Maveryk, Mavarick, Mavarik

Mavis (French) Resembling a songbird
Mavise, Maviss, Mavisse, Mavys, Mavyss, Mavysse

May (Latin) Born during the month of May; form of Mary, meaning "star of the sea / from the sea of bitterness"
Mae, Mai, Maelynn, Maelee, Maj, Mala, Mayana, Maye

*Maya (Indian / Hebrew) An illusion, a dream / woman of the water
Mya

Mayumi (Japanese) One who embodies truth, wisdom, and beauty

Mazarine (French) Having deep-blue eyes
Mazareen, Mazareene, Mazaryn, Mazaryne, Mazine, Mazyne, Mazeene

Mazhira (Hebrew) A shining woman
Mazhirah, Mazheera

McKayla (Gaelic) A fiery woman
McKale, McKaylee, McKaleigh, McKay, McKaye, McKaela

Meara (Gaelic) One who is filled with happiness
Mearah

Medea (Greek) A cunning ruler; in mythology, a sorceress
Madora, Medeia, Media, Medeah, Mediah, Mediya, Mediyah

Medini (Indian) Daughter of the earth
Medinie, Mediny, Mediney, Medinee, Medinea

Meditrina (Latin) The healer; in mythology, goddess of health and wine
Meditreena, Meditryna, Meditriena

Medora (Greek) A wise ruler
Medoria, Medorah, Medorra, Medorea

Medusa (Greek) In mythology, a Gorgon with snakes for hair
Medoosa, Medusah, Medoosah, Medousa, Medousah

Meenakshi (Indian) Having beautiful eyes

Megan (Welsh) Form of Margaret, meaning "resembling a pearl / the child of light"
Maegan, Meg, Magan, Magen, Megin, Maygan, Meagan, Meaghan, Meghan

Mehalia (Hebrew) An affectionate woman
Mehaliah, Mehalea, Mehaleah, Mehaliya, Mehaliyah

Melangell (Welsh) A sweet messenger from heaven
Melangelle, Melangela, Melangella, Melangele, Melangel

*Melanie (Greek) A dark-skinned beauty
Malaney, Malanie, Mel, Mela, Melaina, Melaine, Melainey, Melany

Meli (Native American) One who is bitter
Melie, Melee, Melea, Meleigh, Mely, Meley

Melia (Hawaiian / Greek) Resembling the plumeria / of the ash tree; in mythology, a nymph
Melidice, Melitine, Meliah, Meelia, Melya

Melika (Turkish) A great beauty
Melikah, Melicka, Melicca, Melyka, Melycka, Meleeka, Meleaka

Melinda (Latin) One who is sweet and gentle
Melynda, Malinda, Malinde, Mallie, Mally, Malynda, Melinde, Mellinda, Mindy

Melisande (French) Having the strength of an animal
Malisande, Malissande, Malyssandre, Melesande, Melisandra, Melisandre

Melissa (Greek) Resembling a honeybee; in mythology, a nymph
Malissa, Mallissa, Mel, Melesa, Melessa, Melisa, Melise, Melisse

Melita (Greek) As sweet as honey
Malita, Malitta, Melida, Melitta, Melyta, Malyta, Meleeta, Meleata

Melody (Greek) A beautiful song
Melodee, Melodey, Melodi, Melodia, Melodie, Melodea

Merana (American) Woman of the waters
Meranah, Meranna, Merannah

Mercer (English) A prosperous merchant

Meredith (Welsh) A great ruler; protector of the sea
Maredud, Meridel, Meredithe, Meredyth, Meridith, Merridie, Meradith, Meredydd

Meribah (Hebrew) A quarrelsome woman
Meriba

Meroz (Hebrew) From the cursed plains
Meroza, Merozia, Meroze

Merry (English) One who is lighthearted and joyful
Merree, Merri, Merrie, Merrielle, Merrile, Merrilee, Merrili, Merrily

Mertice (English) A well-known lady

Merton (English) From the village near the pond
Mertan, Mertin, Mertun

Metea (Greek) A gentle woman
Meteah, Metia, Metiah

Metin (Greek) A wise counselor
Metine, Metyn, Metyne

Metis (Greek) One who is industrious
Metiss, Metisse, Metys, Metyss, Metysse

Mettalise (Danish) As graceful as a pearl
Metalise, Mettalisse, Mettalisa, Mettalissa

ᵀMia** (Israeli / Latin) Who is like God? / form of Mary, meaning "star of the sea / from the sea of bitterness"
Miah, Mea, Meah, Meya

Michaela (Celtic, Gaelic, Hebrew, English, Irish) Feminine form of Michael; who is like God?
Macaela, MacKayla, Mak, Mechaela, Meeskaela, Mekea, Micaela

Michelle (French) Feminine form of Michael; who is like God?
Machelle, Mashelle, M'chelle, Mechelle, Meechelle, Me'Shell, Meshella, Mischa

Michewa (Tibetan) Sent from heaven
Michewah

Mide (Irish) One who is thirsty
Meeda, Mida

Midori (Japanese) Having green eyes
Midorie, Midory, Midorey, Midoree, Midorea

Mignon (French) One who is cute and petite

Mikayla (English) Feminine form of Michael, meaning "who is like God?"

^**Mila** (Slavic) One who is industrious and hardworking
Milaia, Milaka, Milla, Milia

Milan (Latin) From the city in Italy; one who is gracious
Milaana

Milena (Slavic) The favored one
Mileena, Milana, Miladena, Milanka, Mlada, Mladena

Miley (American) Form of Mili, meaning "a virtuous woman"
Milee, Mylee, Mareli

Miliana (Latin) Feminine of Emeliano; one who is eager and willing
Milianah, Milianna, Miliane, Miliann, Milianne

Milima (Swahili) Woman from the mountains
Milimah, Mileema, Milyma

Millo (Hebrew) Defender of the sacred city
Milloh, Millowe, Milloe

Mima (Hebrew) Form of Jemima, meaning "our little dove"
Mimah, Mymah, Myma

Minda (Native American, Hindi) Having great knowledge
Mindah, Mynda, Myndah, Menda, Mendah

Mindel (Hebrew) Form of Mary, meaning "star of the sea / from the sea of bitterness"
Mindell, Mindelle, Mindele, Mindela, Mindella

Mindy (English) Form of Melinda, meaning "one who is sweet and gentle"
Minda, Mindee, Mindi, Mindie, Mindey, Mindea

Ming Yue (Chinese) Born beneath the bright moon

Minka (Teutonic) One who is resolute; having great strength
Minkah, Mynka, Mynkah, Minna, Minne

Minowa (Native American) One who has a moving voice
Minowah, Mynowa, Mynowah

Minuit (French) Born at midnight
Minueet

Miracle (American) An act of God's hand
Mirakle, Mirakel, Myracle, Myrakle

Miranda (Latin) Worthy of admiration
Maranda, Myranda, Randi

Mirai (Basque / Japanese) A miracle child / future
Miraya, Mirari, Mirarie, Miraree, Mirae

Miremba (Ugandan) A promoter of peace
Mirembe, Mirem, Mirembah, Mirembeh, Mirema

Miriam (Hebrew) Form of Mary, meaning "star of the sea / from the sea of bitterness"
Mariam, Maryam, Meriam, Meryam, Mirham, Mirjam, Mirjana, Mirriam

Mirinesse (English) Filled with joy
Miriness, Mirinese, Mirines, Mirinessa, Mirinesa

Mirit (Hebrew) One who is strong-willed

Mischa (Russian) Form of Michelle, meaning "who is like God?"
Misha

Mistico (Italian) A mystical woman
Mistica, Mystico, Mystica, Mistiko, Mystiko

Mitali (Indian) A friendly and sweet woman
Mitalie, Mitalee, Mitaleigh, Mitaly, Mitaley, Meeta, Mitalea

Miya (Japanese) From the sacred temple
Miyah

Miyo (Japanese) A beautiful daughter
Miyoko

Mizar (Hebrew) A little woman; petite
Mizarr, Mizarre, Mizare, Mizara, Mizaria, Mizarra

Mliss (Cambodian) Resembling a flower
Mlissa, Mlisse, Mlyss, Mlysse, Mlyssa

Mocha (Arabic) As sweet as chocolate
Mochah

Modesty (Latin) One who is without conceit
Modesti, Modestie, Modestee, Modestus, Modestey, Modesta, Modestia, Modestina

Moesha (American) Drawn from the water
Moisha, Moysha, Moeesha, Moeasha, Moeysha

Mohini (Indian) The most beautiful
Mohinie, Mohinee, Mohiny

Moladah (Hebrew) A giver of life
Molada

*Molly (Irish) Form of Mary, meaning "star of the sea / from the sea of bitterness"
Moll, Mollee, Molley, Molli, Mollie, Molle, Mollea, Mali

Mona (Gaelic) One who is born into the nobility
Moina, Monah, Monalisa, Monalissa, Monna, Moyna, Monalysa, Monalyssa

Moncha (Irish) A solitary woman
Monchah

Monica (Greek / Latin) A solitary woman / one who advises others
Monnica, Monca, Monicka, Monika, Monike

Monique (French) One who provides wise counsel
Moniqua, Moneeque, Moneequa, Moneeke, Moeneek, Moneaque, Moneaqua, Moneake

Monisha (Hindi) Having great intelligence
Monishah, Monesha, Moneisha, Moniesha, Moneysha, Moneasha

Monroe (Gaelic) Woman from the river
Monrow, Monrowe, Monro

Monserrat (Latin) From the jagged mountain
Montserrat

Montana (Latin) Woman of the mountains; from the state of Montana
Montanna, Montina, Monteene, Montese

Morcan (Welsh) Of the bright sea
Morcane, Morcana, Morcania, Morcanea

Moreh (Hebrew) A great archer; a teacher

*⋆ᵀ**Morgan** (Welsh) Circling the bright sea; a sea dweller
Morgaine, Morgana, Morgance, Morgane, Morganica, Morgann, Morganne, Morgayne

Morguase (English) In Arthurian legend, the mother of Gawain
Marguase, Margawse, Morgawse, Morgause, Margause

Morina (Japanese) From the woodland town
Morinah, Moreena, Moryna, Moriena, Moreina, Moreana

Mubarika (Arabic) One who is blessed
Mubaarika, Mubaricka, Mubaryka, Mubaricca, Mubarycca

Mubina (Arabic) One who displays her true image
Mubeena, Mubinah, Mubyna, Mubeana, Mubiena

Mudan (Mandarin) Daughter of a harmonious family
Mudane, Mudana, Mudann, Mudaen, Mudaena

Mufidah (Arabic) One who is helpful to others
Mufeeda, Mufeyda, Mufyda, Mufeida, Mufieda, Mufeada

Mugain (Irish) In mythology, the wife of the king of Ulster
Mugayne, Mugaine, Mugane

Muirne (Irish) One who is dearly loved
Muirna

Munay (African) One who loves and is loved
Manay, Munaye, Munae, Munai

Munazza (Arabic) An independent woman; one who is free
Munazzah, Munaza, Munazah

Muriel (Irish) Of the shining sea
Merial, Meriel, Merrill

Murphy (Celtic) Daughter of a great sea warrior
Murphi, Murphie, Murphey

Musoke (African) Having the beauty of a rainbow

*Mya (American) Form of Maya, meaning "an illusion, woman of the water"
Myah

Myisha (Arabic) Form of Aisha, meaning "lively; womanly"
Myesha, Myeisha, Myeshia, Myiesha, Myeasha

Myka (Hebrew) Feminine of Micah, meaning "who is like God?"
Micah, Mika

Myrina (Latin) In mythology, an Amazon
Myrinah, Myreena, Myreina, Myriena, Myreana

Myrrh (Egyptian) Resembling the fragrant oil

N

Naama (Hebrew) Feminine form of Noam; an attractive woman; good-looking
Naamah

Naava (Hebrew) A lovely and pleasant woman
Naavah, Nava, Navah, Navit

Nabila (Arabic) Daughter born into nobility; a highborn daughter
Nabilah, Nabeela, Nabyla, Nabeelah, Nabylah, Nabeala, Nabealah

Nadda (Arabic) A very generous woman
Naddah, Nada, Nadah

ᵀ**Nadia** (Slavic) One who is full of hope
Nadja, Nadya, Naadiya, Nadine, Nadie, Nadiyah, Nadea, Nadija

Nadirah (Arabic) One who is precious; rare
Nadira, Nadyra, Nadyrah, Nadeera, Nadeerah, Nadra

Naeva (French) Born in the evening
Naevah, Naevia, Naevea, Nayva, Nayvah

Nagge (Hebrew) A radiant woman

Nailah (Arabic) Feminine form of Nail; a successful woman; the acquirer
Na'ila, Na'ilah, Naa'ilah, Naila, Nayla, Naylah, Naela, Naelah

Najia (Arabic) An independent woman; one who is free
Naajia

Najja (African) The second-born child
Najjah

Namid (Native American) A star dancer
Namide, Namyd, Namyde

Namita (Papuan) In mythology, a mother goddess
Namitah, Nameeta, Namyta

Nana (Hawaiian / English) Born during the spring; a star / a grandmother or one who watches over children

Nancy (English) Form of Anna, meaning "a woman graced with God's favor"
Nainsey, Nainsi, Nance, Nancee, Nancey, Nanci, Nancie, Nancsi

Nandalia (Australian) A fiery woman
Nandaliah, Nandalea, Nandaleah, Nandali, Nandalie, Nandalei, Nandalee, Nandaleigh

Nandita (Indian) A delightful daughter
Nanditah, Nanditia, Nanditea

Naomi (Hebrew / Japanese) One who is pleasant / a beauty above all others
Namoie, Nayomi, Naomee

Narella (Greek) A bright woman; intelligent
Narellah, Narela, Narelah, Narelle, Narell, Narele

Nascio (Latin) In mythology, goddess of childbirth

Natalia (Spanish / Latin) form of Natalie; born on Christmas day
Natalya, Natalja

^*T**Natalie** (Latin) Refers to Christ's birthday; born on Christmas Day
*Natala, Natalee, **Nathalie**, Nataline, Nataly, Natasha*

Natane (Native American) Her father's daughter
Natanne

Natasha (Russian) Form of Natalie, meaning "born on Christmas Day"
Nastaliya, Nastalya, Natacha, Natascha, Natashenka, Natashia, Natasia, Natosha

Navida (Iranian) Feminine form of Navid; bringer of good news
Navyda, Navidah, Navyda, Naveeda, Naveedah, Naveada, Naveadah

Navya (Indian) One who is youthful
Navyah, Naviya, Naviyah

Nawal (Arabic) A gift of God
Nawall, Nawalle, Nawala, Nawalla

Nawar (Arabic) Resembling a flower
Nawaar

Nazahah (Arabic) One who is pure and honest
Nazaha, Nazihah, Naziha

Nechama (Hebrew) One who provides comfort
Nehama, Nehamah, Nachmanit, Nachuma, Nechamah, Nechamit

Neda (Slavic) Born on a Sunday
Nedda, Nedah, Nedi, Nedie, Neddi, Neddie, Nedaa

Neena (Hindi) A woman who has beautiful eyes
Neenah, Neanah, Neana, Neyna, Neynah

Nefertiti (Egyptian) A queenly woman
Nefertari, Nefertyty, Nefertity, Nefertitie, Nefertitee, Nefertytie, Nefertitea

Neith (Egyptian) In mythology, goddess of war and hunting
Neitha, Neytha, Neyth, Neit, Neita, Neitia, Neitea, Neithe, Neythe

Nekana (Spanish) Woman of sorrow
Nekane, Nekania, Nekanea

Neo (African) A gift from God

Nerissa (Italian / Greek) A black-haired beauty / sea nymph
Narissa, Naryssa, Nericcia, Neryssa, Narice, Nerice, Neris

Nessa (Hebrew / Greek) A miracle child / form of Agnes, meaning "one who is pure; chaste"
Nesha, Nessah, Nessia, Nessya, Nesta, Neta, Netia, Nessie

Netis (Native American) One who is trustworthy
Netiss, Netisse, Netys, Netyss, Netysse

*ᵀNevaeh (American) Child from heaven

Nevina (Scottish) Feminine form of Nevin; daughter of a saint
Nevinah, Neveena, Nevyna, Nevinne, Nevynne, Neveene, Neveana, Neveane

Newlyn (Gaelic) Born during the spring
Newlynn, Newlynne, Newlin, Newlinn, Newlinne, Newlen, Newlenn, Newlenne

Neziah (Hebrew) One who is pure; a victorious woman
Nezia, Nezea, Nezeah, Neza, Nezah, Neziya, Neziyah

Niabi (Native American) Resembling a fawn
Niabie, Niabee, Niabey, Niaby

Niagara (English) From the famous waterfall
Niagarah, Niagarra, Niagarrah, Nyagara, Nyagarra

ᵀNicole (Greek) Feminine form of Nicholas; of the victorious people
Necole, Niccole, Nichol, Nichole, Nicholle, Nickol, Nickole, Nicol

Nicosia (English) Woman from the capital of Cyprus
Nicosiah, Nicosea, Nicoseah, Nicotia, Nicotea

Nidia (Spanish) One who is gracious
Nydia, Nidiah, Nydiah, Nidea, Nideah, Nibia, Nibiah, Nibea

Nike (Greek) One who brings victory; in mythology, goddess of victory
Nikee, Nikey, Nykee, Nyke

Nilam (Arabic) Resembling a precious blue stone
Neelam, Nylam, Nilima, Nilyma, Nylyma, Nylima, Nealam, Nealama

Nilsine (Scandinavian)
Feminine form of Neil; a
champion

Nimeesha (African) A princess; daughter born to royalty
Nimeeshah, Nimiesha

Nini (African) As solid as a
stone
*Ninie, Niny, Niney, Ninee,
Ninea*

Nishan (African) One who
wins awards
*Nishann, Nishanne, Nishana,
Nishanna, Nyshan, Nyshana*

Nitya (Indian) An eternal
beauty
Nithya, Nithyah, Nityah

Nixie (German) A beautiful
water sprite
*Nixi, Nixy, Nixey, Nixee,
Nixea*

Noelle (French) Born at
Christmastime
Noel, Noela, Noele, Noe

Nolcha (Native American) Of
the sun
Nolchia, Nolchea

Nomusa (African) One who is
merciful
*Nomusah, Nomusha, Nomusia,
Nomusea, Nomushia,
Nomushea*

^**Nora** (English) Form of
Eleanor, meaning "the shin-
ing light"
*Norah, Noora, Norella, Norelle,
Norissa, Norri, Norrie, Norry*

Nordica (German) Woman
from the north
*Nordika, Nordicka, Nordyca,
Nordyka, Nordycka, Norda,
Norell, Norelle*

Nosiwe (African) Mother of
the homeland

Noura (Arabic) Having an
inner light
Nureh, Nourah, Nure

Nyala (African) Resembling an
antelope
Nyalah, Nyalla, Nyallah

Nyneve (English) In Arthurian
legend, another name for the
lady of the lake
*Nineve, Niniane, Ninyane,
Nyniane, Ninieve, Niniveve*

Nyura (Ukrainian) A graceful
woman
*Nyrurah, Nyrurra, Niura,
Neura*

Oaisara (Arabic) A great ruler; an empress
Oaisarah, Oaisarra, Oaisarrah

Oamra (Arabic) Daughter of the moon
Oamrah, Oamira, Oamyra, Oameera

Oba (African) In mythology, the goddess of rivers
Obah, Obba, Obbah

Octavia (Latin) Feminine form of Octavius; the eighth-born child
Octaviana, Octavianne, Octavie, Octiana, Octoviana, Ottavia, Octavi, Octavy

Ode (Egyptian / Greek) Traveler of the road / a lyric poem
Odea

Odessa (Greek) Feminine form of Odysseus; one who wanders; an angry woman
Odissa, Odyssa, Odessia, Odissia, Odyssia, Odysseia

Odina (Latin / Scandinavian) From the mountain / feminine form of Odin, the highest of the gods
Odinah, Odeena, Odeene, Odeen, Odyna, Odyne, Odynn, Odeana

Ogin (Native American) Resembling the wild rose

Oheo (Native American) A beautiful woman

Oira (Latin) One who prays to God
Oyra, Oirah, Oyrah

Okalani (Hawaiian) Form of Kalani, meaning "from the heavens"
Okalanie, Okalany, Okalaney, Okalanee, Okaloni, Okalonie, Okalonee, Okalony, Okaloney, Okeilana, Okelani, Okelani, Okelanie, Okelany, Okelaney, Okelanee, Okalanea, Okalonea, Okelanea

Okei (Japanese) Woman of the ocean

Oksana (Russian) Hospitality
Oksanah, Oksie, Aksana

Ola (Nigerian / Hawaiian / Norse) One who is precious / giver of life; well-being / a relic of one's ancestors
Olah, Olla, Ollah

Olaide (American) A thoughtful woman
Olaid, Olaida, Olayd, Olayde, Olayda, Olaed, Olaede, Olaeda

Olathe (Native American) A lovely young woman

Olayinka (Yoruban) Surrounded by wealth and honor
Olayenka, Olayanka

Oleda (English) Resembling a winged creature
Oldedah, Oleta, Olita, Olida, Oletah, Olitah, Olidah

Olethea (Latin) Form of Alethea, meaning "one who is truthful"
Oletheia, Olethia, Oletha, Oletea, Olthaia, Olithea, Olathea, Oletia

Olina (Hawaiian) One who is joyous
Oline, Oleen, Oleene, Olyne, Oleena, Olyna, Olin

*ᵀOlivia (Latin) Feminine form of Oliver; of the olive tree; one who is peaceful
Oliviah, Oliva, Olive, Oliveea, Olivet, Olivetta, Olivette, Olivija

Olwen (Welsh) One who leaves a white footprint
Olwynn, Olvyen, Olvyin

Olympia (Greek) From Mount Olympus; a goddess
Olympiah, Olimpe, Olimpia, Olimpiada, Olimpiana, Olypme, Olympie, Olympi

Omri (Arabic) A red-haired woman
Omrie, Omree, Omrea, Omry, Omrey

Ona (Hebrew) Filled with grace
Onit, Onat, Onah

Ondrea (Slavic) Form of Andrea, meaning "courageous and strong / womanly"
Ondria, Ondrianna, Ondreia, Ondreina, Ondreya, Ondriana, Ondreana, Ondera

Oneida (Native American) Our long-awaited daughter
Onieda, Oneyda, Onida, Onyda

Onida (Native American) The one who has been expected
Onidah, Onyda, Onydah

Ontina (American) An open-minded woman
Ontinah, Onteena, Onteenah, Onteana, Onteanah, Ontiena, Ontienah, Onteina

Oona (Gaelic) Form of Agnes, meaning "one who is pure; chaste"

Opal (Sanskrit) A treasured jewel; resembling the iridescent gemstone
Opall, Opalle, Opale, Opalla, Opala, Opalina, Opaline, Opaleena

Ophelia (Greek) One who offers help to others
Ofelia, Ofilia, OphÈlie, Ophelya, Ophilia, Ovalia, Ovelia, Opheliah

Ophrah (Hebrew) Resembling a fawn; from the place of dust
Ofra, Ofrit, Ophra, Oprah, Orpa, Orpah, Ofrat, Ofrah

Orange (Latin) Resembling the sweet fruit
Orangetta, Orangia, Orangina, Orangea

Orbelina (American) One who brings excitement
Orbelinah, Orbeleena

Orea (Greek) From the mountains
Oreah

Orenda (Iroquois) A woman with magical powers

Oriana (Latin) Born at sunrise
Oreana, Orianna, Oriane, Oriann, Orianne

Oribel (Latin) A beautiful golden child
Orabel, Orabelle, Orabell, Orabela, Orabella, Oribell, Oribelle, Oribele

Orin (Irish) A dark-haired beauty
Orine, Orina, Oryna, Oryn, Oryne

Orinthia (Hebrew / Gaelic) Of the pine tree / a fair lady
Orrinthia, Orenthia, Orna, Ornina, Orinthea, Orenthea, Orynthia, Orynthea

Oriole (Latin) Resembling the gold-speckled bird
Oreolle, Oriolle, Oreole, Oriola, Oriolla, Oriol, Oreola, Oreolla

Orion (Greek) The huntress; a constellation

Orithna (Greek) One who is natural
Orithne, Orythna, Orythne, Orithnia, Orythnia, Orithnea, Orythnea

Orla (Gaelic) The golden queen
Orlah, Orrla, Orrlah, Orlagh, Orlaith, Orlaithe, Orghlaith, Orghlaithe

Orna (Irish / Hebrew) One who is pale-skinned / of the cedar tree
Ornah, Ornette, Ornetta, Ornete, Orneta, Obharnait, Ornat

Ornella (Italian) Of the flowering ash tree

Ornice (Irish) A pale-skinned woman
Ornyce, Ornise, Orynse, Orneice, Orneise, Orniece, Orniese, Orneece

Orva (Anglo-Saxon / French) A courageous friend / as precious as gold

Orynko (Ukrainian) A peaceful woman
Orinko, Orynka, Orinka

Osaka (Japanese) From the city of industry
Osaki, Osakie, Osakee, Osaky, Osakey, Osakea

Osma (English) Feminine form of Osmond; protected by God
Osmah, Ozma, Ozmah

Otina (American) A fortunate woman
Otinah, Otyna, Otynah, Oteena, Oteenah, Oteana, Oteanah, Otiena

Overton (English) From the upper side of town
Overtown

Owena (Welsh) A high-born woman
Owenah, Owenna, Owennah, Owenia, Owenea

Ozora (Hebrew) One who is wealthy
Ozorah, Ozorra, Ozorrah

P

Pace (American) A charismatic young woman
Paice, Payce, Paece, Pase, Paise, Payse, Paese

Pacifica (Spanish) A peaceful woman
Pacifika, Pacyfyca, Pacyfyka, Pacifyca, Pacifyka, Pacyfica, Pacyfika

Pageant (American) A dramatic woman
Pagent, Padgeant, Padgent

*Paige (English) A young assistant
Page, Payge, Paege

^Paisley (English) Woman of the church

Paki (African) A witness of God
Pakki, Packi, Pacci, Pakie, Pakkie, Paky, Pakky, Pakey

Palba (Spanish) A fair-haired woman

Palemon (Spanish) A kind-hearted woman
Palemond, Palemona, Palemonda

Palesa (African) Resembling a flower
Palessa, Palesah, Palysa, Palisa, Paleesa

Paloma (Spanish) Dove-like
Palloma, Palomita, Palometa, Peloma, Aloma

Pamela (English) A woman who is as sweet as honey
Pamelah, Pamella, Pammeli, Pammelie, Pameli, Pamelie, Pamelia, Pamelea

Panagiota (Greek) Feminine form of Panagiotis; a holy woman

Panchali (Indian) A princess; a high-born woman
Panchalie, Panchaly, Panchalli

Panda (English) Resembling the bamboo-eating animal
Pandah

Pandara (Indian) A good wife
Pandarah, Pandarra, Pandaria, Pandarea

Pandora (Greek) A gifted, talented woman; in mythology, the first mortal woman, who unleashed evil upon the world
Pandorah, Pandorra, Pandoria, Pandorea, Pandoriya

Pantxike (Latin) A woman who is free
Pantxikey, Pantxikye, Pantxeke, Pantxyke

Paras (Indian) A woman against whom others are measured

Parcae (Latin) In mythology, a name that refers to the Fates
Parca, Parcia, Parcee, Parsae, Parsee, Parsia, Parcea

ᵀ**Paris** (English) Woman of the city in France
Pariss, Parisse, Parys, Paryss, Parysse

Parry (Welsh) Daughter of Harry
Parri, Parrie, Parrey, Parree, Parrea

Parvani (Indian) Born during a full moon
Parvanie, Parvany, Parvaney, Parvanee, Parvanea

Parvati (Hindi) Daughter of the mountain; in Hinduism, a name for the wife of Shiva
Parvatie, Parvaty, Parvatey, Parvatee, Pauravi, Parvatea, Pauravie, Pauravy

Paterekia (Hawaiian) An upper-class woman
Paterekea, Pakelekia, Pakelekea

Patience (English) One who is patient; an enduring woman
Patiencia, Paciencia, Pacencia, Pacyncia, Pacincia, Pacienca

Patricia (English) Feminine form of Patrick; of noble descent
Patrisha, Patrycia, Patrisia, Patsy, Patti, Patty, Patrizia, Pattie, Trisha

Patrina (American) Born into the nobility
Patreena, Patriena, Patreina, Patryna, Patreana

Paula (English) Feminine form of Paul; a petite woman
Paulina, Pauline, Paulette, Paola, Pauleta, Pauletta, Pauli, Paulete

Pausha (Hindi) Resembling the moon
Paushah

Pax (Latin) One who is peaceful; in mythology, the goddess of peace
Paxi, Paxie, Paxton, Paxten, Paxtan, Paxy, Paxey, Paxee

^*Payton (English) From the warrior's village
Paton, Paeton, Paiton, Payten, Paiten

Pearl (Latin) A precious gem of the sea
Pearla, Pearle, Pearlie, Pearly, Pearline, Pearlina, Pearli, Pearley

Pelopia (Greek) In mythology, the wife of Thyestes and mother of Aegisthus
Pelopiah, Pelopea, Pelopeah, Pelopiya

Pembroke (English) From the broken hill
Pembrook, Pembrok, Pembrooke

Pendant (French) A decorated woman
Pendent, Pendante, Pendente

^Penelope (Greek) Resembling a duck; in mythology, the faithful wife of Odysseus
Peneloppe, Penelopy, Penelopey, Penelopi, Penelopie, Penelopee, Penella, Penelia

Penia (Greek) In mythology, the personification of poverty
Peniah, Penea, Peniya, Peneah, Peniyah

Penthesilea (Greek) In mythology, a queen of the Amazons

Peony (Greek) Resembling the flower
Peoney, Peoni, Peonie, Peonee, Peonea

Pepin (French) An awe-inspiring woman
Peppin, Pepine, Peppine, Pipin, Pippin, Pepen, Pepan, Peppen

Pepita (Spanish) Feminine form of Joseph; God will add
Pepitah, Pepitta, Pepitia, Pepitina

Perdita (Latin) A lost woman
Perditah, Perditta, Perdy, Perdie, Perdi, Perdee, Perdea, Perdeeta

Perdix (Latin) Resembling a partridge
Perdixx, Perdyx, Perdyxx

Peri (Persian / English) In mythology, a fairy / from the pear tree
Perry, Perri, Perie, Perrie, Pery, Perrey, Perey, Peree

Perpetua (Latin) One who is constant; steadfast

Persephone (Greek) In mythology, the daughter of Demeter and Zeus who was abducted to the underworld
Persephoni, Persephonie, Persephony, Persephoney, Persephonee, Persefone, Persefoni, Persefonie

Persis (Greek) Woman of Persia
Persiss, Persisse, Persys, Persyss, Persysse

Pesha (Hebrew) A flourishing woman
Peshah, Peshia, Peshiah, Peshea, Pesheah, Peshe

Petronela (Latin) Feminine form of Peter, as solid and strong as a rock
Petronella, Petronelle, Petronia, Petronilla, Petronille, Petrona, Petronia, Petronel

Petunia (English) Resembling the flower
Petuniah, Petuniya, Petunea, Petoonia, Petounia

*Peyton (English) From the warrior's village
Peyten

Phaedra (Greek) A bright woman; in mythology, the wife of Theseus
Phadra, Phaidra, Phedra, Phaydra, Phedre, Phaedre

Phailin (Thai) Resembling a sapphire
Phaylin, Phaelin, Phalin

Phashestha (American) One who is decorated
Phashesthea, Phashesthia, Phashesthiya

Pheakkley (Vietnamese) A
faithful woman
*Pheakkly, Pheakkli, Pheakklie,
Pheakklee, Pheakkleigh,
Pheakklea*

Pheodora (Greek) A supreme
gift
Pheodorah, Phedora, Phedorah

Phernita (American) A well-
spoken woman
*Pherneeta, Phernyta, Phernieta,
Pherneita, Pherneata*

Phia (Italian) A saintly woman
Phiah, Phea, Pheah

Philippa (English) Feminine
form of Phillip; a friend of
horses
*Phillippa, Philipa, Phillipa,
Philipinna, Philippine,
Phillipina, Phillipine, Pilis*

Philomena (Greek) A friend of
strength
Filomena, Philomina, Mena

Phoebe (Greek) A bright, shining woman; in mythology,
another name for the goddess
of the moon
*Phebe, Phoebi, Phebi, Phoebie,
Phebie, Pheobe, Phoebee,
Phoebea*

Phoena (Greek) Resembling a
mystical bird
*Phoenah, Phoenna, Phena,
Phenna*

Phoenix (Greek) A dark-red
color; in mythology, an
immortal bird
Phuong, Phoenyx

Phyllis (Greek) Of the foliage;
in mythology, a girl who was
turned into an almond tree
*Phylis, Phillis, Philis, Phylys,
Phyllida, Phylida, Phillida,
Philida*

Pili (Egyptian) The second-
born child
*Pilie, Pily, Piley, Pilee, Pilea,
Pileigh*

Pililani (Hawaiian) Having
great strength
*Pililanie, Pililany, Pililaney,
Pililanee, Pililanea*

Piluki (Hawaiian) Resembling
a small leaf
*Pilukie, Piluky, Pilukey,
Pilukee, Pilukea*

Pineki (Hawaiian) Resembling
a peanut
*Pinekie, Pineky, Pinekey,
Pinekee, Pinekea*

Ping (Chinese) One who is
peaceful
Pyng

Pinga (Inuit) In mythology, goddess of the hunt, fertility, and healing
Pingah, Pyngah, Pyngah

Pinquana (Native American) Having a pleasant fragrance
Pinquan, Pinquann, Pinquanne, Pinquanna, Pinquane

Piper (English) One who plays the flute
Pipere, Piperel, Piperell, Piperele, Piperelle, Piperela, Piperella, Pyper

Pippi (French / English) A friend of horses / a blushing young woman
Pippie, Pippy, Pippey, Pippee, Pippea

Pirouette (French) A ballet dancer
Piroette, Pirouett, Piroett, Piroueta, Piroeta, Pirouetta, Piroetta, Pirouet

Pisces (Latin) The twelfth sign of the zodiac; the fishes
Pysces, Piscees, Pyscees, Piscez, Pisceez

Pithasthana (Hindi) In Hinduism, a name for the wife of Shiva

Platinum (English) As precious as the metal
Platynum, Platnum, Platie, Plati, Platee, Platy, Platey, Platea

Platt (French) From the plains
Platte

Pleshette (American) An extravagent woman
Pleshett, Pleshet, Pleshete, Plesheta, Pleshetta

Pleun (American) One who is good with words
Pleune

Po (Italian) A lively woman

Podarge (Greek) In mythology, one of the Harpies

Poetry (American) A romantic woman
Poetrey, Poetri, Poetrie, Poetree, Poetrea

Polete (Hawaiian) A kind young woman
Polet, Polett, Polette, Poleta, Poletta

Polina (Russian) A small woman
Polinah, Poleena, Poleenah, Poleana, Poleanah, Poliena, Polienah, Poleina

Polyxena (Greek) In mythology, a daughter of Priam and loved by Achilles
Polyxenah, Polyxenia, Polyxenna, Polyxene, Polyxenea

Pomona (Latin) In mythology, goddess of fruit trees
Pomonah, Pomonia, Pomonea, Pamona, Pamonia, Pamonea

Poni (African) The second-born daughter
Ponni, Ponie, Ponnie, Pony, Ponny, Poney, Ponney, Ponee

Poodle (American) Resembling the dog; one with curly hair
Poudle, Poodel, Poudel

Poonam (Hindi) A kind and caring woman
Pounam

Porter (Latin) The doorkeeper

Posala (Native American) Born at the end of spring
Posalah, Posalla, Posallah

Posh (American) A fancy young woman
Poshe, Posha

Potina (Latin) In mythology, goddess of children's food and drink
Potinah, Potyna, Potena, Poteena, Potiena, Poteina, Poteana

Powder (American) A light-hearted woman
Powdar, Powdir, Powdur, Powdor, Powdi, Powdie, Powdy, Powdey

Praise (Latin) One who expresses admiration
Prayse, Praize, Prayze, Praze, Praese, Praeze

Pramada (Indian) One who is indifferent

Pramlocha (Hindi) In Hinduism, a celestial nymph

Precious (American) One who is treasured
Preshis, Preshys

^**Presley** (English) Of the priest's town
Presly, Preslie, Presli, Preslee

Primola (Latin) Resembling a primrose
Primolah, Primolia, Primoliah, Primolea, Primoleah

Princess (English) A high-born daughter; born to royalty
Princessa, Princesa, Princie, Princi, Princy, Princee, Princey, Princea

Prisca (Latin) From an ancient family
Priscilla, Priscella, Precilla, Presilla, Prescilla, Prisilla, Prisella, Prissy, Prissi

Promise (American) A faithful
woman
*Promice, Promyse, Promyce,
Promis, Promiss, Promys,
Promyss*

Prudence (English) One who
is cautious and exercises good
judgment
*Prudencia, Prudensa,
Prudensia, Prudentia,
Predencia, Predentia, Prue, Pru*

Pryce (American / Welsh) One
who is very dear / an enthusiastic child
Price, Prise, Pryse

Pulcheria (Italian) A chubby
baby
*Pulcheriah, Pulcherea,
Pulchereah, Pulcherya,
Pulcheryah, Pulcheriya*

Pulika (African) An obedient
and well-behaved girl
*Pulikah, Pulicca, Pulicka,
Pulyka, Puleeka, Puleaka*

Pyrena (Greek) A fiery woman
*Pyrenah, Pyrina, Pyrinah,
Pyryna, Pyrynah, Pyreena,
Pyreenah, Pyriena*

Pyria (American) One who is
cherished
*Pyriah, Pyrea, Pyreah, Pyriya,
Pyriyah, Pyra*

Qadesh (Syrian) In mythology,
goddess of love and sensuality
*Quedesh, Qadesha, Quedesha,
Qadeshia, Quedeshia,
Quedeshiya*

Qamra (Arabic) Of the moon
*Qamrah, Qamar, Qamara,
Qamrra, Qamaria, Qamrea,
Qamria*

Qimat (Indian) A valuable
woman
*Qimate, Qimatte, Qimata,
Qimatta*

Qitarah (Arabic) Having a nice
fragrance
*Qitara, Qytarah, Qytara,
Qitaria, Qitarra, Qitarria,
Qytarra, Qytarria*

Qoqa (Chechen) Resembling
a dove

Quana (Native American)
One who is aromatic; sweet-
smelling
*Quanah, Quanna, Quannah,
Quania, Quaniya, Quanniya,
Quannia, Quanea*

Querida (Spanish) One who is dearly loved; beloved
Queridah, Queryda, Querydah, Querrida, Queridda, Querridda, Quereeda, Quereada

Queta (Spanish) Head of the household
Quetah, Quetta, Quettah

Quiana (American) Living with grace; heavenly
Quianah, Quianna, Quiane, Quian, Quianne, Quianda, Quiani, Quianita

Quincy (English) The fifth-born child
Quincey, Quinci, Quincie, Quincee, Quincia, Quinncy, Quinnci, Quyncy

Quintana (Latin / English) The fifth girl / queen's lawn
Quintanah, Quinella, Quinta, Quintina, Quintanna, Quintann, Quintara, Quintona

Quintessa (Latin) Of the essence
Quintessah, Quintesa, Quintesha, Quintisha, Quintessia, Quyntessa, Quintosha, Quinticia

Quinyette (American) The fifth-born child
Quinyett, Quinyet, Quinyeta, Quinyette, Quinyete

Quirina (Latin) One who is contentious
Quirinah, Quiryna, Quirynah, Quireena, Quireenah, Quireina, Quireinah, Quiriena

Quiritis (Latin) In mythology, goddess of motherhood
Quiritiss, Quiritisse, Quirytis, Quirytys, Quiritys, Quirityss

Quiterie (French) One who is peaceful; tranquil
Quiteri, Quitery, Quiterey, Quiteree, Quiterye, Quyterie, Quyteri, Quyteree

R

Rabiah (Egyptian / Arabic) Born in the springtime / of the gentle wind
Rabia, Raabia, Rabi'ah, Rabi

Rachana (Hindi) Born of the creation
Rachanna, Rashana, Rashanda, Rachna

*Rachel (Hebrew) The innocent lamb; in the Bible, Jacob's wife
Rachael, Racheal, Rachelanne, Rachelce, Rachele, Racheli, Rachell, Rachelle, Raquel

Radcliffe (English) Of the red cliffs
Radcleff, Radclef, Radclif, Radclife, Radclyffe, Radclyf, Radcliphe, Radclyphe

Radella (English) An elfin counselor
Radell, Radel, Radele, Radella, Radela, Raedself, Radself, Raidself

Radmilla (Slavic) Hard-working for the people
Radilla, Radinka, Radmila, Redmilla, Radilu

Rafi'a (Arabic) An exalted woman
Rafia, Rafi'ah, Rafee'a, Rafeea, Rafeeah, Rafiya, Rafiyah

Ragnara (Swedish) Feminine form of Ragnar; one who provides counsel to the army
Ragnarah, Ragnarra, Ragnaria, Ragnarea, Ragnari, Ragnarie, Ragnary, Ragnarey

Rahi (Arabic) Born during the springtime
Rahii, Rahy, Rahey, Rahee, Rahea, Rahie

Rahimah (Arabic) A compassionate woman; one who is merciful
Rahima, Raheema, Raheemah, Raheima, Rahiema, Rahyma, Rahymah, Raheama

Raina (Polish) Form of Regina, meaning "a queenly woman"
Raenah, Raene, Rainah, Raine, Rainee, Rainey, Rainelle, Rainy

Raja (Arabic) One who is filled with hope
Rajah

Raleigh (English) From the clearing of roe deer
Raileigh, Railey, Raley, Rawleigh, Rawley, Raly, Rali, Ralie

Ramona (Spanish) Feminine form of Ramon; a wise protector
Ramee, Ramie, Ramoena, Ramohna, Ramonda, Ramonde, Ramonita, Ramonna

Randi (English) Feminine form of Randall; shielded by wolves; form of Miranda, meaning "worthy of admiration"
Randa, Randee, Randelle, Randene, Randie, Randy, Randey, Randilyn

Raquel (Spanish) Form of Rachel, meaning "the innocent lamb"
Racquel, Racquell, Raquela, Raquelle, Roquel, Roquela, Rakel, Rakell

Rasha (Arabic) Resembling a
young gazelle
*Rashah, Raisha, Raysha,
Rashia, Raesha*

Ratana (Thai) Resembling a
crystal
*Ratanah, Ratanna, Ratannah,
Rathana, Rathanna*

Rati (Hindi) In Hinduism,
goddess of passion and lust
Ratie, Ratea, Ratee, Raty, Ratey

Ratri (Indian) Born in the
evening
*Ratrie, Ratry, Ratrey, Ratree,
Ratrea*

Rawiyah (Arabic) One who
recites ancient poetry
Rawiya, Rawiyya, Rawiyyah

Rawnie (English) An elegant
lady
*Rawni, Rawny, Rawney,
Rawnee, Rawnea*

Raya (Israeli) A beloved friend
Rayah

Raymonde (German)
Feminine form of Raymond;
one who offers wise protec-
tion
*Raymondi, Raymondie,
Raymondee, Raymondea,
Raymonda, Raymunde,
Raymunda*

Rayna (Hebrew /
Scandinavian) One who is
pure / one who provides wise
counsel
*Raynah, Raynee, Rayni, Rayne,
Raynea, Raynie*

Reba (Hebrew) Form of
Rebecca, meaning "one who
is bound to God"
*Rebah, Reeba, Rheba, Rebba,
Ree, Reyba, Reaba*

Rebecca (Hebrew) One who is
bound to God; in the Bible,
the wife of Isaac
*Rebakah, Rebbeca, Rebbecca,
Rebbecka, Rebeca, Rebeccah,
Rebeccea, Becky, Reba*

Reese (American) Form of
Rhys, meaning "having great
enthusiasm for life"
*Rhyss, Rhysse, Reece, Reice,
Reise, Reace, Rease, Riece*

Regan (Gaelic) Born into roy-
alty; the little ruler
*Raegan, Ragan, Raygan,
Reganne, Regann, Regane,
Reghan, Reagan*

Regina (Latin) A queenly
woman
*Regeena, Regena, Reggi, Reggie,
Régine, Regine, Reginette,
Reginia, Raina*

Rehan (Armenian) Resembling a flower
Rehane, Rehann, Rehanne, Rehana, Rehanna, Rehanan, Rehannan, Rehania

Rehoboth (Hebrew) From the city by the river
Rehobothe, Rehobotha, Rehobothia

Rekha (Indian) One who walks a straight line
Rekhah, Reka, Rekah

Remy (French) Woman from the town of Rheims
Remi, Remie, Remmy, Remmi, Remmie, Remy, Remmey, Remey

Ren (Japanese) Resembling a water lily

Renée (French) One who has been reborn
Ranae, Ranay, Ranée, Renae, Renata, Renay, Renaye, René

Reseda (Latin) Resembling the mignonette flower
Resedah, Reselda, Resedia, Reseldia

Resen (Hebrew) From the head of the stream; refers to a bridle

Reshma (Arabic) Having silky skin
Reshmah, Reshman, Reshmane, Reshmann, Reshmanne, Reshmana, Reshmanna, Reshmaan

Reya (Spanish) A queenly woman
Reyah, Reyeh, Reye, Reyia, Reyiah, Reyea, Reyeah

Reza (Hungarian) Form of Theresa, meaning "a harvester"
Rezah, Rezia, Reziah, Rezi, Rezie, Rezy, Rezee, Resi

Rezeph (Hebrew) As solid as a stone
Rezepha, Rezephe, Rezephia, Rezephah, Rezephiah

Rhea (Greek) Of the flowing stream; in mythology, the wife of Cronus and mother of gods and goddesses
Rea, Rhae, Rhaya, Rhia, Rhiah, Rhiya, Rheya

Rheda (Anglo-Saxon) A divine woman; a goddess
Rhedah

Rhiannon (Welsh) The great and sacred queen
Rheanna, Rheanne, Rhiana, Rhiann, Rhianna, Rhiannan, Rhianon, Rhyan

Rhonda (Welsh) Wielding a good spear
Rhondelle, Rhondene, Rhondiesha, Rhonette, Rhonnda, Ronda, Rondel, Rondelle

Rhys (Welsh) Having great enthusiasm for life
Rhyss, Rhysse, Reece, Reese, Reice, Reise, Reace, Rease

Ria (Spanish) From the river's mouth
Riah

Riane (Gaelic) Feminine form of Ryan; little ruler
Riana, Rianna, Rianne, Ryann, Ryanne, Ryana, Ryanna, Riann

Rica (English) Form of Frederica, meaning "peaceful ruler"; form of Erica, meaning "ever the ruler / resembling heather"
Rhica, Ricca, Ricah, Rieca, Riecka, Rieka, Riqua, Ryca

Riddhi (Indian) A prosperous woman
Riddhie, Riddhy, Riddhey, Riddhee, Riddhea

Rihanna (Arabic) Resembling sweet basil
Rihana

*Riley (Gaelic) From the rye clearing; a courageous woman
Reilley, Reilly, Rilee, Rileigh, Ryley, Rylee, Ryleigh, Rylie

Rini (Japanese) Resembling a young rabbit
Rinie, Rinee, Rinea, Riny, Riney

Rio (Spanish) Woman of the river
Rhio

Risa (Latin) One who laughs often
Risah, Reesa, Riesa, Rise, Rysa, Rysah, Riseh, Risako

Rita (Greek) Precious pearl
Ritta, Reeta, Reita, Rheeta, Riet, Rieta, Ritah, Reta

Roberta (English) Feminine form of Robert; one who is bright with fame
Robertah, Robbie, Robin

Rochelle (French) From the little rock
Rochel, Rochele, Rochell, Rochella, Rochette, Roschella, Roschelle, Roshelle

Roja (Spanish) A red-haired lady
Rojah

Rolanda (German) Feminine form of Roland; well-known throughout the land
Rolandah, Rolandia, Roldandea, Rolande, Rolando, Rollanda, Rollande

Romhilda (German) A glorious battle maiden
Romhilde, Romhild, Romeld, Romelde, Romelda, Romilda, Romild, Romilde

Ronli (Hebrew) My joy is the Lord
Ronlie, Ronlee, Ronleigh, Ronly, Ronley, Ronlea, Ronia, Roniya

Ronni (English) Form of Veronica, meaning "displaying her true image"
Ronnie, Ronae, Ronay, Ronee, Ronelle, Ronette, Roni, Ronica, Ronika

Rosalind (German / English) Resembling a gentle horse / form of Rose, meaning "resembling the beautiful and meaningful flower"
Ros, Rosaleen, Rosalen, Rosalin, Rosalina, Rosalinda, Rosalinde, Rosaline, Chalina

Rose (Latin) Resembling the beautiful and meaningful flower
Rosa, Rosie, Rosalind

Roseanne (English) Resembling the graceful rose
Ranna, Rosana, Rosanagh, Rosanna, Rosannah, Rosanne, Roseann, Roseanna

Rosemary (Latin / English) The dew of the sea / resembling a bitter rose
Rosemaree, Rosemarey, Rosemaria, Rosemarie, Rosmarie, Rozmary, Rosamaria, Rosamarie

Rowan (Gaelic) Of the redberry tree
Rowann, Rowane, Rowanne, Rowana, Rowanna

Rowena (Welsh / German) One who is fair and slender / having much fame and happiness
Rhowena, Roweena, Roweina, Rowenna, Rowina, Rowinna, Rhonwen, Rhonwyn

Ruana (Indian) One who is musically inclined
Ruanah, Ruanna, Ruannah, Ruane, Ruann, Ruanne

Ruby (English) As precious as the red gemstone
Rubee, Rubi, Rubie, Rubyna, Rubea

Rudella (German) A well-known woman
Rudela, Rudelah, Rudell, Rudelle, Rudel, Rudele, Rudy, Rudie

Rue (English, German) A medicinal herb
Ru, Larue

Rufina (Latin) A red-haired woman
Rufeena, Rufeine, Ruffina, Rufine, Ruffine, Rufyna, Ruffyna, Rufyne

Ruhi (Arabic) A spiritual woman
Roohee, Ruhee, Ruhie, Ruhy, Ruhey, Roohi, Roohie, Ruhea

Rukmini (Hindi) Adorned with gold; in Hinduism, the first wife of Krishna
Rukminie, Rukminy, Rukminey, Rukminee, Rukminea, Rukminni, Rukminii

Rumah (Hebrew) One who has been exalted
Ruma, Rumia, Rumea, Rumiah, Rumeah, Rumma, Rummah

Rumina (Latin) In mythology, a protector goddess of mothers and babies
Ruminah, Rumeena, Rumeenah, Rumeina, Rumiena, Rumyna, Rumeinah, Rumienah

Rupali (Indian) A beautiful woman
Rupalli, Rupalie, Rupalee, Rupallee, Rupal, Rupa, Rupaly, Rupaley

Ruqayyah (Arabic) A gentle woman; a daughter of Muhammad
Ruqayya, Ruqayah, Ruqaya

Ruth (Hebrew) A beloved companion
Ruthe, Ruthelle, Ruthellen, Ruthetta, Ruthi, Ruthie, Ruthina, Ruthine

Ryba (Slavic) Resembling a fish
Rybah, Rybba, Rybbah

Ryder (American) An accomplished horsewoman
Rider

Rylee (American) Form of Riley, meaning "from the rye clearing / a courageous woman"

S

Saba (Greek / Arabic) Woman from Sheba / born in the morning
Sabah, Sabaa, Sabba, Sabbah, Sabaah

Sabana (Spanish) From the open plain
Sabanah, Sabanna, Sabann, Sabanne, Sabane, Saban

Sabi (Arabic) A lovely young lady
Sabie, Saby, Sabey, Sabee, Sabbi, Sabbee, Sabea

Sabirah (Arabic) Having great patience
Sabira, Saabira, Sabeera, Sabiera, Sabeira, Sabyra, Sabirra, Sabyrra

Sabra (Hebrew) Resembling the cactus fruit; to rest
Sabrah, Sebra, Sebrah, Sabrette, Sabbra, Sabraa, Sabarah, Sabarra

Sabrina (English) A legendary princess
Sabrinah, Sabrinna, Sabreena, Sabriena, Sabreina, Sabryna, Sabrine, Sabryne, Cabrina, Zabrina

Sachet (Hindi) Having consciousness
Sachett, Sachette

Sada (Japanese) The pure one
Sadda, Sadaa, Sadako, Saddaa

Sadella (American) A beautiful fairylike princess
Sadel, Sadela, Sadelah, Sadele, Sadell, Sadellah, Sadelle, Sydel

Sadhana (Hindi) A devoted woman
Sadhanah, Sadhanna, Sadhannah, Sadhane, Sadhanne, Sadhann, Sadhan

Sadhbba (Irish) A wise woman
Sadhbh, Sadhba

Sadie (English) Form of Sarah, meaning "a princess; lady"
Sadi, Sady, Sadey, Sadee, Saddi, Saddee, Sadiey, Sadye

Sadiya (Arabic) One who is fortunate; lucky
Sadiyah, Sadiyyah, Sadya, Sadyah

Sadzi (American) Having a sunny disposition
Sadzee, Sadzey, Sadzia, Sadziah, Sadzie, Sadzya, Sadzyah, Sadzy

Safa (Arabic) One who is innocent and pure
Safah, Saffa, Sapha, Saffah, Saphah

Saffron (English) Resembling the yellow flower
Saffrone, Saffronn, Saffronne, Safron, Safronn, Safronne, Saffronah, Safrona

Saheli (Indian) A beloved friend
Sahelie, Sahely, Saheley, Sahelee, Saheleigh, Sahyli, Sahelea

Sahila (Indian) One who provides guidance
Sahilah, Saheela, Sahyla, Sahiela, Saheila, Sahela, Sahilla, Sahylla

Sahkyo (Native American) Resembling the mink
Sakyo

Saida (Arabic) Fortunate one; one who is happy
Saidah, Sa'ida, Sayida, Saeida, Saedah, Said, Sayide, Sayidea

Saihah (Arabic) One who is useful; good
Saiha, Sayiha

Sailor (American) One who sails the seas
Sailer, Sailar, Saylor, Sayler, Saylar, Saelor, Saeler, Saelar

Saima (Arabic) A fasting woman
Saimah, Saimma, Sayima

Sajni (Indian) One who is dearly loved
Sajnie, Sajny, Sajney, Sajnee, Sajnea

Sakae (Japanese) One who is prosperous
Sakai, Sakaie, Sakay, Sakaye

Sakari (Native American) A sweet girl
Sakarie, Sakary, Sakarri, Sakarey, Sakaree, Sakarree, Sakarah, Sakarrie

Sakina (Indian / Arabic) A beloved friend / having God-inspired peace of mind
Sakinah, Sakeena, Sakiena, Sakeina, Sakyna, Sakeyna, Sakinna, Sakeana

Sakti (Hindi) In Hinduism, the divine energy
Saktie, Sakty, Sakkti, Sackti, Saktee, Saktey, Saktia, Saktiah

Saku (Japanese) Remembrance of the Lord
Sakuko

Sakura (Japanese) Resembling a cherry blossom
Sakurah, Sakurako, Sakurra

Sala (Hindi) From the sacred sala tree
Salah, Salla, Sallah

Salal (English) An evergreen shrub with flowers and berries
Sallal, Salall, Sallall, Salalle, Salale, Sallale

Salamasina (Samoan) A princess; born to royalty
Salamaseena, Salamasyna, Salamaseana, Salamaseina, Salamasiena

Salina (French) One of a solemn, dignified character
Salin, Salinah, Salinda, Salinee, Sallin, Sallina, Sallinah, Salline

Saloma (Hebrew) One who offers peace and tranquility
Salomah, Salome, Salomia, Salomiah, Schlomit, Shulamit, Salomeaexl, Salomma

Salus (Latin) In mythology, goddess of health and prosperity; salvation
Saluus, Salusse, Saluss

Salwa (Arabic) One who provides comfort; solace
Salwah

Samah (Arabic) A generous, forgiving woman
Sama, Samma, Sammah

*Samantha (Aramaic) One who listens well
Samanthah, Samanthia, Samanthea, Samantheya, Samanath, Samanatha, Samana, Samanitha

Sameh (Arabic) One who forgives
Sammeh, Samaya, Samaiya

Samina (Arabic) A healthy woman
Saminah, Samine, Sameena, Samyna, Sameana, Sameina, Samynah

Samone (Hebrew) Form of Simone, meaning "one who listens well"
Samoan, Samoane, Samon, Samona, Samonia

Samuela (Hebrew) Feminine form of Samuel; asked of God
Samuelah, Samuella, Samuell, Samuelle, Sammila, Sammile, Samella, Samielle

Sana (Persian / Arabic) One who emanates light / brilliance; splendor
Sanah, Sanna, Sanako, Sanaah, Sane, Saneh

Sanaa (Swahili) Beautiful work of art
Sanae, Sannaa

Sandeep (Punjabi) One who is enlightened
Sandeepe, Sandip, Sandipp, Sandippe, Sandeyp, Sandeype

Sandhya (Hindi) Born at twilight; name of the daughter of the god Brahma
Sandhiya, Sandhyah, Sandya, Sandyah

Sandra (Greek) Form of Alexandra, meaning "a helper and defender of mankind"
Sandrah, Sandrine, Sandy, Sandi, Sandie, Sandey, Sandee, Sanda, Sandrica

Sandrica (Greek) Form of Sandra, meaning "a helper and defender of mankind"
Sandricca, Sandricah, Sandricka, Sandrickah, Sandrika, Sandrikah, Sandryca, Sandrycah

Sandrine (Greek) Form of Alexandra, meaning "a helper and defender of mankind"
Sandrin, Sandreana, Sandreanah, Sandreane, Sandreen, Sandreena, Sandreenah, Sandreene

Sangita (Indian) One who is musical
Sangitah, Sangeeta, Sangeita, Sangyta, Sangieta, Sangeata

Saniya (Indian) A moment in time preserved
Saniyah, Sanya, Sanea, Sania

Sanjna (Indian) A conscientious woman

Santana (Spanish) A saintly woman
Santa, Santah, Santania, Santaniah, Santaniata, Santena, Santenah, Santenna

Saoirse (Gaelic) An independent woman; having freedom
Saoyrse

Sapna (Hindi) A dream come true
Sapnah, Sapnia, Sapniah, Sapnea, Sapneah, Sapniya, Sapniyah

★Sarah (Hebrew) A princess; lady; in the Bible, wife of Abraham
Sara, Sari, Sariah, Sarika, Saaraa, Sarita, Sarina, Sarra, Kala, Sadie

Saraid (Irish) One who is excellent; superior
Saraide, Saraed, Saraede, Sarayd, Sarayde

Sarama (African / Hindi) A kind woman / in Hinduism, Indra's dog
Saramah, Saramma, Sarrama, Sarramma

Saran (African) One who brings joy to others
Sarane, Sarran, Saranne, Saranna, Sarana, Sarann

Sarasvati (Hindi) In Hinduism, goddess of learning and the arts
Sarasvatti, Sarasvatie, Sarasvaty, Sarasvatey, Sarasvatee, Sarasvatea

Saraswati (Hindi) Owning water; in Hinduism, a river goddess
Saraswatti, Saraswatie, Saraswaty, Saraswatey, Saraswatee, Saraswatea

Sardinia (Italian) Woman from a mountainous island
Sardiniah, Sardinea, Sardineah, Sardynia, Sardyniah, Sardynea, Sardyneah

Sasa (Japanese) One who is helpful; gives aid
Sasah

^Sasha (Russian) Form of Alexandra, meaning "a helper and defender of mankind"
Sascha, Sashenka, Saskia

Sauda (Swahili) A dark beauty
Saudaa, Sawda, Saudda

*ᵀSavannah (English) From the open grassy plain
Savanna, Savana, Savanne, Savann, Savane, Savanneh

Savarna (Hindi) Daughter of the ocean
Savarnia, Savarnea, Savarniya, Savarneia

Savitri (Hindi) In Hinduism, the daughter of the god of the sun
Savitari, Savitrie, Savitry, Savitarri, Savitarie, Savitree, Savitrea, Savitrey

Savvy (American) Smart and perceptive woman
Savy, Savvi, Savvie, Savvey, Savee, Savvee, Savvea, Savea

Sayyida (Arabic) A mistress
Sayyidah, Sayida, Sayyda, Seyyada, Seyyida, Seyada, Seyida

Scarlett (English) Vibrant red color; a vivacious woman
Scarlet, Scarlette, Skarlet

Scota (Irish) Woman of Scotland
Scotta, Scotah, Skota, Skotta, Skotah

Sea'iqa (Arabic) Thunder and lightning
Seaqa, Seaqua

Season (Latin) A fertile woman; one who embraces change
Seazon, Seeson, Seezon, Seizon, Seasen, Seasan, Seizen, Seizan

Sebille (English) In Arthurian legend, a fairy
Sebylle, Sebill, Sebile, Sebyle, Sebyl

Secunda (Latin) The second-born child
Secundah, Secuba, Secundus, Segunda, Sekunda

Seda (Armenian) Voices of the forest
Sedda, Sedah, Seddah

Sedona (American) Woman from a city in Arizona
Sedonah, Sedonna, Sedonnah, Sedonia, Sedonea

Seema (Greek) A symbol; a sign
Seyma, Syma, Seama, Seima, Siema

Sefarina (Greek) Of a gentle wind
Sefarinah, Sefareena, Sefareenah, Sefaryna, Sefarynah, Sefareana, Sefareanah

Seiko (Japanese) The force of truth

Selene (Greek) Of the moon
Sela, Selena, Selina, Celina, Zalina

Sema (Arabic) A divine omen; a known symbol
Semah

Senalda (Spanish) A sign; a symbol
Senaldah, Senaldia, Senaldiya, Senaldea, Senaldya

September (American) Born in the month of September
Septimber, Septymber, Septemberia, Septemberea

Sequoia (Native American) Of the giant redwood tree
Sekwoya, Lequoia

Serafina (Latin) A seraph; a heavenly winged angel
Serafinah, Serafine, Seraphina, Serefina, Seraphine, Sera

Serena (Latin) Having a peaceful disposition
Serenah, Serene, Sereena, Seryna, Serenity, Serenitie, Serenitee, Serepta, Cerina, Xerena

Serendipity (American) A fateful meeting; having good fortune
Serendipitey, Serendipitee, Serendipiti, Serendipitie, Serendypyty

*Serenity (Latin) peaceful

Sevati (Indian) Resembling the white rose
Sevatie, Sevatti, Sevate, Sevatee, Sevatea, Sevaty, Sevatey, Sevti

Shabana (Arabic) A maiden belonging to the night
Shabanah, Shabanna, Shabaana, Shabanne, Shabane

Shabnan (Persian) A falling raindrop
Shabnane, Shabnann, Shabnanne

Shadha (Arabic) An aromatic fragrance
Shadhah

Shafiqa (Arabic) A compassionate woman
Shafiqah, Shafiqua, Shafeeqa, Shafeequa

Shai (Gaelic) A gift of God
Shay, Shae, Shayla, Shea, Shaye

Sha'ista (Arabic) One who is polite and well-behaved
Shaistah, Shaista, Shaa'ista, Shayista, Shaysta

Shakila (Arabic) Feminine form of Shakil; beautiful one
Shakilah, Shakela, Shakeela, Shakeyla, Shakyla, Shakeila, Shakiela, Shakina

Shakira (Arabic) Feminine form of Shakir; grateful; thankful
Shakirah, Shakiera, Shaakira, Shakeira, Shakyra, Shakeyra, Shakura, Shakirra

Shakti (Indian) A divine woman; having power
Shaktie, Shakty, Shaktey, Shaktee, Shaktye, Shaktea

Shaliqa (Arabic) One who is sisterly
Shaliqah, Shaliqua, Shaleeqa, Shaleequa, Shalyqa, Shalyqua

Shamima (Arabic) A woman full of flavor
Shamimah, Shameema, Shamiema, Shameima, Shamyma, Shameama

Shandy (English) One who is rambunctious; boisterous
Shandey, Shandee, Shandi, Shandie, Shandye, Shandea

Shani (African) A marvelous woman
Shanie, Shany, Shaney, Shanee, Shanni, Shanea, Shannie, Shanny

Shanley (Gaelic) Small and ancient woman
Shanleigh, Shanlee, Shanly, Shanli, Shanlie, Shanlea

Shannon (Gaelic) Having ancient wisdom; river name
Shanon, Shannen, Shannan, Shannin, Shanna, Shannae, Shannun, Shannyn

Shaquana (American) Truth in life
Shaqana, Shaquanah, Shaquanna, Shaqanna, Shaqania

Sharifah (Arabic) Feminine form of Sharif; noble; respected; virtuous
Sharifa, Shareefa, Sharufa, Sharufah, Sharyfa, Sharefa, Shareafa, Shariefa

Sharik (African) One who is a child of God
Shareek, Shareake, Sharicke, Sharick, Sharike, Shareak, Sharique, Sharyk

Sharikah (Arabic) One who is a good companion
Sharika, Shareeka, Sharyka, Shareka, Shariqua, Shareaka

Sharlene (French) Feminine form of Charles; petite and womanly
Sharleene, Sharleen, Sharla, Sharlyne, Sharline, Sharlyn, Sharlean, Sharleane

Sharon (Hebrew) From the plains; a flowering shrub
Sharron, Sharone, Sharona, Shari, Sharis, Sharne, Sherine, Sharun

Shasta (Native American) From the triple-peaked mountain
Shastah, Shastia, Shastiya, Shastea, Shasteya

Shawnee (Native American) A tribal name
Shawni, Shawnie, Shawnea, Shawny, Shawney, Shawnea

Shayla (Irish) Of the fairy palace; form of Shai, meaning "a gift of God"
Shaylah, Shaylagh, Shaylain, Shaylan, Shaylea, Shayleah, Shaylla, Sheyla

Shaylee (Gaelic) From the fairy palace; a fairy princess
Shalee, Shayleigh, Shailee, Shaileigh, Shaelee, Shaeleigh, Shayli, Shaylie

Sheehan (Celtic) Little peaceful one; peacemaker
Shehan, Sheyhan, Shihan, Shiehan, Shyhan, Sheahan

Sheela (Indian) One of cool conduct and character
Sheelah, Sheetal

Sheena (Gaelic) God's gracious gift
Sheenah, Shena, Shiena, Sheyna, Shyna, Sheana, Sheina

Sheherezade (Arabic) One who is a city dweller

Sheila (Irish) Form of Cecilia, meaning "one who is blind"
Sheilah, Sheelagh, Shelagh, Shiela, Shyla, Selia, Sighle, Sheiletta

Shelby (English) From the willow farm
Shelbi, Shelbey, Shelbie, Shelbee, Shelbye, Shelbea

Sheridan (Gaelic) One who is wild and untamed; a searcher
Sheridann, Sheridanne, Sherydan, Sherridan, Sheriden, Sheridon, Sherrerd, Sherida

Sheshebens (Native American) Resembling a small duck

Shifra (Hebrew) A beautiful midwife
Shifrah, Shiphrah, Shiphra, Shifria, Shifriya, Shifrea

Shikha (Indian) Flame burning brightly
Shikhah, Shikkha, Shekha, Shykha

Shima (Native American) Little mother
Shimah, Shimma, Shyma, Shymah

Shina (Japanese) A virtuous woman; having goodness
Shinah, Shinna, Shyna, Shynna

Shobha (Indian) An attractive woman
Shobhah, Shobbha, Shoba, Shobhan, Shobhane

Shoshana (Arabic) Form of Susannah, meaning "white lily"
Shosha, Shoshan, Shoshanah, Shoshane, Shoshanha, Shoshann, Shoshanna, Shoshannah

Shradhdha (Indian) One who is faithful; trusting
Shraddha, Shradha, Shradhan, Shradhane

Shruti (Indian) Having good hearing
Shrutie, Shruty, Shrutey, Shrutee, Shrutye, Shrutea

Shunnareh (Arabic) Pleasing in manner and behavior
Shunnaraya, Shunareh, Shunarreh

Shyann (English) Form of Cheyenne, meaning "unintelligible speaker"
Shyanne, Shyane, Sheyann, Sheyanne, Sheyenne, Sheyene

Shysie (Native American) A quiet child
Shysi, Shysy, Shysey, Shysee, Shycie, Shyci, Shysea, Shycy

Sibyl (English) A prophetess; a seer
Sybil, Sibyla, Sybella, Sibil, Sibella, Sibilla, Sibley, Sibylla

Siddhi (Hindi) Having spiritual power
Sidhi, Syddhi, Sydhi

Sidero (Greek) In mythology, stepmother of Pelias and Neleus
Siderro, Sydero, Sideriyo

Sieglinde (German) Winning a gentle victory

Sienna (Italian) Woman with reddish-brown hair
Siena, Siennya, Sienya, Syenna, Syinna

Sierra (Spanish) From the jagged mountain range
Siera, Syerra, Syera, Seyera, Seeara

Sigfreda (German) A woman who is victorious
Sigfreeda, Sigfrida, Sigfryda, Sigfreyda, Sigfrieda, Sigfriede, Sigfrede

Sigismonda (Teutonic) A victorious defender
Sigismunda

Signia (Latin) A distinguishing sign
Signiya, Signea, Signeia, Signeya, Signa

Sigyn (Norse) In mythology, the wife of Loki

Sihu (Native American) As delicate as a flower

Silka (Latin) Form of Cecelia, meaning "one who is blind"
Silke, Silkia, Silkea, Silkie, Silky, Silkee, Sylka, Sylke

Sima (Arabic) One who is treasured; a prize
Simma, Syma, Simah, Simia, Simiya

Simone (French) One who listens well
Sim, Simonie, Symone, Samone

Sine (Scottish) Form of Jane, meaning "God is gracious"
Sinead, Sineidin, Sioned, Sionet, Sion, Siubhan, Siwan, Sineh

Sinobia (Greek) Form of Zenobia, meaning "child of Zeus"
Sinobiah, Sinobya, Sinobe, Sinobie, Sinovia, Senobia, Senobya, Senobe

Sinopa (Native American) Resembling a fox

Sinope (Greek) In mythology, one of the daughters of Asopus

Siran (Armenian) An alluring and lovely woman

Siren (Greek) In mythology, a sea nymph whose beautiful singing lured sailors to their deaths; refers to a seductive and beautiful woman
Sirene, Sirena, Siryne, Siryn, Syren, Syrena, Sirine, Sirina

Siria (Spanish / Persian) Bright like the sun / a glowing woman
Siriah, Sirea, Sireah, Siriya, Siriyah, Sirya, Siryah

Siroun (Armenian) A lovely woman
Sirune

Sirpuhi (Armenian) One who is holy; pious
Sirpuhie, Sirpuhy, Sirpuhey, Sirpuhea, Sirpuhee

Sissy (English) Form of Cecilia, meaning "one who is blind"
Sissey, Sissie, Sisley, Sisli, Sislee, Sissel, Sissle, Syssy

Sita (Hindi) In Hinduism, goddess of the harvest and wife of Rama

Sive (Irish) A good and sweet girl
Sivney, Sivny, Sivni, Sivnie, Sivnee, Sivnea

Skylar (English) One who is learned, a scholar
Skylare, Skylarr, Skyler, Skylor, Skylir

Sloane (Irish) A strong protector; a woman warrior
Sloan, Slone

Smita (Indian) One who smiles a lot

Snow (American) Frozen rain
Snowy, Snowie, Snowi, Snowey, Snowee, Snowea, Sno

Snowdrop (English) Resembling a small white flower

Solana (Latin / Spanish) Wind from the east / of the sunshine
Solanah, Solanna, Solann, Solanne

Solange (French) One who is religious and dignified

Solaris (Greek) Of the sun
Solarise, Solariss, Solarisse, Solarys, Solaryss, Solarysse, Sol, Soleil

Solita (Latin) One who is solitary
Solitah, Solida, Soledad, Soledada, Soledade

Somatra (Indian) Of the excellent moon

Sona (Arabic) The golden one
Sonika, Sonna

Sonora (Spanish) A pleasant-sounding woman
Sonorah, Sonoria, Sonorya, Sonoriya

Soo (Korean) Having an excellent long life

*T**Sophia** (Greek) Form of Sophie, meaning great wisdom and foresight
Sofia, Sofiya

*T**Sophie** (Greek) Wisdom
Sophia, Sofiya, Sofie, Sofia, Sofi, Sofiyko, Sofronia, Sophronia, Zofia

Sorina (Romanian) Feminine form of Sorin; of the sun
Sorinah, Sorinna, Sorinia, Soriniya, Sorinya, Soryna, Sorynia, Sorine

Sorrel (French) From the surele plant
Sorrell, Sorrelle, Sorrele, Sorrela, Sorrella

Sparrow (English) Resembling a small songbird
Sparro, Sparroe, Sparo, Sparow, Sparowe, Sparoe

Sslama (Egyptian) One who is peaceful

Stacey (English) Form of Anastasia, meaning "one who shall rise again"
Stacy, Staci, Stacie, Stacee, Stacia, Stasia, Stasy, Stasey

Stella (English) Star of the sea
Stela, Stelle, Stele, Stellah, Stelah

Stephanie (Greek) Feminine form of Stephen; crowned in victory
Stephani, Stephany, Stephaney, Stephanee, Stephene, Stephana, Stefanie, Stefani

Stevonna (Greek) A crowned lady
Stevonnah, Stevona, Stevonah, Stevonia, Stevonea, Stevoniya

Styx (Greek) In mythology, the river of the underworld
Stixx, Styxx, Stix

Suave (American) A smooth and courteous woman
Swave

Subhadra (Hindi) In Hinduism, the sister of Krishna

Subhaga (Indian) A fortunate person

Subhuja (Hindi) An auspicious celestial damsel

Subira (African) One who is patient
Subirah, Subirra, Subyra, Subyrra, Subeera, Subeara, Subeira, Subiera

Suhaila (Arabic) Feminine form of Suhail; the second brightest star
Suhayla, Suhaela, Suhala, Suhailah, Suhaylah, Suhaelah, Suhalah

Sulwyn (Welsh) One who shines as bright as the sun
Sulwynne, Sulwynn, Sulwinne, Sulwin, Sulwen, Sulwenn, Sulwenne

Sumana (Indian) A good-natured woman
Sumanah, Sumanna, Sumane, Sumanne, Sumann

Sumi (Japanese) One who is elegant and refined
Sumie

Sumitra (Indian) A beloved friend
Sumitrah, Sumita, Sumytra, Sumyta, Sumeetra, Sumeitra, Sumietra, Sumeatra

Summer (American) Refers to the season; born in summer
Sommer, Sumer, Somer, Somers

Suna (Turkish) A swan-like woman

Sunanda (Indian) Having a sweet character
Sunandah, Sunandia, Sunandiya, Sunandea, Sunandya

Sunila (Indian) Feminine form of Sunil; very blue
Sunilah, Sunilla, Sunilya, Suniliya

Sunniva (English) Gift of the sun
Synnove, Synne, Synnove, Sunn

Surabhi (Indian) Having a lovely fragrance
Surbhii, Surabhie, Surabhy, Surabhey, Surabhee, Surabhea

Susannah (Hebrew) White lily
*Susanna, Susanne, Susana,
Susane, Susan, Suzanna,
Suzannah, Suzanne,
Shoshana, Huhana*

Sushanti (Indian) A peaceful
woman; tranquil
*Sushantie, Sushanty,
Sushantey, Sushantee,
Sushantea*

Suzu (Japanese) One who is
long-lived
Suzue, Suzuko

Swanhilda (Norse) A woman
warrior; in mythology, the
daughter of Sigurd
*Swanhild, Swanhilde,
Svanhilde, Svanhild, Svenhilde,
Svenhilda*

Swarupa (Indian) One who is
devoted to the truth

*Sydney (English) Of the wide
meadow
*Sydny, Sydni, Sydnie, Sydnea,
Sydnee, Sidney, Sidne, Sidnee*

T

Taariq (Swahili) Resembling
the morning star
Tariq, Taarique, Tarique

Tabia (African / Egyptian) One
who makes incantations / a
talented woman
*Tabiah, Tabya, Tabea, Tabeah,
Tabiya*

Tabita (African) A graceful
woman
*Tabitah, Tabyta, Tabytah,
Tabeeta, Tabeata, Tabieta,
Tabeita*

Tabitha (Greek) Resembling a
gazelle; known for beauty and
grace
*Tabithah, Tabbitha, Tabetha,
Tabbetha, Tabatha, Tabbatha,
Tabotha, Tabbotha*

Tabora (Spanish) One who
plays a small drum
*Taborah, Taborra, Taboria,
Taborya*

Tacincala (Native American)
Resembling a deer
*Tacincalah, Tacyncala,
Tacyncalah, Tacincalla,
Tacyncalla*

Tahsin (Arabic) Beautification; one who is praised
Tahseen, Tahsene, Tahsyne, Tasine, Tahseene, Tahsean, Tahseane

Tahzib (Arabic) One who is educated and cultured
Tahzeeb, Tahzebe, Tahzybe, Tazib, Tazyb, Tazeeb, Tahzeab, Tazeab

Taithleach (Gaelic) A quiet and calm young lady

Takako (Japanese) A lofty child

Takoda (Native American) Friend to everyone
Takodah, Takodia, Takodya, Takota

Tala (Native American) A stalking wolf
Talah, Talla

Talia (Hebrew / Greek) Morning dew from heaven / blooming
Taliah, Talea, Taleah, Taleya, Tallia, Talieya, Taleea, Taleia

Talihah (Arabic) One who seeks knowledge
Taliha, Talibah, Taliba, Talyha, Taleehah, Taleahah

Taline (Armenian) Of the monestary
Talene, Taleen, Taleene, Talyne, Talinia, Talinya, Taliniya

Talisa (American) Consecrated to God
Talisah, Talysa, Taleesa, Talissa, Talise, Taleese, Talisia, Talisya

Talisha (American) A damsel; an innocent
Talesha, Taleisha, Talysha, Taleesha, Tylesha, Taleysha, Taleshia, Talishia

Talitha (Arabic) A maiden; young girl
Talithah, Taletha, Taleetha, Talytha, Talithia, Talethia, Tiletha, Talith

Tamanna (Indian) One who is desired
Tamannah, Tamana, Tamanah, Tammana, Tammanna

Tamasha (African) Pageant winner
Tamasha, Tomosha, Tomasha, Tamashia, Tamashya

Tamesis (Celtic) In mythology, the goddess of water; source of the name for the river Thames
Tamesiss, Tamesys, Tamesyss

Tangia (American) The angel
Tangiah, Tangya, Tangiya, Tangeah

Tani (Japanese / Melanesian / Tonkinese) From the valley / a sweetheart / a young woman
Tanie, Tany, Taney, Tanee, Tanni, Tanye, Tannie, Tanny

Tania (Russian) Queen of the fairies
Tanya, Tannie, Tanny, Tanika

Tanner (English) One who tans hides
Taner, Tannar, Tannor, Tannis

Tansy (English / Greek) An aromatic yellow flower / having immortality
Tansey, Tansi, Tansie, Tansee, Tansye, Tansea, Tancy, Tanzy

Tanushri (Indian) One who is beautiful; attractive
Tanushrie, Tanushry, Tanushrey, Tanushree, Tanushrea

Tanvi (Indian) Slender and beautiful woman
Tanvie, Tanvy, Tanvey, Tanvee, Tanvye, Tannvi, Tanvea

Tapati (Indian) In mythology, the daughter of the sun god
Tapatie, Tapaty, Tapatey, Tapatee, Tapatye, Tapatea

Taphath (Hebrew) In the Bible, Solomon's daughter
Tafath, Taphathe, Tafathe

Tara (Gaelic / Indian) Of the tower; rocky hill / star; in mythology, an astral goddess
Tarah, Tarra, Tayra, Taraea, Tarai, Taralee, Tarali, Taraya

Tarachand (Indian) Silver star
Tarachande, Tarachanda, Tarachandia, Tarachandea, Tarachandiya, Tarachandya

Taree (Japanese) A bending branch
Tarea, Tareya

Taregan (Native American) Resembling a crane
Tareganne, Taregann

Tareva-chine(shanay) (Native American) One with beautiful eyes

Tariana (American) From the holy hillside
Tariana, Tarianna, Taryana, Taryanna

Tarika (Indian) A starlet
Tarikah, Taryka, Tarykah, Taricka, Tarickah

Tarisai (African) One to behold; to look at
Tarysai

Tasanee (Thai) A beautiful view
Tasane, Tasani, Tasanie, Tasany, Tasaney, Tasanye, Tasanea

Taskin (Arabic) One who provides peace; satisfaction
Taskine, Taskeen, Taskeene, Taskyne, Takseen, Taksin, Taksyn

Tasnim (Arabic) From the fountain of paradise
Tasnime, Tasneem, Tasneeme, Tasnyme, Tasnym, Tasneam, Tasneame

Tatum (English) Bringer of joy; spirited
Tatom, Tatim, Tatem, Tatam, Tatym

Tavi (Aramaic) One who is well-behaved
Tavie, Tavee, Tavy, Tavey, Tavea

***T Taylor** (English) Cutter of cloth; one who alters garments
Tailor, Taylore, Taylar, Tayler, Talour, Taylre, Tailore, Tailar

Teagan (Gaelic) One who is attractive
Teegan

Tehya (Native American) One who is precious
Tehyah, Tehiya, Tehiyah

Teigra (Greek) Resembling a tiger
Teigre

Telephassa (Latin) In mythology, the queen of Tyre
Telephasa, Telefassa, Telefasa

Temperance (English) Having self-restraint
Temperence, Temperince, Temperancia, Temperanse, Temperense, Temperinse

Tendai (African) Thankful to God
Tenday, Tendae, Tendaa, Tendaye

Tender (American) One who is sensitive; young and vulnerable
Tendere, Tendera, Tenderia, Tenderre, Tenderiya

Teranika (Gaelic) Victory of the earth
Teranikah, Teranieka, Teraneika, Teraneeka, Teranica, Teranicka, Teranicca, Teraneaka

Teresa (Greek) A harvester
Theresa, Theresah, Theresia, Therese, Thera, Tresa, Tressa, Tressam, Reese, Reza

Terpsichore (Greek) In mythology, the muse of dancing and singing
Terpsichora, Terpsichoria, Terpsichoriya

rm of Patricia,
ble descent"
, Tricia, Trish,

In mythology,
he deceased,
ves
ia, Trishniah,
eah, Trishniya,
nya

he one

, Trisniah,
h, Trisniya,
ya

Form of
ing "adored

rudie, Trude,
Truda, Trudia

tate of being

Truptey,
Truptea

h) In
d, a fairy prin-

monne,
nonna

e third-born

Tsifira (Hebrew) One who is
crowned
Tsifirah, Tsifyra, Tsiphyra,
Tsiphira, Tsipheera, Tsifeera

Tuccia (Latin) A vestal virgin

Tula (Hindi) Balance; a sign of
the zodiac
Tulah, Tulla, Tullah

Tullia (Irish) One who is
peaceful
Tulliah, Tullea, Tulleah,
Tullya, Tulia, Tulea, Tuleah,
Tulya

Tusti (Hindi) One who brings
happiness and peace
Tustie, Tusty, Tustey, Tustee,
Tuste, Tustea

Tutilina (Latin) In mythol-
ogy, the protector goddess of
stored grain
Tutilinah, Tutileena, Tutileana,
Tutilyna, Tutileina, Tutiliena,
Tutilena, Tutylina

Tuuli (Finnish) Of the wind
Tuulie, Tuulee, Tuula, Tuuly,
Tuuley, Tuulea

Tuyet (Vietnamese) Snow
white woman
Tuyett, Tuyete, Tuyette, Tuyeta,
Tuyetta

Tyler (English) Tiler of roofs

Terra (Latin) From the earth;
in mythology, an earth god-
dess
Terrah, Terah, Teralyn, Terran,
Terena, Terenah, Terenna,
Terrena

Terrian (Greek) One who is
innocent
Terriane, Terrianne, Terriana,
Terianna, Terian, Terianne

Tessa (Greek) Form of Teresa,
meaning "a harvester"

Tetsu (Japanese) A strong
woman
Tetsue

Tetty (English) Form of
Elizabeth, meaning "my God
is bountiful; God's promise"
Tettey, Tetti, Tettie, Tettee,
Tettea

Tevy (Cambodian) An angel
Tevey, Tevi, Tevie, Tevee, Tevea

Thandiwe (African) The loving
one
Thandywe, Thandiewe,
Thandeewe, Thandie, Thandi,
Thandee, Thandy, Thandey

Thara (Arabic) One who is
wealthy; prosperous
Tharah, Tharra, Tharrah,
Tharwat

Thelma (Greek) One who is
ambitious and willful
Thelmah, Telma, Thelmai,
Thelmia, Thelmalina

Thelred (English) One who is
well-advised
Thelrede, Thelread, Thelredia,
Thelredina, Thelreid, Thelreed,
Thelryd

Thema (African) A queen
Themah, Theema, Thyma,
Theyma, Theama

Theora (Greek) A watcher
Theorra, Theoria, Theoriya,
Theorya

Theta (Greek) Eighth letter of
the Greek alphabet
Thetta

Thistle (English) Resembling
the prickly, flowered plant
Thistel, Thissle, Thissel

Thomasina (Hebrew)
Feminine form of Thomas;
a twin
Thomasine, Thomsina,
Thomasin, Tomasina,
Tomasine, Thomasa,
Thomaseena, Thomaseana

Thoosa (Greek) In mythology,
a sea nymph
Thoosah, Thoosia, Thoosiah,
Thusa, Thusah, Thusia,
Thusiah, Thousa

Thorberta (Norse) Brilliance of Thor
Thorbiartr, Thorbertha

Thordia (Norse) Spirit of Thor
Thordiah, Thordis, Tordis, Thordissa, Tordissa, Thoridyss

Thuy (Vietnamese) One who is gentle and pure
Thuye, Thuyy, Thuyye

Thy (Vietnamese / Greek) A poet / one who is untamed
Thye

Tia (Spanish / Greek) An aunt / daughter born to royalty
Tiah, Tea, Teah, Tiana, Teea, Tya, Teeya, Tiia

Tiberia (Italian) Of the Tiber river
Tiberiah, Tiberiya, Tiberya, Tibeeria, Tibearia, Tibieria, Tibeiria

Tiegan (Aztec) A little princess in a big valley
Tiegann, Tieganne

Tierney (Gaelic) One who is regal; lordly
Tiernie, Tierni, Tiernee, Tierny, Tiernea

Tiffany (Greek) Lasting love
Tiffaney, Tiffani, Tiffanie, Tiffanee, Tifany, Tifaney, Tifanee, Tifani

Timothea (English) Feminine form of Timothy; honoring God
Timotheah, Timothia, Timothya, Timothiya

Tina (English) From the river; also shortened form of names ending in -tina
Tinah, Teena, Tena, Teyna, Tyna, Tinna, Teana

Ting (Chinese) Graceful and slim woman

Tirza (Hebrew) One who is pleasant; a delight
Tirzah

Tisa (African) The ninth-born child
Tisah, Tiza

Tita (Latin) Holding a title of honor
Titah, Teeta, Tyta, Teata

Tivona (Hebrew) Lover of nature
Tivonna, Tivone, Tivonia, Tivoniya

Toan (Vietnamese) Form of An-toan, meaning "safe and secure"
Toane, Toanne

Toinette (French) Form of Antoinette, meaning "praiseworthy"
Toinett, Toinete, Toinet, Toineta, Toinetta, Tola

Toki (Japanese / Korean) One who grasps opportunity; hopeful / resembling a rabbit
Tokie, Toky, Tokey, Tokye, Tokiko, Tokee, Tokea

Tola (Polish / Cambodian) Form of Toinette, meaning "praiseworthy" / born during October
Tolah, Tolla, Tollah

Topanga (Native American) From above or a high place
Topangah

Topaz (Latin) Resembling a yellow gemstone
Topazz, Topaza, Topazia, Topaziya, Topazya, Topazea

Tordis (Norse) A goddess
Tordiss, Tordisse, Tordys, Tordyss, Tordysse

Torny (Norse) New; just discovered
Torney, Tornie, Torni, Torn, Torn, Tornee, Tornea

Torunn (Norse) Thor's love
Torun, Torrun, Torrunn

Trisha (Latin) meaning "of n
Trishah, Trishi, Trissa, Trisa

Trishna (Polish) the goddess of protector of gr
Trishnah, Trish, Trishnea, Trish, Trishniyah, Tri

Trisna (Indian) desired
Trisnah, Trisni, Trisnea, Trisne, Trisniyah, Trisn

Trudy (German) Gertrude, mea warrior"
Trudey, Trudi, Trudye, Trudee,

Trupti (Indian) satisfied
Truptie, Trupty, Truptee, Trupte

Tryamon (Engli Arthurian lege cess
Tryamonn, Try Tryamona, Try

Tryna (Greek) T child
Trynah

Tyme (English) The aromatic herb thyme
Time, Thyme, Thime

Tyne (English) Of the river
Tyna

Tyro (Greek) In mythology, a woman who bore twin sons to Poseidon

Tzidkiya (Hebrew) Righteousness of the Lord
Tzidkiyah, Tzidkiyahu

Tzigane (Hungarian) A gypsy
Tzigan, Tzigain, Tzigaine, Tzigayne

U

Uadjit (Egyptian) In mythology, a snake goddess
Ujadet, Uajit, Udjit, Ujadit

Ualani (Hawaiian) Of the heavenly rain
Ualanie, Ualany, Ualaney, Ualanee, Ualanea, Ualania, Ualana

Udavine (American) A thriving woman
Udavyne, Udavina, Udavyna, Udevine, Udevyne, Udevina, Udevyna

Udele (English) One who is wealthy; prosperous
Udelle, Udela, Udella, Udelah, Udellah, Uda, Udah

Uela (American) One who is devoted to God
Uelah, Uella, Uellah

Uganda (African) From the country in Africa
Ugandah, Ugaunda, Ugaundah, Ugawnda, Ugawndah, Ugonda, Ugondah

Ugolina (German) Having a bright spirit; bright mind
Ugolinah, Ugoleena, Ugoliana, Ugolyna, Ugoline, Ugolyn, Ugolyne

Ulalia (Greek) Form of Eulalia, meaning "well-spoken"
Ulaliah, Ulalya, Ulalyah

Ulan (African) Firstborn of twins
Ulann, Ulanne

Ulima (Arabic) One who is wise and astute
Ulimah, Ullima, Ulimma, Uleema, Uleama, Ulyma, Uleima, Uliema

Ulla (German) A willful
woman
Ullah, Ullaa, Ullai, Ullae

Uma (Hindi) Mother; in
mythology, the goddess of
beauty and sunlight
Umah, Umma

Umberla (French) Feminine
form of Umber; providing
shade; of an earth color
*Umberlah, Umberly, Umberley,
Umberlee, Umberleigh,
Umberli, Umberlea, Umberlie*

Ummi (African) Born of my
mother
*Ummie, Ummy, Ummey,
Ummee, Umi*

Unity (American) Woman who
upholds oneness; together-
ness
*Unitey, Unitie, Uniti, Unitee,
Unitea, Unyty, Unytey, Unytie*

Ura (Indian) Loved from the
heart
Urah, Urra

Ural (Slavic) From the mountains
Urall, Urale, Uralle

Urbai (American) One who is
gentle
Urbae, Urbay, Urbaye

Urbana (Latin) From the city;
city dweller
*Urbanah, Urbanna, Urbane,
Urbania, Urbanya, Urbanne*

Uriela (Hebrew) The angel of
light
*Uriella, Urielle, Uriel, Uriele,
Uriell*

Urta (Latin) Resembling the
spiny plant
Urtah

Utah (Native American) People
of the mountains; from the
state of Utah

Uzoma (African) One who
takes the right path
Uzomah, Uzomma, Uzommah

Uzzi (Hebrew / Arabic) God
is my strength / a strong
woman
*Uzzie, Uzzy, Uzzey, Uzzee,
Uzi, Uzie, Uzy, Uzey*

V

Vala (German) The chosen
one; singled out
Valah, Valla

Valda (Teutonic / German) Spirited in battle / famous ruler
Valdah, Valida, Velda, Vada, Vaida, Vayda, Vaeda

Valdis (Norse) In mythology, the goddess of the dead
Valdiss, Valdys, Valdyss

Valencia (Spanish) One who is powerful; strong; from the city of Valencia
Valenciah, Valyncia, Valencya, Valenzia, Valancia, Valenica, Valanca, Valecia

Valentina (Latin) One who is vigorous and healthy
Valentinah, Valentine, Valenteena, Valenteana, Valentena, Valentyna, Valantina, Valentyne

*ᵀValeria (Latin) Form of Valerie, meaning "strong and valiant"
Valara, Valera, Valaria, Valeriana, Veleria, Valora

Valerie (Latin) Feminine form of Valerius; strong and valiant
Valeri, Valeree, Valerey, Valery, Valarie, Valari, Vallery

Vandani (Hindi) One who is honorable and worthy
Vandany, Vandaney, Vandanie, Vandanee, Vandania, Vandanya

*ᵀVanessa (Greek) Resembling a butterfly
Vanessah, Vanesa, Vannesa, Vannessa, Vanassa, Vanasa, Vanessia, Vanysa, Yanessa

Vanity (English) Having excessive pride
Vanitey, Vanitee, Vaniti, Vanitie, Vanitty, Vanyti, Vanyty, Vanytie

Vanmra (Russian) A stranger; from a foreign place
Vanmrah

Varda (Hebrew) Resembling a rose
Vardah, Vardia, Vardina, Vardissa, Vardita, Vardysa, Vardyta, Vardit

Varuna (Hindi) Wife of the sea
Varunah, Varuna, Varun, Varunani, Varuni

Vashti (Persian) A lovely woman
Vashtie, Vashty, Vashtey, Vashtee

Vasta (Persian) One who is pretty
Vastah

Vasteen (American) A capable woman
Vasteene, Vastiene, Vastien, Vastein, Vasteine, Vastean, Vasteane

Vasuda (Hindi) Of the earth
Vasudah, Vasudhara, Vasundhara, Vasudhra, Vasundhra

Vayu (Hindi) A vital life force; the air
Vayyu

Vedette (French) From the guard tower
Vedete, Vedett, Vedet, Vedetta, Vedeta

Vedi (Sanskrit) Filled with wisdom
Vedie, Vedy, Vedey, Vedee, Vedea, Vedeah

Vega (Latin) A falling star
Vegah

Vellamo (Finnish) In mythology, the goddess of the sea
Velamo, Vellammo

Ventana (Spanish) As transparent as a window
Ventanah, Ventanna, Ventane, Ventanne

Venus (Greek) In mythology, the goddess of love and beauty
Venis, Venys, Vynys, Venusa, Venusina, Venusia

Veradis (Latin) One who is genuine; truthful
Veradise, Veradys, Veradisa, Verdissa, Veradysa, Veradyssa, Veradisia, Veraditia

Verda (Latin) Springlike; one who is young and fresh
Verdah, Verdea, Virida, Verdy, Verdey, Verde, Verdi, Verdie

Verenase (Swedish) One who is flourishing
Verenese, Verennase, Vyrenase, Vyrennase, Vyrenese, Verenace, Vyrenace

Veronica (Latin) Displaying her true image
Veronicah, Veronic, Veronicca, Veronicka, Veronika, Veronicha, Veronique, Veranique, Ronni

Vesna (Slavic) Messenger; in mythology, the goddess of spring
Vesnah, Vezna, Vesnia, Vesnaa

Vespera (Latin) Evening star; born in the evening
Vesperah, Vespira, Vespeera, Vesperia, Vesper

Vevila (Gaelic) Woman with a melodious voice
Vevilah, Veveela, Vevyla, Vevilla, Vevylla, Vevylle, Vevyle, Vevillia

Vibeke (Danish) A small
woman
*Vibekeh, Vibeek, Vibeeke,
Vybeke, Viheke*

Vibhuti (Hindi) Of the sacred
ash; a symbol
Vibuti, Vibhutie, Vibhutee

*****Victoria** (Latin) Victorious
woman; winner; conqueror
*Victoriah, Victorea, Victoreah,
Victorya, Victorria, Victoriya,
Vyctoria, Victorine, Tory*

Vidya (Indian) Having great
wisdom
Vidyah

Viet (Vietnamese) A woman
from Vietnam
Vyet, Viett, Vyett, Viette, Vyette

Vigilia (Latin) Wakefulness;
watchfulness
*Vigiliah, Vygilia, Vygylia,
Vijilia, Vyjilia*

Vignette (French) From the
little vine
*Vignete, Vignet, Vignetta,
Vignett, Vigneta, Vygnette,
Vygnete, Vygnet*

Vilina (Hindi) One who is
dedicated
*Vilinah, Vileena, Vileana,
Vylina, Vyleena, Vyleana,
Vylyna, Vilinia*

Villette (French) From the
small village
*Vilette, Villete, Vilete, Vilet,
Vilett, Villet, Villett, Vylet*

Vimala (Indian) Feminine
form of Vamal; clean and
pure
Vimalah, Vimalia, Vimalla

Vincentia (Latin) Feminine
form of Vincent; conquerer;
triumphant
*Vincentiah, Vincenta,
Vincensia, Vincenzia,
Vyncentia, Vyncyntia,
Vyncenzia, Vycenzya*

Violet (French) Resembling
the purplish-blue flower
*Violett, Violette, Violete, Vyolet,
Vyolett, Vyolette, Vyolete,
Violeta*

Virginia (Latin) One who is
chaste; virginal; from the state
of Virginia
*Virginiah, Virginnia, Virgenya,
Virgenia, Virgeenia, Virgeena,
Virgena, Ginny*

Virtue (Latin) Having moral
excellence, chastity, and
goodness
*Virtu, Vyrtue, Vyrtu, Vertue,
Vertu*

Viveka (German) Little woman of the strong fortress
Vivekah, Vivecka, Vyveka, Viveca, Vyveca, Vivecca, Vivika, Vivieka

Vivian (Latin) Lively woman
Viv, Vivi, Vivienne, Bibiana

Vixen (American) A flirtatious woman
Vixin, Vixi, Vixie, Vixee, Vixea, Vixeah, Vixy, Vixey

Vlasta (Slavic) A friendly and likeable woman
Vlastah, Vlastia, Vlastea, Vlastiah, Vlasteah

Voleta (Greek) The veiled one
Voletah, Voletta, Volita, Volitta, Volyta, Volytta, Volet, Volett

Volva (Scandinavian) In mythology, a female shaman
Volvah, Volvya, Volvaa, Volvae, Volvai, Volvay, Volvia

Vondila (African) Woman who lost a child
Vondilah, Vondilla, Vondilya, Vondilia, Vondyla, Vondylya

Vonna (French) Form of Yvonne, meaning "young archer"
Vonnah, Vona, Vonah, Vonnia, Vonnya, Vonia, Vonya, Vonny

Vonshae (American) One who is confident
Vonshay, Vonshaye, Vonshai

Vor (Norse) In mythology, an omniscient goddess
Vore, Vorr, Vorre

Vulpine (English) A cunning woman; like a fox
Vulpyne, Vulpina, Vulpyna

Vyomini (Indian) A gift of the divine
Vyominie, Vyominy, Vyominey, Vyominee, Vyomyni, Vyomyny, Viomini, Viomyni

W

Wafa (Arabic) One who is faithful; devoted
Wafah, Wafaa, Waffa, Wapha, Waffah, Waphah

Wagaye (African) My sense of value; my price
Wagay, Wagai, Wagae

Wainani (Hawaiian) Of the beautiful waters
Wainanie, Wainany, Wainaney, Wainanee, Wainanea, Wainaneah

Wajihah (Arabic) One who is
distinguished; eminent
*Wajiha, Wajeeha, Wajyha,
Wajeehah, Wajyhah, Wajieha,
Wajiehah, Wajeiha*

Wakanda (Native American)
One who possesses magical
powers
*Wakandah, Wakenda,
Wakinda, Wakynda*

Wakeishah (American) Filled
with happiness
*Wakeisha, Wakieshah,
Wakiesha, Wakesha*

Walda (German) One who has
fame and power
*Waldah, Wallda, Walida,
Waldine, Waldina, Waldyne,
Waldyna, Welda*

Walker (English) Walker of the
forests
Wallker, Walkher

Walta (African) One who acts
as a shield
Waltah

Wanetta (English) A pale-
skinned woman
*Wanettah, Wanette, Wannette,
Wannetta, Wonetta, Wonette,
Wonitta, Wonitte*

Wangari (African) Resembling
the leopard
*Wangarie, Wangarri, Wangary,
Wangarey, Wangaria,
Wangaree*

Wanyika (African) Of the bush
*Wanyikka, Wanyicka,
Wanyicca, Wanyica*

Waqi (Arabic) Falling;
swooping
Waqqi

Warma (American) A caring
woman
*Warm, Warme, Warmia,
Warmiah, Warmea, Warmeah*

Warna (German) One who
defends her loved ones
Warnah

Washi (Japanese) Resembling
an eagle
*Washie, Washy, Washey,
Washee, Washea, Washeah*

Waynette (English) One who
makes wagons
*Waynett, Waynet, Waynete,
Wayneta, Waynetta*

Wednesday (American) Born
on a Wednesday
*Wensday, Winsday,
Windnesday, Wednesdae,
Wensdae, Winsdae,
Windnesdae, Wednesdai*

Welcome (English) A welcome guest
Welcom, Welcomme

Wendy (Welsh) Form of Gwendolyn, meaning "one who is fair; of the white ring"
Wendi, Wendie, Wendee, Wendey, Wenda, Wendia, Wendea, Wendya

Wesley (English) From the western meadow
Wesly, Weslie, Wesli, Weslee, Weslia, Wesleigh, Weslea, Weslei

Whisper (English) One who is soft-spoken
Whysper, Wisper, Wysper

Whitley (English) From the white meadow
Whitly, Whitlie, Whitli, Whitlee, Whitleigh, Whitlea, Whitlia, Whitlya

Whitney (English) From the white island
Whitny, Whitnie, Whitni, Whitnee, Whittney, Whitneigh, Whytny, Whytney

Wicapi Wakan (Native American) A holy star

Wijida (Arabic) An excited seeker
Wijidah, Weejida, Weejidah, Wijeeda, Wijeedah, Wijyda, Wijydah, Wijieda

Wileen (Teutonic) A firm defender
Wiline, Wilean, Wileane, Wilyn, Wileene, Wilene, Wyleen, Wyline

Wilhelmina (German) Feminine form of Wilhelm; determined protector
Wilhelminah, Wylhelmina, Wylhelmyna, Willemina, Wilhelmine, Wilhemina, Wilhemine, Helma, Ilma

Willa (English) Feminine version of William, meaning "protector"
Willah, Wylla

^**Willow** (English) One who is hoped for; desired.
Willo, Willough

Winetta (American) One who is peaceful
Wineta, Wynetta, Wyneta, Winet, Winett, Winette, Wynet, Wynett

Winnielle (African) A victorious woman
Winniell, Winniele, Winniel, Winniella

Winola (German) Gracious and charming friend
Winolah, Wynola, Winolla, Wynolla, Wynolah, Winollah, Wynollah

Winta (African) One who is desired
Wintah, Whinta, Wynta, Whynta, Whintah, Wyntah, Whyntah

Wisconsin (French) Gathering of waters; from the state of Wisconsin
Wisconsyn, Wisconsen

Woody (American) A woman of the forest
Woodey, Woodi, Woodie, Woodee, Woodea, Woodeah, Woods

Wren (English) Resembling a small songbird
Wrenn, Wrene, Wrena, Wrenie, Wrenee, Wreney, Wrenny, Wrenna

Wynda (Scottish) From the narrow passage
Wyndah, Winda, Windah

Xalvadora (Spanish) A savior
Xalvadorah, Xalbadora, Xalbadorah, Xalvadoria, Xalbadoria

Xanadu (African) From the exotic paradise

Xantara (American) Protector of the Earth
Xantarah, Xanterra, Xantera, Xantarra, Xantarrah, Xanterah, Xanterrah

Xaquelina (Galician) Form of Jacqueline, meaning "the supplanter"
Xaqueline, Xaqueleena, Xaquelyna, Xaquelayna, Xaqueleana

Xerena (Latin) Form of Serena, meaning "having a peaceful disposition"
Xerenah, Xerene, Xeren, Xereena, Xeryna, Xereene, Xerenna

Xhosa (African) Leader of a nation
Xosa, Xhose, Xhosia, Xhosah, Xosah

Xiang (Chinese) Having a nice fragrance
Xyang, Xeang, Xhiang, Xhyang, Xheang

Xiao Hong (Chinese) Of the morning rainbow

Xin Qian (Chinese) Happy and beautiful woman

Xinavane (African) A mother;
to propagate
*Xinavana, Xinavania,
Xinavain, Xinavaine,
Xinavaen, Xinavaene*

Xirena (Greek) Form of Sirena,
meaning "enchantress"
*Xirenah, Xireena, Xirina,
Xirene, Xyrena, Xyreena,
Xyrina, Xyryna*

Xi-Wang (Chinese) One with
hope

Xochiquetzal (Aztec)
Resembling a flowery feather;
in mythology, the goddess of
love, flowers, and the earth

Xola (African) Stay in peace
Xolah, Xolia, Xolla, Xollah

Xue (Chinese) Woman of
snow

Yachne (Hebrew) One who is
gracious and hospitable
*Yachnee, Yachney, Yachnie,
Yachni, Yachnea, Yachneah*

Yadra (Spanish) Form of
Madre, meaning "mother"
Yadre, Yadrah

Yaffa (Hebrew) A beautiful
woman
Yaffah, Yaffit, Yafit, Yafeal

Yakini (African) An honest
woman
*Yakinie, Yakiney, Yakiny,
Yackini, Yackinie, Yackiney,
Yackiny, Yakinee*

Yalena (Greek) Form of Helen,
meaning "the shining light"
*Yalenah, Yalina, Yaleena,
Yalyna, Yalana, Yaleana,
Yalane, Yaleene*

Yama (Japanese) From the
mountain
Yamma, Yamah, Yammah

Yamin (Hebrew) Right hand
*Yamine, Yamyn, Yamyne,
Yameen, Yameene, Yamein,
Yameine, Yamien*

Yana (Hebrew) He answers
Yanna, Yaan, Yanah, Yannah

Yanessa (American) Form of
Vanessa, meaning "resem-
bling a butterfly"
*Yanessah, Yanesa, Yannesa,
Yannessa, Yanassa, Yanasa,
Yanessia, Yanysa*

Yanka (Slavic) God is good
Yancka, Yancca, Yankka

Yara (Brazilian) In mythology, the goddess of the river; a mermaid
Yarah, Yarrah, Yarra

Yareli (American) The Lord is my light
Yarelie, Yareley, Yarelee, Yarely, Yaresly, Yarelea, Yareleah

^Yaretzi (Spanish) Always beloved
Yaretzie, Yaretza, Yarezita

Yashira (Japanese) Blessed with God's grace
Yashirah, Yasheera, Yashyra, Yashara, Yashiera, Yashierah, Yasheira, Yasheirah

Yashona (Hindi) A wealthy woman
Yashonah, Yashawna, Yashauna, Yaseana, Yashawnah, Yashaunah, Yaseanah

Yasmine (Persian) Resembling the jasmine flower
Yasmin, Yasmene, Yasmeen, Yasmeene, Yasmen, Yasemin, Yasemeen, Yasmyn

Yatima (African) An orphan
Yatimah, Yateema, Yatyma, Yateemah, Yatymah, Yatiema, Yatiemah, Yateima

Yedidah (Hebrew) A beloved friend
Yedida, Yedyda, Yedydah, Yedeeda, Yedeedah

Yeira (Hebrew) One who is illuminated
Yeirah, Yaira, Yeyra, Yairah, Yeyrah

Yenge (African) A hardworking woman
Yenga, Yengeh, Yengah

Yeshi (African) For a thousand
Yeshie, Yeshey, Yeshy, Yeshee, Yeshea, Yesheah

Yessica (Hebrew) Form of Jessica, meaning "the Lord sees all"
Yesica, Yessika, Yesika, Yesicka, Yessicka, Yesyka, Yesiko

Yetta (English) Form of Henrietta, meaning "ruler of the house"
Yettah, Yeta, Yette, Yitta, Yettie, Yetty

Yi Min (Chinese) An intelligent woman

Yi Ze (Chinese) Happy and shiny as a pearl

Yihana (African) One deserving congratulations
Yihanah, Yhana, Yihanna, Yihannah, Yhanah, Yhanna, Yhannah

Yinah (Spanish) A victorious
woman
Yina, Yinna, Yinnah

Yitta (Hebrew) One who
emanates light
Yittah, Yita, Yitah

Ynes (French) Form of Agnes,
meaning "pure; chaste"
Ynez, Ynesita

Yogi (Hindi) One who
practices yoga
*Yogini, Yoginie, Yogie, Yogy,
Yogey, Yogee, Yogea, Yogeah*

Yohance (African) A gift from
God
Yohanse

Yoki (Native American) Of the
rain
*Yokie, Yokee, Yoky, Yokey,
Yokea, Yokeah*

Yolanda (Greek) Resembling
the violet flower
Yola, Yolana, Yolandah, Colanda

Yomaris (Spanish) I am the
sun
Yomariss, Yomarise, Yomarris

Yon (Korean) Resembling a
lotus blossom

Yoruba (African) Woman from
Nigeria
Yorubah, Yorubba, Yorubbah

Yoshi (Japanese) One who is
respectful and good
*Yoshie, Yoshy, Yoshey, Yoshee,
Yoshiyo, Yoshiko, Yoshino,
Yoshea*

Ysabel (Spanish) Form of
Isabel, meaning "my God is
bountiful; God's promise"
*Ysabelle, Ysabela, Ysabele,
Ysabell, Ysabella, Ysbel, Ysibel,
Ysibela*

Ysbail (Welsh) A spoiled girl
*Ysbale, Ysbayle, Ysbaile, Ysbayl,
Ysbael, Ysbaele*

Yue (Chinese) Of the
moonlight

Yuette (American) A capable
woman
*Yuett, Yuete, Yuet, Yueta,
Yuetta*

Yulan (Spanish) A splendid
woman
Yulann

Yuna (African) A gorgeous
woman
Yunah, Yunna, Yunnah

Yuta (Hebrew / Japanese) One
who is awarded praise / one
who is superior
Yutah, Yoota, Yootah

Yvonne (French) Young archer
Yvone, Vonne, Vonna

Z

Zabrina (American) Form of Sabrina, meaning "a legendary princess"
Zabreena, Zabrinah, Zabrinna, Zabryna, Zabryne, Zabrynya, Zabreana, Zabreane

Zachah (Hebrew) Feminine form of Zachary; God is remembered
Zacha, Zachie, Zachi, Zachee, Zachea, Zacheah

Zafara (Hebrew) One who sings
Zaphara, Zafarra, Zapharra, Zafarah, Zafarrah, Zapharah, Zapharrah

Zagir (Armenian) Resembling a flower
Zagiri, Zagirie, Zagiree, Zagirea, Zagireah, Zagiry, Zagirey, Zagira

Zahiya (Arabic) A brilliant woman; radiant
Zahiyah, Zehiya, Zehiyah, Zeheeya, Zaheeya, Zeheeyah, Zaheeyah, Zaheiya

Zahra (Arabic / Swahili) White-skinned / flowerlike
Zahrah, Zahraa, Zahre, Zahreh, Zahara, Zaharra, Zahera, Zahira

Zainab (Arabic) A fragrant flowering plant
Zaynab, Zaenab

Zainabu (Swahili) One who is known for her beauty
Zaynabu, Zaenabu

Zalina (French) Form of Selene, meaning "of the moon"; in mythology Selene was the Greek goddess of the moon
Zalinah, Zaleana, Zaleena, Zalena, Zalyna, Zaleen, Zaleene, Zalene

Zama (Latin) One from the town of Zama
Zamah, Zamma, Zammah

Zambda (Hebrew) One who meditates
Zambdah

Zamella (Zulu) One who strives to succeed
Zamellah, Zamy, Zamie, Zami, Zamey, Zamee, Zamea, Zameah

Zamilla (Greek) Having the strength of the sea
Zamillah, Zamila, Zamilah, Zamylla, Zamyllah, Zamyla, Zamylah

Zamora (Spanish) From the city of Zamora
Zamorah, Zamorrah, Zamorra

Zana (Romanian / Hebrew) In mythology, the three graces / shortened form of Susanna, meaning "lily"
Zanna, Zanah, Zannah

Zane (Scandinavian) One who is bold
Zain, Zaine, Zayn, Zayne, Zaen, Zaene

Zanta (Swahili) A beautiful young woman
Zantah

Zarahlinda (Hebrew) Of the beautiful dawn
Zaralinda, Zaralynda, Zarahlindah, Zaralyndah, Zarahlynda, Zarahlyndah, Zaralenda, Zarahlenda

^Zariah (Russian / Slavic) Born at sunrise
Zarya, Zariah, Zaryah

Zarifa (Arabic) One who is successful; moves with grace
Zarifah, Zaryfa, Zaryfah, Zareefa, Zareefah, Zariefa, Zariefah, Zareifa

Zarna (Hindi) Resembling a spring of water
Zarnah, Zarnia, Zarniah

Zarqa (Arabic) Having bluish-green eyes; from the city of Zarqa
Zarqaa

Zaylee (English) A heavenly woman
Zayleigh, Zayli, Zaylie, Zaylea, Zayleah, Zayley, Zayly, Zalee

Zaypana (Tibetan) A beautiful woman
Zaypanah, Zaypo, Zaypanna, Zaypannah

Zaza (Hebrew / Arabic) Belonging to all / one who is flowery
Zazah, Zazu, Zazza, Zazzah, Zazzu

Zdenka (Slovene) Feminine form of Zdenek, meaning "from Sidon"
Zdena, Zdenuska, Zdenicka, Zdenika, Zdenyka, Zdeninka, Zdenynka

Zebba (Persian) A known beauty
Zebbah, Zebara, Zebarah, Zebarra, Zebarrah

Zelia (Greek / Spanish) Having great zeal / of the sunshine
Zeliah, Zelya, Zelie, Zele, Zelina, Zelinia

Zenaida (Greek) White-winged dove; in mythology, a daughter of Zeus
Zenaidah, Zenayda, Zenaide, Zenayde, Zinaida, Zenina, Zenna, Zenaydah

Zenechka (Russian) Form of Eugenia, meaning "a well-born woman"

Zenobia (Greek) Child of Zeus
Sinobia

Zephyr (Greek) Of the west wind
Zephyra, Zephira, Zephria, Zephra, Zephyer, Zefiryn, Zefiryna, Zefyrin

Zera (Hebrew) A sower of seeds
Zerah, Zeria, Zeriah, Zera'im, Zerra, Zerrah

Zeraldina (Polish) One who rules with the spear
Zeraldinah, Zeraldeena, Zeraldeenah, Zeraldiena, Zeraldienah, Zeraldeina, Zeraldeinah, Zeraldyna

Zerdali (Turkish) Resembling the wild apricot
Zerdalie, Zerdaly, Zerdaley, Zerdalya, Zerdalia, Zerdalee, Zerdalea, Zerdalea

Zesta (American) One with energy and gusto
Zestah, Zestie, Zestee, Zesti, Zesty, Zestey, Zestea, Zesteah

Zetta (Portuguese) Resembling the rose
Zettah

Zhen (Chinese) One who is precious and chaste
Zen, Zhena, Zenn, Zhenni

Zhi (Chinese) A woman of high moral character

Zhong (Chinese) An honorable woman

Zi (Chinese) A flourishing young woman

Zia (Arabic) One who emanates light; splendor
Ziah, Zea, Zeah, Zya, Zyah

Zilias (Hebrew) A shady woman; a shadow
Zilyas, Zylias, Zylyas

Zillah (Hebrew) The shadowed one
Zilla, Zila, Zyla, Zylla, Zilah, Zylah, Zyllah

Zilpah (Hebrew) One who is frail but dignified; in the Bible, a concubine of Jacob
Zilpa, Zylpa, Zilpha, Zylpha, Zylpah, Zilphah, Zylphah

Zimbab (African) Woman from Zimbabwe
Zymbab, Zimbob, Zymbob

Zinat (Arabic) A decoration; graceful beauty
Zeenat, Zynat, Zienat, Zeinat, Zeanat

Zinchita (Incan) One who is dearly loved
Zinchitah, Zinchyta, Zinchytah, Zincheeta, Zincheetah, Zinchieta, Zinchietah, Zincheita

Zintkala Kinyan (Native American) Resembling a flying bird
Zintkalah Kinyan

Ziona (Hebrew) One who symbolizes goodness
Zionah, Zyona, Zyonah

Zipporah (Hebrew) A beauty; little bird; in the Bible, the wife of Moses
Zippora, Ziporah, Zipora, Zypora, Zyppora, Ziproh, Zipporia

Zira (African) The pathway
Zirah, Zirra, Zirrah, Zyra, Zyrah, Zyrra, Zyrrah

Zisel (Hebrew) One who is sweet
Zissel, Zisal, Zysel, Zysal, Zyssel, Zissal, Zyssal

Zita (Latin / Spanish) Patron of housewives and servants / little rose
Zitah, Zeeta, Zyta, Zeetah

Ziwa (Swahili) Woman of the lake
Ziwah, Zywa, Zywah

Zizi (Hungarian) Dedicated to God
Zeezee, Zyzy, Ziezie, Zeazea, Zeyzey

Zoa (Greek) One who is full of life; vibrant

*★T***Zoe** (Greek) A life-giving woman; alive
Zoee, Zowey, Zowie, Zowe, Zoelie, Zoeline, Zoelle, **Zoey**

Zofia (Slavic) Form of Sophia, meaning "wisdom"
Zofiah, Zophia, Zophiah, Zophya, Zofie, Zofee, Zofey

Zora (Slavic) Born at dawn; aurora
Zorah, Zorna, Zorra, Zorya, Zorane, Zory, Zorrah, Zorey

Zoria (Basque) One who is lucky
Zoriah

Zoriona (Basque) One who is happy

Zubeda (Swahili) The best one
Zubedah

Zudora (Arabic) A laborer; hardworking woman
Zudorah, Zudorra

Zula (African) One who is brilliant; from the town of Zula
Zul, Zulay, Zulae, Zulai, Zulah, Zulla, Zullah

Zuni (Native American) One who is creative
Zunie, Zuny, Zuney, Zunee, Zunea, Zuneah

Zurafa (Arabic) A lovely woman
Zurafah, Zirafa, Zirafah, Ziraf, Zurufa, Zurufah

Zuri (Swahili / French) A beauty / lovely and white
Zurie, Zurey, Zuria, Zuriaa, Zury, Zuree, Zurya, Zurisha

Zuwena (African) One who is pleasant and good
Zuwenah, Zwena, Zwenah, Zuwenna, Zuwennah, Zuwyna, Zuwynah

Zuyana (Sioux) One who has a brave heart
Zuyanah, Zuyanna

Zuzena (Basque) One who is correct
Zuzenah, Zuzenna

Zwi (Scandinavian) Resembling a gazelle
Zui, Zwie, Zwee, Zwey

Boys

Aabha (Indian) One who shines
Abha, Abbha

Aabharan (Hindu) One who is treasured; jewel
Abharan, Abharen, Aabharen, Aabharon

^**Aaden** (Irish) Form of Aidan, meaning "a fiery young man"
Adan, Aden

Aage (Norse) Representative of ancestors
Age, Ake, Aake

Aarif (Arabic) A learned man
Arif, Aareef, Areef, Aareaf, Areaf, Aareif, Areif, Aarief

*****Aaron** (Hebrew) One who is exalted; from the mountain of strength
Aaran, Aaren, Aarin, Aaro, Aaronas, Aaronn, Aarron, Aaryn, Eron, Aron, Eran

Abdi (Hebrew) My servant
Abdie, Abdy, Abdey, Abdee

Abdul (Arabic) A servant of God
Abdal, Abdall, Abdalla, Abdallah, Abdel, Abdell, Abdella, Abdellah

Abedi (African) One who worships God
Abedie, Abedy, Abedey, Abedee, Abedea

Abednago (Aramaic) Servant of the god of wisdom, Nabu
Abednego

Abejundio (Spanish) Resembling a bee
Abejundo, Abejundeo, Abedjundiyo, Abedjundeyo

Abel (Hebrew) The life force, breath
Abele, Abell, Abelson, Able, Avel, Avele

Abraham (Hebrew) Father of a multitude; father of nations
Abarran, Avraham, Aberham, Abrahamo, Abrahan, Abrahim, Abram, Abrami, Ibrahim

^**Abram** (Hebrew) Form of Abraham, meaning "father of nations"

Absalom (Hebrew) The father of peace
Absalon, Abshalom, Absolem, Absolom, Absolon, Avshalom, Avsholom

Abu (African) A father
Abue, Aboo, Abou

Abundio (Spanish) A man of plenty
Abbondio, Abondio, Aboundio, Abundo, Abundeo, Aboundeo

Adael (Hebrew) God witnesses
Adaele, Adayel, Adayele

*****Adam** (Hebrew) Of the earth
Ad, Adamo, Adams, Adan, Adao, Addam, Addams, Addem

Adamson (English) The son of Adam
Adamsson, Addamson, Adamsun, Adamssun

Addy (Teutonic) One who is awe-inspiring
Addey, Addi, Addie, Addee, Addea, Adi, Ady, Adie

Adelpho (Greek) A brotherly man
Aldelfo, Adelfus, Adelfio, Adelphe

Adil (Arabic) A righteous man; one who is fair and just
Adyl, Adiel, Adeil, Adeel, Adeal, Adyeel

Aditya (Hindi) Of the sun
Adithya, Adithyan, Adityah, Aditeya, Aditeyah

Adonis (Greek) In mythology, a handsome young man loved by Aphrodite
Addonia, Adohnes, Adonys

*****Adrian** (Latin) A man from Hadria
Adrien, Adrain, Adrean, Adreean, Adreyan, Adreeyan, Adriaan

Adriel (Hebrew) From God's flock
Adriell, Adriele, Adryel, Adryell, Adryele

Afif (Arabic) One who is chaste; pure
Afeef, Afief, Afeif, Affeef, Affif, Afyf, Afeaf

Agamemnon (Greek) One who works slowly; in mythology, the leader of the Greeks at Troy
Agamemno, Agamenon

^**Ahmad** (Arabic) One who always thanks God; a name of Muhammed
Ahmed

*ᵀ**Aidan** (Irish) A fiery young man
Aiden, Aedan, Aeden, Aidano, Aidyn, Ayden, Aydin, Aydan

Aiken (English) Constructed of oak; sturdy
Aikin, Aicken, Aickin, Ayken, Aykin, Aycken, Ayckin

Ainsworth (English) From Ann's estate
Answorth, Annsworth, Ainsworthe, Answorthe, Annsworthe

Ajax (Greek) In mythology, a hero of the Trojan war
Aias, Aiastes, Ajaxx, Ajaxe

Ajit (Indian) One who is invincible
Ajeet, Ajeat, Ajeit, Ajiet, Ajyt

Akiko (Japanese) Surrounded by bright light
Akyko

Akin (African) A brave man; a hero
Akeen, Akean, Akein, Akien, Akyn

Akiva (Hebrew) One who protects or provides shelter
Akyva, Akeeva, Akeava, Akieva, Akeiva, Akeyva

Akmal (Arabic) A perfect man
Aqmal, Akmall, Aqmall, Acmal, Acmall, Ackmal, Ackmall

Alaire (French) Filled with joy
Alair, Alaer, Alaere, Alare, Alayr, Alayre

Alamar (Arabic) Covered with gold
Alamarr, Alemar, Alemarr, Alomar, Alomarr

Alan (German / Gaelic) One who is precious / resembling a little rock
Alain, Alann, Allan, Alson, Allin, Allen, Allyn

Alard (German) Of noble strength
Aliard, Allard, Alliard

Albert (German) One who is noble and bright
Alberto, Albertus, Alburt, Albirt, Aubert, Albyrt, Albertos, Albertino

Alden (English) An old friend
Aldan, Aldin, Aldyn, Aldon, Aldun

Aldo (German) Old or wise one; elder
Aldous, Aldis, Aldus, Alldo, Aldys

Aldred (English) An old advisor
Alldred, Aldraed, Alldraed, Aldread, Alldread

Alejandro (Spanish) Form of Alexander, meaning "a helper and defender of mankind"
Alejandrino, Alejo

*ᵀAlex (English) Form of Alexander, meaning "a helper and defender of mankind"
*Aleks, Alecks, Alecs, Allex, Alleks, Allecks, **Alexis***

*ᵀAlexander (Greek) A helper and defender of mankind
Alex, Alec, Alejandro, Alaxander, Aleksandar, Aleksander, Aleksandr, Alessandro, Alexzander, Zander

Alfonso (Italian) Prepared for battle; eager and ready
Alphonso, Alphonse, Affonso, Alfons, Alfonse, Alfonsin, Alfonsino, Alfonz, Alfonzo

Ali (Arabic) The great one; one who is exalted
Alie, Aly, Aley, Alee

Alijah (American) Form of Elijah, meaning "Jehovah is my god"

Alon (Hebrew) Of the oak tree
Allona, Allon, Alonn

Alonzo (Spanish) Form of Alfonso, meaning "prepared for battle; eager and ready"
Alonso, Alanso, Alanzo, Allonso, Allonzo, Allohnso, Allohnzo, Alohnso

Aloysius (German) A famous warrior
Ahlois, Aloess, Alois, Aloisio, Aloisius, Aloisio, Aloj, Alojzy

Alpha (Greek) The first-born child; the first letter of the Greek alphabet
Alphah, Alfa, Alfah

Alter (Hebrew) One who is old
Allter, Altar, Alltar

Alton (English) From the old town
Aldon, Aldun, Altun, Alten, Allton, Alltun, Allten

Alvin (English) Friend of the elves
Alven, Alvan, Alvyn

Amani (African / Arabic) One who is peaceful / one with wishes and dreams
Amanie, Amany, Amaney, Amanee, Amanye, Amanea, Amaneah

Amari (African) Having great strength; a builder
Amarie, Amaree, Amarea, Amary, Amarey

Amil (Hindi) One who is invaluable
Ameel, Ameal, Ameil, Amiel, Amyl

Amit (Hindi) Without limit; endless
Ameet, Ameat, Ameit, Ameit, Amyt

Amory (German) Ruler and lover of one's home
Aimory, Amery, Amorey, Amry, Amori, Amorie, Amoree, Amorea

Amos (Hebrew) To carry; hardworking
Amoss, Aymoss, Aymos

Andino (Italian) Form of Andrew, meaning "one who is manly; a warrior"
Andyno, Andeeno, Andeano, Andieno, Andeino

Andre (French) Form of Andrew, meaning "manly, a warrior"
Andreas, Andrei, Andrej, Andres, Andrey

*T**Andrew** (Greek) One who is manly; a warrior
Andy, Aindrea, Andreas, Andie, Andonia, Andor, Andresj, Anderson

Andrik (Slavic) Form of Andrew, meaning "one who is manly; a warrior"
Andric, Andrick, Andryk, Andryck, Andryc

*Angel** (Greek) A messenger of God
Andjelko, Ange, Angelino, Angell, Angelmo, Angelo, Angie, Angy

Angus (Scottish) One force; one strength; one choice
Aengus, Anngus, Aonghus

Anicho (German) An ancestor
Anico, Anecho, Aneco, Anycho, Anyco

Ankur (Indian) One who is blossoming; a sapling

Annan (Celtic) From the brook
Anan

Ansley (English) From the noble's pastureland
Ansly, Anslie, Ansli, Anslee, Ansleigh, Anslea, Ansleah, Anslye

Antenor (Spanish) One who antagonizes
Antener, Antenar, Antenir, Antenyr, Antenur

*T**Anthony** (Latin) A flourishing man; of an ancient Roman family
*Antal, Antony, Anthoney, Anntoin, Antin, Anton, Antone, Antonello, **Antonio***

Antoine (French) Form of Anthony, meaning "a flourishing man; of an ancient Roman family"
Antione, Antjuan, Antuan, Antuwain, Antuwaine, Antuwayne, Antuwon, Antwahn

Antonio (Italian) Form of Anthony, meaning "a flourishing man, from an ancient Roman family"
Antonin, Antonino, Antonius, Antonyo

Ara (Armenian / Latin) A legendary king / of the altar; the name of a constellation
Araa, Aira, Arah, Arae, Ahraya

Aram (Assyrian) One who is exalted
Arram

Arcadio (Greek) From an ideal country paradise
Alcadio, Alcado, Alcedio, Arcadios, Arcadius, Arkadi, Arkadios, Arkadius

Arcelio (Spanish) From the altar of heaven
Arcelios, Arcelius, Aricelio, Aricelios, Aricelius

Archard (German) A powerful holy man
Archerd, Archird, Archyrd

Archelaus (Greek) The ruler of the people
Archelaios, Arkelaos, Arkelaus, Arkelaios, Archelaos

Ardal (Gaelic) Having the valor of a bear
Ardghal

Ardell (Latin) One who is eager
Ardel, Ardelle, Ardele

Arden (Latin / English) One who is passionate and enthusiastic / from the valley of the eagles
Ardan, Arrden, Arrdan, Ardin, Arrdin, Ard, Ardyn, Arrdyn

Arduino (German) A valued friend
Ardwino, Arrduino, Ardueno

Ari (Hebrew) Resembling a lion or an eagle
Aree, Arie, Aristide, Aristides, Arri, Ary, Arye, Arrie

Ariel (Hebrew) A lion of God
Arielle, Ariele, Ariell, Arriel, Ahriel, Airial, Arieal, Arial

Aries (Latin) Resembling a ram; the first sign of the zodiac; a constellation
Arese, Ariese

Arion (Greek) A poet or musician
Arian, Arien, Aryon

Aristotle (Greek) Of high quality
Aristotelis, Aristotellis

Arius (Greek) Enduring life; everlasting; immortal
Areos, Areus, Arios

Arley (English) From the hare's meadow
Arlea, Arleigh, Arlie, Arly, Arleah, Arli, Arlee

Arliss (Hebrew) Of the pledge
Arlyss, Aryls, Arlis, Arlisse, Arlysse

Arnold (German) The eagle ruler
Arnaldo, Arnaud, Arnauld, Arnault, Arnd, Arndt, Arnel, Arnell

Arthur (Celtic) As strong as a bear; a hero
Aart, Arrt, Art, Artair, Arte, Arther, Arthor, Arthuro

Arvad (Hebrew) A wanderer; voyager
Arpad

Arvin (English) A friend to everyone
Arvinn, Arvinne, Arven, Arvenn, Arvenne, Arvyn, Arvynn, Arvynne

Asa (Hebrew) One who heals others
Asah

Asaph (Hebrew) One who gathers or collects
Asaf, Asaphe, Asafe, Asiph, Asiphe, Asif, Asife

Ash (English) From the ash tree
Ashe

Asher (Hebrew) Filled with happiness
Ashar, Ashor, Ashir, Ashyr, Ashur

Ashley (English) From the meadow of ash trees
Ashely, Asheley, Ashelie, Ashlan, Ashleigh, Ashlen, Ashli, Ashlie

ᵀ**Ashton** (English) From the ash-tree town
Asheton, Ashtun, Ashetun, Ashtin, Ashetin, Ashtyn, Ashetyn, Aston

Aslan (Turkish) Resembling a lion
Aslen, Azlan, Azlen

Athens (Greek) From the capital of Greece
Athenios, Athenius, Atheneos, Atheneus

Atticus (Latin) A man from Athens
Attikus, Attickus, Aticus, Atickus, Atikus

Atwell (English) One who lives at the spring
Attwell, Atwel, Attwel

Aubrey (English) One who rules with elf-wisdom
Aubary, Aube, Aubery, Aubry, Aubury, Aubrian, Aubrien, Aubrion

Auburn (Latin) Having a reddish-brown color
Aubirn, Auburne, Aubyrn, Abern, Abirn, Aburn, Abyrn, Aubern

Audley (English) From the old meadow
Audly, Audleigh, Audlee, Audlea, Audleah, Audli, Audlie

^**August** (Irish) One who is venerable; majestic
Austin, Augustine, Agoston, Aguistin, Agustin, Augustin, Augustyn, Avgustin, Augusteen, Agosteen

*****Austin** (English) Form of August, meaning "one who is venerable; majestic"
Austen, Austyn, Austan, Auston, Austun

Avery (English) One who is a wise ruler; of the nobility
Avrie, Averey, Averie, Averi, Averee

Aviram (Hebrew) My Father is mighty
Avyram, Avirem, Avyrem

Axel (German / Latin / Hebrew) Source of life; small oak / axe / peace
Aksel, Ax, Axe, Axell, Axil, Axill, Axl

Aya (Hebrew) Resembling a bird
Ayah

*****Ayden** (Irish) form of Aiden, meaning "a fiery young man"

Ayo (African) Filled with happiness
Ayoe, Ayow, Ayowe

Azamat (Arabic) A proud man; one who is majestic

Azi (African) One who is youthful
Azie, Azy, Azey, Azee, Azea

Azmer (Islamic) Resembling a lion
Azmar, Azmir, Azmyr, Azmor, Azmur

B

Baakir (African) The eldest child
Baakeer, Baakyr, Baakear, Baakier, Baakeir

Bachir (Hebrew) The oldest son
Bacheer, Bachear, Bachier, Bacheir, Bachyr

Baha (Arabic) A glorious and splendid man
Bahah

Bailintin (Irish) A valiant man
Bailinten, Bailentin, Bailenten, Bailintyn, Bailentyn

Bain (Irish) A fair-haired man
Baine, Bayn, Bayne, Baen, Baene, Bane, Baines, Baynes

Bajnok (Hungarian) A victorious man
Bajnock, Bajnoc

Bakari (Swahili) One who is promised
Bakarie, Bakary, Bakarey, Bakaree, Bakarea

Bakhit (Arabic) A lucky man
Bakheet, Bakheat, Bakheit, Bakhiet, Bakhyt, Bakht

Bala (Hindi) One who is youthful
Balu, Balue, Balou

Balark (Hindi) Born with the rising sun

Balasi (Basque) One who is flat-footed
Balasie, Balasy, Balasey, Balasee, Balasea

Balbo (Latin) One who mutters
Balboe, Balbow, Balbowe, Ballbo, Balbino, Balbi, Balbie, Balby

Baldwin (German) A brave friend
Baldwine, Baldwinn, Baldwinne, Baldwen, Baldwenn, Baldwenne, Baldwyn, Baldwynn

Balint (Latin) A healthy and strong man
Balent, Balin, Balen, Balynt, Balyn

Balloch (Scottish) From the grazing land

Bancroft (English) From the bean field
Bancrofte, Banfield, Banfeld, Bankroft, Bankrofte

Bandana (Spanish) A brightly colored headwrap
Bandanah, Bandanna, Bandannah

Bandy (American) A fiesty man
Bandey, Bandi, Bandie, Bandee, Bandea

Bansi (Indian) One who plays the flute
Bansie, Bansy, Bansey, Bansee, Bansea

Bao (Vietnamese / Chinese) To order / one who is prized

Baqir (Arabic) A learned man
Baqeer, Baqear, Baqier, Baqeir, Baqyr, Baqer

Barak (Hebrew) Of the lightning flash
Barrak, Barac, Barrac, Barack, Barrack

Baram (Hebrew) The son of the nation
Barem, Barum, Barom, Barim, Barym

Bard (English) A minstrel; a poet
Barde, Bardo

Barden (English) From the barley valley; from the boar's valley
Bardon, Bardun, Bardin, Bardyn, Bardan, Bardene

Bardol (Basque) A farmer
Bardo, Bartol

Bardrick (Teutonic) An axe ruler
Bardric, Bardrik, Bardryck, Bardryk, Bardryc, Bardarick, Bardaric, Bardarik

Barek (Arabic) One who is noble
Barec, Bareck

Barend (German) The hard bear
Barende, Barind, Barinde, Barynd, Barynde

Barnett (English) Of honorable birth
Barnet, Baronet, Baronett

Baron (English) A title of nobility
Barron

Barr (English) A lawyer
Barre, Bar

Barra (Gaelic) A fair-haired man

Barrett (German / English) Having the strength of a bear / one who argues
Baret, Barrat, Barratt, Barret, Barrette

Barry (Gaelic) A fair-haired man
Barrey, Barri, Barrie, Barree, Barrea, Barrington, Barryngton, Barringtun

Bartholomew (Aramaic) The son of the farmer
Bart, Bartel, Barth, Barthelemy, Bartho, Barthold, Bartholoma, Bartholomaus, Bartlett, Bartol

Bartlett (French) Form of Bartholomew, meaning "the son of the farmer"
Bartlet, Bartlitt, Bartlit, Bartlytt, Bartlyt

Bartley (English) From the meadow of birch trees
Bartly, Bartli, Bartlie, Bartlee, Bartlea, Bartleah, Bartleigh

Bartoli (Spanish) Form of Bartholomew, meaning "the son of the farmer"
Bartolie, Bartoly, Bartoley, Bartolee, Bartoleigh, Bartolea, Bartolo, Bartolio

Barton (English) From the barley town
Bartun, Barten, Bartan, Bartin, Bartyn

Barwolf (English) The ax-wolf
Barrwolf, Barwulf, Barrwulf

Basant (Arabic) One who smiles often
Basante

Bassett (English) A little person
Baset, Basset, Basett

Basy (American) A homebody
Basey, Basi, Basie, Basee, Basea, Basye

Baurice (American) Form of Maurice, meaning "a dark-skinned man; Moorish".
Baurell, Baureo, Bauricio, Baurids, Baurie, Baurin

Bay (Vietnamese / English) The seventh-born child; born during the month of July / from the bay
Baye, Bae, Bai

Beal (French) A handsome man
Beals, Beale, Beall, Bealle

Beamer (English) One who plays the trumpet
Beamor, Beamir, Beamyr, Beamur, Beamar, Beemer, Beemar, Beemir

Beau (French) A handsome man, an admirer
Bo

Becher (Hebrew) The firstborn son

^**Beckett** (English) From the small stream; from the brook
Becket

Bedar (Arabic) One who is attentive
Beder, Bedor, Bedur, Bedyr, Bedir

Beircheart (Anglo-Saxon) Of the intelligent army

Bela (Slavic) A white-skinned man
Belah, Bella, Bellah

Belden (English) From the beautiful valley
Beldan, Beldon, Beldun, Beldin, Beldyn, Bellden, Belldan, Belldon, Belldun, Belldin, Belldyn

Belen (Greek) Of an arrow
Belin, Belyn, Belan, Belon, Belun

Belindo (English) A handsome and tender man
Belyndo, Belindio, Belyndio, Belindeo, Belyndeo, Belindiyo, Belyndiyo, Belindeyo

Bellarmine (Italian) One who is handsomely armed
Bellarmin, Bellarmeen, Bellarmeene, Bellarmean, Bellarmeane, Bellarmyn, Bellarmyne

Belton (English) From the beautiful town
Bellton, Beltun, Belltun, Belten, Bellten

Belvin (American) Form of Melvin, meaning "a friend who offers counsel"
Belven, Belvyn, Belvon, Belvun, Belvan

Bem (African) A peaceful man

Ben (English) Form of Benjamin, meaning "son of the south; son of the right hand"
Benn, Benni, Bennie, Bennee, Benney, Benny, Bennea, Benno

*ᵀBenjamin (Hebrew) Son of the south; son of the right hand
Ben, Benejamen, Beniamino, Benjaman, Benjamen, Benjamino, Benjamon, Benjiman, Benjimen

^Bennett (English) Form of Benedict, meaning "one who is blessed"
Benett, Bennet, Benet

Bentley (English) From the meadow of bent grass
Bently, Bentleigh, Bentlee, Bentlie

Berdy (German) Having a brilliant mind
Berdey, Berdee, Berdea, Berdi, Berdie

Beresford (English) From the barley ford
Beresforde, Beresfurd, Beresfurde, Beresferd, Beresferde, Berford, Berforde, Berfurd

Berkeley (English) From the meadow of birch trees
Berkely, Berkeli, Berkelie, Berkelea, Berkeleah, Berkelee, Berkeleigh, Berkley

Bernard (German) As strong and brave as a bear
Barnard, Barnardo, Barnhard, Barnhardo, Bearnard, Bernardo, Bernarr, Bernd

Berry (English) Resembling a berry fruit
Berrey, Berri, Berrie, Berree, Berrea

Bert (English) One who is illustrious
Berte, Berti, Bertie, Bertee, Bertea, Berty, Bertey

Bethel (Hebrew) The house of God
Bethell, Bethele, Bethelle, Betuel, Betuell, Betuele, Betuelle

Bevis (Teutonic) An archer
Beviss, Bevys, Bevyss, Beavis, Beaviss, Beavys, Beavyss

Biagio (Italian) One who has a stutter
Biaggio

Birney (English) From the island with the brook
Birny, Birnee, Birnea, Birni, Birnie

Black (English) A dark-skinned man
Blak, Blac, Blacke

Blackwell (English) From the dark spring
Blackwel, Blackwelle, Blackwele

Blade (English) One who wields a sword or knife
Blayd, Blayde, Blaid, Blaide, Blaed, Blaede

Blagden (English) From the dark valley
Blagdon, Blagdan, Blagdun, Blagdin, Blagdyn

Blaine (Scottish / Irish) A saint's servant / a thin man
Blayne, Blane, Blain, Blayn, Blaen, Blaene, Blainy, Blainey

Blaise (Latin / American) One with a lisp or a stutter / a fiery man
Blaze, Blaize, Blaiz, Blayze, Blayz, Blaez, Blaeze

*Blake (English) A dark, handsome man
Blayk, Blayke, Blaik, Blaike, Blaek, Blaeke

Bliss (English) Filled with happiness
Blis, Blyss, Blys

Blondell (English) A fair-haired boy
Blondel, Blondele, Blondelle

Boaz (Hebrew) One who is swift
Boaze, Boas, Boase

Bob (English) Form of Robert, meaning "one who is bright with fame"
Bobbi, Bobbie, Bobby, Bobbey, Bobbee, Bobbea

Bogart (French) One who is strong with the bow
Bogaard, Bogaart, Bogaerd, Bogey, Bogie, Bogi, Bogy, Bogee

Bolivar (Spanish) A mighty warrior
Bolevar, Bolivarr, Bolevarr, Bollivar, Bollivarr, Bollevar, Bollevarr

Bonaventure (Latin) One who undertakes a blessed venture
Bonaventura, Buenaventure, Buenaventura, Bueaventure, Bueaventura

Booker (English) One who binds books; a scribe
Bookar, Bookir, Bookyr, Bookur, Bookor

Bosley (English) From the meadow near the forest
Bosly, Boslee, Boslea, Bosleah, Bosleigh, Bosli, Boslie, Bozley

Boston (English) From the town near the forest; from the city of Boston
Bostun, Bostin, Bostyn, Bosten, Bostan

Boyce (French) One who lives near the forest
Boice, Boyse, Boise

Boyd (Celtic) A blond-haired man
Boyde, Boid, Boide, Boyden, Boydan, Boydin, Boydyn, Boydon

Boynton (Irish) From the town near the river Boyne
Boyntun, Boynten, Boyntin, Boyntan, Boyntyn

Bracken (English) Resembling the large fern
Braken, Brackan, Brakan, Brackin, Brakin, Brackyn

Braddock (English) From the broadly spread oak
Bradock, Braddoc, Bradoc, Braddok, Bradok

Braden (Gaelic / English)
Resembling salmon / from
the wide valley
*Bradan, Bradon, Bradin,
Bradyn, Braeden, Braddan,
Braddin, Brayden*

Bradford (English) From the
wide ford
*Bradforde, Bradferd, Bradferde,
Bradfurd*

Bradley (English) From the
wide meadow
*Bradly, Bradlea, Bradleah,
Bradlee, Bradleigh, Bradli*

Brady (Irish) The son of a
large-chested man
*Bradey, Bradee, Bradea, Bradi,
Bradie, Braidy, Braidey,
Braidee*

Bramley (English) From the
wild gorse meadow; from the
raven's meadow
*Bramly, Bramlee, Bramlea,
Bramleah, Bramleigh, Bramli,
Bramlie*

Branch (Latin) An extension
Branche

*ᵀ**Brandon** (English) From the
broom or gorse hill
*Brandun, Brandin, Brandyn,
Brandan, Branden, Brannon,
Brannun, Brannen*

Branson (English) The son of
Brand or Brandon
*Bransun, Bransen, Bransan,
Bransin, Bransyn*

Braxton (English) From
Brock's town
*Braxtun, Braxten, Braxtan,
Braxtyn*

***Brayden** (Gaelic / English)
Form of Braden, meaning
"resembling salmon / from
the wide valley"
*Braydon, Braydan, Braydin,
Braydyn*

^**Braylen** (American)
Combination of Brayden and
Lynn
Braylon

Brendan (Irish) Born to
royalty; a prince
*Brendano, Brenden, Brendin,
Brendon, Brendyn, Brendun*

Brennan (Gaelic) A sorrowful
man; a teardrop
*Brenan, Brenn, Brennen,
Brennin, Brennon, Brenin,
Brennun, Brennyn*

Brent (English) From the hill
*Brendt, Brennt, Brentan,
Brenten, Brentin, Brenton,
Brentun, Brentyn*

Brett (Latin) A man from Britain or Brittany
Bret, Breton, Brette, Bretton, Brit, Briton, Britt, Brittain

Brewster (English) One who brews
Brewer, Brewstere

*ᵀBrian (Gaelic / Celtic) Of noble birth / having great strength
*Briano, Briant, Brien, Brion, **Bryan**, Bryant, Bryen, Bryent*

Briar (English) Resembling a thorny plant
Brier, Bryar, Bryer

Brock (English) Resembling a badger
Broc

Broderick (English) From the wide ridge
Broderik, Broderic, Brodrick, Brodryk, Brodyrc, Brodrik, Broderyc, Brodrig

*Brody (Gaelic / Irish) From the ditch
Brodie, Brodey, Brodi, Brodee

Brogan (Gaelic) One who is sturdy
Broggan, Brogen, Broggen, Brogon, Broggon, Brogun, Broggun, Brogin, Broggin, Brogyn

^Brooks (English) From the running stream
Brookes

Bruce (Scottish) A man from Brieuse; one who is well-born; from an influential family
Brouce, Brooce, Bruci, Brucie, Brucey, Brucy

Bruno (German) A brown-haired man
Brunoh, Brunoe, Brunow, Brunowe, Bruin, Bruine, Brunon, Brunun

Bryce (Scottish / Anglo-Saxon) One who is speckled / the son of a nobleman
Brice, Bricio, Brizio, Brycio

Bryson (Welsh) The son of Brice
*Brisen, Brysin, Brysun, Brysyn, **Brycen***

Bud (English) One who is brotherly
Budd, Buddi, Buddie, Buddee, Buddey, Buddy

Budha (Hindi) Another name for the planet Mercury
Budhan, Budhwar

Bulat (Russian) Having great strength
Bulatt

Burbank (English) From the riverbank of burrs
Burrbank, Burhbank

Burgess (German) A free citizen of the town
Burges, Burgiss, Burgis, Burgyss, Burgys, Burgeis

Burne (English) Resembling a bear; from the brook; the brown-haired one
Burn, Beirne, Burnis, Byrn, Byrne, Burns, Byrnes

Burnet (French) Having brown hair
Burnett, Burnete, Burnette, Bernet, Bernett, Bernete, Bernette

Burton (English) From the fortified town
Burtun, Burten, Burtin, Burtyn, Burtan

Butler (English) The keeper of the bottles (wine, liquor)
Buttler, Butlar, Butlor, Butlir, Buttlir, Butlyr

^Byron (English) One who lives near the cow sheds
Byrom, Beyren, Beyron, Biren, Biron, Buiron, Byram, Byran

C

Cable (French) One who makes rope
Cabel, Caibel, Caible, Caybel, Cayble, Caebel, Caeble, Cabe

Caddis (English) Resembling a worsted fabric
Caddys, Caddiss, Caddice

Cade (English / French) One who is round / of the cask
Caid, Caide, Cayd, Cayde, Caed, Caede

Cadell (Welsh) Having the spirit of battle
Cadel, Caddell, Caddel

Caden (Welsh) Spirit of Battle
Caiden, Cayden

Cadmus (Greek) A man from the east; in mythology, the man who founded Thebes
Cadmar, Cadmo, Cadmos, Cadmuss

Cadogan (Welsh) Having glory and honor during battle
Cadogawn, Cadwgan, Cadwgawn, Cadogaun

Caesar (Latin) An emperor
Caezar, Casar, Cezar, Chezare, Caesarius, Ceasar, Ceazer

Cain (Hebrew) One who wields a spear; something acquired; in the Bible, Adam and Eve's first son who killed his brother Abel
Cayn, Caen, Cane, Caine, Cayne, Caene

Caird (Scottish) A traveling metal worker
Cairde, Cayrd, Cayrde, Caerd, Caerde

Cairn (Gaelic) From the mound of rocks
Cairne, Cairns, Caern, Caerne, Caernes

Caith (Irish) Of the battlefield
Caithe, Cayth, Caythe, Cathe, Caeth, Caethe

Calbert (English) A cowboy
Calberte, Calburt, Calburte, Calbirt, Calbirte, Calbyrt, Calbyrte

Cale (English) Form of Charles, meaning "one who is manly and strong / a free man"
Cail, Caile, Cayl, Cayle, Cael, Caele

ᵀCaleb** (Hebrew) Resembling a dog
Cayleb, Caileb, Caeleb, Calob, Cailob, Caylob, Caelob, Kaleb

Calian (Native American) A warrior of life
Calien, Calyan, Calyen

Callum (Gaelic) Resembling a dove
Calum

Calvin (French) The little bald one
Cal, Calvyn, Calvon, Calven, Calvan, Calvun, Calvino

Camara (African) One who teaches others

Camden (Gaelic) From the winding valley
Camdene, Camdin, Camdyn, Camdan, Camdon, Camdun

Cameo (English) A small, perfect child
Cammeo

*Cameron (Scottish) Having a crooked nose
Cameren, Cameran, Camerin, Cameryn, Camerun, Camron, Camren, Camran, Tameron

Campbell (Scottish) Having a crooked mouth
Campbel, Cambell, Cambel, Camp, Campe, Cambeul, Cambeull, Campbeul

Candan (Turkish) A sincere man
Canden, Candin, Candyn, Candon, Candun

Cannon (French) An official of the church
Canon, Cannun, Canun, Cannin, Canin

Canyon (Spanish / English) From the footpath / from the deep ravine
Caniyon, Canyun, Caniyun

Capricorn (Latin) The tenth sign of the zodiac; the goat

Cargan (Gaelic) From the small rock
Cargen, Cargon, Cargun, Cargin, Cargyn

Carl (German) Form of Karl, meaning "a free man"
Carel, Carlan, Carle, Carlens, Carlitis, Carlin, Carlo, Carlos

*****Carlos** (Spanish) Form of Karl, meaning "a free man"
Carolos, Carolo, Carlito

Carlsen (Scandinavian) The son of Carl
Carlssen, Carlson, Carlsson, Carlsun, Carllsun, Carlsin, Carllsin, Carlsyn

Carlton (English) From the free man's town
Carltun, Carltown, Carston, Carstun, Carstown, Carleton, Carletun, Carlten

Carmichael (Scottish) A follower of Michael

Carmine (Latin / Aramaic) A beautiful song / the color crimson
Carman, Carmen, Carmin, Carmino, Carmyne, Carmon, Carmun, Carmyn

*****Carson** (Scottish) The son of a marsh dweller
Carsen, Carsun, Carsan, Carsin, Carsyn

*****Carter** (English) One who transports goods; one who drives a cart
Cartar, Cartir, Cartyr, Cartor, Cartur, Cartere, Cartier, Cartrell

Cartland (English) From Carter's land
Carteland, Cartlan, Cartlend, Cartelend, Cartlen

Cary (Celtic / Welsh / Gaelic) From the river / from the fort on the hill / having dark features
Carey, Cari, Carie, Caree, Carea, Carry, Carrey, Carri

Case (French) Refers to a chest or box
Cace

Cash (Latin) money

Cassander (Spanish) A brother of heroes
Casander, Casandro, Cassandro, Casandero

Cassius (Latin) One who is empty; hollow; vain
Cassios, Cassio, Cach, Cache, Cashus, Cashos, Cassian, Cassien

Castel (Spanish) From the castle
Castell, Castal, Castall, Castol, Castoll, Castul, Castull, Castil

Castor (Greek) Resembling a beaver; in mythology, one of the Dioscuri
Castur, Caster, Castar, Castir, Castyr, Castorio, Castoreo, Castoro

Cat (American) Resembling the animal
Catt, Chait, Chaite

Cathmore (Irish) A renowned fighter
Cathmor, Cathemore

Cato (Latin) One who is all-knowing
Cayto, Caito, Caeto

Caton (Spanish) One who is knowledgable
Caten, Catun, Catan, Catin, Catyn

Cavell (Teutonic) One who is bold
Cavel, Cavele, Cavelle

Caxton (English) From the lump settlement
Caxtun, Caxten

Celesto (Latin) From heaven
Célestine, Celestino, Celindo, Celestyne, Celestyno

Cephas (Hebrew) As solid as a rock

Cesar (Spanish) form of Caesar, meaning "emperor"
Cesare, Cesaro, Cesario

Chad (English) One who is warlike
Chaddie, Chadd, Chadric, Chadrick, Chadrik, Chadryck, Chadryc, Chadryk

Chadwick (English) From Chad's dairy farm
Chadwik, Chadwic, Chadwyck, Chadwyk, Chadwyc

Chai (Hebrew) A giver of life
Chaika, Chaim, Cahyim, Cahyyam

Chalkley (English) From the chalk meadow
Chalkly, Chalkleigh, Chalklee, Chalkleah, Chalkli, Chalklie, Chalklea

Champion (English) A warrior; the victor
Champeon, Champiun, Champeun, Champ

Chan (Spanish / Sanskrit) Form of John, meaning "God is gracious" / a shining man
Chayo, Chano, Chawn, Chaun

Chanan (Hebrew) God is compassionate
Chanen, Chanin, Chanyn, Chanun, Chanon

ᵀ**Chance** (English) Having good fortune

Chandler (English) One who makes candles
Chandlar, Chandlor

Chaniel (Hebrew) The grace of God
Chanyel, Chaniell, Chanyell

Channing (French / English) An official of the church / resembling a young wolf
Channyng, Canning, Cannyng

Chao (Chinese) The great one

Chappel (English) One who works in the chapel
Capel, Capell, Capello, Cappel, Chappell

*****Charles** (English / German) One who is manly and strong / a free man
Charls, Chas, Charli, Charlie, Charley, Charly, Charlee, Charleigh, Cale, Chuck, Chick

Charleson (English) The son of Charles
Charlesen, Charlesin, Charlesyn, Charlesan, Charlesun

Charlton (English) From the free man's town
Charleton, Charltun, Charletun, Charleston, Charlestun

Charro (Spanish) A cowboy
Charo

*ᵀ**Chase** (English) A huntsman
Chace, Chasen, Chayce, Chayse, Chaise, Chaice, Chaece, Chaese

Chatwin (English) A warring friend
Chatwine, Chatwinn, Chatwinne, Chatwen, Chatwenn, Chatwenne, Chatwyn, Chatwynn

Chaviv (Hebrew) One who is dearly loved
Chaveev, Chaveav, Chaviev, Chaveiv, Chavyv, Chavivi, Chavivie, Chavivy

Chay (Gaelic) From the fairy place
Chaye, Chae

Chelsey (English) From the landing place for chalk
Chelsee, Chelseigh, Chelsea, Chelsi, Chelsie, Chelsy, Chelcey, Chelcy

Cheslav (Russian) From the fortified camp
Cheslaw

Chester (Latin) From the camp of the soldiers
Chet, Chess, Cheston, Chestar, Chestor, Chestur, Chestir, Chestyr

Chico (Spanish) A boy; a lad

Chien (Vietnamese) A combative man

Chiron (Greek) A wise tutor
Chyron, Chirun, Chyrun

Chogan (Native American) Resembling a blackbird
Chogen, Chogon, Chogun, Chogin, Chogyn

Choni (Hebrew) A gracious man
Chonie, Chony, Choney, Chonee, Chonea

*ᵀ**Christian** (Greek) A follower of Christ
Chrestien, Chretien, Chris, Christan, Christer, Christiano, Cristian

*ᵀ**Christopher** (Greek) One who bears Christ inside
Chris, Kit, Christof, Christofer, Christoffer, Christoforo, Christoforus, Christoph, Christophe, Cristopher, Cristofer

Chuchip (Native American) A deer spirit

Chuck (English) Form of Charles, meaning "one who is manly and strong / a free man"
Chucke, Chucki, Chuckie, Chucky, Chuckey, Chuckee, Chuckea

Chul (Korean) One who stands firm

Chun (Chinese) Born during the spring

Cid (Spanish) A lord
Cyd

Cillian (Gaelic) One who suffers strife

Ciqala (Native American) The little one

Cirrus (Latin) A lock of hair; resembling the cloud
Cyrrus

Clair (Latin) One who is bright
Clare, Clayr, Claer, Clairo, Claro, Claero

Clancy (Celtic) Son of the red-haired warrior
Clancey, Clanci, Clancie, Clancee, Clancea, Clansey, Clansy, Clansi

Clark (English) A cleric; a clerk
Clarke, Clerk, Clerke, Clerc

Claude (English) One who is lame
Claud, Claudan, Claudell, Claidianus, Claudicio, Claudien, Claudino, Claudio

Clay (English) Of the earth's clay

Clayton (English) From the town settled on clay
Claytun, Clayten, Claytin, Claytyn, Claytan, Cleyton, Cleytun, Cleytan

Cleon (Greek) A well-known man
Cleone, Clion, Clione, Clyon, Clyone

Clifford (English) From the ford near the cliff
Cliff, Clyfford, Cliford, Clyford

Cliffton (English) From the town near the cliff
Cliff, Cliffe, Clyff, Clyffe, Clifft, Clift, Clyfft, Clyft

Clinton (English) From the town on the hill
Clynton, Clintun, Clyntun, Clint, Clynt, Clinte, Clynte

Clive (English) One who lives near the cliff
Clyve, Cleve

Cluny (Irish) From the meadow
Cluney, Cluni, Clunie, Clunee, Clunea, Cluneah

Cobden (English) From the cottage in the valley
Cobdenn, Cobdale, Cobdail, Cobdaile, Cobdell, Cobdel, Cobdayl, Cobdayle

Coby (English) Form of Jacob, meaning "he who supplants"
Cobey

Cody (Irish / English) One who is helpful; a wealthy man / acting as a cushion
Codi, Codie, Codey, Codee, Codeah, Codea, Codier, Codyr

Colbert (French) A famous and bright man
Colvert, Culbert, Colburt, Colbirt, Colbyrt, Colbart, Culburt, Culbirt

Colby (English) From the coal town
Colbey, Colbi, Colbie, Colbee, Collby, Coalby, Colbea, Colbeah

*Cole (English) Having dark features; having coal-black hair
Coley, Coli, Coly, Colie, Colee, Coleigh, Colea, Colson

Coleridge (English) From the dark ridge
Colerige, Colridge, Colrige

Colgate (English) From the dark gate
Colegate, Colgait, Colegait, Colgayt, Colegayt, Colgaet

Colin (Scottish) A young man; a form of Nicholas, meaning "of the victorious people"
Cailean, Colan, Colyn, Colon, Colen, Collin, Collan

^Colt (English) A young horse; from the coal town
Colte

Colter (English) A horse herdsman
Coltere, Coltar, Coltor, Coltir, Coltyr, Coulter, Coultar, Coultir

*Colton (English) From the coal town
Colten, Coltun, Coltan, Coltin, Coltyn, Coltrain

Comanche (Native American) A tribal name
Comanchi, Comanchie, Comanchee, Comanchea, Comanchy, Comanchey

Comus (Latin) In mythology, the god of mirth and revelry
Comas, Comis, Comys

Conan (English / Gaelic) Resembling a wolf / one who is high and mighty
Conant

Condon (Celtic) A dark, wise man
Condun, Condan, Conden, Condin, Condyn

Cong (Chinese) A clever man

Conn (Irish) The chief
Con

Connecticut (Native American) From the place beside the long river / from the state of Connecticut

Connery (Scottish) A daring man
Connary, Connerie, Conneri, Connerey, Connarie, Connari, Connarey, Conary

*ᵀ**Connor** (Gaelic) A wolf lover
*Conor, Conner, Coner, Connar,
Conar, Connur, Conur, Connir,
Conir*

Conroy (Irish) A wise advisor
Conroye, Conroi

Constantine (Latin) One who
is steadfast; firm
Dinos

Consuelo (Spanish) One who
offers consolation
*Consuel, Consuelio, Consueleo,
Consueliyo, Consueleyo*

Conway (Gaelic) The hound
of the plain; from the sacred
river
*Conwaye, Conwai, Conwae,
Conwy*

Cook (English) One who
prepares meals for others
Cooke

Cooney (Irish) A handsome
man
*Coony, Cooni, Coonie, Coonee,
Coonea*

*****Cooper** (English) One who
makes barrels
*Coop, Coopar, Coopir, Coopyr,
Coopor, Coopur, Coopersmith,
Cupere*

Corbett (French) Resembling
a young raven
*Corbet, Corbete, Corbette,
Corbit, Corbitt, Corbite,
Corbitte*

Corcoran (Gaelic) Having a
ruddy complexion
Cochran

Cordero (Spanish) Resembling
a lamb
*Corderio, Corderiyo, Cordereo,
Cordereyo*

Corey (Irish) From the hollow;
of the churning waters
*Cory, Cori, Corie, Coree, Corea,
Correy, Corry, Corri*

Coriander (Greek) A romantic
man; resembling the spice
*Coryander, Coriender,
Coryender*

Corlan (Irish) One who wields
a spear
*Corlen, Corlin, Corlyn, Corlon,
Corlun*

Corrado (German) A bold
counselor
Corrade, Corradeo, Corradio

Corridon (Irish) One who
wields a spear
*Corridan, Corridun, Corriden,
Corridin, Corridyn*

Cortez (Spanish) A courteous man
Cortes

Cosmo (Greek) The order of the universe
Cosimo, Cosmé, Cosmos, Cosmas, Cozmo, Cozmos, Cozmas

Cotton (American) Resembling or farmer of the plant
Cottin, Cotten, Cottyn, Cottun, Cottan

Courtney (English) A courteous man; courtly
Cordney, Cordni, Cortenay, Corteney, Cortni, Cortnee, Cortneigh, Cortney

Covert (English) One who provides shelter
Couvert

Covey (English) A brood of birds
Covy, Covi, Covie, Covee, Covea, Covvey, Covvy, Covvi

Covington (English) From the town near the cave
Covyngton, Covingtun, Covyngtun

Cox (English) A coxswain
Coxe, Coxi, Coxie, Coxey, Coxy, Coxee, Coxea

Coyle (Irish) A leader during battle
Coyl, Coil, Coile

Craig (Gaelic) From the rocks; from the crag
Crayg, Craeg, Craige, Crayge, Craege, Crage, Crag

Crandell (English) From the valley of cranes
Crandel, Crandale, Crandail, Crandaile, Crandayl, Crandayle, Crandael, Crandaele

Crawford (English) From the crow's ford
Crawforde, Crawferd, Crawferde, Crawfurd, Crawfurde

Creed (Latin) A guiding principle; a belief
Creede, Cread, Creade, Creedon, Creadon, Creedun, Creadun, Creedin

Creek (English) From the small stream
Creeke, Creak, Creake, Creik, Creike

Creighton (Scottish) From the border town
Creightun, Crayton, Craytun, Craiton, Craitun, Craeton, Craetun, Crichton

Crescent (French) One who creates; increasing; growing
Creissant, Crescence, Cressant, Cressent, Crescant

Cruz (Spanish) Of the cross

Cuarto (Spanish) The fourth-born child
Cuartio, Cuartiyo, Cuarteo

^**Cullen** (Gaelic) A good-looking young man
Cullin, Cullyn, Cullan, Cullon, Cullun

Cunningham (Gaelic) From the village of milk
Conyngham, Cuningham, Cunnyngham, Cunyngham

Curcio (French) One who is courteous
Curceo

Cuthbert (English) One who is bright and famous
Cuthbeorht, Cuthburt, Cuthbirt, Cuthbyrt

Cyneley (English) From the royal meadow
Cynely, Cyneli, Cynelie, Cynelee, Cynelea, Cyneleah, Cyneleigh

Czar (Russian) An emperor

D

Dacey (Gaelic / Latin) A man from the south / a man from Dacia
Dacy, Dacee, Dacea, Daci, Dacie, Daicey, Daicy

Dack (English) From the French town of Dax
Dacks, Dax

Daedalus (Greek) A craftsman
Daldalos, Dedalus

Dag (Scandinavian) Born during the daylight
Dagney, Dagny, Dagnee, Dagnea, Dagni, Dagnie, Daeg, Dagget

Daijon (American) A gift of hope
Dayjon, Daejon, Dajon

Dainan (Australian) A kind-hearted man
Dainen, Dainon, Dainun, Dainyn, Dainin, Daynan, Daynen, Daynon

Daire (Irish) A wealthy man
Dair, Daere, Daer, Dayr, Dayre, Dare, Dari, Darie

Daivat (Hindi) A powerful man

Dakarai (African) Filled with happiness

Dakota (Native American) A friend to all
Daccota, Dakoda, Dakodah, Dakotah, Dakoeta, Dekota, Dekohta, Dekowta

Dallan (Irish) One who is blind
Dalan, Dallen, Dalen, Dalin, Dallin, Dallyn, Dalyn, Dallon, Dalon, Dallun, Dalun

Dallas (Scottish) From the dales
Dalles, Dallis, Dallys, Dallos

Dalton (English) from the town in the valley
Daltun, Dalten, Daltan, Daltin, Daltyn, Daleten, Dalte, Daulten

Damario (Greek / Spanish) Resembling a calf / one who is gentle
Damarios, Damarius, Damaro, Damero, Damerio, Damereo, Damareo, Damerios

Damian (Greek) One who tames or subdues others
Daemon, Daimen, Daimon, Daman, Damen, Dameon, Damiano, Damianos

Dane (English) A man from Denmark
Dain, Daine, Dayn, Dayne

Danely (Scandinavian) A man from Denmark
Daneley, Daneli, Danelie, Danelee, Daneleigh, Danelea, Daineley, Dainely

Daniachew (African) A mediator

*T**Daniel** (Hebrew) God is my judge
Dan, Danal, Daneal, Danek, Danell, Danial, Daniele, Danil, Danilo

Danso (African) A reliable man
Dansoe, Dansow, Dansowe

Dante (Latin) An enduring man; everlasting
Dantae, Dantay, Dantel, Daunte, Dontae, Dontay, Donte, Dontae

Daoud (Arabian) Form of David, meaning "the beloved one"
Daoude, Dawud, Doud, Daud, Da'ud

Daphnis (Greek) In mythology, the son of Hermes
Daphnys

Dar (Hebrew) Resembling a pearl
Darr

Darcel (French) Having dark features
Darcell, Darcele, Darcelle, Darcio, Darceo

Dardanus (Greek) In mythology, the founder of Troy
Dardanio, Dardanios, Dardanos, Dard, Darde

Darek (English) Form of Derek, meaning "the ruler of the tribe"
Darrek, Darec, Darrec, Darreck, Dareck

Darion (Greek) A gift
Darian, Darien, Dariun, Darrion, Darrian, Darrien, Daryon, Daryan

Darius (Greek) A kingly man; one who is wealthy
Darias, Dariess, Dario, Darious, Darrius, Derrius, Derrious, Derrias

Darlen (American) A sweet man; a darling
Darlon, Darlun, Darlan, Darlin, Darlyn

Darnell (English) From the hidden place
Darnall, Darneil, Darnel, Darnele, Darnelle

Darold (English) Form of Harold, meaning "the ruler of an army"
Darrold, Derald, Derrald, Derold, Derrold

Darren (Gaelic / English) A great man / a gift from God
Darran, Darrin, Darryn, Darron, Darrun, Daren, Darin, Daran

Dart (English / American) From the river / one who is fast
Darte, Darrt, Darrte, Darti, Dartie, Dartee, Dartea, Darty

Darvell (French) From the eagle town
Darvel, Darvele, Darvelle

Dasras (Indian) A handsome man

Dasya (Indian) A servant

⊤*David** (Hebrew) The beloved one
Dave, Davey, Davi, Davidde, Davide, Davie, Daviel, Davin, Daoud

Davis (English) The son of David
Davies, Daviss, Davys, Davyss

Davu (African) Of the beginning
Davue, Davoo, Davou, Davugh

Dawson (English) The son of David
Dawsan, Dawsen, Dawsin, Dawsun

Dax (French) From the French town Dax
Daxton

Dayton (English) From the sunny town

Deacon (Greek) The dusty one; a servant
Deecon, Deakon, Deekon, Deacun, Deecun, Deakun, Deekun, Deacan

Dean (English) From the valley; a church official
Deane, Deen, Deene, Dene, Deans, Deens, Deani, Deanie

DeAndre (American) A manly man
D'André, DeAndrae, DeAndray, Diandray, Diondrae, Diondray

Dearon (American) One who is much loved
Dearan, Dearen, Dearin, Dearyn, Dearun

Decker (German / Hebrew) One who prays / a piercing man
Deker, Decer, Dekker, Deccer, Deck, Decke

Declan (Irish) The name of a saint

Dedrick (English) Form of Dietrich, meaning "the ruler of the tribe"
Dedryck, Dedrik, Dedryk, Dedric, Dedryc

Deegan (Irish) A black-haired man
Deagan, Degan, Deegen, Deagen, Degen, Deegon, Deagon, Degon

Deinorus (American) A lively man
Denorius, Denorus, Denorios, Deinorius, Deinorios

Dejuan (American) A talkative man
Dejuane, Dewon, Dewonn, Dewan, Dewann, Dwon, Dwonn, Dajuan

Delaney (Irish / French) The dark challenger / from the elder-tree grove
Delany, Delanee, Delanea, Delani, Delanie, Delainey, Delainy, Delaini

Delaware (English) From the state of Delaware
Delawair, Delaweir, Delwayr, Delawayre, Delawaire, Delawaer, Delawaere

Delius (Greek) A man from
Delos
Delios, Delos, Delus, Delo

Dell (English) From the small
valley
Delle, Del

Delmon (English) A man of
the mountain
*Delmun, Delmen, Delmin,
Delmyn, Delmont, Delmonte,
Delmond, Delmonde*

Delsi (American) An easygo-
ing guy
*Delsie, Delsy, Delsey, Delsee,
Delsea, Delci, Delcie, Delcee*

Delvin (English) A godly friend
*Delvinn, Delvinne, Delvyn,
Delvynn, Delvynne, Delven,
Delvenn, Delvenne*

Demarcus (American) The son
of Marcus
*DeMarcus, DaMarkiss,
DeMarco, Demarkess,
DeMarko, Demarkus,
DeMarques, DeMarquez*

Dembe (African) A peaceful
man
*Dembi, Dembie, Dembee,
Dembea, Dembey, Demby*

Denali (American) From the
national park
*Denalie, Denaly, Denaley,
Denalee, Denalea, Denaleigh*

Denley (English) From the
meadow near the valley
*Denly, Denlea, Denleah,
Denlee, Denleigh, Denli, Denlie*

Denman (English) One who
lives in the valley
*Denmann, Denmin, Denmyn,
Denmen, Denmon, Denmun*

Dennis (French) A follower of
Dionysus
*Den, Denies, Denis, Dennes,
Dennet, Denney, Dennie,
Denys, Dennys*

Dennison (English) The son of
Dennis
*Denison, Dennisun, Denisun,
Dennisen, Denisen, Dennisan,
Denisan*

Deo (Greek) A godly man

Deonte (French) An outgoing
man
*Deontay, Deontaye, Deontae,
Dionte, Diontay, Diontaye,
Diontae*

Deotis (American) A learned
man; a scholar
*Deotiss, Deotys, Deotyss,
Deotus, Deotuss*

Derek (English) The ruler of
the tribe
*Dereck, Deric, Derick, Derik,
Deriq, Derk, Derreck, Derrek,
Derrick*

Dervin (English) A gifted friend
Dervinn, Dervinne, Dervyn, Dervynn, Dervynne, Dervon, Dervan, Dervun

Deshan (Hindi) Of the nation
Deshal, Deshad

Desiderio (Latin) One who is desired; hoped for
Derito, Desi, Desideratus, Desiderios, Desiderius, Desiderus, Dezi, Diderot

Desmond (Gaelic) A man from South Munster
Desmonde, Desmund, Desmunde, Dezmond, Dezmonde, Dezmund, Dezmunde, Desmee

Desperado (Spanish) A renegade

Destin (French) Recognizing one's certain fortune; fate
Destyn, Deston, Destun, Desten, Destan

Destrey (American) A cowboy
Destry, Destree, Destrea, Destri, Destrie

Deutsch (German) A German

Devanshi (Hindi) A divine messenger
Devanshie, Devanshy, Devanshey, Devanshee

Devante (Spanish) One who fights wrongdoing

Deverell (French) From the riverbank
Deverel, Deveral, Deverall, Devereau, Devereaux, Devere, Deverill, Deveril

Devlin (Gaelic) Having fierce bravery; a misfortunate man
Devlyn, Devlon, Devlen, Devlan, Devlun

Devon (English) From the beautiful farmland; of the divine
Devan, Deven, Devenn, Devin, Devonn, Devone, Deveon, Devonne

Dewitt (Flemish) A blond-haired man
DeWitt, Dewytt, DeWytt, Dewit, DeWit, Dewyt, DeWyt

Dexter (Latin) A right-handed man; one who is skillful
Dextor, Dextar, Dextur, Dextir, Dextyr, Dexton, Dextun, Dexten

Dhyanesh (Indian) One who meditates
Dhianesh, Dhyaneshe, Dhianeshe

Dice (American) A gambling man
Dyce

Dichali (Native American) One who talks a lot
Dichalie, Dichaly, Dichaley, Dichalee, Dichalea, Dichaleigh

*Diego (Spanish) Form of James, meaning "he who supplants"
Dyego, Dago

Diesel (American) Having great strength
Deisel, Diezel, Deizel, Dezsel

Dietrich (German) The ruler of the tribe
Dedrick

Digby (Norse) From the town near the ditch
Digbey, Digbee, Digbea, Digbi, Digbie

Diji (African) A farmer
Dijie, Dijee, Dijea, Dijy, Dijey

Dillon (Gaelic) Resembling a lion; a faithful man
Dillun, Dillen, Dillan, Dillin, Dillyn, Dilon, Dilan, Dilin

Dino (Italian) One who wields a little sword
Dyno, Dinoh, Dynoh, Deano, Deanoh, Deeno, Deenoh, Deino

Dinos (Greek) Form of Constantine, meaning "one who is steadfast; firm"
Dynos, Deanos, Deenos, Deinos, Dinose, Dinoz

Dins (American) One who climbs to the top
Dinz, Dyns, Dynz

Dionysus (Greek) The god of wine and revelry
Dion, Deion, Deon, Deonn, Deonys, Deyon, Diandre

Dior (French) The golden one
D'Or, Diorr, Diorre, Dyor, Deor, Dyorre, Deorre

Diron (American) Form of Darren, meaning "a great man / a gift from God"
Dirun, Diren, Diran, Dirin, Diryn, Dyron, Dyren

Dixon (English) The son of Dick
Dixen, Dixin, Dixyn, Dixan, Dixun

Doane (English) From the rolling hills
Doan

Dobber (American) An independent man
Dobbar, Dobbor, Dobbur, Dobbir, Dobbyr

Dobbs (English) A fiery man
Dobbes, Dobes, Dobs

Domevlo (African) One who doesn't judge others
Domivlo, Domyvlo

Domingo (Spanish) Born on a Sunday
Domyngo, Demingo, Demyngo

***Dominic** (Latin) A lord
Demenico, Dom, Domenic, Domenico, Domenique, Domini, Dominick, Dominico

Domnall (Gaelic) A world ruler
Domhnall, Domnull, Domhnull

Don (Scottish) Form of Donald, meaning "ruler of the world"
Donn, Donny, Donney, Donnie, Donni, Donnee, Donnea, Donne

Donald (Scottish) Ruler of the world
Don, Donold, Donuld, Doneld, Donild, Donyld

Donato (Italian) A gift from God

Donovan (Irish) A brown-haired chief
Donavan, Donavon, Donevon, Donovyn

Dor (Hebrew) Of this generation
Doram, Doriel, Dorli, Dorlie, Dorlee, Dorlea, Dorleigh, Dorly

Doran (Irish) A stranger; one who has been exiled
Doren, Dorin, Doryn

Dorsey (Gaelic) From the fortress near the sea
Dorsy, Dorsee, Dorsea, Dorsi, Dorsie

Dost (Arabic) A beloved friend
Doste, Daust, Dauste, Dawst, Dawste

Dotson (English) The son of Dot
Dotsen, Dotsan, Dotsin, Dotsyn, Dotsun, Dottson, Dottsun, Dottsin

Dove (American) A peaceful man
Dovi, Dovie, Dovy, Dovey, Dovee, Dovea

Drade (American) A serious-minded man
Draid, Draide, Drayd, Drayde, Draed, Draede, Dradell, Dradel

Drake (English) Resembling a dragon
Drayce, Drago, Drakie

Drew (Welsh) One who is wise
Drue, Dru

Driscoll (Celtic) A mediator; one who is sorrowful; a messenger
Dryscoll, Driscol, Dryscol, Driskoll, Dryskoll, Driskol, Dryskol, Driskell

Druce (Gaelic / English) A wise man; a druid / the son of Drew
Drews, Drewce, Druece, Druse, Druson, Drusen

Drummond (Scottish) One who lives on the ridge
Drummon, Drumond, Drumon, Drummund, Drumund, Drummun

Duane (Gaelic) A dark or swarthy man
Dewain, Dewayne, Duante, Duayne, Duwain, Duwaine, Duwayne, Dwain

Dublin (Irish) From the capital of Ireland
Dublyn, Dublen, Dublan, Dublon, Dublun

Duc (Vietnamese) One who has upstanding morals

Due (Vietnamese) A virtuous man

Duke (English) A title of nobility; a leader
Dooke, Dook, Duki, Dukie, Dukey, Duky, Dukee, Dukea

Dumi (African) One who inspires others
Dumie, Dumy, Dumey, Dumee, Dumea

Dumont (French) Man of the mountain
Dumonte, Dumount, Dumounte

Duncan (Scottish) A dark warrior
Dunkan, Dunckan, Dunc, Dunk, Dunck

Dundee (Scottish) From the town on the Firth of Tay
Dundea, Dundi, Dundie, Dundy, Dundey

Dung (Vietnamese) A brave man; a heroic man

Dunton (English) From the town on the hill
Duntun, Dunten, Duntan, Duntin, Duntyn

Durin (Norse) In mythology, one of the fathers of the dwarves
Duryn, Duren, Duran, Duron, Durun

Durjaya (Hindi) One who is difficult to defeat

Durrell (English) One who is strong and protective
Durrel, Durell, Durel

Dustin (English / German) From the dusty area / a courageous warrior
Dustyn, Dusten, Dustan, Duston, Dustun, Dusty, Dustey, Dusti

Duvall (French) From the valley
Duval, Duvale

Dwade (English) A dark traveler
Dwaid, Dwaide, Dwayd, Dwayde, Dwaed, Dwaede

Dwight (Flemish) A white- or blond-haired man
Dwite, Dwhite, Dwyght, Dwighte

Dyami (Native American) Resembling an eagle
Dyamie, Dyamy, Dyamey, Dyamee, Dyamea, Dyame

Dyer (English) A creative man
Dier, Dyar, Diar, Dy, Dye, Di, Die

*ᵀ**Dylan** (Welsh) Son of the sea
Dyllan, Dylon, Dyllon, Dylen, Dyllen, Dylun, Dyllun, Dylin

Dzigbode (African) One who is patient

E

Eagan (Irish) A fiery man
Eegan, Eagen, Eegen, Eagon, Eegon, Eagun, Eegun

Eagle (Native American) Resembling the bird
Eegle, Eagel, Eegel

Eamon (Irish) Form of Edmund, meaning "a wealthy protector"
Eaman, Eamen, Eamin, Eamyn, Eamun, Eamonn, Eames, Eemon

Ean (Gaelic) Form of John, meaning "God is gracious"
Eion, Eyan, Eyon, Eian

Earl (English) A nobleman
Earle, Erle, Erl, Eorl

Easey (American) An easygoing man
Easy, Easi, Easie, Easee, Easea, Eazey, Eazy, Eazi

Eastman (English) A man from the east
East, Easte, Eeste

^**Easton** (English) Eastern place.
Eastan, Easten, Eastyn

Eckhard (German) Of the brave sword point
Eckard, Eckardt, Eckhardt, Ekkehard, Ekkehardt, Ekhard, Ekhardt

Ed (English) Form of
Edward, meaning "a wealthy
protector"
*Edd, Eddi, Eddie, Eddy, Eddey,
Eddee, Eddea, Edi*

Edan (Celtic) One who is full
of fire
Edon, Edun

Edbert (English) One who is
prosperous and bright
*Edberte, Edburt, Edburte,
Edbirt, Edbirte, Edbyrt, Edbyrte*

Edenson (English) Son of
Eden
*Eadenson, Edensun, Eadensun,
Edinson*

Edgar (English) A powerful
and wealthy spearman
Eadger, Edgardo, Edghur, Edger

Edison (English) Son of
Edward
*Eddison, Edisun, Eddisun,
Edisen, Eddisen, Edisyn,
Eddisyn, Edyson*

Edlin (Anglo-Saxon) A wealthy
friend
*Edlinn, Edlinne, Edlyn, Edlynn,
Edlynne, Eadlyn, Eadlin, Edlen*

Edmund (English) A wealthy
protector
Ed, Eddie, Edmond, Eamon

Edom (Hebrew) A red-haired
man
*Edum, Edam, Edem, Edim,
Edym*

Edred (Anglo-Saxon) A king
Edread, Edrid, Edryd

Edward (English) A wealthy
protector
*Ed, Eadward, Edik, Edouard,
Eduard, Eduardo, Edvard,
Edvardas, Edwardo*

Edwardson (English) The son
of Edward
*Edwardsun, Eadwardsone,
Eadwardsun*

Edwin (English) A wealthy
friend
*Edwinn, Edwinne, Edwine,
Edwyn, Edwynn, Edwynne,
Edwen, Edwenn*

Effiom (African) Resembling a
crocodile
*Efiom, Effyom, Efyom, Effeom,
Efeom*

Efigenio (Greek) Form
of Eugene, meaning "a
well-born man"
*Ephigenio, Ephigenios,
Ephigenius, Efigenios*

Efrain (Spanish) Form of Ephraim, meaning "one who is fertile; productive"
Efraine, Efrayn, Efrayne, Efraen, Efraene, Efrane

Efrat (Hebrew) One who is honored
Efratt, Ephrat, Ephratt

Egesa (Anglo-Saxon) One who creates terror
Egessa, Egeslic, Egeslick, Egeslik

Eghert (German) An intelligent man
Egherte, Eghurt, Eghurte, Eghirt, Eghirte, Eghyrt

Egidio (Italian) Resembling a young goat
Egydio, Egideo, Egydeo, Egidiyo, Egydiyo, Egidius

Eilert (Scandinavian) Of the hard point
Elert, Eilart, Elart, Eilort, Elort, Eilurt, Elurt, Eilirt

Eilon (Hebrew) From the oak tree
Eilan, Eilin, Eilyn, Eilen, Eilun

Einar (Scandinavian) A leading warrior
Einer, Ejnar, Einir, Einyr, Einor, Einur, Ejnir, Ejnyr

Einri (Teutonic) An intelligent man
Einrie, Einry, Einrey, Einree, Einrea

Eisig (Hebrew) One who laughs often
Eisyg

Eladio (Spanish) A man from Greece
Eladeo, Eladiyo, Eladeyo

Elbert (English / German) A well-born man / a bright man
Elberte, Elburt, Elburte, Elbirt, Elbirte, Ethelbert, Ethelburt, Ethelbirt

Eldan (English) From the valley of the elves

Eldon (English) From the sacred hill
Eldun

Eldorado (Spanish) The golden man

Eldred (English) An old, wise advisor
Eldrid, Eldryd, Eldrad, Eldrod, Edlrud, Ethelred

Eldrick (English) An old, wise ruler
Eldrik, Eldric, Eldryck, Eldryk, Eldryc, Eldrich

Eleazar (Hebrew) God will
help
*Elazar, Eleasar, Eliezer,
Elazaro, Eleazaro, Elazer*

*****Eli** (Hebrew) One who has
ascended; my God on High
Ely

Eliachim (Hebrew) God will
establish
*Eliakim, Elyachim, Elyakim,
Eliakym*

Elian (Spanish) A spirited man
*Elyan, Elien, Elyen, Elion,
Elyon, Eliun, Elyun*

Elias (Hebrew) Form of Elijah,
meaning "Jehovah is my god"
Eliyas

Elihu (Hebrew) My God is He
Elyhu, Elihue, Elyhue

*****ᵀElijah** (Hebrew) Jehovah is
my God
*Elija, Eliyahu, Eljah, Elja,
Elyjah, Elyja, Elijuah, Elyjuah*

Elimu (African) Having
knowledge of science
*Elymu, Elimue, Elymue,
Elimoo, Elymoo*

Elisha (Hebrew) God is my
salvation
*Elisee, Eliseo, Elisher, Eliso,
Elisio, Elysha, Elysee, Elyseo*

Elliott (English) Form of
Elijah, meaning "Jehovah is
my God"
Eliot, Eliott, Elliot, Elyot

Ellory (Cornish) Resembling
a swan
*Ellorey, Elloree, Ellorea, Ellori,
Ellorie, Elory, Elorey*

Ellsworth (English) From the
nobleman's estate
*Elsworth, Ellswerth, Elswerth,
Ellswirth, Elswirth, Elzie*

Elman (English) A nobleman
Elmann, Ellman, Ellmann

Elmo (English / Latin) A
protector / an amiable man
Elmoe, Elmow, Elmowe

Elmot (American) A lovable
man
Elmott, Ellmot, Ellmott

Elof (Swedish) The only heir
*Eluf, Eloff, Eluff, Elov, Ellov,
Eluv, Elluv*

Elois (German) A famous
warrior
Eloys, Eloyis, Elouis

Elpidio (Spanish) A fearless
man; having heart
*Elpydio, Elpideo, Elpydeo,
Elpidios, Elpydios, Elpidius*

Elroy (Irish / English) A red-haired young man / a king
Elroi, Elroye, Elric, Elryc, Elrik, Elryk, Elrick, Elryck

Elston (English) From the nobleman's town
Ellston, Elstun, Ellstun, Elson, Ellson, Elsun, Ellsun

Elton (English) From the old town
Ellton, Eltun, Elltun, Elten, Ellten, Eltin, Elltin, Eltyn

Eluwilussit (Native American) A holy man

Elvey (English) An elf warrior
Elvy, Elvee, Elvea, Elvi, Elvie

Elvis (Scandinavian) One who is wise
Elviss, Elvys, Elvyss

Elzie (English) Form of Ellsworth, meaning "from the nobleman's estate"
Elzi, Elzy, Elzey, Elzee, Elzea, Ellzi, Ellzie, Ellzee

Emest (German) One who is serious
Emeste, Emesto, Emestio, Emestiyo, Emesteo, Emesteyo, Emo, Emst

Emil (Latin) One who is eager; an industrious man
Emelen, Emelio, Emile, Emilian, Emiliano, Emilianus, Emilio, Emilion

^**Emiliano** (Spanish) form of Emil, meaning "one who is eager"

Emmanuel (Hebrew) God is with us
Manuel, Manny, Em, Eman, Emmannuel

^**Emmett** (German) A universal man
Emmet, Emmit, Emmitt, Emmot

Emrys (Welsh) An immortal man

Enapay (Native American) A brave man
Enapaye, Enapai, Enapae

Enar (Swedish) A great warrior
Ener, Enir, Enyr, Enor, Enur

Engelbert (German) As bright as an angel
Englebert, Englbert, Engelburt, Engleburt, Englburt, Englebirt, Engelbirt, Englbirt

Enoch (Hebrew) One who is dedicated to God
Enoc, Enok, Enock

Enrique (Spanish) The ruler of the estate
Enrico, Enriko, Enricko, Enriquez, Enrikay, Enreekay, Enrik, Enric

Enyeto (Native American) One who walks like a bear

Enzo (Italian) The ruler of the estate
Enzio, Enzeo, Enziyo, Enzeyo

Eoin Baiste (Irish) Refers to John the Baptist

Ephraim (Hebrew) One who is fertile; productive
Eff, Efraim, Efram, Efrem, Efrain

*Eric (Scandinavian) Ever the ruler
Erek, Erich, Erick, Erik, Eriq, Erix, Errick, Eryk

Ernest (English) One who is sincere and determined; serious
Earnest, Ernesto, Ernestus, Ernst, Erno, Ernie, Erni, Erney

Eron (Spanish) Form of Aaron, meaning "one who is exalted"
Erun, Erin, Eran, Eren, Eryn

Errigal (Gaelic) From the small church
Errigel, Errigol, Errigul, Errigil, Errigyl, Erigal, Erigel, Erigol

Erskine (Gaelic) From the high cliff
Erskin, Erskyne, Erskyn, Erskein, Erskeine, Erskien, Erskiene

Esam (Arabic) A safeguard
Essam

Esben (Scandinavian) Of God
Esbin, Esbyn, Esban, Esbon, Esbun

Esmé (French) One who is esteemed
Esmay, Esmaye, Esmai, Esmae, Esmeling, Esmelyng

Esmun (American) A kind man
Esmon, Esman, Esmen, Esmin, Esmyn

Esperanze (Spanish) Filled with hope
Esperance, Esperence, Esperenze, Esperanzo, Esperenzo

Estcott (English) From the eastern cottage
Estcot

Esteban (Spanish) One who is crowned in victory
Estebon, Estevan, Estevon, Estefan, Estefon, Estebe, Estyban, Estyvan

*ᵀEthan (Hebrew) One who is firm and steadfast
Ethen, Ethin, Ethyn, Ethon, Ethun, Eitan, Etan, Eithan

Ethanael (American) God has given me strength
Ethaniel, Ethaneal, Ethanail, Ethanale

Ethel (Hebrew) One who is noble
Ethal, Etheal

Etlelooaat (Native American) One who shouts

Eudocio (Greek) One who is respected
Eudoceo, Eudociyo, Eudoceyo, Eudoco

*Eugene (Greek) A well-born man
*Eugean, Eugenie, Ugene, Efigenio, Gene, **Owen***

Eulogio (Greek) A reasonable man
Eulogiyo, Eulogo, Eulogeo, Eulogeyo

Euodias (Greek) Having good fortune
Euodeas, Euodyas

Euphemios (Greek) One who is well-spoken
Eufemio, Eufemius, Euphemio, Eufemios, Euphemius, Eufemius

Euphrates (Turkish) From the great river
Eufrates, Euphraites, Eufraites, Euphraytes, Eufraytes

Eusebius (Greek) One who is devout
Esabio, Esavio, Esavius, Esebio, Eusabio, Eusaio, Eusebio, Eusebios

Eustace (Greek) Having an abundance of grapes
Eustache, Eustachios, Eustachius, Eustachy, Eustaquio, Eustashe, Eustasius, Eustatius

*Evan (Welsh) Form of John, meaning "God is gracious"
Evann, Evans, Even, Evin, Evon, Evyn, Evian, Evien

Evander (Greek) A benevolent man
Evandor, Evandar, Evandir, Evandur, Evandyr

^Everett (English) Form of Everhard, meaning "as strong as a bear"

Evett (American) A bright man
Evet, Evatt, Evat, Evitt, Evit, Evytt, Evyt

Eyal (Hebrew) Having great strength

Eze (African) A king

Ezeji (African) The king of yams
Ezejie, Ezejy, Ezejey, Ezejee, Ezejea

Ezekiel (Hebrew) Strengthened by God
Esequiel, Ezechiel, Eziechiele, Eziequel, Ezequiel, Ezekial, Ezekyel, Esquevelle, Zeke

F

Factor (English) A business-man
Facter, Factur, Factir, Factyr, Factar

Fairbairn (Scottish) A fair-haired boy
Fayrbairn, Faerbairn, Fairbaern, Fayrbaern, Faerbaern, Fairbayrn, Fayrbayrn, Faerbayrn

Fairbanks (English) From the bank along the path
Fayrbanks, Faerbanks, Farebanks

Faisal (Arabic) One who is decisive; resolute
Faysal, Faesal, Fasal, Feisal, Faizal, Fasel, Fayzal, Faezal

Fakhir (Arabic) A proud man
Fakheer, Fakhear, Fakheir, Fakhier, Fakhyr, Faakhir, Faakhyr, Fakhr

Fakih (Arabic) A legal expert
Fakeeh, Fakeah, Fakieh, Fakeih, Fakyh

Falco (Latin) Resembling a falcon; one who works with falcons
Falcon, Falconer, Falconner, Falk, Falke, Falken, Falkner, Faulconer

Fam (American) A family-oriented man

Fang (Scottish) From the sheep pen
Faing, Fayng, Faeng

Faraji (African) One who provides consolation
Farajie, Farajy, Farajey, Farajee, Farajea

Fardoragh (Irish) Having dark features

Fargo (American) One who is jaunty
Fargoh, Fargoe, Fargouh

Farha (Arabic) Filled with happiness
Farhah, Farhad, Farhan, Farhat, Farhani, Farhanie, Farhany, Farhaney

Fariq (Arabic) One who holds rank as lieutenant general
Fareeq, Fareaq, Fareiq, Farieq, Faryq, Farik, Fareek, Fareak

Farnell (English) From the fern hill
Farnel, Farnall, Farnal, Fernauld, Farnauld, Fernald, Farnald

Farold (English) A mighty traveler
Farould, Farald, Farauld, Fareld

Farran (Irish / Arabic / English) Of the land / a baker / one who is adventurous
Fairran, Fayrran, Faerran, Farren, Farrin, Farron, Ferrin, Ferron

Farrar (English) A blacksmith
Farar, Farrer, Farrier, Ferrar, Ferrars, Ferrer, Ferrier, Farer

Farro (Italian) Of the grain
Farroe, Faro, Faroe, Farrow, Farow

Fatik (Indian) Resembling a crystal
Fateek, Fateak, Fatyk, Fatiek, Fateik

Faust (Latin) Having good luck
Fauste, Faustino, Fausto, Faustos, Faustus, Fauston, Faustin, Fausten

Fawcett (American) An audacious man
Fawcet, Fawcette, Fawcete, Fawce, Fawci, Fawcie, Fawcy, Fawcey

Fawwaz (Arabic) A successful man
Fawaz, Fawwad, Fawad

Fay (Irish) Resembling a raven
Faye, Fai, Fae, Feich

Februus (Latin) A pagan god

Fedor (Russian) A gift from God
Faydor, Feodor, Fyodor, Fedyenka, Fyodr, Fydor, Fjodor

Feechi (African) One who worships God
Feechie, Feechy, Feechey, Feechee, Feachi, Feachie

Feivel (Hebrew) The brilliant one
Feival, Feivol, Feivil, Feivyl, Feivul, Feiwel, Feiwal, Feiwol

Felim (Gaelic) One who is always good
Felym, Feidhlim, Felimy, Felimey, Felimee, Felimea, Felimi, Felimie

Felipe (Spanish) Form of Phillip, meaning "one who loves horses"
Felippe, Filip, Filippo, Fillip, Flip, Fulop, Fullop, Fulip

Felix (Latin) One who is happy and prosperous

Felton (English) From the town near the field
Feltun, Felten, Feltan, Feltyn, Feltin

Fenn (English) From the marsh
Fen

Ferdinand (German) A courageous voyager
Ferdie, Ferdinando, Fernando

Fergus (Gaelic) The first and supreme choice
Fearghas, Fearghus, Feargus, Fergie, Ferguson, Fergusson, Furgus, Fergy

Ferrell (Irish) A brave man; a hero
Ferell, Ferel, Ferrel

Fiacre (Celtic) Resembling a raven
Fyacre, Fiacra, Fyacra, Fiachra, Fyachra, Fiachre, Fyachre

Fielding (English) From the field
Fieldyng, Fielder, Field, Fielde, Felding, Feldyng, Fields

Fiero (Spanish) A fiery man
Fyero

Finbar (Irish) A fair-haired man
Finnbar, Finnbarr, Fionn, Fionnbharr, Fionnbar, Fionnbarr, Fynbar, Fynnbar

Finch (English) Resembling the small bird
Fynch, Finche, Fynche, Finchi, Finchie, Finchy, Finchey, Finchee

Fineas (Egyptian) A dark-skinned man
Fyneas, Finius, Fynius

Finian (Irish) A handsome man; fair
Finan, Finnian, Fionan, Finien, Finnien, Finghin, Finneen, Fineen

Finn (Gaelic) A fair-haired man
Fin, Fynn, Fyn, Fingal, Fingall

Finnegan (Irish) A fair-haired man
Finegan, Finnegen, Finegen, Finnigan, Finigan

Finnley (Gaelic) A fair-haired hero
Findlay, Findley, Finly, Finlay, Finlee, Finnly, Finnley

Fiorello (Italian) Resembling a little flower
Fiorelo, Fiorelio, Fioreleo, Fiorellio, Fiorelleo

Fisher (English) A fisherman
Fischer, Fysher

Fitch (English) Resembling an
ermine
*Fytch, Fich, Fych, Fitche,
Fytche*

Fitzgerald (English) The son of
Gerald
Fytzgerald

Flann (Irish) One who has a
ruddy complexion
*Flan, Flainn, Flannan,
Flannery, Flanneri, Flannerie,
Flannerey*

Fletcher (English) One who
makes arrows
Fletch, Fletche, Flecher

Flynn (Irish) One who has a
ruddy complexion
*Flyn, Flinn, Flin, Flen, Flenn,
Floinn*

Fogarty (Irish) One who has
been exiled
*Fogartey, Fogartee, Fogartea,
Fogarti, Fogartie, Fogerty,
Fogertey, Fogerti*

Foley (English) A creative man
Foly, Folee, Foli, Folie

Folker (German) A guardian of
the people
*Folkar, Folkor, Folkur, Folkir,
Folkyr, Folke, Folko, Folkus*

Fonso (German) Form of
Alfonso, meaning "prepared
for battle; eager and ready"
*Fonzo, Fonsie, Fonzell, Fonzie,
Fonsi, Fonsy, Fonsey, Fonsee*

Fontaine (French) From the
water source
*Fontayne, Fontaene, Fontane,
Fonteyne, Fontana, Fountain*

Ford (English) From the river
crossing
*Forde, Forden, Fordan, Fordon,
Fordun, Fordin, Fordyn, Forday*

Fouad (Arabic) One who
has heart
Fuad

Francisco (Spanish) A man
from France
*Francesco, Franchesco,
Fransisco*

Frank (Latin) Form of Francis,
meaning "a man from
France; one who is free."
Franco, Frankie

Fred (German) Form of
Frederick, meaning "a
peaceful ruler"
*Freddi, Freddie, Freddy,
Freddey, Freddee, Freddea,
Freddis, Fredis*

Frederick (German) A peaceful ruler
Fred, Fredrick, Federico, Federigo, Fredek, Frederic, Frederich, Frederico, Frederik, Fredric

Freeborn (English) One who was born a free man
Freeborne, Freebourn, Freebourne, Freeburn, Freeburne, Free

Fremont (French) The protector of freedom
Freemont, Fremonte

Frigyes (Hungarian) A mighty and peaceful ruler

Frode (Norse) A wise man
Froad, Froade

Froyim (Hebrew) A kind man
Froiim

Fructuoso (Spanish) One who is fruitful
Fructo, Fructoso, Fructuso

Fu (Chinese) A wealthy man

Fudail (Arabic) Of high moral character
Fudaile, Fudayl, Fudayle, Fudale, Fudael, Fudaele

Fulbright (English) A brilliant man
Fullbright, Fulbrite, Fullbrite, Fulbryte, Fullbryte, Fulbert, Fullbert

Fulki (Indian) A spark
Fulkie, Fulkey, Fulky, Fulkee, Fulkea

Fullerton (English) From Fuller's town
Fullertun, Fullertin, Fullertyn, Fullertan, Fullerten

Fursey (Gaelic) The name of a missionary saint
Fursy, Fursi, Fursie, Fursee, Fursea

Fyfe (Scottish) A man from Fifeshire
Fife, Fyffe, Fiffe, Fibh

Fyren (Anglo-Saxon) A wicked man
Fyrin, Fyryn, Fyran, Fyron, Fyrun

G

Gabai (Hebrew) A delightful man

Gabbana (Italian) A creative man
Gabbanah, Gabana, Gabanah, Gabbanna, Gabanna

Gabbo (English) To joke or
scoff
Gabboe, Gabbow, Gabbowe

Gabor (Hebrew) God is my
strength
*Gabur, Gabar, Gaber, Gabir,
Gabyr*

Gabra (African) An offering
Gabre

*ᵀ**Gabriel** (Hebrew) A hero of
God
*Gabrian, Gabriele, Gabrielli,
Gabriello, Gaby, Gab, Gabbi,
Gabbie*

Gad (Hebrew / Native
American) Having good for-
tune / from the juniper tree
*Gadi, Gadie, Gady, Gadey,
Gadee, Gadea*

Gadiel (Arabic) God is my
fortune
*Gadiell, Gadiele, Gadielle,
Gaddiel, Gaddiell, Gadil,
Gadeel, Gadeal*

Gaffney (Irish) Resembling a
calf
*Gaffny, Gaffni, Gaffnie,
Gaffnee, Gaffnea*

Gage (French) Of the pledge
Gaige, Gaege, Gauge

Gahuj (African) A hunter

Gair (Gaelic) A man of short
stature
*Gayr, Gaer, Gaire, Gayre,
Gaere, Gare*

Gaius (Latin) One who rejoices
Gaeus

Galal (Arabic) A majestic man
Galall, Gallal, Gallall

Galbraith (Irish) A foreigner;
a Scot
*Galbrait, Galbreath, Gallbraith,
Gallbreath, Galbraithe,
Gallbraithe, Galbreathe,
Gallbreathe*

Gale (Irish / English) A for-
eigner / one who is cheerful
*Gail, Gaill, Gaille, Gaile, Gayl,
Gayle, Gaylle, Gayll*

Galen (Greek) A healer; one
who is calm
*Gaelan, Gaillen, Galan,
Galin, Galyn, Gaylen, Gaylin,
Gaylinn*

Gali (Hebrew) From the foun-
tain
*Galie, Galy, Galey, Galee,
Galea, Galeigh*

Galip (Turkish) A victorious
man
*Galyp, Galup, Galep, Galap,
Galop*

Gallagher (Gaelic) An eager
helper
*Gallaghor, Gallaghar,
Gallaghur, Gallaghir, Gallaghyr,
Gallager, Gallagar, Gallagor*

Galt (English) From the high,
wooded land
Galte, Gallt, Gallte

Galtero (Spanish) Form
of Walter, meaning "the
commander of the army"
*Galterio, Galteriyo, Galtereo,
Galtereyo, Galter, Galteros,
Galterus, Gualterio*

Gamaliel (Hebrew) God's
reward
*Gamliel, Gamalyel, Gamlyel,
Gamli, Gamlie, Gamly,
Gamley, Gamlee*

Gameel (Arabic) A handsome
man
*Gameal, Gamil, Gamiel,
Gameil, Gamyl*

Gamon (American) One who
enjoys playing games
*Gamun, Gamen, Gaman,
Gamin, Gamyn, Gammon,
Gammun, Gamman*

Gan (Chinese) A wanderer

Gandy (American) An
adventurer
*Gandey, Gandi, Gandie,
Gandee, Gandea*

Gann (English) One who
defends with a spear
Gan

Gannon (Gaelic) A fair-
skinned man
*Gannun, Gannen, Gannan,
Gannin, Gannyn, Ganon,
Ganun, Ganin*

Garcia (Spanish) One who is
brave in battle
*Garce, Garcy, Garcey, Garci,
Garcie, Garcee, Garcea*

Gared (English) Form of
Gerard, meaning "one who is
mighty with a spear"
*Garad, Garid, Garyd, Garod,
Garud*

Garman (English) A spearman
*Garmann, Garmen, Garmin,
Garmon, Garmun, Garmyn,
Gar, Garr*

Garrett (English) Form of
Gerard, meaning "one who is
mighty with a spear"
*Garett, Garret, Garretson, Garritt,
Garrot, Garrott, Gerrit, Gerritt*

Garrison (French) Prepared
Garris, Garrish, Garry, Gary

Garson (English) The son of
Gar (Garrett, Garrison, etc.)
*Garrson, Garsen, Garrsen,
Garsun, Garrsun, Garsone,
Garrsone*

Garth (Scandinavian) The keeper of the garden
Garthe, Gart, Garte

Garvey (Gaelic) A rough but peaceful man
Garvy, Garvee, Garvea, Garvi, Garvie, Garrvey, Garrvy, Garrvee

Garvin (English) A friend with a spear
Garvyn, Garven, Garvan, Garvon, Garvun

Gary (English) One who wields a spear
Garey, Gari, Garie, Garea, Garee, Garry, Garrey, Garree

Gassur (Arabic) A courageous man
Gassor, Gassir, Gassyr, Gassar, Gasser

Gaston (French) A man from Gascony
Gastun, Gastan, Gasten, Gascon, Gascone, Gasconey, Gasconi, Gasconie

Gate (American) One who is close-minded
Gates, Gait, Gaite, Gaits

*Gavin (Welsh) A little white falcon
Gavan, Gaven, Gavino, Gavyn, Gavynn, Gavon, Gavun, Gavyno

Gazali (African) A mystic
Gazalie, Gazaly, Gazaley, Gazalee, Gazalea, Gazaleigh

Geirleif (Norse) A descendant of the spear
Geirleaf, Geerleif, Geerleaf

Geirstein (Norse) One who wields a rock-hard spear
Geerstein, Gerstein

Gellert (Hungarian) A mighty soldier
Gellart, Gellirt, Gellyrt, Gellort, Gellurt

Genaro (Latin) A dedicated man
Genaroh, Genaroe, Genarow, Genarowe

Gene (English) Form of Eugene, meaning "a well-born man"
Genio, Geno, Geneo, Gino, Ginio, Gineo

Genet (African) From Eden
Genat, Genit, Genyt, Genot, Genut

Genoah (Italian) From the city of Genoa
Genoa, Genovise, Genovize

Geoffrey (English) Form of Jeffrey, meaning "a man of peace"
Geffrey, Geoff, Geoffery, Geoffroy, Geoffry, Geofrey, Geofferi, Geofferie

George (Greek) One who works the earth; a farmer
Georas, Geordi, Geordie, Georg, Georges, Georgi, Georgie, Georgio, Yegor, Jurgen, Joren

Gerald (German) One who rules with the spear
Jerald, Garald, Garold, Gearalt, Geralde, Geraldo, Geraud, Gere, Gerek

Gerard (French) One who is mighty with a spear
Gerord, Gerrard, Gared, Garrett

Geremia (Italian) Form of Jeremiah, meaning "one who is exalted by the Lord"
Geremiah, Geremias, Geremija, Geremiya, Geremyah, Geramiah, Geramia

Germain (French / Latin) A man from Germany / one who is brotherly
Germaine, German, Germane, Germanicus, Germano, Germanus, Germayn, Germayne

Gerry (German) Short form of names beginning with Ger-, such as Gerald or Gerard
Gerrey, Gerri, Gerrie, Gerrea, Gerree

Gershom (Hebrew) One who has been exiled
Gersham, Gershon, Gershoom, Gershem, Gershim, Gershym, Gershum, Gersh

Getachew (African) Their master

Ghazi (Arabic) An invader; a conqueror
Ghazie, Ghazy, Ghazey, Ghazee, Ghazea

Ghoukas (Armenian) Form of Lucas, meaning "a man from Lucania"
Ghukas

Giancarlo (Italian) One who is gracious and mighty
Gyancarlo

Gideon (Hebrew) A mighty warrior; one who fells trees
Gideone, Gidi, Gidon, Gidion, Gid, Gidie, Gidy, Gidey

Gilam (Hebrew) The joy of the people
Gylam, Gilem, Gylem, Gilim, Gylim, Gilym, Gylym, Gilom

Gilbert (French / English) Of the bright promise / one who is trustworthy
Gib, Gibb, Gil, Gilberto, Gilburt, Giselbert, Giselberto, Giselbertus

Gildas (Irish / English) One who serves God / the golden one
Gyldas, Gilda, Gylda, Gilde, Gylde, Gildea, Gyldea, Gildes

Giles (Greek) Resembling a young goat
Gyles, Gile, Gil, Gilles, Gillis, Gilliss, Gyle, Gyl

Gill (Gaelic) A servant
Gyll, Gilly, Gilley, Gillee, Gillea, Gilli, Gillie, Ghill

Gillivray (Scottish) A servant of God
Gillivraye, Gillivrae, Gillivrai

Gilmat (Scottish) One who wields a sword
Gylmat, Gilmet, Gylmet

Gilmer (English) A famous hostage
Gilmar, Gilmor, Gilmur, Gilmir, Gilmyr, Gillmer, Gillmar, Gillmor

Gilon (Hebrew) Filled with joy
Gilun, Gilen, Gilan, Gilin, Gilyn, Gilo

Ginton (Arabic) From the garden
Gintun, Gintan, Ginten, Gintin, Gintyn

Giovanni (Italian) Form of John, meaning "God is gracious"
Geovani, Geovanney, Geovanni, Geovanny, Geovany, Giannino, Giovan, Giovani, Yovanny

Giri (Indian) From the mountain
Girie, Giry, Girey, Giree, Girea

Girvan (Gaelic) The small rough one
Gyrvan, Girven, Gyrven, Girvin, Gyrvin, Girvyn, Gyrvyn, Girvon

Giulio (Italian) One who is youthful
Giuliano, Giuleo

Giuseppe (Italian) Form of Joseph, meaning "God will add"
Giuseppi, Giuseppie, Giuseppy, Giuseppee, Giuseppea, Giuseppey, Guiseppe, Guiseppi

Gizmo (American) One who is playful
Gismo, Gyzmo, Gysmo, Gizmoe, Gismoe, Gyzmoe, Gysmoe

Glade (English) From the clearing in the woods
Glayd, Glayde, Glaid, Glaide, Glaed, Glaede

Glaisne (Irish) One who is calm; serene
Glaisny, Glaisney, Glaisni, Glaisnie, Glaisnee, Glasny, Glasney, Glasni

Glasgow (Scottish) From the city in Scotland
Glasgo

Glen (Gaelic) From the secluded narrow valley
Glenn, Glennard, Glennie, Glennon, Glenny, Glin, Glinn, Glyn

Glover (English) One who makes gloves
Glovar, Glovir, Glovyr, Glovur, Glovor

Gobind (Sanskrit) The cow finder
Gobinde, Gobinda, Govind, Govinda, Govinde

Goby (American) An audacious man
Gobi, Gobie, Gobey, Gobee, Gobea

Godfrey (German) God is peace
Giotto, Godefroi, Godfry, Godofredo, Goffredo, Gottfrid, Gottfried, Godfried

Godfried (German) God is peace
Godfreed, Gjord

Gogo (African) A grandfatherly man

Goldwin (English) A golden friend
Goldwine, Goldwinn, Goldwinne, Goldwen, Goldwenn, Goldwenne, Goldwyn, Goldwynn

Goode (English) An upstanding man
Good, Goodi, Goodie, Goody, Goodey, Goodee, Goodea

Gordon (Gaelic) From the great hill; a hero
Gorden, Gordin, Gordyn, Gordun, Gordan, Gordi, Gordie, Gordee

Gormley (Irish) The blue spearman
Gormly, Gormlee, Gormlea, Gormleah, Gormleigh, Gormli, Gormlie, Gormaly

Goro (Japanese) The fifth-born child

Gotzon (Basque) A heavenly messenger; an angel

Gower (Welsh) One who is pure; chaste
Gwyr, Gowyr, Gowir, Gowar, Gowor, Gowur

Gozal (Hebrew) Resembling a baby bird
Gozall, Gozel, Gozell, Gozale, Gozele

Grady (Gaelic) One who is famous; noble
Gradey, Gradee, Gradea, Gradi, Gradie, Graidy, Graidey, Graidee

Graham (English) From the gravelled area; from the gray home
Graem

Grand (English) A superior man
Grande, Grandy, Grandey, Grandi, Grandie, Grandee, Grandea, Grander

Granger (English) A farmer
Grainger, Graynger, Graenger, Grange, Graynge, Graenge, Grainge, Grangere

Grant (English) A tall man; a great man
Grante, Graent

Granville (French) From the large village
Granvylle, Granvil, Granvyl, Granvill, Granvyll, Granvile, Granvyle, Grenvill

Gray (English) A gray-haired man
Graye, Grai, Grae, Greye, Grey, Graylon, Graylen, Graylin

Grayson (English) The son of a gray-haired man
Graysen, Graysun, Graysin, Greyson, Graysan, Graison, Graisun, Graisen

Greenwood (English) From the green forest
Greenwode

Gregory (Greek) One who is vigilant; watchful
Greg, Greggory, Greggy, Gregori, Gregorie, Gregry, Grigori

Gremian (Anglo-Saxon) One who enrages others
Gremien, Gremean, Gremyan

Gridley (English) From the flat meadow
Gridly, Gridlee, Gridlea, Gridleah, Gridleigh, Gridli, Gridlie

Griffin (Latin) Having a hooked nose
Griff, Griffen, Griffon, Gryffen, Gryffin, Gryphen

Griffith (Welsh) A mighty chief
Griffyth, Gryffith, Gryffyth

Grimsley (English) From the dark meadow
Grimsly, Grimslee, Grimslea, Grimsleah, Grimsleigh, Grimsli, Grimslie

Griswold (German) From the gray forest
Griswald, Gryswold, Gryswald, Greswold, Greswald

Guban (African) One who has been burnt
Guben, Gubin, Gubyn, Gubon, Gubun

Guedado (African) One who is unwanted

Guerdon (English) A warring man
Guerdun, Guerdan, Guerden, Guerdin, Guerdyn

Guido (Italian) One who acts as a guide
Guidoh, Gwedo, Gwido, Gwydo, Gweedo

Guillaume (French) Form of William, meaning "the determined protector"
Gillermo, Guglielmo, Guilherme, Guillermo, Gwillyn, Gwilym, Guglilmo

Gulshan (Hindi) From the gardens

^**Gunner** (Scandinavian) A bold warrior
Gunnar, Gunnor, Gunnur, Gunnir, Gunnyr

Gunnolf (Norse) A warrior wolf
Gunolf, Gunnulf, Gunulf

Gur (Hebrew) Resembling a lion cub
Guryon, Gurion, Guriel, Guriell, Guryel, Guryell, Guri, Gurie

Gurpreet (Indian) A devoted follower
Gurpreat, Gurpriet, Gurpreit, Gurprit, Gurpryt

Guru (Indian) A teacher; a religious head

Gurutz (Basque) Of the holy cross
Guruts

Gus (German) A respected man; one who is exalted
Guss

Gustav (Scandinavian) Of the staff of the gods
Gus, Gustave, Gussie, Gustaf, Gustof, Tavin

Gusty (American) Of the wind; a revered man
Gustey, Gustee, Gustea, Gusti, Gustie, Gusto

Guwayne (American) Form of Wayne, meaning "one who builds wagons"
Guwayn, Guwain, Guwaine, Guwaen, Guwaene, Guwane

Gwalchmai (Welsh) A battle hawk

Gwandoya (African) Suffering a miserable fate

Gwydion (Welsh) In mythology, a magician
Gwydeon, Gwydionne, Gwydeonne

Gylfi (Scandinavian) A king
Gylfie, Gylfee, Gylfea, Gylfi, Gylfie, Gylphi, Gylphie, Gylphey

Gypsy (English) A wanderer; a nomad
Gipsee, Gipsey, Gipsy, Gypsi, Gypsie, Gypsey, Gypsee, Gipsi

Habimama (African) One who believes in God
Habymama

Hadden (English) From the heather-covered hill
Haddan, Haddon, Haddin, Haddyn, Haddun

Hadriel (Hebrew) The splendor of God
Hadryel, Hadriell, Hadryell

Hadwin (English) A friend in war
Hadwinn, Hadwinne, Hadwen, Hadwenn, Hadwenne, Hadwyn, Hadwynn, Hadwynne

Hafiz (Arabic) A protector
Haafiz, Hafeez, Hafeaz, Hafiez, Hafeiz, Hafyz, Haphiz, Haaphiz

Hagar (Hebrew) A wanderer

Hagen (Gaelic) One who is youthful
Haggen, Hagan, Haggan, Hagin, Haggin, Hagyn, Haggyn, Hagon

Hagop (Armenian) Form of James, meaning "he who supplants"
Hagup, Hagap, Hagep, Hagip, Hagyp

Hagos (African) Filled with happiness

Hahnee (Native American) A beggar
Hahnea, Hahni, Hahnie, Hahny, Hahney

Haim (Hebrew) A giver of life
Hayim, Hayyim

Haines (English) From the vined cottage; from the hedged enclosure
Haynes, Haenes, Hanes, Haine, Hayne, Haene, Hane

Hajari (African) One who takes flight
Hajarie, Hajary, Hajarey, Hajaree, Hajarea

Haji (African) Born during the hajj
Hajie, Hajy, Hajey, Hajee, Hajea

Hakan (Norse / Native American) One who is noble / a fiery man

Hakim (Arabic) One who is wise; intelligent
Hakeem, Hakeam, Hakeim, Hakiem, Hakym

Hal (English) A form of Henry, meaning "the ruler of the house"; a form of Harold, meaning "the ruler of an army"

Halford (English) From the hall by the ford
Hallford, Halfurd, Hallfurd, Halferd, Hallferd

Halil (Turkish) A beloved friend
Haleel, Haleal, Haleil, Haliel, Halyl

Halla (African) An unexpected gift
Hallah, Hala, Halah

Hallberg (Norse) From the rocky mountain
Halberg, Hallburg, Halburg

Halle (Norse) As solid as a rock

Halley (English) From the hall near the meadow
Hally, Halli, Hallie, Halleigh, Hallee, Halleah, Hallea

Halliwell (English) From the holy spring
Haligwell

Hallward (English) The guardian of the hall
Halward, Hallwerd, Halwerd, Hallwarden, Halwarden, Hawarden, Haward, Hawerd

Hamid (Arabic / Indian) A praiseworthy man / a beloved friend
Hameed, Hamead, Hameid, Hamied, Hamyd, Haamid

Hamidi (Swahili) One who is commendable
Hamidie, Hamidy, Hamidey, Hamidee, Hamidea, Hamydi, Hamydie, Hamydee

Hamilton (English) From the flat-topped hill
Hamylton, Hamiltun, Hamyltun, Hamilten, Hamylten, Hamelton, Hameltun, Hamelten

Hamlet (German) From the little home
Hamlett, Hammet, Hammett, Hamnet, Hamnett, Hamlit, Hamlitt, Hamoelet

Hammer (German) One who makes hammers; a carpenter
Hammar, Hammor, Hammur, Hammir, Hammyr

Hampden (English) From the home in the valley
Hampdon, Hampdan, Hampdun, Hampdyn, Hampdin

Hancock (English) One who owns a farm
Hancok, Hancoc

Hanford (English) From the high ford
Hanferd, Hanfurd, Hanforde, Hanferde, Hanfurde

Hanisi (Swahili) Born on a Thursday
Hanisie, Hanisy, Hanisey, Hanisee, Hanisea, Hanysi, Hanysie, Hanysy

Hank (English) Form of Henry, meaning "the ruler of the house"
Hanke, Hanks, Hanki, Hankie, Hankee, Hankea, Hanky, Hankey

Hanley (English) From the high meadow
Hanly, Hanleigh, Hanleah, Hanlea, Hanlie, Hanli

Hanoch (Hebrew) One who is dedicated
Hanock, Hanok, Hanoc

Hanraoi (Irish) Form of Henry, meaning "the ruler of the house"

Hansraj (Hindi) The swan king

Hardik (Indian) One who has heart
Hardyk, Hardick, Hardyck, Hardic, Hardyc

Hare (English) Resembling a rabbit

Harence (English) One who is swift
Harince, Harense, Harinse

Hari (Indian) Resembling a lion
Harie, Hary, Harey, Haree, Harea

Harim (Arabic) A superior man
Hareem, Haream, Hariem, Hareim, Harym

Harkin (Irish) Having dark red hair
Harkyn, Harken, Harkan, Harkon, Harkun

Harlemm (American) A soulful man
Harlam, Harlom, Harlim, Harlym, Harlem

Harlow (English) From the army on the hill
Harlowe, Harlo, Harloe

Harold (Scandinavian) The ruler of an army
Hal, Harald, Hareld, Harry, Darold

Harper (English) One who plays or makes harps
Harpur, Harpar, Harpir, Harpyr, Harpor, Hearpere

Harrington (English) From Harry's town; from the herring town
Harringtun, Harryngton, Harryngtun, Harington, Haringtun, Haryngton, Haryntun

Harrison (English) The son of Harry
Harrisson, Harris, Harriss, Harryson

Harshad (Indian) A bringer of joy
Harsh, Harshe, Harsho, Harshil, Harshyl, Harshit, Harshyt

Hartford (English) From the stag's ford
Harteford, Hartferd, Harteferd, Hartfurd, Hartefurd, Hartforde, Harteforde, Hartferde

Haru (Japanese) Born during the spring

Harvey (English / French) One who is ready for battle / a strong man
Harvy, Harvi, Harvie, Harvee, Harvea, Harv, Harve, Hervey

Hasim (Arabic) One who is decisive
Haseem, Haseam, Hasiem, Haseim, Hasym

Haskel (Hebrew) An intelligent man
Haskle, Haskell, Haskil, Haskill, Haske, Hask

Hasso (German) Of the sun
Hassoe, Hassow, Hassowe

Hassun (Native American) As solid as a stone

Hastiin (Native American) A man

Hastin (Hindi) Resembling an elephant
Hasteen, Hastean, Hastien, Hastein, Hastyn

Hawes (English) From the hedged place
Haws, Hayes, Hays, Hazin, Hazen, Hazyn, Hazon, Hazan

Hawiovi (Native American) One who descends on a ladder
Hawiovie, Hawiovy, Hawiovey, Hawiovee, Hawiovea

Hawkins (English) Resembling a small hawk
Haukins, Hawkyns, Haukyn

Hawthorne (English) From the hawthorn tree
Hawthorn

*☆ᵀ**Hayden** (English) From the hedged valley
Haydan, Haydon, Haydun, Haydin, Haydyn, Haden, Hadan, Hadon

Haye (Scottish) From the stockade
Hay, Hae, Hai

Hazaiah (Hebrew) God will decide
Hazaia, Haziah, Hazia

Hazleton (English) From the hazel-tree town
Hazelton, Hazletun, Hazelton, Hazleten, Hazelten

Heath (English) From the untended land of flowering shrubs
Heathe, Heeth, Heethe

Heaton (English) From the town on high ground
Heatun, Heeton, Heetun, Heaten, Heeten

Heber (Hebrew) A partner or companion
Heeber, Hebar, Heebar, Hebor, Heebor, Hebur, Heebur, Hebir

Hector (Greek) One who is steadfast; in mythology, the prince of Troy
Hecter, Hekter, Heckter

Helio (Greek) Son of the sun
Heleo, Helios, Heleos

Hem (Indian) The golden son

Hemendu (Indian) Born beneath the golden moon
Hemendue, Hemendoo

Hemi (Maori) Form of James, meaning "he who supplants"
Hemie, Hemy, Hemee, Hemea, Hemey

Henderson (Scottish) The son of Henry
Hendrie, Hendries, Hendron, Hendri, Hendry, Hendrey, Hendree, Hendrea

Hendrick (English) Form of Henry, meaning "the ruler of the house"
Hendryck, Hendrik, Hendryk, Hendric, Hendryc

Henley (English) From the high meadow
Henly, Henleigh, Henlea, Henleah, Henlee, Henli, Henlie

*Henry (German) The ruler of the house
Hal, Hank, Harry, Henny, Henree, Henri, Hanraoi, Hendrick

Heraldo (Spanish) Of the divine

Hercules (Greek) In mythology, a son of Zeus who possessed superhuman strength
Herakles, Hercule, Herculi, Herculie, Herculy, Herculey, Herculee

Herman (German) A soldier
Hermon, Hermen, Hermun, Hermin, Hermyn, Hermann, Hermie

Herne (English) Resembling a heron
Hern, Hearn, Hearne

Hero (Greek) The brave defender
Heroe, Herow, Herowe

Hershel (Hebrew) Resembling a deer
Hersch, Herschel, Herschell, Hersh, Hertzel, Herzel, Herzl, Heschel

Herwin (Teutonic) A friend of war
Herwinn, Herwinne, Herwen, Herwenn, Herwenne, Herwyn, Herwynn, Herwynne

Hesed (Hebrew) A kind man

Hesutu (Native American) A rising yellow-jacket nest
Hesutou, Hesoutou

Hewson (English) The son of Hugh
Hewsun

Hiawatha (Native American)
He who makes rivers
*Hiawathah, Hyawatha,
Hiwatha, Hywatha*

Hickok (American) A famous
frontier marshal
*Hickock, Hickoc, Hikock,
Hikoc, Hikok, Hyckok,
Hyckock, Hyckoc*

Hidalgo (Spanish) The noble
one
Hydalgo

Hideaki (Japanese) A clever
man; having wisdom
*Hideakie, Hideaky, Hideakey,
Hideakee, Hideakea*

Hieronim (Polish) Form of
Jerome, meaning "of the
sacred name"
*Hieronym, Hieronymos,
Hieronimos, Heronim,
Heronym, Heronymos,
Heronimos*

Hietamaki (Finnish) From the
sand hill
*Hietamakie, Hietamaky,
Hietamakey, Hietamakee,
Hietamakea*

Hieu (Vietnamese) A pious
man

Hikmat (Islamic) Filled with
wisdom
Hykmat

Hildefuns (German) One who
is ready for battle
Hildfuns, Hyldefuns, Hyldfuns

Hillel (Hebrew) One who is
praised
*Hyllel, Hillell, Hyllell, Hilel,
Hylel, Hilell, Hylell*

Hiranmay (Indian) The golden
one
*Hiranmaye, Hiranmai,
Hiranmae, Hyranmay,
Hyranmaye, Hyranmai,
Hyranmae*

Hiroshi (Japanese) A generous
man
*Hiroshie, Hiroshy, Hiroshey,
Hiroshee, Hiroshea, Hyroshi,
Hyroshie, Hyroshey*

Hirsi (African) An amulet
*Hirsie, Hirsy, Hirsey, Hirsee,
Hirsea*

Hisoka (Japanese) One who is
secretive
*Hysoka, Hisokie, Hysokie,
Hisoki, Hysoki, Hisokey,
Hysokey, Hisoky*

Hitakar (Indian) One who
wishes others well
Hitakarin, Hitakrit

Hobart (American) Form of Hubert, meaning "having a shining intellect"
Hobarte, Hoebart, Hoebarte, Hobert, Hoberte, Hoburt, Hoburte, Hobirt

Hohberht (German) One who is high and bright
Hohbert, Hohburt, Hohbirt, Hohbyrt, Hoh

Holcomb (English) From the deep valley
Holcom, Holcombe

Holden (English) From a hollow in the valley
Holdan, Holdyn, Holdon

Holland (American) From the Netherlands
Hollend, Hollind, Hollynd, Hollande, Hollende, Hollinde, Hollynde

Hollis (English) From the holly tree
Hollys, Holliss, Hollyss, Hollace, Hollice, Holli, Hollie, Holly

Holman (English) A man from the valley
Holmann, Holmen, Holmin, Holmyn, Holmon, Holmun

Holt (English) From the forest
Holte, Holyt, Holyte, Holter, Holtar, Holtor, Holtur, Holtir

Honaw (Native American) Resembling a bear
Honawe, Honau

Hondo (African) A warring man
Hondoh, Honda, Hondah

Honesto (Spanish) One who is honest
Honestio, Honestiyo, Honesteo, Honesteyo, Honestoh

Honon (Native American) Resembling a bear
Honun, Honen, Honan, Honin, Honyn

Honovi (Native American) Having great strength
Honovie, Honovy, Honovey, Honovee, Honovea

Honza (Czech) A gift from God

Horsley (English) From the horse meadow
Horsly, Horslea, Horsleah, Horslee, Horsleigh, Horsli, Horslie

Horst (German) From the thicket
Horste, Horsten, Horstan, Horstin, Horstyn, Horston, Horstun, Horstman

Hoshi (Japanese) Resembling a star
Hoshiko, Hoshyko, Hoshie, Hoshee, Hoshea, Hoshy, Hoshey

Hototo (Native American) One who whistles; a warrior spirit that sings

Houston (Gaelic/English) From Hugh's town, from the town on the hill
Huston, Houstyn, Hustin, Husten, Hustin, Houstun

Howard (English) The guardian of the home
Howerd, Howord, Howurd, Howird, Howyrd, Howi, Howie, Howy

Howi (Native American) Resembling a turtle dove

Hrothgar (Anglo-Saxon) A king
Hrothgarr, Hrothegar, Hrothegarr, Hrothgare, Hrothegare

Hubert (German) Having a shining intellect
Hobart, Huberte, Huburt, Huburte, Hubirt, Hubirte, Hubyrt, Hubyrte, Hubie, Uberto

Hudson (English) The son of Hugh; from the river
Hudsun, Hudsen, Hudsan, Hudsin, Hudsyn

Hugin (Norse) A thoughtful man
Hugyn, Hugen, Hugan, Hugon, Hugun

Humam (Arabic) A generous and brave man

Hungan (Haitian) A spirit master or priest
Hungen, Hungon, Hungun, Hungin, Hungyn

Hungas (Irish) A vigorous man

T*Hunter** (English) A great huntsman and provider
Huntar, Huntor, Huntur, Huntir, Huntyr, Hunte, Hunt, Hunting

Husky (American) A big man; a manly man
Huski, Huskie, Huskey, Huskee, Huskea, Husk, Huske

Huslu (Native American) Resembling a hairy bear
Huslue, Huslou

Husto (Spanish) A righteous man
Hustio, Husteo, Hustiyo, Husteyo

Huynh (Vietnamese) An older brother

I

Iakovos (Hebrew) Form of Jacob, meaning "he who supplants"
Iakovus, Iakoves, Iakovas, Iakovis, Iakovys

*Ian (Gaelic) Form of John, meaning "God is gracious"
Iain, Iaine, Iayn, Iayne, Iaen, Iaene, Iahn

Iavor (Bulgarian) From the sycamore tree
Iaver, Iavur, Iavar, Iavir, Iavyr

Ibrahim (Arabic) Form of Abraham, meaning "father of a multitude; father of nations"
Ibraheem, Ibraheim, Ibrahiem, Ibraheam, Ibrahym

Ichabod (Hebrew) The glory has gone
Ikabod, Ickabod, Icabod, Ichavod, Ikavod, Icavod, Ickavod, Icha

Ichtaca (Nahuatl) A secretive man
Ichtaka, Ichtacka

Ida (Anglo-Saxon) A king
Idah

Idi (African) Born during the holiday of Idd
Idie, Idy, Idey, Idee, Idea

Ido (Arabic / Hebrew) A mighty man / to evaporate
Iddo, Idoh, Iddoh

Idris (Welsh) An eager lord
Idrys, Idriss, Idrisse, Idryss, Idrysse

Iefan (Welsh) Form of John, meaning "God is gracious"
Iefon, Iefen, Iefin, Iefyn, Iefun, Ifan, Ifon, Ifen

Ifor (Welsh) An archer
Ifore, Ifour, Ifoure

Igasho (Native American) A wanderer
Igashoe, Igashow, Igashowe

Ignatius (Latin) A fiery man; one who is ardent
Ignac, Ignace, Ignacio, Ignacius, Ignatious, Ignatz, Ignaz, Ignazio

Igor (Scandinavian / Russian) A hero / Ing's soldier
Igoryok

Ihit (Indian) One who is honored
Ihyt, Ihitt, Ihytt

Ihsan (Arabic) A charitable man
Ihsann, Ihsen, Ihsin, Ihsyn, Ihson, Ihsun

Ike (Hebrew) Form of Isaac, meaning "full of laughter"
Iki, Ikie, Iky, Ikey, Ikee, Ikea

Iker (Basque) A visitor
Ikar, Ikir, Ikyr, Ikor, Ikur

Ilario (Italian) A cheerful man
Ilareo, Ilariyo, Ilareyo, Ilar, Ilarr, Ilari, Ilarie, Ilary

Ilhuitl (Nahuatl) Born during the daytime

Illanipi (Native American) An amazing man
Illanipie, Illanipy, Illanipey, Illanipee, Illanipea

Iluminado (Spanish) One who shines brightly
Illuminado, Iluminato, Illuminato, Iluminados, Iluminatos, Illuminados, Illuminatos

Imaran (Indian) Having great strength
Imaren, Imaron, Imarun, Imarin, Imaryn

Inaki (Basque) An ardent man
Inakie, Inaky, Inakey, Inakee, Inakea, Inacki, Inackie, Inackee

Ince (Hungarian) One who is innocent
Inse

Indiana (English) From the land of the Indians; from the state of Indiana
Indianna, Indyana, Indyanna

Ingemar (Scandinavian) The son of Ing
Ingamar, Ingemur, Ingmar, Ingmur, Ingar, Ingemer, Ingmer

Inger (Scandinavian) One who is fertile
Inghar, Ingher

Ingo (Scandinavian / Danish) A lord / from the meadow
Ingoe, Ingow, Ingowe

Ingram (Scandinavian) A raven of peace
Ingra, Ingrem, Ingrim, Ingrym, Ingrum, Ingrom, Ingraham, Ingrahame, Ingrams

Iniko (African) Born during troubled times
Inicko, Inico, Inyko, Inycko, Inyco

Iranga (Sri Lankan) One who is special

Irenbend (Anglo-Saxon) From the iron bend
Ironbend

Irwin (English) A friend of the wild boar
Irwinn, Irwinne, Irwyn, Irwynne, Irwine, Irwen, Irwenn, Irwenne

*ᵀ**Isaac** (Hebrew) Full of laughter
Ike, Isaack, Isaak, Isac, Isacco, Isak, Issac, Itzak

*ᵀ**Isaiah** (Hebrew) God is my salvation
Isa, Isaia, Isais, Isia, Isiah, Issiah, Izaiah, Iziah

Iseabail (Hebrew) One who is devoted to God
Iseabaile, Iseabayl, Iseabyle, Iseabael, Iseabaele

Isham (English) From the iron one's estate
Ishem, Ishom, Ishum, Ishim, Ishym, Isenham

Isidore (Greek) A gift of Isis
Isador, Isadore, Isidor, Isidoro, Isidorus, Isidro

Iskander (Arabic) Form of Alexander, meaning "a helper and defender of mankind"
Iskinder, Iskandar, Iskindar, Iskynder, Iskyndar, Iskender, Iskendar

Israel (Hebrew) God perseveres
Israeli, Israelie, Isreal, Izrael

Istvan (Hungarian) One who is crowned
Istven, Istvin, Istvyn, Istvon, Istvun

Iulian (Romanian) A youthful man
Iulien, Iulio, Iuleo

Ivan (Slavic) Form of John, meaning "God is gracious"
Ivann, Ivanhoe, Ivano, Iwan, Iban, Ibano, Ivanti, Ivantie

Ives (Scandinavian) The archer's bow; of the yew wood
Ivair, Ivar, Iven, Iver, Ivo, Ivon, Ivor, Ivaire

Ivy (English) Resembling the evergreen vining plant
Ivee, Ivey, Ivie, Ivi, Ivea

Iyar (Hebrew) Surrounded by light
Iyyar, Iyer, Iyyer

J

Ja (Korean / African) A handsome man / one who is magnetic

Jabari (African) A valiant man
Jabarie, Jabary, Jabarey, Jabaree, Jabarea

Jabbar (Indian) One who consoles others
Jabar

Jabin (Hebrew) God has built; one who is perceptive

Jabon (American) A fiesty man
Jabun, Jabin, Jabyn, Jaben, Jaban

Jace (Hebrew) God is my salvation
Jacen, Jacey, Jacian, Jacy, Jaice, Jayce, Jaece, Jase

Jacinto (Spanish) Resembling a hyacinth
Jacynto, Jacindo, Jacyndo, Jacento, Jacendo, Jacenty, Jacentey, Jacentee

*⋆ᵀ***Jack** (English) Form of John, meaning "God is gracious"
Jackie, Jackman, Jacko, Jacky, Jacq, Jacqin, Jak, Jaq

*⋆***Jackson** (English) The son of Jack or John
Jacksen, Jacksun, Jacson, Jakson, Jaxen, Jaxon, Jaxun, Jaxson, Jaxson

*⋆ᵀ***Jacob** (Hebrew) He who supplants
Jake, James, Kuba, Iakovos, Yakiv, Yankel, Yaqub, Jaco, Jacobo, Jacobi, Jacoby, Jacobie, Jacobey, Jacobo

Jacoby (Hebrew) Form of Jacob, meaning "he who supplants"

Jadal (American) One who is punctual
Jadall, Jadel, Jadell

Jade (Spanish) Resembling the green gemstone
Jadee, Jadie, Jayde, Jaden

*^⋆ᵀ***Jaden** (Hebrew / English) One who is thankful to God; God has heard / form of Jade, meaning "resembling the green gemstone"
Jaiden, Jadyn, Jaeden, Jaidyn, Jayden, Jaydon

Jagan (English) One who is self-confident
Jagen, Jagin, Jagyn, Jagon, Jagun, Jago

Jahan (Indian) Man of the world
Jehan, Jihan, Jag, Jagat, Jagath

Jaidayal (Indian) The victory of kindness
Jadayal, Jaydayal, Jaedayal

Jaime (Spanish) Form of James, meaning "he who supplants"
Jamie, Jaime, Jaimee, Jaimey, Jaimi, Jaimie, Jaimy, Jamee

Jaimin (French) One who is loved
Jaimyn, Jamin, Jamyn, Jaymin, Jaymyn, Jaemin, Jaemyn

Jairdan (American) One who enlightens others
Jardan, Jayrdan, Jaerdan, Jairden, Jarden, Jayrden, Jaerden

Jaja (African) A gift from God

Jajuan (American) One who loves God

Jake (English) Form of Jacob, meaning "he who supplants"
Jaik, Jaike, Jayk, Jayke, Jakey, Jaky

Jakome (Basque) Form of James, meaning "he who supplants"
Jackome, Jakom, Jackom, Jacome

^T**Jalen** (American) One who heals others; one who is tranquil
Jaylon, Jaelan, Jalon, Jaylan, Jaylen, Jalan, Jaylin

Jamal (Arabic) A handsome man
Jamail, Jahmil, Jam, Jamaal, Jamy, Jamar

Jamar (American) Form of Jamal, meaning "a handsome man"
Jamarr, Jemar, Jemarr, Jimar, Jimarr, Jamaar, Jamari, Jamarie

*T**James** (Hebrew) Form of Jacob, meaning "he who supplants"
Jaimes, Jaymes, Jame, Jaym, Jaim, Jaem, Jaemes, Jamese, Jim, Jaime, Diego, Hagop, Hemi, Jakome

^**Jameson** (English) The son of James
Jaimison, Jamieson, Jaymeson, Jamison, Jaimeson, Jaymison, Jaemeson, Jaemison

Jamin (Hebrew) The right hand of favor
Jamian, Jamiel, Jamon, Jaymin, Jaemin, Jaymon

Janesh (Hindi) A leader of the people
Janeshe

Japa (Indian) One who chants
Japeth, Japesh, Japendra

Japheth (Hebrew) May he expand; in the Bible, one of Noah's sons
Jaypheth, Jaepheth, Jaipheth, Jafeth, Jayfeth

Jarah (Hebrew) One who is as sweet as honey
Jarrah, Jara, Jarra

Jared (Hebrew) of the descent; descending
Jarad, Jarod, Jarrad, Jarryd, Jarred, Jarrod, Jaryd, Jerod, Jerrad, Jered

Jarman (German) A man from Germany
Jarmann, Jerman, Jermann

Jaron (Israeli) A song of rejoicing
Jaran, Jaren, Jarin, Jarran, Jarren, Jarrin, Jarron, Jaryn

Jaroslav (Slavic) Born with the beauty of spring
Jaroslaw

Jarrett (English) One who is strong with the spear
Jaret, Jarret, Jarrott, Jerett, Jarritt, Jaret

*Jason (Hebrew / Greek) God is my salvation / a healer; in mythology, the leader of the Argonauts
Jacen, Jaisen, Jaison, Jasen, Jasin, Jasun, Jayson, Jaysen

^Jaspar (Persian) One who holds the treasure
Jasper, Jaspir, Jaspyr, Jesper, Jespar, Jespir, Jespyr

Jatan (Indian) One who is nurturing

Javan (Hebrew) Man from Greece; in the Bible, Noah's grandson
Jayvan, Jayven, Jayvon, Javon, Javern, Javen

Javier (Spanish) the owner of a new house
Javiero

Jax (American) Form of Jackson, meaning, "son of Jack or John"

Jay (Latin / Sanskrit) Resembling a jaybird / one who is victorious
Jae, Jai, Jaye, Jayron, Jayronn, Jey

Jean (French) Form of John, meaning "God is gracious"
Jeanne, Jeane, Jene, Jeannot, Jeanot

Jedidiah (Hebrew) One who is loved by God
Jedadiah, Jedediah, Jed, Jedd, Jedidiya, Jedidiyah, Jedadia, Jedadiya

Jeffrey (English) A man of peace
Jeff, Geoffrey, Jeffery, Jeffree

Jehu (Hebrew) He is God
Jayhu, Jahu, Jehue, Jeyhu, Jeyhue, Jayhue, Jahue, Jehew

Jelani (African) One who is mighty; strong
Jelanie, Jelany, Jelaney, Jelanee, Jelanea

Jennett (Hindi) One who is heaven-sent
Jenett, Jennet, Jenet, Jennitt, Jenitt, Jennit, Jenit

Jerald (English) Form of Gerald, meaning "one who rules with the spear"
Jeraldo, Jerold, Jerrald, Jerrold

*Jeremiah (Hebrew) One who is exalted by the Lord
Jeremia, Jeremias, Jeremija, Jeremiya, Jeremyah, Jeramiah, Jeramia, Jerram, Geremia

Jeremy (Hebrew) Form of Jeremiah, meaning "one who is exalted by the Lord"
Jeramey, Jeramie, Jeramy, Jerami, Jereme, Jeromy

Jermaine (French / Latin) A man from Germany / one who is brotherly
Jermain, Jermane, Jermayne, Jermin, Jermyn, Jermayn, Jermaen, Jermaene

Jerome (Greek) Of the sacred name
Jairome, Jeroen, Jeromo, Jeronimo, Jerrome, Jerom, Jerolyn, Jerolin, Hieronim

Jerram (Hebrew) Form of Jeremiah, meaning "one who is exalted by the Lord"
Jeram, Jerrem, Jerem, Jerrym, Jerym

Jesimiel (Hebrew) The Lord establishes
Jessimiel

Jesse (Hebrew) God exists; a gift from God; God sees all
Jess, Jessey, Jesiah, Jessie, Jessy, Jese, Jessi, Jessee

*Jesus (Hebrew) God is my salvation
*Jesous, Jesues, **Jesús**, Xesus*

^Jett (English) Resembling the jet-black lustrous gemstone
Jet, Jette

Jibril (Arabic) Refers to the archangel Gabriel
Jibryl, Jibri, Jibrie, Jibry, Jibrey, Jibree

Jim (English) Form of James, meaning "he who supplants"
Jimi, Jimmee, Jimmey, Jimmie, Jimmy, Jimmi, Jimbo

Jimoh (African) Born on a Friday
Jymoh, Jimo, Jymo

Jivan (Hindi) A giver of life
Jivin, Jiven, Jivyn, Jivon

Joab (Hebrew) The Lord is my father
Joabb, Yoav

Joachim (Hebrew) One who is established by God; God will judge
Jachim, Jakim, Joacheim, Joaquim, Joaquin, Josquin, Joakim, Joakeen

Joe (English) Form of Joseph, meaning "God will add"
Jo, Joemar, Jomar, Joey, Joie, Joee, Joeye

Joel (Hebrew) Jehovah is God; God is willing

Johan (German) Form of John, meaning "God is gracious"

*ᵀJohn (Hebrew) God is gracious; in the Bible, one of the Apostles
Sean, Jack, Juan, Ian, Ean, Evan, Giovanni, Hanna, Hovannes, Iefan, Ivan, Jean, Xoan, Yochanan, Yohan, Johnn, Johnny, Jhonny

Jonah (Hebrew) Resembling a dove; in the Bible, the man swallowed by a whale

Jonas (Greek) Form of Jonah, meaning "resembling a dove"

*Jonathan (Hebrew) A gift of God
Johnathan, Johnathon, Jonathon, Jonatan, Jonaton, Jonathen, Johnathen, Jonaten, Yonatan

*ᵀJordan (Hebrew) Of the down-flowing river; in the Bible, the river where Jesus was baptized
Johrdan, Jordain, Jordaine, Jordane, Jordanke, Jordann, Jorden, Jordaen

Jorge (Spanish) Form of George, meaning "one who works the earth; a farmer"

*Jose (Spanish) Form of Joseph, meaning "God will add"
José, Joseito, Joselito

*ᵀJoseph (Hebrew) God will add
Joe, Guiseppe, Yosyp, Jessop, Jessup, Joop, Joos, José, Jose, Josef, Joseito

*ᵀJoshua (Hebrew) God is salvation
Josh, Joshuah, Josua, Josue, Joushua, Jozua, Joshwa, Joshuwa

*ᵀJosiah (Hebrew) God will help
Josia, Josias, Joziah, Jozia, Jozias

Journey (American) One who likes to travel
Journy, Journi, Journie, Journee, Journye, Journea

*****Juan** (Spanish) Form of John, meaning "God is gracious"
Juanito, Juwan, Jwan

^Judah (Hebrew) One who praises God
Juda, Jude, Judas, Judsen, Judson, Judd, Jud

Jude (Latin) Form of Judah, meaning "one who praises God"

*****Julian** (Greek) The child of Jove; one who is youthful
Juliano, Julianus, Julien, Julyan, Julio, Jolyon, Jullien, Julen

Julius (Greek) One who is youthful
Juleus, Yuliy

Juma (African) Born on a Friday
Jumah

Jumbe (African) Having great strength
Jumbi, Jumbie, Jumby, Jumbey, Jumbee

Jumoke (African) One who is dearly loved
Jumok, Jumoak

Jun (Japanese) One who is obedient

Junaid (Arabic) A warrior
Junaide, Junayd, Junayde

Jung (Korean) A righteous man

Jurgen (German) Form of George, meaning "one who works the earth; a farmer"
Jorgen, Jurgin, Jorgin

Justice (English) One who upholds moral rightness and fairness
Justyce, Justiss, Justyss, Justis, Justus, Justise

*****ᵀJustin** (Latin) One who is just and upright
Joost, Justain, Justan, Just, Juste, Justen, Justino, Justo

Justinian (Latin) An upright ruler
Justinien, Justinious, Justinius, Justinios, Justinas, Justinus

K

Kabir (Indian) A spiritual leader
Kabeer, Kabear, Kabier, Kabeir, Kabyr, Kabar

Kabonesa (African) One who is born during difficult times

Kacancu (African) The first-born child
Kacancue, Kakancu, Kakancue, Kacanku, Kacankue

Kacey (Irish) A vigilant man; one who is alert
Kacy, Kacee, Kacea, Kaci, Kacie, Kasey, Kasy, Kasi

Kachada (Native American) A white-skinned man

ᵀ**Kaden** (Arabic) A beloved companion
Kadan, Kadin, Kadon, Kaidan, Kaiden, Kaidon, Kaydan, **Kayden**

Kadmiel (Hebrew) One who stands before God
Kamiell

Kaemon (Japanese) Full of joy; one who is right-handed
Kamon, Kaymon, Kaimon

Kagen (Irish) A fiery man; a thinker
Kaigen, Kagan, Kaigan, Kaygen, Kaygan, Kaegen, Kaegan

Kahoku (Hawaiian) Resembling a star
Kahokue, Kahokoo, Kahokou

Kai (Hawaiian / Welsh / Greek) Of the sea, the keeper of the keys / of the earth
Kye

Kaimi (Hawaiian) The seeker
Kaimie, Kaimy, Kaimey, Kaimee, Kaimea

Kalama (Hawaiian) A source of light
Kalam, Kalame

Kale (English) Form of Charles, meaning "one who is manly and strong / a free man"

Kaleb (Hebrew) Resembling an aggressive dog
Kaileb, Kaeleb, Kayleb, Kalob, Kailob, Kaelob

Kalidas (Hindi) A poet or musician; a servant of Kali
Kalydas

Kalki (Indian) Resembling a white horse
Kalkie, Kalky, Kalkey, Kalkee, Kalkea

Kalkin (Hindi) The tenth-born child
Kalkyn, Kalken, Kalkan, Kalkon, Kalkun

Kamden (English) From the winding valley
Kamdun, Kamdon, Kamdan, Kamdin, Kamdyn

Kane (Gaelic) The little warrior
*Kayn, Kayne, Kaen, Kaene,
Kahan, Kahane*

Kang (Korean) A healthy man

Kano (Japanese) A powerful
man
Kanoe, Kanoh

Kantrava (Indian) Resembling
a roaring animal

Kaper (American) One who is
capricious
Kahper, Kapar, Kahpar

Kapono (Hawaiian) A righteous man

Karcsi (French) A strong,
manly man
*Karcsie, Karcsy, Karcsey,
Karcsee, Karcsea*

Karl (German) A free man
*Carl, Karel, Karlan, Karle,
Karlens, Karli, Karlin, Karlo,
Karlos*

Karman (Gaelic) The lord of
the manor
*Karmen, Karmin, Karmyn,
Karmon, Karmun*

Karson (Scottish) Form of
Carson, meaning son of a
marsh dweller
Karsen

Kasem (Asian) Filled with joy

Kashvi (Indian) A shining man
*Kashvie, Kashvy, Kashvey,
Kashvee, Kashvea*

Kasib (Arabic) One who is
fertile
*Kaseeb, Kaseab, Kasieb, Kaseib,
Kasyb*

Kasim (Arabic) One who is
divided
*Kassim, Kaseem, Kasseem,
Kaseam, Kasseam, Kasym,
Kassym*

Kasimir (Slavic) One who
demands peace
*Kasimeer, Kasimear, Kasimier,
Kasimeir, Kasimyr, Kaz,
Kazimierz*

^**Kason** (Basque) Protected by
a helmet
*Kasin, Kasyn, Kasen, Kasun,
Kasan*

Katzir (Hebrew) The harvester
*Katzyr, Katzeer, Katzear,
Katzier, Katzeir*

Kaushal (Indian) One who is
skilled
Kaushall, Koshal, Koshall

Kazim (Arabic) An even-tempered man
*Kazeem, Kazeam, Kaziem,
Kazeim, Kazym*

Keahi (Hawaiian) Of the flames
Keahie, Keahy, Keahey, Keahee, Keahea

Kealoha (Hawaiian) From the bright path
Keeloha, Kieloha

Kean (Gaelic / English) A warrior / one who is sharp
Keane, Keen, Keene, Kein, Keine, Keyn, Keyne, Kien

Keandre (American) One who is thankful
Kiandre, Keandray, Kiandray, Keandrae, Kiandrae, Keandrai, Kiandrai

Keanu (Hawaiian) Of the mountain breeze
Keanue, Kianu, Kianue, Keanoo, Kianoo, Keanou

Keaton (English) From the town of hawks
Keatun, Keeton, Keetun, Keyton, Keytun

Kedar (Arabic) A powerful man
Keder, Kedir, Kedyr, Kadar, Kader, Kadir, Kadyr

Kefir (Hebrew) Resembling a young lion
Kefyr, Kefeer, Kefear, Kefier, Kefeir

Keegan (Gaelic) A small and fiery man
Kegan, Keigan, Keigan, Keagan, Keagen, Keegen

Keith (Scottish) Man from the forest
Keithe, Keath, Keathe, Kieth, Kiethe, Keyth, Keythe, Keithen

Kellach (Irish) One who suffers strife during battle
Kelach, Kellagh, Kelagh, Keallach

Kellen (Gaelic/German) One who is slender/from the swamp
Kellan, Kellon, Kellun, Kellin

Kelley (Celtic / Gaelic) A warrior / one who defends
Kelly, Kelleigh, Kellee, Kellea, Kelleah, Kelli, Kellie

Kendi (African) One who is much loved
Kendie, Kendy, Kendey, Kendee, Kendea

Kendrick (English / Gaelic) A royal ruler / the champion
Kendric, Kendricks, Kendrik, Kendrix, Kendryck, Kenrick, Kenrik, Kenricks

Kenley (English) From the king's meadow
Kenly, Kenlee, Kenleigh, Kenlea, Kenleah, Kenli, Kenlie

Kenn (Welsh) Of the bright waters

Kennedy (Gaelic) A helmeted chief
Kennedi, Kennedie, Kennedey, Kennedee, Kennedea, Kenadie, Kenadi, Kenady

Kenneth (Irish) Born of the fire; an attractive man
Kennet, Kennett, Kennith, Kennit, Kennitt

Kent (English) From the edge or border
Kentt, Kennt, Kentrell

Kenton (English) From the king's town
Kentun, Kentan, Kentin, Kenten, Kentyn

Kenyon (Gaelic) A blond-haired man
Kenyun, Kenyan, Kenyen, Kenyin

Kepler (German) One who makes hats
Keppler, Kappler, Keppel, Keppeler

Kerbasi (Basque) A warrior
Kerbasie, Kerbasee, Kerbasea, Kerbasy, Kerbasey

Kershet (Hebrew) Of the rainbow

Kesler (American) An energetic man; one who is independent
Keslar, Keslir, Keslyr, Keslor, Keslur

Keung (Chinese) A universal spirit

*Kevin (Gaelic) A beloved and handsome man
Kevyn, Kevan, Keven, Keveon, Kevinn, Kevion, Kevis, Kevon

Khairi (Swahili) A kingly man
Khairie, Khairy, Khairey, Khairee, Khairea

Khalon (American) A strong warrior
Khalun, Khalen, Khalan, Khalin, Khalyn

Khayri (Arabic) One who is charitable
Khayrie, Khayry, Khayrey, Khayree, Khayrea

Khouri (Arabic) A spiritual man; a priest
Khourie, Khoury, Khourey, Khouree, Kouri, Kourie, Koury, Kourey

Khushi (Indian) Filled with happiness
Khushie, Khushey, Khushy, Khushee

Kibbe (Native American) A
nocturnal bird
Kybbe

Kibo (African) From the high-
est moutain peak
*Keybo, Keebo, Keabo, Keibo,
Kiebo*

Kidd (English) Resembling a
young goat
Kid, Kydd, Kyd

Kiefer (German) One who
makes barrels
*Keefer, Keifer, Kieffer, Kiefner,
Kieffner, Kiefert, Kuefer,
Kueffner*

Kildaire (Irish) From county of
Kildare
*Kyldaire, Kildare, Kyldare,
Kildair, Kyldair, Killdaire,
Kylldaire, Kildayr*

Kim (Vietnamese) As precious
as gold
Kym

Kimoni (African) A great man
*Kimonie, Kimony, Kimoney,
Kimonee, Kymoni, Kymonie,
Kymony, Kymoney*

Kincaid (Celtic) The leader
during battle
*Kincade, Kincayd, Kincayde,
Kincaide, Kincaed, Kincaede,
Kinkaid, Kinkaide*

Kindin (Basque) The fifth-born
child
*Kinden, Kindan, Kindyn,
Kindon, Kindun*

Kindle (American) To set
aflame
Kindel, Kyndle, Kyndel

^**King** (English) The royal ruler
Kyng

Kingston (English) From the
king's town
Kingstun, Kinston, Kindon

Kinnard (Irish) From the tall
hill
*Kinard, Kinnaird, Kinaird,
Kynnard, Kynard, Kynnaird,
Kynaird*

Kinsey (English) The victori-
ous prince
*Kynsey, Kinsi, Kynsi, Kinsie,
Kynsie, Kinsee, Kynsee, Kinsea*

Kione (African) One who has
come from nowhere

Kioshi (Japanese) One who is
quiet
*Kioshe, Kioshie, Kioshy,
Kioshey, Kioshee, Kyoshi,
Kyoshe, Kyoshie*

Kipp (English) From the small
pointed hill
*Kip, Kipling, Kippling, Kypp,
Kyp, Kiplyng, Kipplyng, Kippi*

Kiri (Vietnamese) Resembling the mountains
Kirie, Kiry, Kirey, Kiree, Kirea

Kirk (Norse) A man of the church
Kyrk, Kerk, Kirklin, Kirklyn

Kirkland (English) From the church's land
Kirklan, Kirklande, Kyrkland, Kyrklan, Kyrklande

Kirkley (English) From the church's meadow
Kirkly, Kirkleigh, Kirklea, Kirkleah, Kirklee, Kirkli, Kirklie

Kit (English) Form of Christopher, meaning "one who bears Christ inside"
Kitt, Kyt, Kytt

Kitchi (Native American) A brave young man
Kitchie, Kitchy, Kitchey, Kitchee, Kitchea

Kitoko (African) A handsome man
Kytoko

Kivi (Finnish) As solid as stone
Kivie, Kivy, Kivey, Kivee, Kivea

Knight (English) A noble solidier
Knights

Knoton (Native American) Of the wind
Knotun, Knotan, Knoten, Knotin, Knotyn

Knud (Danish) A kind man
Knude

Kobe (African / Hungarian) Tortoise / Form of Jacob, meaning "he who supplants"
Kobi, Koby

Kody (English) One who is helpful
Kodey, Kodee, Kodea, Kodi, Kodie

Koen (German) An honest advisor
Koenz, Kunz, Kuno

Kohana (Native American / Hawaiian) One who is swift / the best

Kohler (German) One who mines coal
Koler

Kojo (African) Born on a Monday
Kojoe, Koejo, Koejoe

Koka (Hawaiian) A man from Scotland

Kolton (American) Form of Colton, meaning from the coal town
Kolten, Koltan

Konane (Hawaiian) Born beneath the bright moon
Konain, Konaine, Konayn, Konayne, Konaen, Konaene

Konnor (English) A wolf lover; one who is strong-willed
Konnur, Konner, Konnar, Konnir, Konnyr

Koofrey (African) Remember me
Koofry, Koofri, Koofrie, Koofree

Kordell (English) One who makes cord
Kordel, Kord, Kordale

Koresh (Hebrew) One who digs in the earth; a farmer
Koreshe

Kory (Irish) From the hollow; of the churning waters
Korey, Kori, Korie, Koree, Korea, Korry, Korrey, Korree

Kozma (Greek) One who is decorated
Kozmah

Kozue (Japanese) Of the tree branches
Kozu, Kozoo, Kozou

Kraig (Gaelic) From the rocky place; as solid as a rock
Kraige, Krayg, Krayge, Kraeg, Kraege, Krage

Kramer (German) A shop-keeper
Kramar, Kramor, Kramir, Kramur, Kramyr, Kraymer, Kraimer, Kraemer

Krany (Czech) A man of short stature
Kraney, Kranee, Kranea, Krani, Kranie

Krikor (Armenian) A vigilant watchman
Krykor, Krikur, Krykur

Kristian (Scandinavian) An annointed Christian
Kristan, Kristien, Krist, Kriste, Krister, Kristar, Khristian, Khrist

Kristopher (Scandinavian) A follower of Christ
Khristopher, Kristof, Kristofer, Kristoff, Kristoffer, Kristofor, Kristophor, Krystof

Kuba (Polish) Form of Jacob, meaning "he who supplants"
Kubas

Kuckunniwi (Native American) Resembling a little wolf
Kukuniwi

Kuleen (Indian) A high-born man
Kulin, Kulein, Kulien, Kulean, Kulyn

Kumar (Indian) A prince;
a male child

Kuri (Japanese) Resembling
a chestnut
*Kurie, Kury, Kurey, Kuree,
Kurea*

Kuron (African) One who gives
thanks
*Kurun, Kuren, Kuran, Kurin,
Kuryn*

Kurt (German) A brave
counselor
Kurte

Kushal (Indian) A talented
man; adroit
Kushall

Kwaku (African) Born on a
Wednesday
*Kwakue, Kwakou, Kwako,
Kwakoe*

Kwan (Korean) Of a bold
character
Kwon

Kwintyn (Polish) The fifth-
born child
*Kwentyn, Kwinton, Kwenton,
Kwintun, Kwentun, Kwintan,
Kwentan, Kwinten*

*Kyle (Gaelic) From the narrow
channel
*Kile, Kiley, Kye, Kylan, Kyrell,
Kylen, Kily, Kili*

Kylemore (Gaelic) From the
great wood
Kylmore, Kylemor, Kylmor

Kyrone (English) Form of
Tyrone, meaning "from
Owen's land"
*Kyron, Keirohn, Keiron,
Keirone, Keirown, Kirone*

L

Lacey (French) Man from
Normandy; as delicate as lace
Lacy, Laci, Lacie, Lacee, Lacea

Lachlan (Gaelic) From the land
of lakes
*Lachlen, Lachlin, Lachlyn,
Locklan, Locklen, Locklin,
Locklyn, Loklan*

Lachman (Gaelic) A man from
the lake
*Lachmann, Lockman,
Lockmann, Lokman, Lokmann,
Lakman, Lakmann*

Ladan (Hebrew) One who is
alert and aware
*Laden, Ladin, Ladyn, Ladon,
Ladun*

Ladd (English) A servant;
a young man
*Lad, Laddey, Laddie, Laddy,
Laddi, Laddee, Laddea, Ladde*

Ladislas (Slavic) A glorious
ruler
*Lacko, Ladislaus, Laslo, Laszlo,
Lazlo, Ladislav, Ladislauv,
Ladislao*

Lagrand (American) A
majestic man
Lagrande

Laibrook (English) One who
lives on the road near the
brook
*Laebrook, Laybrook, Laibroc,
Laebroc, Laybroc, Laibrok,
Laebrok, Laybrok*

Laird (Scottish) The lord of the
manor
*Layrd, Laerd, Lairde, Layrde,
Laerde*

Laken (American) Man from
the lake
*Laike, Laiken, Laikin, Lakin,
Lakyn, Lakan, Laikyn, Laeken*

Lalam (Indian) The best
Lallam, Lalaam, Lallaam

Lam (Vietnamese) Having a
full understanding

Laman (Arabic) A bright and
happy man
Lamaan, Lamann, Lamaann

Lamar (German / French)
From the renowned land / of
the sea
*Lamarr, Lamarre, Lemar,
Lemarr*

Lambert (Scandinavian) The
light of the land
*Lambart, Lamberto, Lambirt,
Landbert, Lambirto, Lambrecht,
Lambret, Lambrett*

Lambi (Norse) In mythology,
the son of Thorbjorn
*Lambie, Lamby, Lambey,
Lambe, Lambee*

Lameh (Arabic) A shining man

Lamorak (English) In
Arthurian legend, the brother
of Percival
*Lamerak, Lamurak, Lamorac,
Lamerac, Lamurac, Lamorack,
Lamerack, Lamurack*

Lance (English) Form of
Lancelot, meaning an
attendant, a knight of the
Round Table

Lander (English) One who
owns land
*Land, Landers, Landis, Landiss,
Landor, Lande, Landry, Landri*

*T Landon (English) From the
long hill
*Landyn, Landan, Landen,
Landin, Lando, Langdon,
Langden, Langdan*

Lane (English) One who takes the narrow path
Laine, Lain, Laen, Laene, Layne, Layn

Langhorn (English) Of the long horn
Langhorne, Lanhorn, Lanhorne

Langilea (Polynesian) Having a booming voice, like thunder
Langileah, Langilia, Langiliah

Langston (English) From the tall man's town
Langsten, Langstun, Langstown, Langstin, Langstyn, Langstan, Langton, Langtun

Langundo (Native American / Polynesian) A peaceful man / one who is graceful

Langworth (English) One who lives near the long paddock
Langworthe, Lanworth, Lanworthe

Lanier (French) One who works with wool

Lantos (Hungarian) One who plays the lute
Lantus

Lapidos (Hebrew) One who carries a torch
Lapydos, Lapidot, Lapydot, Lapidoth, Lapydoth, Lapidus, Lapydus

Laquinton (American) Form of Quinton, meaning "from the queen's town or settlement"
Laquinntan, Laquinnten, Laquinntin, Laquinnton, Laquintain, Laquintan, Laquintyn, Laquintynn

Lar (Anglo-Saxon) One who teaches others

Larson (Scandinavian) The son of Lawrence
Larsan, Larsen, Larsun, Larsin, Larsyn

Lasalle (French) From the hall
Lasall, Lasal, Lasale

Lashaun (American) An enthusiastic man
Lashawn, Lasean, Lashon, Lashond

Lassit (American) One who is open-minded
Lassyt, Lasset

Lathan (American) Form of Nathan, meaning "a gift from God"
Lathen, Lathun, Lathon, Lathin, Lathyn, Latan, Laten, Latun

Latimer (English) One who serves as an interpreter
Latymer, Latimor, Latymor, Latimore, Latymore, Lattemore, Lattimore

Latty (English) A generous
man
*Lattey, Latti, Lattie, Lattee,
Lattea*

Laurian (English) One who
lives near the laurel trees
*Laurien, Lauriano, Laurieno,
Lawrian, Lawrien, Lawriano,
Lawrieno*

Lave (Italian) Of the burning
rock
Lava

Lawford (English) From the
ford near the hill
*Lawforde, Lawferd, Lawferde,
Lawfurd, Lawfurde*

Lawler (Gaelic) A soft-spoken
man; one who mutters
*Lauler, Lawlor, Loller, Lawlar,
Lollar, Loller, Laular, Laulor*

Lawley (English) From the
meadow near the hill
*Lawly, Lawli, Lawlie, Lawleigh,
Lawlee, Lawlea, Lawleah*

Lawrence (Latin) Man from
Laurentum; crowned with
laurel
*Larance, Laranz, Larenz,
Larrance, Larrence, Larrens,
Larrey, Larry*

Laziz (Arabic) One who is
pleasant
*Lazeez, Lazeaz, Laziez,
Lazeiz, Lazyz*

Leaman (American) A
powerful man
*Leeman, Leamon, Leemon,
Leamond, Leamand*

Lear (Greek) Of the royalty
Leare, Leer, Leere

Leather (American) As tough
as hide
Lether

Leavitt (English) A baker
*Leavit, Leavytt, Leavyt, Leavett,
Leavet*

Leben (English) Filled with
hope

Lech (Slavic) In mythology, the
founder of the Polish people
Leche

Ledyard (Teutonic) The
protector of the nation
Ledyarde, Ledyerd, Ledyerde

Lee (English) From the
meadow
Leigh, Lea, Leah, Ley

Leeto (African) One who
embarks on a journey
Leato, Leito, Lieto

Legend (American) One who is memorable
Legende, Legund, Legunde

Leighton (English) From the town near the meadow
Leightun, Layton, Laytun, Leyton, Leytun

Lekhak (Hindi) An author
Lekhan

^**Leland** (English) From the meadow land

Lema (African) One who is cultivated
Lemah, Lemma, Lemmah

Lemon (American) Resembling the fruit
Lemun, Lemin, Lemyn, Limon, Limun, Limin, Limyn, Limen

Len (Native American) One who plays the flute

Lencho (African) Resembling a lion
Lenchos, Lenchio, Lenchiyo, Lencheo, Lencheyo

Lennon (English) Son of love
Lennan

Lennor (English) A courageous man

Lennox (Scottish) One who owns many elm trees
Lenox, Lenoxe, Lennix, Lenix, Lenixe

Lensar (English) One who stays with his parents
Lenser, Lensor, Lensur

Lenton (American) A pious man
Lentin, Lentyn, Lentun, Lentan, Lenten, Lent, Lente

Leo (Latin) Having the strength of a lion
Lio, Lyo, Leon

^**Leon** (Greek) Form of Leo, meaning "resembling a lion"

Leonard (German) Having the strength of a lion
Len, Lenard, Lenn, Lennard, Lennart, Lennerd, Leonardo

Leor (Latin) One who listens well
Leore

Lerato (Latin) The song of my soul
Leratio, Lerateo

Leron (French / Arabic) The circle / my song
Lerun, Leran, Leren, Lerin, Leryn

Leroy (French) The king
*Leroi, Leeroy, Leeroi, Learoy,
Learoi*

*Levi (Hebrew) We are united
as one; in the Bible, one of
Jacob's sons
*Levie, Levin, Levyn, Levy, Levey,
Levee*

Li (Chinese) Having great
strength

*Liam (Gaelic) Form of
William, meaning "the determined protector"

Lian (Chinese) Of the willow

Liang (Chinese) A good man
Lyang

Lidmann (Anglo-Saxon) A man
of the sea; a sailor
Lidman, Lydmann, Lydman

Lif (Scandinavian) An energetic man; lively

Lihau (Hawaiian) A spirited
man

Like (Asian) A soft-spoken
man
Lyke

Lilo (Hawaiian) One who is
generous
*Lylo, Leelo, Lealo, Leylo, Lielo,
Leilo*

Lincoln (English) From the vil-
lage near the lake
*Lincon, Lyncon, Linc, Lynk,
Lync*

Lindford (English) From the
linden-tree ford
*Linford, Lindforde, Linforde,
Lyndford, Lynford, Lyndforde,
Lynforde*

Lindhurst (English) From the
village by the linden trees
*Lyndhurst, Lindenhurst,
Lyndenhurst, Lindhirst,
Lindherst, Lyndhirst, Lyndherst,
Lindenhirst*

Lindley (English) From the
meadow of linden trees
*Lindly, Lindleigh, Lindlea,
Lindleah, Lindlee, Lindli*

Lindman (English) One who
lives near the linden trees
Lindmann, Lindmon

Line (English) From the bank

Lipût (Hungarian) A brave
young man

Lisimba (African) One who
has been attacked by a lion
Lisymba, Lysimba, Lysymba

Liu (Asian) One who is quiet;
peaceful

Llewellyn (Welsh) Resembling a lion
Lewellen, Lewellyn, Llewellen, Llewelyn, Llwewellin, Llew, Llewe, Llyweilun

Lochan (Hindi / Irish) The eyes / one who is lively

***Logan** (Gaelic) From the little hollow
Logann, Logen, Login, Logyn, Logenn, Loginn, Logynn

Lolonyo (African) The beauty of love
Lolonyio, Lolonyeo, Lolonio, Lolonea

Loman (Gaelic) One who is small and bare
Lomann, Loeman, Loemann

Lombard (Latin) One who has a long beard
Lombardi, Lombardo, Lombardie, Lombardy, Lombardey, Lombardee

London (English) From the capital of England
Lundon, Londen, Lunden

Lonzo (Spanish) One who is ready for battle
Lonzio, Lonzeo

Lootah (Native American) Refers to the color red
Loota, Loutah, Louta, Lutah, Luta

Lorcan (Irish) The small fierce one
Lorcen, Lorcin, Lorcyn, Lorcon, Lorcun, Lorkan, Lorken, Lorkin

Lord (English) One who has authority and power
Lorde, Lordly, Lordley, Lordlee, Lordlea, Lordleigh, Lordli, Lordlie

Lore (Basque / English) Resembling a flower / form of Lawrence, meaning "man from Laurentum; crowned with laurel"
Lorea

Lorimer (Latin) One who makes harnesses
Lorrimer, Lorimar, Lorrimar, Lorymar, Lorrymar, Lorymer, Lorrymer

Louis (German) A famous warrior
Lew, Lewes, Lewis, Lodewick, Lodovico, Lou, Louie, Lucho, Luis

Luba (Yugoslavian) One who loves and is loved
Lubah

***Lucas** (English) A man from Lucania
Lukas, Loucas, Loukas, Luckas, Louckas, Lucus, Lukus, Ghoukas

Lucian (Latin) Surrounded by light
Luciano, Lucianus, Lucien, Lucio, Lucjan, Lukianos, Lukyan, Luce

Lucky (English) A fortunate man
Luckey, Luckee, Luckea, Lucki, Luckie

Ludlow (English) The ruler of the hill
Ludlowe

*****Luis** (Spanish) Form of Louis, meaning "a famous warrior"
Luiz

*ᵀ**Luke** (Greek) A man from Lucania
Luc, Luken

Lunt (Scandinavian) From the grove
Lunte

Luthando (Latin) One who is dearly loved

Luther (German) A soldier of the people
Louther, Luter, Luthero, Lutero, Louthero, Luthus, Luthas, Luthos

Lux (Latin) A man of the light
Luxe, Luxi, Luxie, Luxee, Luxea, Luxy, Luxey

Ly (Vietnamese) A reasonable man

Lynn (English) A man of the lake
Linn, Lyn, Lynne, Linne

M

Maahes (Egyptian) Resembling a lion

Mac (Gaelic) The son of Mac (Macarthur, Mackinley, etc.)
Mack, Mak, Macky, Macky, Macki, Mackie, Mackee, Mackea

Macadam (Gaelic) The son of Adam
Macadhamh, MacAdam, McAdam, MacAdhamh

Macallister (Gaelic) The son of Alistair
MacAlister, McAlister, McAllister, Macalister

Macardle (Gaelic) The son of great courage
MacArdle, McCardle, Macardell, MacArdell, McCardell

Macartan (Gaelic) The son of
Artan
*MacArtan, McArtan,
Macarten, MacArten, McArten*

Macarthur (Gaelic) The son of
Arthur
*MacArthur, McArthur,
Macarther, MacArther,
McArther*

Macauslan (Gaelic) The son of
Absalon
*MacAuslan, McAuslan,
Macauslen, MacAuslen,
McAuslen*

Maccoll (Gaelic) The son of
Coll
McColl, Maccoll, MacColl

Maccrea (Gaelic) The son of
grace
*McCrea, Macrae, MacCrae,
MacCray, MacCrea*

Macedonio (Greek) A man
from Macedonia
*Macedoneo, Macedoniyo,
Macedoneyo*

Macgowan (Gaelic) The son of
a blacksmith
*MacGowan, Magowan,
McGowan, McGowen,
McGown, MacCowan,
MacCowen*

Machau (Hebrew) A gift from
God

Machenry (Gaelic) The son of
Henry
MacHenry, McHenry

Machk (Native American)
Resembling a bear

Macintosh (Gaelic) The son of
the thane
*MacIntosh, McIntosh,
Macintoshe, MacIntoshe,
McIntoshe, Mackintosh,
MacKintosh*

Mackay (Gaelic) The son of
fire
*MacKay, McKay, Mackaye,
MacKaye, McKaye*

Mackinley (Gaelic) The son of
the white warrior
*MacKinley, McKinley,
MacKinlay, McKinlay,
Mackinlay, Mackinlie,
MacKinlie*

Macklin (Gaelic) The son of
Flann
*Macklinn, Macklyn, Macklynn,
Macklen, Macklenn*

Maclaine (Gaelic) The son of
John's servant
*MacLaine, Maclain, MacLain,
Maclayn, McLaine, McLain,
Maclane, MacLane*

Macleod (Gaelic) The son of
the ugly one
*MacLeod, McLeod, McCloud,
MacCloud*

Macmurray (Gaelic) The son
of Murray
*MacMurray, McMurray,
Macmurra, MacMurra*

Macnab (Gaelic) The son of
the abbot
MacNab, McNab

Macon (English / French)
To make / from the city in
France
*Macun, Makon, Makun,
Maken, Mackon, Mackun*

Macqueen (Gaelic) The son of
the good man
MacQueen, McQueen

Macrae (Gaelic) The son of
Ray
*MacRae, McRae, Macray,
MacRay, McRay, Macraye,
MacRaye, McRaye*

Madden (Pakistani) One who
is organized; a planner
*Maddon, Maddan, Maddin,
Maddyn, Maddun, Maden,
Madon, Madun*

Maddox (Welsh) The son of
the benefactor
Madox, Madocks, Maddocks

Madhur (Indian) A sweet man

Magee (Gaelic) The son of
Hugh
*MacGee, McGee, MacGhee,
Maghee*

Maguire (Gaelic) The son of
the beige one
*Magwire, MacGuire, McGuire,
MacGwire, McGwire*

Magus (Latin) A sorcerer
*Magis, Magys, Magos, Magas,
Mages*

Mahan (American) A cowboy
*Mahahn, Mahen, Mayhan,
Maihan, Maehan, Mayhen,
Maihen, Maehen*

Mahant (Indian) Having a
great soul
Mahante

Mahatma (Hindi) Of great
spiritual development

Mahfouz (Arabic) One who is
protected
*Mafouz, Mahfooz, Mafooz,
Mahfuz, Mafuz*

Mahkah (Native American) Of
the earth
Mahka, Makah, Maka

Mahmud (Arabic) One who is
praiseworthy
*Mahmood, Mahmoud,
Mehmood, Mehmud, Mehmoud*

Mailhairer (French) An ill-fated man

Maimon (Arabic) One who is dependable; having good fortune
Maymon, Maemon, Maimun, Maymun, Maemun, Mamon, Mamun

Maitland (English) From the meadow land
Maytland, Maetland, Maitlande, Maytlande, Maetlande

Majdy (Arabic) A glorious man
Majdey, Majdi, Majdie, Majdee, Majdea

Makaio (Hawaiian) A gift from God

Makena (Hawaiian) Man of abundance
Makenah

Makin (Arabic) Having great strength
Makeen, Makean, Makein, Makien, Makyn

Makis (Hebrew) A gift from God
Madys, Makiss, Makyss, Makisse, Madysse

Malachi (Hebrew) A messenger of God
Malachie, Malachy, Malaki, Malakia, Malakie, Malaquias, Malechy, Maleki

Malawa (African) A flourishing man

Malcolm (Gaelic) Follower of St. Columbus
Malcom, Malcolum, Malkolm, Malkom, Malkolum

Mali (Indian) A ruler; the firstborn son
Malie, Maly, Maley, Malee, Malea

Mamoru (Japanese) Of the earth
Mamorou, Mamorue, Mamorew, Mamoroo

Manchester (English) From the city in England
Manchestar, Manchestor, Manchestir, Manchestyr, Manchestur

Mandan (Native American) A tribal name
Manden, Mandon, Mandun, Mandin, Mandyn

Mandhatri (Indian) A prince; born to royalty
Mandhatrie, Mandhatry, Mandhatrey, Mandhatree, Mandhatrea

Mani (African) From the mountain
Manie, Many, Maney, Manee, Manea

Manjit (Indian) A conqueror of the mind; having great knowledge
Manjeet, Manjeat, Manjeit, Manjiet, Manjyt

Manley (English) From the man's meadow; from the hero's meadow
Manly, Manli, Manlie, Manlea, Manleah, Manlee, Manleigh

Manmohan (Indian) A handsome and pleasing man
Manmohen, Manmohin, Manmohyn

Mannheim (German) From the hamlet in the swamp
Manheim

Mano (Hawaiian) Resembling a shark
Manoe, Manow, Manowe

Manohar (Indian) A delightful and captivating man
Manoharr, Manohare

Mansel (English) From the clergyman's house
Mansle, Mansell, Mansele, Manselle, Manshel, Manshele, Manshell, Manshelle

Mansfield (English) From the field near the small river
Mansfeld, Maunfield, Maunfeld

Manton (English) From the man's town; from the hero's town
Mantun, Manten, Mannton, Manntun, Mannten

Manu (African) The second-born child
Manue, Manou, Manoo

Manuel (Spanish) Form of Emmanuel, meaning "God is with us"
Manuelo, Manuello, Manolito, Manolo, Manollo, Manny, Manni

Manya (Indian) A respected man
Manyah

Manzo (Japanese) The third son with ten-thousand-fold strength

Mar (Spanish) Of the sea
Marr, Mare, Marre

Marcel (French) The little warrior
Marceau, Marcelin, Marcellin, Marcellino, Marcell, Marcello, Marcellus, Marcelo

Marcus (Latin) Form of Mark,
meaning "dedicated to Mars,
the god of war"
*Markus, Marcas, Marco,
Markos*

Mariatu (African) One who is
pure; chaste
Mariatue, Mariatou, Mariatoo

Marid (Arabic) A rebellious
man
Maryd

Mario (Latin) A manly man
*Marius, Marios, Mariano,
Marion, Mariun, Mareon*

Mark (Latin) Dedicated to
Mars, the god of war
*Marc, Markey, Marky, Marki,
Markie, Markee, Markea,
Markov*

Marmion (French) Our little
one
Marmyon, Marmeon

Marsh (English) From the
marshland
Marshe

Marshall (French / English) A
caretaker of horses / a stew-
ard
*Marchall, Marischal,
Marischall, Marschal, Marshal,
Marshell, Marshel, Marschall*

Marston (English) From the
town near the marsh
*Marstun, Marsten, Marstin,
Marstyn, Marstan*

Martin (Latin) Dedicated to
Mars, the god of war
*Martyn, Mart, Martel, Martell,
Marten, Martenn, Marti,
Martie*

Marvin (Welsh) A friend of
the sea
*Marvinn, Marvinne, Marven,
Marvenn, Marvenne, Marvyn,
Marvynn, Marvynne, Mervin*

Maryland (English) Honoring
Queen Mary; from the state
of Maryland
*Mariland, Maralynd, Marylind,
Marilind*

Masanao (Japanese) A good
man

Masao (Japanese) A righteous
man

TMason** (English) One who
works with stone
*Masun, Masen, Masan, Masin,
Masyn, Masson, Massun,
Massen*

Masselin (French) A young
Thomas
*Masselyn, Masselen, Masselan,
Masselon, Masselun, Maselin,
Maselyn, Maselon*

Masura (Japanese) A good
destiny
Masoura

Mataniah (Hebrew) A gift
from God
*Matania, Matanya,
Matanyahu, Mattania,
Mattaniah, Matanyah*

Matata (African) One who
causes trouble

Matin (Arabic) Having great
strength
*Maten, Matan, Matyn, Maton,
Matun*

Matisse (French) One who is
gifted
*Matiss, Matysse, Matyss,
Matise, Matyse*

Matlock (American) A rancher
Matlok, Matloc

^**Matteo** (Italian) Form of
Matthew, meaning "a gift
from God"

*ᵀ**Matthew** (Hebrew) A gift
from God
*Matt, Mathew, Matvey,
Mateas, Mattix, Madteos,
Matthias, Mat, Mateo, Matteo,
Mateus*

Matunde (African) One who is
fruitful
Matundi, Matundie

Matvey (Russian) Form of
Matthew, meaning "a gift
from God"
*Matvy, Matvee, Matvea, Matvi,
Matvie, Motka, Matviyko*

Matwau (Native American)
The enemy

Maurice (Latin) A dark-
skinned man; Moorish
*Maurell, Maureo, Mauricio,
Maurids, Maurie, Maurin,
Maurio, Maurise, Baurice*

Maverick (English) An
independent man; a non-
conformist
*Maveric, Maverik, Mavrick,
Mavric, Mavrik*

Mawulol (African) One who
gives thanks to God

^**Maximilian** (Latin) The
greatest
*Max, Macks, Maxi, Maxie,
Maxy, Maxey, Maxee, Maxea,
Maximiliano*

Maxfield (English) From
Mack's field
Mackfield, Maxfeld, Macksfeld

ᵀ**Maxwell** (English) From
Mack's spring
*Maxwelle, Mackswell, Maxwel,
Mackswel, Mackwelle, Maxwill,
Maxwille, Mackswill*

Mayer (Latin / German / Hebrew) A large man / a farmer / one who is shining bright
Maier, Mayar, Mayor, Mayir, Mayur, Meyer, Meir, Myer

Mayfield (English) From the strong one's field
Mayfeld, Maifield, Maifeld, Maefield, Maefeld

Mayo (Gaelic) From the yew tree plain
Mayoe, Maiyo, Maeyo, Maiyoe, Maeyoe, Mayoh, Maioh

Mccoy (Gaelic) The son of Coy
McCoy

McKenna (Gaelic) The son of Kenna; to ascend
McKennon, McKennun, McKennen, McKennan

Mckile (Gaelic) The son of Kyle
McKile, Mckyle, McKyle, Mackile, Mackyle, MacKile, MacKyle

Medad (Hebrew) A beloved friend
Meydad

Medgar (German) Having great strength
Medgarr, Medgare, Medgard, Medárd

Medwin (German) A strong friend
Medwine, Medwinn, Medwinne, Medwen, Medwenn, Medwenne, Medwyn, Medwynn

Meged (Hebrew) One who has been blessed with goodness

Mehdi (Arabian) One who is guided
Mehdie, Mehdy, Mehdey, Mehdee, Mehdea

Mehetabel (Hebrew) One who is favored by God
Mehetabell, Mehitabel, Mehitabell, Mehytabel, Mehytabell

Meilyr (Welsh) A regal ruler

Meinrad (German) A strong counselor
Meinred, Meinrod, Meinrud, Meinrid, Meinryd

Meka (Hawaiian) Of the eyes
Mekah

Melancton (Greek) Resembling a black flower
Melankton, Melanctun, Melanktun, Melancten, Melankten, Melanchton, Melanchten, Melanchthon

Mele (Hawaiian) One who is happy

Melesio (Spanish) An attentive man; one who is careful
Melacio, Melasio, Melecio, Melicio, Meliseo, Milesio

Meletius (Greek) A cautious man
Meletios, Meletious, Meletus, Meletos

Meli (Native American) One who is bitter
Melie, Mely, Meley, Melee, Melea, Meleigh

Melker (Swedish) A king
Melkar, Melkor, Melkur, Melkir, Melkyr

Melton (English) From the mill town
Meltun, Meltin, Meltyn, Melten, Meltan

Melville (English) From the mill town
Melvill, Melvil, Melvile, Melvylle, Melvyll, Melvyl, Melvyle

Melvin (English) A friend who offers counsel
Melvinn, Melvinne, Melven, Melvenn, Melvenne, Melvyn, Melvynn, Melvynne, Belvin

Memphis (American) From the city in Tennessee
Memfis, Memphys, Memfys, Memphus, Memfus

Menachem (Hebrew) One who provides comfort
Menaheim, Menahem, Menachim, Menachym, Menahim, Menahym, Machum, Machem

Menassah (Hebrew) A forgetful man
Menassa, Menass, Menas, Menasse, Menasseh

Menefer (Egyptian) Of the beautiful city
Menefar, Menefir, Menefyr, Menefor, Menefur

Menelik (African) The son of a wise man
Menelick, Menelic, Menelyk, Menelyck, Menelyc

Merewood (English) From the forest with the lake
Merwood, Merewode, Merwode

Merlin (Welsh) Of the sea fortress; in Arthurian legend, the wizard and mentor of King Arthur
Merlyn, Merlan, Merlon, Merlun, Merlen, Merlinn, Merlynn, Merlonn

Merrill (English) Of the shining sea
Meril, Merill, Merrel, Merrell, Merril, Meryl, Merryll, Meryll

Merton (English) From the town near the lake
Mertun, Mertan, Merten, Mertin, Mertyn, Murton, Murtun, Murten

Mervin (Welsh) Form of Marvin, meaning "a friend of the sea"
Mervinn, Mervinne, Mervyn, Mervynn, Mervynne, Merven, Mervenn, Mervenne

Meshach (Hebrew) An enduring man
Meshack, Meshac, Meshak, Meeshach, Meeshack, Meeshak, Meeshac

Mhina (African) One who is delightful
Mhinah, Mheena, Mheenah, Mheina, Mheinah, Mhienah, Mhienah, Mhyna

Micah (Hebrew) Form of Michael, meaning "who is like God?"
Mica, Mycah

*ᵀMichael (Hebrew) Who is like God?
Makai, Micael, Mical, Micha, Michaelangelo, Michail, Michal, Micheal, **Miguel,** *Mick*

Mick (English) Form of Michael, meaning "who is like God?"
Micke, Mickey, Micky, Micki, Mickie, Mickee, Mickea, Mickel

Mieko (Japanese) A bright man

*Miguel (Portuguese / Spanish) Form of Michael, meaning "who is like God?"
Migel, Myguel

Milan (Latin) An eager and hardworking man
Mylan

Miles (German / Latin) One who is merciful / a soldier
Myles, Miley, Mily, Mili, Milie, Milee

Milford (English) From the mill's ford
Millford, Milfurd, Millfurd, Milferd, Millferd, Milforde, Millforde, Milfurde

Miller (English) One who works at the mill
Millar, Millor, Millur, Millir, Millyr, Myller, Millen, Millan

Milo (German) Form of Miles, meaning "one who is merciful"
Mylo

Milson (English) The son of Miles
Milsun, Milsen, Milsin, Milsyn, Milsan

Mimir (Norse) In mythology, a giant who guarded the well of wisdom
Mymir, Mimeer, Mimyr, Mymeer, Mymyr, Meemir, Meemeer, Meemyr

Miner (Latin / English) One who works in the mines / a youth
Minor, Minar, Minur, Minir, Minyr

Mingan (Native American) Resembling a gray wolf
Mingen, Mingin, Mingon, Mingun, Mingyn

Minh (Vietnamese) A clever man

Minster (English) Of the church
Mynster, Minstar, Mynstar, Minstor, Mynstor, Minstur, Mynstur, Minstir

Miracle (American) An act of God's hand
Mirakle, Mirakel, Myracle, Myrakle

Mirage (French) An illusion
Myrage

Mirumbi (African) Born during a period of rain
Mirumbie, Mirumby, Mirumbey, Mirumbee, Mirumbea

Missouri (Native American) From the town of large canoes; from the state of Missouri
Missourie, Mizouri, Mizourie, Missoury, Mizoury, Missuri, Mizuri, Mizury

Mitchell (English) Form of Michael, meaning "who is like God?"
Mitch, Mitchel, Mytch, Mitchum, Mytchill, Mitcham

Mitsu (Japanese) Of the light
Mytsu, Mitsue, Mytsue

Mochni (Native American) Resembling a talking bird
Mochnie, Mochny, Mochney, Mochnee, Mochnea

Modesty (Latin) One who is without conceit
Modesti, Modestie, Modestee, Modestus, Modestey, Modesto, Modestio, Modestine

Mogens (Dutch) A powerful man
Mogen, Mogins, Mogin, Mogyns, Mogyn, Mogan, Mogans

Mohajit (Indian) A charming man
Mohajeet, Mohajeat, Mohajeit, Mohajiet, Mohajyt

^**Mohammed** (Arabic) One who is greatly praised; the name of the prophet and founder of Islam
Mahomet, Mohamad, Mohamed, Mohamet, Mohammad, Muhammad, Muhammed, Mehmet

Mohave (Native American) A tribal name
Mohav, Mojave

Mojag (Native American) One who is never quiet

Molan (Irish) The servant of the storm
Molen

Momo (American) A warring man

Mona (African) A jealous man
Monah

Mongo (African) A well-known man
Mongoe, Mongow, Mongowe

Mongwau (Native American) Resembling an owl

Monroe (Gaelic) From the mouth of the river Roe
Monro, Monrow, Monrowe, Munro, Munroe, Munrow, Munrowe

Montenegro (Spanish) From the black mountain

Montgomery (French) From Gomeric's mountain
Monty, Montgomerey, Montgomeri, Montgomerie, Montgomeree, Montgomerea

Monty (English) Form of Montgomery, meaning "from Gomeric's mountain"
Montey, Monti, Montie, Montee, Montea, Montes, Montez

Moon (American) Born beneath the moon; a dreamer

Mooney (Irish) A wealthy man
Moony, Mooni, Moonie, Maonaigh, Moonee, Moonea, Moone

Moose (American) Resembling the animal; a big, strong man
Moos, Mooze, Mooz

Moran (Irish) A great man
Morane, Morain, Moraine, Morayn, Morayne, Moraen, Moraene

Morathi (African) A wise man
Morathie, Morathy, Morathey, Morathee, Morathea

Moreland (English) From the moors
Moorland, Morland

Morley (English) From the meadow on the moor
Morly, Morleigh, Morlee, Morlea, Morleah, Morli, Morlie, Moorley

Morpheus (Greek) In mythology, the god of dreams
Morfeus, Morphius, Mofius

Mortimer (French) Of the still water; of the dead sea
Mortymer, Morty, Mortey, Morti, Mortie, Mortee, Mortea, Mort, Morte

Moses (Hebrew) A savior; in the Bible, the leader of the Israelites; drawn from the water
Mioshe, Mioshye, Mohsen, Moke, Moise, Moises, Mose, Moshe

Mostyn (Welsh) From the mossy settlement
Mostin, Mosten, Moston, Mostun, Mostan

Moswen (African) A light-skinned man
Moswenn, Moswenne, Moswin, Moswinn, Moswinne, Moswyn, Moswynn, Moswynne

Moubarak (Arabian) One who is blessed
Mubarak, Moobarak

Mounafes (Arabic) A rival

Muhannad (Arabic) One who wields a sword
Muhanned, Muhanad, Muhaned, Muhunnad, Muhunad, Muhanned, Muhaned

Mukhtar (Arabic) The chosen one
Muktar

Mukisa (Ugandan) Having good fortune
Mukysa

Mulcahy (Irish) A war chief
Mulcahey, Mulcahi, Mulcahie, Mulcahee, Mulcahea

Mundhir (Arabic) One who cautions others
Mundheer, Mundhear, Mundheir, Mundhier, Mundhyr

Murdock (Scottish) From the sea
Murdok, Murdoc, Murdo, Murdoch, Murtagh, Murtaugh, Murtogh, Murtough

Murfain (American) Having a warrior spirit
Murfaine, Murfayn, Murfayne, Murfaen, Murfaene, Murfane

Muriel (Gaelic) Of the shining sea
Muryel, Muriell, Muryell, Murial, Muriall, Muryal, Muryall, Murell

Murphy (Gaelic) A warrior of the sea
Murphey, Murphee, Murphea, Murphi, Murphie, Murfey, Murfy, Murfee

Murray (Gaelic) The lord of the sea
Murrey, Murry, Murri, Murrie, Murree, Murrea, Murry

Murron (Celtic) A bitter man
Murrun, Murren, Murran, Murrin, Murryn

Murtadi (Arabic) One who is content
Murtadie, Murtady, Murtadey, Murtadee, Murtadea

Musad (Arabic) One who is lucky
Musaad, Mus'ad

Mushin (Arabic) A charitable man
Musheen, Mushean, Mushein, Mushien, Mushyn

Muskan (Arabic) One who smiles often
Musken, Muskon, Muskun, Muskin, Muskyn

Muslim (Arabic) An adherent of Islam
Muslym, Muslem, Moslem, Moslim, Moslym

Mustapha (Arabic) The chosen one
Mustafa, Mostapha, Mostafa, Moustapha, Moustafa

Muti (Arabic) One who is obedient
Mutie, Muty, Mutey, Mutee, Mutea, Muta

Myron (Greek) Refers to myrrh, a fragrant oil
Myrun, Myran, Myren, Myrin, Myryn, Miron, Mirun, Miran

Mystique (French) A man with an air of mystery
Mystic, Mistique, Mysteek, Misteek, Mystiek, Mistiek, Mysteeque, Misteeque

N

Nabendu (Indian) Born beneath the new moon
Nabendue, Nabendoo, Nabendou

Nabhi (Indian) The best
Nabhie, Nabhy, Nabhey, Nabhee, Nabhea

Nabhomani (Indian) Of the sun
Nabhomanie, Nabhomany, Nabhomaney, Nabhomanee, Nabhomanea

Nabil (Arabic) A highborn man
Nabeel, Nabeal, Nabeil, Nabiel, Nabyl

Nabu (Babylonian) In mythology, the god of writing and wisdom
Nabue, Naboo, Nabo, Nebo, Nebu, Nebue, Neboo

Nachshon (Hebrew) An adventurous man; one who is daring
Nachson

Nadav (Hebrew) A generous man
Nadaav

Nadif (African) One who is born between seasons
Nadeef, Nadief, Nadeif, Nadyf, Nadeaf

Nadim (Arabic) A beloved friend
Nadeem, Nadeam, Nadiem, Nadeim, Nadym

Naftali (Hebrew) A struggling man; in the Bible, one of Jacob's sons
Naphtali, Naphthali, Neftali, Nefthali, Nephtali, Nephthali, Naftalie, Naphtalie

Nagel (German) One who makes nails
Nagle, Nagler, Naegel, Nageler, Nagelle, Nagele, Nagell

Nahir (Hebrew) A clear-headed and bright man
Naheer, Nahear, Naheir, Nahier, Nahyr, Naher

Nahum (Hebrew) A compassionate man
Nahom, Nahoum, Nahoom, Nahuem

Naji (Arabic) One who is safe
Najea, Naje, Najee, Najie, Najy, Najey, Nanji, Nanjie

Najib (Arabic) Of noble descent; a highborn man
Najeeb, Najeab, Najeib, Najieb, Najyb, Nageeb, Nageab, Nagyb

Nally (Irish) A poor man
Nalley, Nalli, Nallie, Nallee, Nallea, Nalleigh

Namir (Israeli) Resembling a leopard
Nameer, Namear, Namier, Nameir, Namyr

Nandan (Indian) One who is pleasing
Nanden, Nandin, Nandyn, Nandon, Nandun

Naotau (Indian) Our new son
Naotou

Napier (French / English) A mover / one who takes care of the royal linens
Neper

Napoleon (Italian / German) A man from Naples / son of the mists
Napolean, Napolion, Napoleone, Napoleane, Napolione

Narcissus (Greek) Resembling a daffodil; self-love; in mythology, a youth who fell in love with his reflection
Narciso, Narcisse, Narkissos, Narses, Narcisus, Narcis, Narciss

Naresh (Indian) A king
Nareshe, Natesh, Nateshe

Nasih (Arabic) One who advises others
Nasyh

Natal (Spanish) Born at Christmastime
Natale, Natalino, Natalio, Natall, Natalle, Nataleo, Natica

***ᵀNathan** (Hebrew) Form of Nathaniel, meaning "a gift from God"
Nat, Natan, Nate, Nathen, Nathon, Nathin, Nathyn, Nathun, Lathan

***Nathaniel** (Hebrew) A gift from God
Nathan, Natanael, Nataniel, Nathanael, Nathaneal, Nathanial, Nathanyal, Nathanyel, Nethanel

Nature (American) An outdoorsy man
Natural

Navarro (Spanish) From the plains
Navaro, Navarrio, Navario, Navarre, Navare, Nabaro, Nabarro

Naveed (Persian) Our best wishes
Navead, Navid, Navied, Naveid, Navyd

Nazim (Arabian) Of a soft
breeze
*Nazeem, Nazeam, Naziem,
Nazeim, Nazym*

Nebraska (Native American)
From the flat water land;
from the state of Nebraska

Neckarios (Greek) Of the
nectar; one who is immortal
*Nectaire, Nectarios, Nectarius,
Nektario, Nektarius, Nektarios,
Nektaire*

Neelotpal (Indian) Resembling
the blue lotus
*Nealotpal, Nielotpal, Neilotpal,
Nilothpal, Neelothpal*

Negm (Arabian) Resembling
a star

Nehal (Indian) Born during a
period of rain
Nehall, Nehale, Nehalle

Nehemiah (Hebrew) God
provides comfort
*Nehemia, Nechemia,
Nechemiah, Nehemya,
Nehemyah, Nechemya,
Nechemyah*

Neil (Gaelic) The champion
*Neal, Neale, Neall, Nealle,
Nealon, Neel, Neilan, Neile*

Neirin (Irish) Surrounded by
light
*Neiryn, Neiren, Neerin, Neeryn,
Neeren*

Nelek (Polish) Resembling a
horn
Nelec, Neleck

Nelson (English) The son of
Neil; the son of a champion
*Nealson, Neilson, Neillson,
Nelsen, Nilson, Nilsson, Nelli,
Nellie*

Neptune (Latin) In mythology,
god of the sea
*Neptun, Neptoon, Neptoone,
Neptoun, Neptoune*

Neroli (Italian) Resembling an
orange blossom
*Nerolie, Neroly, Neroley,
Neroleigh, Nerolea, Nerolee*

Nevan (Irish) The little saint
Naomhan

Neville (French) From the new
village
*Nev, Nevil, Nevile, Nevill,
Nevylle, Nevyl, Nevyle, Nevyll*

Newcomb (English) From the
new valley
*Newcom, Newcome, Newcombe,
Neucomb, Neucombe, Neucom,
Neucome*

Newlin (Welsh) From the new pond
Newlinn, Newlyn, Newlynn, Neulin, Neulinn, Neulyn, Neulynn

Newman (English) A newcomer
Newmann, Neuman, Neumann

Nhat (Vietnamese) Having a long life
Nhatt, Nhate, Nhatte

Niaz (Persian) A gift
Nyaz

Nibaw (Native American) One who stands tall
Nybaw, Nibau, Nybau

*ᵀ**Nicholas** (Greek) Of the victorious people
Nick, Nicanor, Niccolo, Nichol, Nicholai, Nicholaus, Nikolai, Nicholl, Nichols, Colin, Nicolas, Nico

Nick (English) Form of Nicholas, meaning "of the victorious people"
Nik, Nicki, Nickie, Nickey, Nicky, Nickee, Nickea, Niki

Nickler (American) One who is swift
Nikler, Nicler, Nyckler, Nykler, Nycler

Nicomedes (Greek) One who thinks of victory
Nikomedes, Nicomedo, Nikomedo

Nihal (Indian) One who is content
Neehal, Neihal, Niehal, Neahal, Neyhal, Nyhal

Nihar (Indian) Covered with the morning's dew
Neehar, Niehar, Neihar, Neahar, Nyhar

Nikan (Persian) One who brings good things
Niken, Nikin, Nikyn, Nikon, Nikun

Nikshep (Indian) One who is treasured
Nykshep

Nikunja (Indian) From the grove of trees

Nino (Italian / Spanish) God is gracious / a young boy
Ninoshka

Nirad (Indian) Of the clouds
Nyrad

Niran (Thai) The eternal one
Nyran, Niren, Nirin, Niryn, Niron, Nirun, Nyren, Nyrin

Nirav (Indian) One who is quiet
Nyrav

Nirbheet (Indian) A fearless man
Nirbhit, Nirbhyt, Nirbhay, Nirbhaye, Nirbhai, Nirbhae

Niremaan (Arabic) One who shines as brightly as fire
Nyremaan, Nireman, Nyreman

Nishan (Armenian) A sign or symbol

Nishok (Indian) Filled with happiness
Nyshok, Nishock, Nyshock

Nissan (Hebrew) A miracle child
Nisan

Niyol (Native American) Of the wind

Njord (Scandinavian) A man from the north
Njorde, Njorth, Njorthe

*★T**Noah** (Hebrew) A peaceful wanderer
Noa

Nodin (Native American) Of the wind
Nodyn, Noden, Nodan, Nodon, Nodun

Nolan (Gaelic) A famous and noble man; a champion of the people
Nolen, Nolin, Nolon, Nolun, Nolyn, Noland, Nolande

North (English) A man from the north
Northe

Northcliff (English) From the northern cliff
Northcliffe, Northclyf, Northclyff, Northclyffe

Norval (Scottish) From the northern valley
Norvall, Norvale, Norvail, Norvaile, Norvayl, Norvayle, Norvael, Norvaele

Norward (English) A guardian of the north
Norwarde, Norwerd, Norwerde, Norwurd, Norwurde

Noshi (Native American) A fatherly man
Noshie, Noshy, Noshey, Noshee, Noshea, Nosh, Noshe

Notaku (Native American) Resembling a growling bear
Notakou, Notakue, Notakoo

Nuhad (Arabic) A brave young man
Nuehad, Nouhad, Neuhad

Nukpana (Native American) An evil man
Nukpanah, Nukpanna, Nukpannah, Nuckpana, Nucpana

Nulte (Irish) A man from Ulster
Nulti, Nultie, Nulty, Nultey, Nultee, Nultea

Nuncio (Spanish) A messenger
Nunzio

Nuriel (Hebrew) God's light
Nuriell, Nuriele, Nurielle, Nuryel, Nuryell, Nuryele, Nuryelle, Nooriel

Nuru (African) My light
Nurue, Nuroo, Nurou, Nourou, Nooroo

Nyack (African) One who is persistent
Niack, Nyak, Niak, Nyac, Niac

Nye (English) One who lives on the island
Nyle, Nie, Nile

O

Obedience (American) A well-behaved man
Obediance, Obedyence, Obedeynce

Oberon (German) A royal bear; having the heart of a bear
Oberron

Obert (German) A wealthy and bright man
Oberte, Oberth, Oberthe, Odbart, Odbarte, Odbarth, Odbarthe, Odhert

Ochi (African) Filled with laughter
Ochie, Ochee, Ochea, Ochy, Ochey

Odam (English) A son-in-law
Odom, Odem, Odum

Ode (Egyptian / Greek) Traveler of the road / a lyric poem

Oded (Hebrew) One who is supportive and encouraging

Oder (English) From the river
Odar, Odir, Odyr, Odur

Odin (Norse) In mythology, the supreme deity
Odyn, Odon, Oden, Odun

Odinan (Hungarian) One who is wealthy and powerful
Odynan, Odinann, Odynann

Odion (African) The first-born of twins
Odiyon, Odiun, Odiyun

Odissan (African) A wanderer;
traveler
*Odyssan, Odisan, Odysan,
Odissann, Odyssann, Odisann,
Odysann*

Ofir (Hebrew) The golden son
*Ofeer, Ofear, Ofyr, Ofier, Ofeir,
Ofer*

Ogaleesha (Native American)
A man wearing a red shirt
*Ogaleasha, Ogaleisha,
Ogaleysha, Ogalesha,
Ogaliesha, Ogalisha*

Oghe (Irish) One who rides
horses
*Oghi, Oghie, Oghee, Oghea,
Oghy, Oghey*

Oguz (Hungarian) An arrow
Oguze, Oguzz, Oguzze

Ohanko (Native American) A
reckless man
Ohankio, Ohankiyo

Ojaswit (Indian) A powerful
and radiant man
*Ojaswyt, Ojaswin, Ojaswen,
Ojaswyn, Ojas*

Okal (African) To cross
Okall

Okan (Turkish) Resembling a
horse
Oken, Okin, Okyn

Okapi (African) Resembling
an animal with a long neck
*Okapie, Okapy, Okapey,
Okapee, Okapea, Okape*

Okechuku (African) Blessed
by God

Oki (Japanese) From the
center of the ocean
Okie, Oky, Okey, Okee, Okea

Oklahoma (Native American)
Of the red people; from the
state of Oklahoma

Oktawian (African) The
eighth-born child
*Oktawyan, Oktawean,
Octawian, Octawyan,
Octawean*

Olaf (Scandinavian) The
remaining of the ancestors
*Olay, Ole, Olef, Olev, Oluf,
Uolevi*

Olafemi (African) A lucky
young man
*Olafemie, Olafemy, Olafemey,
Olafemee, Olafemea*

Oleg (Russian) One who is
holy
Olezka

*Oliver (Latin) From the olive
tree
*Oliviero, Olivero, Olivier,
Oliviero, Olivio, Ollie*

Olney (English) From the loner's field
Olny, Olnee, Olnea, Olni, Olnie, Ollaneg, Olaneg

Olujimi (African) One who is close to God
Olujimie, Olujimy, Olujimey, Olujimee, Olujimea

Olumide (African) God has arrived
Olumidi, Olumidie, Olumidy, Olumidey, Olumidee, Olumidea, Olumyde, Olumydi

Omar (Arabic) A flourishing man; one who is well-spoken
Omarr, Omer

Omeet (Hebrew) My light
Omeete, Omeit, Omeite, Omeyt, Omeyte, Omit, Omeat, Omeate

Omega (Greek) The last great one; the last letter of the Greek alphabet
Omegah

Onaona (Hawaiian) Having a pleasant scent

Ond (Hungarian) The tenth-born child
Onde

Ondrej (Czech) A manly man
Ondrejek, Ondrejec, Ondrousek, Ondravsek

Onkar (Indian) The purest one
Onckar, Oncar, Onkarr, Onckarr, Oncarr

Onofrio (Italain) A defender of peace
Onofre, Onofrius, Onophrio, Onophre, Onfrio, Onfroi

Onslow (Arabic) From the hill of the enthusiast
Onslowe, Ounslow, Ounslowe

Onyebuchi (African) God is in everything
Onyebuchie, Onyebuchy, Onyebuchey, Onyebuchee, Onyebuchea

Oqwapi (Native American) Resembling a red cloud
Oqwapie, Oqwapy, Oqwapey, Oqwapee, Oqwapea

Oram (English) From the enclosure near the riverbank
Oramm, Oraham, Orahamm, Orham, Orhamm

Ordell (Latin) Of the beginning
Ordel, Ordele, Ordelle, Orde

Ordway (Anglo-Saxon) A fighter armed with a spear
Ordwaye, Ordwai, Ordwae

Oren (Hebrew / Gaelic) From the pine tree / a pale-skinned man
Orenthiel, Orenthiell, Orenthiele, Orenthielle, Orenthiem, Orenthium, Orin

Orleans (Latin) The golden child
Orlean, Orleane, Orleens, Orleen, Orleene, Orlins, Olryns, Orlin

Orly (Hebrew) Surrounded by light
Orley, Orli, Orlie, Orlee, Orleigh, Orlea

Ormod (Anglo-Saxon) A sorrowful man

Ormond (English) One who defends with a spear / from the mountain of bears
Ormonde, Ormund, Ormunde, Ormemund, Ormemond, Ordmund, Ordmunde, Ordmond

Ornice (Irish / Hebrew) A pale-skinned man / from the cedar tree
Ornyce, Ornise, Orynse, Orneice, Orneise, Orniece, Orniese, Orneece

Orris (Latin) One who is inventive
Orriss, Orrisse, Orrys, Orryss, Orrysse

Orson (Latin) Resembling a bear; raised by a bear
Orsen, Orsin, Orsini, Orsino, Orsis, Orsonio, Orsinie, Orsiny

Orth (English) An honest man
Orthe

Orton (English) From the settlement by the shore
Ortun, Oraton, Oratun

Orville (French) From the gold town
Orvell, Orvelle, Orvil, Orvill, Orvele, Orvyll, Orvylle, Orvyl

Orwel (Welsh) Of the horizon
Orwell, Orwele, Orwelle

Os (English) The divine

Osborn (Norse) A bear of God
Osborne, Osbourn, Osbourne, Osburn, Osburne

Oscar (English / Gaelic) A spear of the gods / a friend of deer
Oskar, Osker, Oscer, Osckar, Oscker, Oszkar, Oszcar

Osher (Hebrew) A man of good fortune

Osias (Greek) Salvation
Osyas

Osileani (Polynesian) One who talks a lot
Osileanie, Osileany, Osileaney, Osileanee, Osileanea

Oswald (English) The power of God
Oswalde, Osvald, Osvaldo, Oswaldo, Oswell, Osvalde, Oswallt, Osweald

Oswin (English) A friend of God
Oswinn, Oswinne, Oswen, Oswenn, Oswenne, Oswyn, Oswynn, Oswynne

Othniel (Hebrew) God's lion
Othniell, Othnielle, Othniele, Othnyel, Othnyell, Othnyele, Othnyelle

Otmar (Teutonic) A famous warrior
Otmarr, Othmar, Othmarr, Otomar, Ottomar

Otoahhastis (Native American) Resembling a tall bull

Ottokar (German) A spirited warrior
Otokar, Otokarr, Ottokarr, Ottokars, Otokars, Ottocar, Otocar, Ottocars

Ouray (Native American) The arrow
Ouraye, Ourae, Ourai

Ourson (French) Resembling a little bear
Oursun, Oursoun, Oursen, Oursan, Oursin, Oursyn

Ovid (Latin) A shepherd; an egg
Ovyd, Ovidio, Ovido, Ovydio, Ovydo, Ovidiu, Ovydiu, Ofydd

*ᵀ**Owen** (Welsh / Gaelic) Form of Eugene, meaning "a well-born man" / a youthful man
Owenn, Owenne, Owin, Owinn, Owinne, Owyn, Owynn, Owynne

Oxton (English) From the oxen town
Oxtun, Oxtown, Oxnaton, Oxnatun, Oxnatown

Oz (Hebrew) Having great strength
Ozz, Ozzi, Ozzie, Ozzy, Ozzey, Ozzee, Ozzea, Ozi

Ozni (Hebrew) One who knows God
Oznie, Ozny, Ozney, Oznee, Oznea

Ozuru (Japanese) Resembling a stork
Ozurou, Ozourou, Ozuroo, Ozooroo

P

Paavo (Finnish) Form of Paul, meaning "a small or humble man"
Paaveli

Pace (Hebrew / English) Refers to Passover / a peaceful man
Paice, Payce, Paece, Pacey, Pacy, Pacee, Paci, Pacie

Pacho (Spanish) An independent man; one who is free

Pachu'a (Native American) Resembling a water snake

Paco (Spanish) A man from France
Pacorro, Pacoro, Paquito

Padgett (French) One who strives to better himself
Padget, Padgette, Padgete, Padgeta, Padgetta, Padge, Paget, Pagett

Padman (Indian) Resembling the lotus
Padmann

Padruig (Scottish) Of the royal family

Paine (Latin) Man from the country; a peasant
Pain, Payn, Payne, Paen, Paene, Pane, Paien

Palamedes (English) In Arthurian legend, a knight
Palomydes, Palomedes, Palamydes, Palsmedes, Palsmydes, Pslomydes

Palban (Spanish) A blond-haired man
Palben, Palbin, Palbyn, Palbon, Palbun

Paley (English) Form of Paul, meaning "a small or humble man"
Paly, Pali, Palie, Palee, Palea

Palladin (Greek) Filled with wisdom
Palladyn, Palladen, Palladan, Paladin, Paladyn, Paladen, Paladan

Palmer (English) A pilgrim bearing a palm branch
Pallmer, Palmar, Pallmar, Palmerston, Palmiro, Palmeero, Palmeer, Palmire

Pan (Greek) In mythology, god of the shepherds
Pann

Panama (Spanish) From the canal

Pancho (Spanish) A man from France

Pankaj (Indian) Resembling the lotus flower

Panya (African) Resembling a mouse
Panyah

Panyin (African) The first-born of twins
Panyen

Paras (Hindi) A touchstone
Parasmani, Parasmanie, Parasmany, Parasmaney, Parasmanee

*Parker (English) The keeper of the park
Parkar, Parkes, Parkman, Park

Parley (Scottish) A reluctant man
Parly, Parli, Parlie, Parlee, Parlea, Parle

Parmenio (Spanish) A studious man; one who is intelligent
Parmenios, Parmenius

Parounag (Armenian) One who is thankful

Parrish (Latin) Man of the church
Parish, Parrishe, Parishe, Parrysh, Parysh, Paryshe, Parryshe, Parisch

Parry (Welsh) The son of Harry
Parrey, Parri, Parrie, Parree, Parrea

Parthenios (Greek) One who is pure; chaste
Parthenius

Parthik (Greek) One who is pure; chaste
Parthyk, Parthick, Parthyck, Parthic, Parthyc

Pascal (Latin) Born during Easter
Pascale, Pascalle, Paschal, Paschalis, Pascoe, Pascual, Pascuale, Pasqual

Patamon (Native American) Resembling a tempest
Patamun, Patamen, Pataman, Patamyn, Patamin

Patch (American) Form of Peter, meaning "as solid and strong as a rock"
Pach, Patche, Patchi, Patchie, Patchy, Patchey, Patchee

Patrick (Latin) A nobleman; patrician
Packey, Padric, Pat, Patrece, Patric, Patrice, Patreece, Patricio

Patton (English) From the
town of warriors
*Paten, Patin, Paton, Patten,
Pattin, Paddon, Padden,
Paddin*

Patwin (Native American) A
manly man
*Patwinn, Patwinne, Patwyn,
Patwynne, Patwynn, Patwen,
Patwenn, Patwenne*

Paul (Latin) A small or humble
man
*Pauley, Paulie, Pauly, Paley,
Paavo*

Paurush (Indian) A coura-
geous man
*Paurushe, Paurushi, Paurushie,
Paurushy, Paurushey,
Paurushee*

Pavanjit (Indian) Resembling
the wind
*Pavanjyt, Pavanjeet, Pavanjeat,
Pavanjete*

^Paxton (English) From the
peaceful town
*Packston, Paxon, Paxten,
Paxtun, Packstun, Packsten*

Pazel (Hebrew) God's gold;
treasured by God
Pazell, Pazele, Pazelle

Pearroc (English) Man of the
forest
*Pearoc, Pearrok, Pearok,
Pearrock, Pearock*

Pecos (American) From the
river; a cowboy
Pekos, Peckos

Pedro (Spanish) Form of
Peter, meaning "as solid and
strong as a rock"
*Pedrio, Pepe, Petrolino, Piero,
Pietro*

Pelham (English) From the
house of furs; from Peola's
home
Pellham, Pelam, Pellam

Pell (English) A clerk or one
who works with skins
Pelle, Pall, Palle

Pelon (Spanish) Filled with joy
Pellon

Pelton (English) From the
town by the lake
*Pellton, Peltun, Pelltun, Peltan,
Pelltan, Pelten, Pellten, Peltin*

Penda (African) One who is
dearly loved
Pendah, Penha, Penhah

Penley (English) From the
enclosed meadow
*Penly, Penleigh, Penli, Penlie,
Penlee, Penlea, Penleah, Pennley*

Penrod (German) A respected commander

Pentele (Hungarian) A merciful man
Pentelle, Pentel, Pentell

Penuel (Hebrew) The face of God
Penuell, Penuele, Penuelle

Percival (French) One who can pierce the vale"
Purcival, Percy, Percey, Perci, Percie, Percee, Percea, Persy, Persey, Persi

Peregrine (Latin) One who travels; a wanderer
Perry, Perree, Perrea, Perri, Perrie, Perregrino

Perez (Hebrew) To break through
Peretz

Pericles (Greek) One who is in excess of glory
Perricles, Perycles, Perrycles, Periclees, Perriclees, Peryclees, Perryclees, Periclez

Perk (American) One who is cheerful and jaunty
Perke, Perky, Perkey, Perki, Perkie, Perkee, Perkea

Perkinson (English) The son of Perkin; the son of Peter
Perkynson

Perseus (Greek) In mythology, son of Zeus who slew Medusa
Persius, Persyus, Persies, Persyes

Perth (Celtic) From the thorny thicket
Perthe, Pert, Perte

Perye (English) From the pear tree

Peter (Greek) As solid and strong as a rock
Peder, Pekka, Per, Petar, Pete, Peterson, Petr, Petre, Pierce, Patch, Pedro

Petuel (Hindi) The Lord's vision
Petuell, Petuele, Petuelle

Peyton (English) From the village of warriors
Payton, Peytun, Paytun, Peyten, Payten, Paiton, Paitun, Paiten

Pharis (Irish) A heroic man
Pharys, Pharris, Pharrys

Phex (American) A kind man
Phexx

Philemon (Hebrew) A loving man
Phylemon, Philimon, Phylimon, Philomon, Phylomon, Philamon, Phylamon

Philetus (Greek) A collector
Phyletus, Philetos, Phyletos

Phillip (Greek) One who loves horses
Phil, Philip, Felipe, Filipp, Phillie, Philly

Philo (Greek) One who loves and is loved

Phoebus (Greek) A radiant man
Phoibos

Phomello (African) A successful man
Phomelo

Phong (Vietnamese) Of the wind

Phuc (Vietnamese) One who is blessed
Phuoc

Picardus (Hispanic) An adventurous man
Pycardus, Picardos, Pycardos, Picardas, Pycardas, Picardis, Pycardis, Picardys

Pickworth (English) From the woodcutter's estate
Pikworth, Picworth, Pickworthe, Pikworthe, Picworthe

Pierce (English) Form of Peter, meaning "as solid and strong as a rock"
Pearce, Pears, Pearson, Pearsson, Peerce, Peirce, Pierson, Piersson

Pin (Vietnamese) Filled with joy
Pyn

Pio (Latin) A pious man
Pyo, Pios, Pius, Pyos, Pyus

Pirro (Greek) A red-haired man
Pyrro

Pitney (English) From the island of the stubborn man
Pitny, Pitni, Pitnie, Pitnee, Pitnea, Pytney, Pytny, Pytni

Pittman (English) A laborer
Pyttman, Pitman, Pytman

Plantagenet (French) Resembling the broom flower

Poetry (American) A romantic man
Poetrey, Poetri, Poetrie, Poetree, Poetrea, Poet, Poete

Pollux (Greek) One who is crowned
Pollock, Pollok, Polloc, Pollack, Polloch

Polo (African) Resembling an alligator
Poloe, Poloh

Ponce (Spanish) The fifth-born child
Ponse

Pongor (Hungarian) A mighty man
Pongorr, Pongoro, Pongorro

Poni (African) The second-born son
Ponni, Ponie, Ponnie, Pony, Ponny, Poney, Ponney, Ponee

Pons (Latin) From the bridge
Pontius, Ponthos, Ponthus

Poornamruth (Indian) Full of sweetness
Pournamruth

Poornayu (Indian) Full of life; blessed with a full life
Pournayu, Poornayou, Pournayou, Poornayue, Pournayue

Porat (Hebrew) A productive man

Porfirio (Greek) Refers to a purple coloring
Porphirios, Prophyrios, Porfiro, Porphyrios

Powhatan (Native American) From the chief's hill

Prabhakar (Hindu) Of the sun

Prabhat (Indian) Born during the morning

Pragun (Indian) One who is straightforward; honest

Pramod (Indian) A delightful young man

Pranit (Indian) One who is humble; modest
Pranyt, Praneet, Praneat

Prasad (Indian) A gift from God

Prashant (Indian) One who is peaceful; calm
Prashante, Prashanth, Prashanthe

Pratap (Hindi) A majestic man

Pravat (Thai) History

Prem (Indian) An affectionate man

Prentice (English) A student; an apprentice
Prentyce, Prentise, Prentyse, Prentiss, Prentis

Prescott (English) From the priest's cottage
Prescot, Prestcot, Prestcott, Preostcot

Preston (English) From the priest's town
Prestin, Prestyn, Prestan, Prestun, Presten, Pfeostun

Prewitt (French) A brave young one
Prewet, Prewett, Prewit, Pruitt, Pruit, Pruet, Pruett

Prine (English) One who surpasses others
Pryne

Prometheus (Greek) In mythology, he stole fire from the heavens and gave it to man
Promitheus, Promethius, Promithius

Prop (American) A fun-loving man
Propp, Proppe

Prosper (Latin) A fortunate man
Prospero, Prosperus

Pryderi (Celtic) Son of the sea
Pryderie, Prydery, Pryderey, Pryderee, Pryderea

Prydwen (Welsh) A handsome man
Prydwenn, Prydwenne, Prydwin, Prydwinne, Prydwinn, Prydwyn, Prydwynn, Prydwynne

Pullman (English) One who works on a train
Pulman, Pullmann, Pulmann

Pyralis (Greek) Born of fire
Pyraliss, Pyralisse, Pyralys, Pyralyss, Pyralysse, Pyre

Q

Qabil (Arabic) An able-bodied man
Qabyl, Qabeel, Qabeal, Qabeil, Qabiel

Qadim (Arabic) From an ancient family
Qadeem, Qadiem, Qadeim, Qadym, Qadeam

Qaiser (Arabic) A king; a ruler
Qeyser

Qamar (Arabic) Born beneath the moon
Qamarr, Quamar, Quamarr

Qimat (Hindi) A highly valued man
Qymat

Qing (Chinese) Of the deep water
Qyng

Quaashie (American) An ambitious man
Quashie, Quashi, Quashy, Quashey, Quashee, Quashea, Quaashi, Quaashy

Quaddus (American) A bright man
Quadus, Quaddos, Quados

Quade (Latin) The fourth-born child
Quadrees, Quadres, Quadrys, Quadries, Quadreis, Quadreys, Quadreas, Quadrhys

Quaid (Irish) Form of Walter, meaning "the commander of the army"
Quaide, Quayd, Quayde, Quaed, Quaede

Quashawn (American) A tenacious man
Quashaun, Quasean, Quashon, Quashi, Quashie, Quashee, Quashea, Quashy

Qued (Native American) Wearing a decorated robe

Quentin (Latin) The fifth-born child
Quent, Quenten, Quenton, Quentun, Quentan, Quentyn, Quente, Qwentin

Quick (American) One who is fast; a witty man
Quik, Quicke, Quic

Quillan (Gaelic) Resembling a cub
Quilan, Quillen, Quilen, Quillon, Quilon

Quilliam (Gaelic) Form of William, meaning "the determined protector"
Quilhelm, Quilhelmus, Quilliams, Quilliamson

Quimby (Norse) From the woman's estate
Quimbey, Quimbee, Quimbea, Quimbi, Quimbie

Quincy (English) The fifth-born child; from the fifth son's estate
Quincey, Quinci, Quincie, Quincee, Quinncy, Quinnci, Quyncy, Quyncey

Quinlan (Gaelic) A strong and healthy man
Quindlan, Quinlen, Quindlen, Quinian, Quinlin, Quindlin, Quinlyn, Quindlyn

Quinn (Gaelic) One who provides counsel; an intelligent man
Quin, Quinne, Qwinn, Quynn, Qwin, Quiyn, Quyn, Qwinne

Quintavius (American) The fifth-born child
Quintavios, Quintavus, Quintavies

Quinto (Spanish) The fifth-born child
Quynto, Quintus, Quintos, Quinty, Quinti, Quintie

Quinton (Latin) From the queen's town or settlement
Laquinton

Quintrell (English) An elegant and dashing man
Quintrel, Quintrelle, Quyntrell, Quyntrelle, Quyntrel, Quyntrele, Quintrele

Quirinus (Latin) One who wields a spear
Quirinos, Quirynus, Quirynos, Quirinius, Quirynius

Quito (Spanish) A lively man
Quyto, Quitos, Quytos

Quoc (Vietnamese) A patriot
Quok, Quock

Qutub (Indian) One who is tall

R

Rabbaanee (African) An easy-going man

Rabbi (Hebrew) The master

Rach (African) Resembling a frog

Radames (Egyptian) A hero
Radamays, Radamayes, Radamais, Radamaise

Radford (English) From the red ford
Radforde, Radferd, Radfurd, Radferde, Radfurde

Rafael (Spanish) Form of Raphael, meaning "one who is healed by God"
Raphael, Raphaello, Rafaello

Rafe (Irish) A tough man
Raffe, Raff, Raf, Raif, Rayfe, Raife, Raef, Raefe

Rafi (Arabic) One who is exalted
Rafie, Rafy, Rafey, Rafea, Rafee, Raffi, Raffie, Raffy

Rafiki (African) A gentle friend
Rafikie, Rafikea, Rafikee, Rafiky, Rafikey

Rafiya (African) A dignified man
Rafeeya, Rafeaya, Rafeiya, Rafieya

Raghib (Arabic) One who is desired
Ragheb, Ragheeb, Ragheab, Raghyb, Ragheib, Raghieb

Ragnar (Norse) A warrior who places judgment
Ragnor, Ragner, Ragnir, Ragnyr, Ragnur, Regnar

Rahim (Arabic) A compassionate man
Rahym, Raheim, Rahiem, Raheem, Raheam

Raiden (Japanese) In mythology, the god of thunder and lightning
Raidon, Rayden, Raydon, Raeden, Raedon, Raden

Raimi (African) A compassionate man
Raimie, Raimy, Raimey, Raimee, Raimea

Rajab (African) A glorified man

Rajan (Indian) A king
Raj, Raja, Rajah

Rajarshi (Indian) The king's sage
Rajarshie, Rajarshy, Rajarshey, Rajarshee, Rajarshea

Rajesh (Hindi) The king's rule

Rajit (Indian) One who is decorated
Rajeet, Rajeit, Rajiet, Rajyt, Rajeat

Rajiv (Hindi) To be striped
Rajyv, Rajeev, Rajeav

Ralph (English) Wolf counsel
Ralf, Ralphe, Ralfe, Ralphi, Ralphie, Ralphee, Ralphea, Ralphy, Raoul

Ram (Hebrew / Sanskrit) A superior man / one who is pleasing
Rahm, Rama, Rahma, Ramos, Rahmos, Ram, Ramm

Rambert (German) Having great strength; an intelligent man
Ramberte, Ramberth, Ramberthe, Ramburt

Rami (Arabic) A loving man
Ramee, Ramea, Ramie, Ramy, Ramey

Ramiro (Portuguese) A famous counselor; a great judge
Ramyro, Rameero, Rameyro, Ramirez, Ramyrez, Rameerez

Ramsey (English) From the raven island; from the island of wild garlic
Ramsay, Ramsie, Ramsi, Ramsee, Ramsy, Ramsea, Ramzy, Ramzey

Rand (German) One who shields others
Rande

Randall (German) The wolf shield
Randy, Randal, Randale, Randel, Randell, Randl, Randle, Randon, Rendall

Randolph (German) The wolf shield
Randy, Randolf, Ranolf, Ranolph, Ranulfo, Randulfo, Randwulf, Ranwulf, Randwolf

Randy (English) Form of Randall or Randolph, meaning "the wolf shield"
Randey, Randi, Randie, Randee, Randea

Rang (English) Resembling a raven
Range

Rangey (English) From raven's island
Rangy, Rangi, Rangie, Rangee, Rangea

Rangle (American) A cowboy
Rangel

Ranjan (Indian) A delightful boy

Raoul (French) Form of Ralph, meaning "wolf counsel"
Raoule, Raul, Roul, Rowl, Raule, Roule, Rowle

Raqib (Arabic) A glorified man
Raqyb, Raqeeb, Raqeab, Rakib, Rakeeb, Rakeab, Rakyb

Rashard (American) A good-hearted man
Rasherd, Rashird, Rashurd, Rashyrd

Rashaun (American) Form of Roshan, meaning "born during the daylight"
Rashae, Rashane, Rashawn, Rayshaun, Rayshawn, Raishaun, Raishawn, Raeshaun

Ratul (Indian) A sweet man
Ratule, Ratoul, Ratoule, Ratool, Ratoole

Raulo (Spanish) One who is wise
Rawlo

Ravi (Hindi) From the sun
Ravie, Ravy, Ravey, Ravee, Ravea

Ravid (Hebrew) A wanderer; one who searches
Ravyd, Raveed, Ravead, Raviyd, Ravied, Raveid

Ravindra (Indian) The strength of the sun
Ravyndra

Ravinger (English) One who lives near the ravine
Ravynger

Rawlins (French) From the renowned land
Rawlin, Rawson, Rawlinson, Rawlings, Rawling, Rawls, Rawl, Rawle

Ray (English) Form of Raymond, meaning "a wise protector"
Rae, Rai, Rayce, Rayder, Rayse, Raye, Rayford, Raylen

Rayfield (English) From the field of roe deer
Rayfeld

Rayhurn (English) From the roe deer's stream
Rayhurne, Rayhorn, Rayhorne, Rayhourn, Rayhourne

Raymond (German) A wise protector
Ray, Raemond, Raemondo, Raimond, Raimondo, Raimund, Raimundo, Rajmund, Ramon

Rebel (American) An outlaw
Rebell, Rebele, Rebelle, Rebe, Rebbe, Rebbi, Rebbie, Rebbea

Redwald (English) Strong counsel
Redwalde, Raedwalde, Raedwald

Reeve (English) A bailiff
Reve, Reave, Reeford, Reeves, Reaves, Reves, Reaford

Regal (American) Born into royalty
Regall

Regan (Gaelic) Born into royalty; the little ruler
Raegan, Ragan, Raygan, Reganne, Regann, Regane, Reghan, Reagan

Regenfrithu (English) A peaceful raven

Reggie (Latin) Form of Reginald, meaning "the king's advisor"
Reggi, Reggy, Reggey, Reggea, Reggee, Reg

Reginald (Latin) The king's advisor
Reggie, Reynold, Raghnall, Rainault, Rainhold, Raonull, Raynald, Rayniero, Regin, Reginaldo

Regine (French) One who is artistic
Regeen, Regeene, Regean, Regeane, Regein, Regeine, Regien, Regiene

Reid (English) A red-haired man; one who lives near the reeds
Read, Reade, Reed, Reede, Reide, Raed

Reilly (Gaelic) An outgoing man
Reilley, Reilli, Reillie, Reillee, Reilleigh, Reillea

Remington (English) From the town of the raven's family
Remyngton, Remingtun, Remyngtun

Renweard (Anglo-Saxon) The guardian of the house
Renward, Renwarden, Renwerd

Renzo (Japanese) The third-born son

Reuben (Hebrew) Behold, a son!
Reuban, Reubin, Reuven, Rouvin, Rube, Ruben, Rubin, Rubino

Rev (American) One who is distinct
Revv, Revin, Reven, Revan, Revyn, Revon, Revun

Rex (Latin) A king
Reks, Recks, Rexs

Rexford (English) From the king's ford
Rexforde, Rexferd, Rexferde, Rexfurd, Rexfurde

Reynold (English) Form of Reginald, meaning "the king's advisor"
Reynald, Reynaldo, Reynolds, Reynalde, Reynolde

Rhett (Latin) A well-spoken man
Rett, Rhet

Rhydderch (Welsh) Having reddish-brown hair

Richard (English) A powerful ruler
Rick, Rich, Ricard, Ricardo, Riccardo, Richardo, Richart, Richerd, Rickard, Rickert

Richmond (French / German) From the wealthy hill / a powerful protector
Richmonde, Richmund, Richmunde

Rick (English) Form of Richard, meaning "a powerful ruler"
Ric, Ricci, Ricco, Rickie, Ricki, Ricky, Rico, Rik

Rickward (English) A strong protector
Rickwerd, Rickwood, Rikward, Ricward, Rickweard, Rikweard, Ricweard

Riddock (Irish) From the smooth field
Ridock, Riddoc, Ridoc, Ryddock, Rydock, Ryddoc, Rydoc, Ryddok

Ridgeway (English) One who lives on the road near the ridge
Rydgeway, Rigeway, Rygeway

Rigg (English) One who lives near the ridge
Rig, Ridge, Rygg, Ryg, Rydge, Rige, Ryge, Riggs

Riley (English) From the rye clearing
Ryly, Ryli, Rylie, Rylee,Ryleigh, Rylea, Ryleah

Riordain (Irish) A bright man
Riordane, Riordayn, Riordaen, Reardain, Reardane, Reardayn, Reardaen

Riordan (Gaelic) A royal poet; a bard or minstrel
Riorden, Rearden, Reardan, Riordon, Reardon

Ripley (English) From the noisy meadow
Riply, Ripleigh, Ripli, Riplie, Riplea, Ripleah, Riplee, Rip

Rishley (English) From the untamed meadow
Rishly, Rishli, Rishlie, Rishlee, Rishlea, Rishleah, Rishleigh

Rishon (Hebrew) The first-born son
Ryshon, Rishi, Rishie, Rishea, Rishee, Rishy, Rishey

Risley (English) From the brushwood meadow
Risly, Risli, Rislie, Risleigh, Rislea, Risleah, Rislee

Riston (English) From the brushwood settlement
Ryston, Ristun, Rystun

Ritter (German) A knight
Rytter, Ritt, Rytt

River (American) From the river
Ryver, Rivers, Ryvers

Roald (Norse) A famous ruler
Roal

Roam (American) One who wanders, searches
Roami, Roamie, Roamy, Roamey, Roamea, Roamee

Roark (Gaelic) A champion
Roarke, Rorke, Rourke, Rork, Rourk, Ruark, Ruarke

*Robert (German) One who is bright with fame
Bob, Rupert, Riobard, Roban, Robers, Roberto, Robertson, Robartach

Rochester (English) From the stone fortress

Rockford (English) From the rocky ford
Rockforde, Rokford, Rokforde, Rockferd, Rokferd, Rockfurd, Rokfurd

Roderick (German) A famous ruler
Rod, Rodd, Roddi, Roddie, Roddy, Roddee, Roddea

Rodney (German / English) From the famous one's island / from the island's clearing
Rodny, Rodni, Rodnie

Rogelio (Spanish) A famous soldier
Rogelo, Rogeliyo, Rogeleo, Rogeleyo, Rojelio, Rojeleo

Roland (German) From the renowned land
Roeland, Rolando, Roldan, Roley, Rollan, Rolland, Rollie, Rollin

Roman (Latin) A citizen of Rome
Romain, Romaine, Romeo

^Romeo (Italian) Traveler to Rome

Ronald (Norse) The king's advisor
Ranald, Renaldo, Ronal, Ronaldo, Rondale, Roneld, Ronell, Ronello

Ronan (Gaelic) Resembling a little seal

Rong (Chinese) Having glory

Rook (English) Resembling a raven
Rooke, Rouk, Rouke, Ruck, Ruk

Rooney (Gaelic) A red-haired man
Roony, Rooni, Roonie, Roonea, Roonee, Roon, Roone

Roosevelt (Danish) From the field of roses
Rosevelt

Roper (English) One who makes rope
Rapere

Rory (Gaelic) A red-haired man
Rori, Rorey, Rorie, Rorea, Roree, Rorry, Rorrey, Rorri

Roshan (Hindi) Born during the daylight
Rashaun

Roslin (Gaelic) A little red-haired boy
Roslyn, Rosselin, Rosslyn, Rozlin, Rozlyn, Rosling, Rozling

Roswald (German) Of the mighty horses
Rosswald, Roswalt, Rosswalt

Roswell (English) A fascinating man
Rosswell, Rozwell, Roswel, Rozwel

Roth (German) A red-haired man
Rothe

Rousseau (French) A little red-haired boy
Roussell, Russo, Rousse, Roussel, Rousset, Rousskin

Rowdy (English) A boisterous man
Rowdey, Rowdi, Rowdie, Rowdee, Rowdea

Roy (Gaelic / French) A red-haired man / a king
Roye, Roi, Royer, Ruy

Royce (German / French) A famous man / son of the king
Roice, Royse, Roise

Ruadhan (Irish) A red-haired man; the name of a saint
Ruadan, Ruadhagan, Ruadagan

Ruarc (Irish) A famous ruler
Ruarck, Ruarcc, Ruark, Ruarkk, Ruaidhri, Ruaidri

Rubio (Spanish) Resembling a ruby

Rudeger (German) A friendly man
Rudegar, Rudger, Rudgar, Rudiger, Rudigar

Rudolph (German) A famous wolf
Rodolfo, Rodolph, Rodolphe, Rodolpho, Rudy, Rudey, Rudi, Rudie

Rudyard (English) From the red paddock

Rufus (Latin) A red-haired man
Ruffus, Rufous, Rufino

Ruiz (Spanish) A good friend

Rujul (Indian) An honest man
Rujool, Rujoole, Rujule, Rujoul, Rujoule

Rumford (English) From the broad ford
Rumforde, Rumferd, Rumferde, Rumfurd

Rupert (English) Form of Robert, meaning "one who is bright with fame"
Ruprecht

Rushford (English) From the ford with rushes
Rusheford, Rushforde, Rusheforde, Ryscford

Russell (French) A little red-haired boy
Russel, Roussell, Russ, Rusel, Rusell

Russom (African) The chief;
the boss
Rusom, Russome, Rusome

Rusty (English) One who
has red hair or a ruddy
complexion
*Rustey, Rusti, Rustie, Rustee,
Rustea, Rust, Ruste, Rustice*

Rutherford (English) From the
cattle's ford
*Rutherfurd, Rutherferd,
Rutherforde, Rutherfurde*

*ᵀRyan (Gaelic) The little ruler;
little king
*Rian, Rien, Rion, Ryen, Ryon,
Ryun, Rhyan, Rhyen*

^Ryder (English) An accom-
plished horseman
*Rider, Ridder, Ryden, Rydell,
Rydder*

^Ryker (Danish) Form of
Richard, meaning "a powerful
ruler"
Riker

Rylan (English) Form of
Ryland, meaning "from the
place where rye is grown"
Ryelan, Ryle

S

Saarik (Hindi) Resembling a
small songbird
*Saarick, Saaric, Sarik, Sarick,
Saric, Saariq, Sareek, Sareeq*

Saber (French) Man of the
sword
Sabere, Sabr, Sabre

Sabir (Arabic) One who is
patient
*Sabyr, Sabeer, Sabear, Sabeir,
Sabier, Sabri, Sabrie, Sabree*

Saddam (Arabic) A powerful
ruler; the crusher
Saddum, Saddim, Saddym

Sadiq (Arabic) A beloved
friend
*Sadeeq, Sadyq, Sadeaq, Sadeek,
Sadeak, Sadyk, Sadik*

Saga (American) A storyteller
Sago

Sagar (Indian / English) A
king / one who is wise
Saagar, Sagarr, Saagarr

Sagaz (Spanish) One who is
clever
Sagazz

Sagiv (Hebrew) Having great strength
Sagev, Segiv, Segev

Sahaj (Indian) One who is natural

Saieshwar (Hindi) A well-known saint
Saishwar

Sailor (American) Man who sails the seas
Sailer, Sailar, Saylor, Sayler, Saylar, Saelor

Saith (English) One who is well-spoken
Saithe, Sayth, Saythe, Saeth, Saethe, Sath, Sathe

Sajal (Indian) Resembling a cloud
Sajall, Sajjal, Sajjall

Sajan (Indian) One who is dearly loved
Sajann, Sajjan, Sajjann

Saki (Japanese) One who is cloaked
Sakie, Saky, Sakey, Sakee, Sakea

Salaam (African) Resembling a peach

Salehe (African) A good man
Saleh, Salih

Salim (Arabic) One who is peaceful
Saleem, Salem, Selim

Salute (American) A patriotic man
Saloot, Saloote, Salout

Salvador (Spanish) A savior
Sal, Sally, Salvadore, Xalvador

Samanjas (Indian) One who is proper

Samarth (Indian) A powerful man; one who is efficient
Samarthe

Sameen (Indian) One who is treasured
Samine, Sameene, Samean, Sameane, Samyn, Samyne

Sami (Arabic) One who has been exalted
Samie, Samy, Samey, Samee, Samea

Sammohan (Indian) An attractive man

Sampath (Indian) A wealthy man
Sampathe, Sampat

Samson (Hebrew) As bright as the sun; in the Bible, a man with extraordinary strength
Sampson, Sansom, Sanson, Sansone

*T**Samuel** (Hebrew) God has
heard
*Sam, Sammie, Sammy,
Samuele, Samuello, Samwell,
Samuelo, Sammey*

Samuru (Japanese) The name
of God

Sandburg (English) From the
sandy village
*Sandbergh, Sandberg,
Sandburgh*

Sandon (English) From the
sandy hill
*Sanden, Sandan, Sandun,
Sandyn, Sandin*

Sanford (English) From the
sandy crossing
*Sandford, Sanforde, Sandforde,
Sanfurd, Sanfurde, Sandfurd,
Sandfurde*

Sang (Vietnamese) A bright
man
Sange

Sanjiro (Japanese) An admirable man
Sanjyro

Sanjiv (Indian) One who lives
a long life
*Sanjeev, Sanjyv, Sanjeiv,
Sanjiev, Sanjeav, Sanjivan*

Sanorelle (American) An
honest man
Sanorell, Sanorel, Sanorele

Santana (Spanish) A saintly
man
*Santanna, Santanah,
Santannah, Santa*

Santiago (Spanish) refers to
St. James

Santo (Italian) A holy man
*Sante, Santino, Santos, Santee,
Santi, Santie, Santea, Santy*

Sapan (Indian) A dream or
vision
Sapann

Sar (Anglo-Saxon) One who
inflicts pain
Sarlic, Sarlik

Sarbajit (Indian) The
conquerer
*Sarbajeet, Sarbajyt, Sarbajeat,
Sarbajet, Sarvajit, Sarvajeet,
Sarvajyt, Sarvajeat*

Sarojin (Hindu) Resembling
a lotus
Saroj

Sarosh (Persian) One who
prays
Saroshe

Satayu (Hindi) In Hinduism,
the brother of Amavasu and
Vivasu
Satayoo, Satayou, Satayue

Satoshi (Japanese) Born from the ashes
Satoshie, Satoshy, Satoshey, Satoshee, Satoshea

Satparayan (Indian) A good-natured man

Saturn (Latin) In mythology, the god of agriculture
Saturnin, Saturno, Saturnino

Satyankar (Indian) One who speaks the truth
Satyancar, Satyancker

Saville (French) From the willow town
Savil, Savile, Savill, Savyile, Savylle, Savyle, Sauville, Sauvile

Savir (Indian) A great leader
Savire, Saveer, Saveere, Savear, Saveare, Savyr, Savyre

Sawyer (English) One who works with wood
Sayer, Saer

Saxon (English) A swordsman
Saxen, Saxan, Saxton, Saxten, Saxtan

Sayad (Arabic) An accomplished hunter

Scadwielle (English) From the shed near the spring
Scadwyelle, Scadwiell, Scadwyell, Scadwiel, Scadwyel, Scadwiele, Scadwyele

Scand (Anglo-Saxon) One who is disgraced
Scande, Scandi, Scandie, Scandee, Scandea

Sceotend (Anglo-Saxon) An archer

Schaeffer (German) A steward
Schaffer, Shaeffer, Shaffer, Schaeffur, Schaffur, Shaeffur, Shaffur

Schelde (English) From the river
Shelde

Schneider (German) A tailor
Shneider, Sneider, Snider, Snyder

Schubert (German) One who makes shoes
Shubert, Schuberte, Shuberte, Schubirt, Shubirt, Schuburt, Shuburt

Scirocco (Italian) Of the warm wind
Sirocco, Scyrocco, Syrocco

Scott (English) A man from Scotland
Scot, Scottie, Scotto, Scotty, Scotti, Scottey, Scottee, Scottea

Scowyrhta (Anglo-Saxon) One who makes shoes

Seabury (English) From the village by the sea
Seaburry, Sebury, Seburry, Seaberry, Seabery, Seberry

Seaman (English) A mariner

*****Sean** (Irish) Form of John, meaning "God is gracious"
Shaughn, Shawn, Shaun, Shon, Shohn, Shonn, Shaundre, Shawnel

Seanachan (Irish) One who is wise

Seanan (Hebrew / Irish) A gift from God / an old, wise man
Sinon, Senen, Siobhan

*****Sebastian** (Greek) The revered one
Sabastian, Seb, Sebastiano, Sebastien, Sebestyen, Sebo, Sebastyn, Sebestyen

Sedgwick (English) From the place of sword grass
Sedgewick, Sedgewyck, Sedgwyck, Sedgewic, Sedgewik, Sedgwic, Sedgwik, Sedgewyc

Seerath (Indian) A great man
Seerathe, Searath, Searathe

Sef (Egyptian) Son of yesterday
Sefe

Seferino (Greek) Of the west wind
Seferio, Sepherino, Sepherio, Seferyno, Sepheryno

Seignour (French) Lord of the house

Selas (African) Refers to the Trinity
Selassi, Selassie, Selassy, Selassey, Selassee, Selassea

Selestino (Spanish) One who is heaven-sent
Selestyno, Selesteeno, Selesteano

Sellers (English) One who dwells in the marshland
Sellars, Sellurs, Selliers, Sellyrs

Seminole (Native American) A tribal name
Semynole

Seppanen (Finnish) A blacksmith
Sepanen, Seppenen, Sepenen, Seppanan, Sepanan

September (American) Born in the month of September
Septimber, Septymber, Septemberia, Septemberea

Septimus (Latin) The seventh-born child
Septymus

Seraphim (Hebrew) The
burning ones; heavenly
winged angels
*Sarafino, Saraph, Serafin,
Serafino, Seraph, Seraphimus,
Serafim*

Sereno (Latin) One who is
calm; tranquil

Serfati (Hebrew) A man from
France
*Sarfati, Serfatie, Sarfatie,
Serfaty, Sarfaty, Serfatey,
Sarfatey, Serfatee*

Sergio (Latin) An attendant;
a servant
*Seargeoh, Serge, Sergei, Sergeo,
Sergey, Sergi, Sergios, Sergiu*

Seth (Hebrew) One who has
been appointed
Sethe, Seath, Seathe, Zeth

Seung (Korean) A victorious
successor

Seven (American) Refers to
the number; the seventh-born
child
Sevin, Sevyn

Sewati (Native American)
Resembling a bear claw
*Sewatie, Sewaty, Sewatey,
Sewatee, Sewatea*

Sexton (English) The church's
custodian
Sextun, Sextan, Sextin, Sextyn

Seymour (French) From the
French town of Saint Maur
*Seamore, Seamor, Seamour,
Seymore*

Shaan (Hebrew) A peaceful
man

Shade (English) A secretive
man
*Shaid, Shaide, Shayd, Shayde,
Shaed, Shaede*

Shadi (Persian / Arabic) One
who brings happiness and joy
/ a singer
Shadie, Shady, Shadey

Shadrach (Hebrew) Under the
command of the moon god
Aku
Shadrack, Shadrick, Shad

Shah (Persian) The king

Shai (Hebrew) A gift from God

Shail (Indian) A mountain
rock
*Shaile, Shayl, Shayle, Shael,
Shaele, Shale*

Shaka (African) A tribal leader
Shakah

Shakir (Arabic) One who is
grateful
*Shakeer, Shaqueer, Shakier,
Shakeir, Shakear, Shakar,
Shaker, Shakyr*

Shane (English) Form of John, meaning "God is gracious"
Shayn, Shayne, Shaine, Shain

Shannon (Gaelic) Having ancient wisdom
Shanan, Shanen, Shannan, Shannen, Shanon

Shardul (Indian) Resembling a tiger
Shardule, Shardull, Shardulle

Shashi (Indian) Of the moonbeam
Shashie, Shashy, Shashey, Shashee, Shashea, Shashhi

Shavon (American) One who is open-minded
Shavaughn, Shavonne, Shavaun, Shovon, Shovonne, Shovaun

Shaw (English) From the woodland
Shawe

Shaykeen (American) A successful man
Shaykean, Shaykein, Shakeyn, Shakine

Shea (Gaelic) An admirable man / from the fairy fortress
Shae, Shai, Shay, Shaye, Shaylon, Shays

Sheen (English) A shining man
Sheene, Shean, Sheane

Sheffield (English) From the crooked field
Sheffeld

Sheldon (English) From the steep valley
Shelden, Sheldan, Sheldun, Sheldin, Sheldyn, Shel

Shelley (English) From the meadow's ledge
Shelly, Shelli, Shellie, Shellee, Shellea, Shelleigh, Shelleah

Shelton (English) From the farm on the ledge
Shellton, Sheltown, Sheltun, Shelten, Shelny, Shelney, Shelni, Shelnie

Shem (Hebrew) Having a well-known name

Shepherd (English) One who herds sheep
Shepperd, Shep, Shepard, Shephard, Shepp, Sheppard

Sheridan (Gaelic) A seeker
Sheredan, Sheridon, Sherridan, Seireadan, Sheriden, Sheridun, Sherard, Sherrard

Sherlock (English) A fairhaired man
Sherlocke, Shurlock, Shurlocke

Sherman (English) One who cuts wool cloth
Shermon, Scherman, Schermann, Shearman, Shermann, Sherm, Sherme

Sherrerd (English) From the open field
Shererd, Sherrard, Sherard

Shields (Gaelic) A faithful protector
Sheelds, Shealds

Shikha (Indian) A fiery man
Shykha

Shiloh (Hebrew) He who was sent
Shilo, Shyloh, Shylo

Shing (Chinese) A victorious man
Shyng

Shino (Japanese) A bamboo stem
Shyno

Shipton (English) From the ship town; from the sheep town

Shiro (Japanese) The fourth-born son
Shyro

Shorty (American) A man who is small in stature
Shortey, Shorti, Shortie, Shortee, Shortea

Shreshta (Indian) The best; one who is superior

Shubhang (Indian) A handsome man

Shuraqui (Arabic) A man from the east

Siamak (Persian) A bringer of joy
Syamak, Siamack, Syamack, Siamac, Syamac

Sidor (Russian) One who is talented
Sydor

Sierra (Spanish) From the jagged mountain range
Siera, Syerra, Syera, Seyera, Seeara

Sigehere (English) One who is victorious
Sygehere, Sigihere, Sygihere

Sigenert (Anglo-Saxon) A king
Sygenert, Siginert, Syginert

Sigmund (German) The victorious protector
Siegmund, Sigmond, Zsigmond, Zygmunt

Sihtric (Anglo-Saxon) A king
Sihtrik, Sihtrick, Syhtric, Syhtrik, Syhtrick, Sihtryc, Sihtryk, Sihtryck

Sik'is (Native American) A friendly man

^**Silas** (Latin) Form of Silvanus, meaning "a woodland dweller"

Silny (Czech) Having great strength
Silney, Silni, Silnie, Silnee, Silnea

Simbarashe (African) The power of God
Simbarashi, Simbarashie, Simbarashy, Simbarashey, Simbarashee

Simcha (Hebrew) Filled with joy
Symcha, Simha, Symha

Simmons (Hebrew) The son of Simon
Semmes, Simms, Syms, Simmonds, Symonds, Simpson, Symms, Simson

Simon (Hebrew) God has heard
Shimon, Si, Sim, Samien, Semyon, Simen, Simeon, Simone

Sinai (Hebrew) From the clay desert

Sinclair (English) Man from Saint Clair
Sinclaire, Sinclare, Synclair, Synclaire, Synclare

Singer (American) A vocalist
Synger

Sion (Armenian) From the fortified hill
Sionne, Syon, Syonne

Sirius (Greek) Resembling the brightest star
Syrius

Siyavash (Persian) One who owns black horses
Siyavashe

Skerry (Norse) From the rocky island
Skereye, Skerrey, Skerri, Skerrie, Skerree, Skerrea

Slade (English) Son of the valley
Slaid, Slaide, Slaed, Slaede, Slayd, Slayde

Sladkey (Slavic) A glorious man
Sladky, Sladki, Sladkie, Sladkee, Sladkea

Smith (English) A blacksmith
Smyth, Smithe, Smythe, Smedt, Smid, Smitty, Smittee, Smittea

Snell (Anglo-Saxon) One who is bold
Snel, Snelle, Snele

Solange (French) An angel of the sun

Solaris (Greek) Of the sun
*Solarise, Solariss, Solarisse,
Solarys, Solaryss, Solarysse,
Solstice, Soleil*

Somer (French) Born during
the summer
*Somers, Sommer, Sommers,
Sommar, Somar*

Somerset (English) From the
summer settlement
*Sommerset, Sumerset,
Summerset*

Songaa (Native American)
Having great strength
Songan

Sophocles (Greek) An ancient
playwright
Sofocles

Sorley (Irish) Of the summer
vikings
*Sorly, Sorlee, Sorlea, Sorli,
Sorlie*

Soumil (Indian) A beloved
friend
*Soumyl, Soumille, Soumylle,
Soumill, Soumyll*

Southern (English) Man from
the south
Sothern, Suthern

Sovann (Cambodian) The
golden son
Sovan, Sovane

Spark (English / Latin) A
gallant man / to scatter
*Sparke, Sparki, Sparkie,
Sparky, Sparkey, Sparkee,
Sparkea*

Spencer (English) One who
dispenses provisions
Spenser

Squire (English) A knight's
companion; the shield-bearer
*Squier, Squiers, Squires,
Squyre, Squyres*

Stanford (English) From the
stony ford
*Standford, Standforde,
Standforde, Stamford*

Stanhope (English) From the
stony hollow
Stanhop

Stanton (English) From the
stone town
*Stantown, Stanten, Staunton,
Stantan, Stantun*

Stark (German) Having great
strength
Starke, Starck, Starcke

Stavros (Greek) One who is
crowned

Steadman (English) One who
lives at the farm
*Stedman, Steadmann,
Stedmann, Stedeman*

Steed (English) Resembling a stallion
Steede, Stead, Steade

Stephen (Greek) Crowned with garland
Staffan, Steba, Steben, Stefan, Stefano, Steffan, Steffen, Steffon, Steven, Steve

Sterling (English) One who is highly valued
Sterlyng, Stirling, Sterlyn

Stian (Norse) A voyager; one who is swift
Stig, Styg, Stygge, Stieran, Steeran, Steeren, Steeryn, Stieren

Stilwell (Anglo-Saxon) From the quiet spring
Stillwell, Stilwel, Stylwell, Styllwell, Stylwel, Stillwel

Stobart (German) A harsh man
Stobarte, Stobarth, Stobarthe

Stockley (English) From the meadow of tree stumps
Stockly, Stockli, Stocklie, Stocklee, Stockleigh

Storm (American) Of the tempest; stormy weather; having an impetuous nature
Storme, Stormy, Stormi, Stormie, Stormey, Stormee, Stormea

Stowe (English) A secretive man
Stow, Stowey, Stowy, Stowee, Stowea, Stowi, Stowie

Stratford (English) From the street near the river ford
Strafford, Stratforde, Straford, Strafforde, Straforde

Stratton (Scottish) A homebody
Straton, Stratten, Straten, Strattan, Stratan, Strattun, Stratun

Strider (English) A great warrior
Stryder

Striker (American) An aggressive man
Strike, Stryker, Stryke

Struthers (Irish) One who lives near the brook
Struther, Sruthair, Strother, Strothers

Stuart (English) A steward; the keeper of the estate
Steward, Stewart, Stewert, Stuert, Stu, Stew

Suave (American) A smooth and sophisticated man
Swave

Subhi (Arabic) Born during
the early morning hours
*Subhie, Subhy, Subhey,
Subhee, Subhea*

Suffield (English) From the
southern field
Suffeld, Suthfeld, Suthfield

Sullivan (Gaelic) Having dark
eyes
Sullavan, Sullevan, Sullyvan

Sully (English) From the
southern meadow
*Sulley, Sulli, Sullie, Sulleigh,
Sullee, Sullea, Sulleah, Suthley*

Sultan (African / American) A
ruler / one who is bold
*Sultane, Sulten, Sultun, Sulton,
Sultin, Sultyn*

Suman (Hindi) A wise man

Sundiata (African) Resembling
a hungry lion
*Sundyata, Soundiata,
Soundyata, Sunjata*

Sundown (American) Born at
dusk
Sundowne

Su'ud (Arabic) One who has
good luck
Suoud

Swahili (Arabic) Of the coastal
people
*Swahily, Swahiley, Swahilee,
Swahiley, Swaheeli, Swaheelie,
Swaheely, Swaheeley*

Sylvester (Latin) Man from the
forest
*Silvester, Silvestre, Silvestro,
Sylvestre, Sylvestro, Sly,
Sevester, Seveste*

Syon (Indian) One who is
followed by good fortune

Szemere (Hungarian) A man
of small stature
*Szemir, Szemeer, Szemear,
Szemyr*

T

Tabari (Arabic) A famous his-
torian
*Tabarie, Tabary, Tabarey,
Tabaree, Tabarea*

Tabbai (Hebrew) A well-
behaved boy
Tabbae, Tabbay, Tabbaye

Tabbart (German) A brilliant
man
*Tabbert, Tabart, Tabert,
Tahbert, Tahberte*

Tacari (African) As strong as a warrior
Tacarie, Tacary, Tacarey, Tacaree, Tacarea

Tadao (Japanese) One who is satisfied

Tadeusuz (Polish) One who is worthy of praise
Tadesuz

Tadi (Native American) Of the wind
Tadie, Tady, Tadey, Tadee, Tadea

Tadzi (American / Polish) Resembling the loon / one who is praised
Tadzie, Tadzy, Tadzey, Tadzee, Tadzea

Taft (French / English) From the homestead / from the marshes
Tafte

Taggart (Gaelic) Son of a priest
Taggert, Taggort, Taggirt, Taggyrt

Taghee (Native American) A chief
Taghea, Taghy, Taghey, Taghi, Taghie

Taheton (Native American) Resembling a hawk

Tahoe (Native American) From the big water
Taho

Tahoma (Native American) From the snowy mountain peak
Tehoma, Tacoma, Takoma, Tohoma, Tocoma, Tokoma, Tekoma, Tecoma

Taishi (Japanese) An ambitious man
Taishie, Taishy, Taishey, Taishee, Taishea

Taj (Indian) One who is crowned
Tahj, Tajdar

Tajo (Spanish) Born during the daytime

Taksony (Hungarian) One who is content; well-fed
Taksoney, Taksoni, Taksonie, Taksonee, Taksonea, Tas

Talasi (Native American) Resembling a cornflower
Talasie, Talasy, Talasey, Talasee, Talasea

Talford (English) From the high ford
Talforde, Tallford, Tallforde

Talfryn (Welsh) From the high hill
Talfrynn, Talfrin, Talfrinn, Talfren, Talfrenn, Tallfryn, Tallfrin, Tallfren

Talmai (Hebrew) From the furrows
Talmae, Talmay, Talmaye

Talmon (Hebrew) One who is oppressed
Talman, Talmin, Talmyn, Talmen

Talo (Finnish) From the homestead

Tam (Vietnamese / Hebrew) Having heart / one who is truthful

Taman (Hindi) One who is needed

Tamarius (American) A stubborn man
Tamarias, Tamarios, Tamerius, Tamerias, Tamerios

Tameron (American) Form of Cameron, meaning "having a crooked nose"
Tameren, Tameryn, Tamryn, Tamerin, Tamren, Tamrin, Bamron

Tammany (Native American) A friendly chief
Tammani, Tammanie, Tammaney, Tammanee, Tammanea

Tanafa (Polynesian) A drum-beat

Taneli (Hebrew) He will be judged by God
Tanelie, Tanely, Taneley, Tanelee, Tanelea

Tanish (Indian) An ambitious man
Tanishe, Taneesh, Taneeshe, Taneash, Taneashe, Tanysh, Tanyshe

Tanjiro (Japanese) The prized second-born son
Tanjyro

Tank (American) A man who is big and strong
Tankie, Tanki, Tanky, Tankey, Tankee, Tankea

Tanner (English) One who makes leather
Tannere, Tannor, Tannar, Tannir, Tannyr, Tannur, Tannis

Tannon (German) From the fir tree
Tannan, Tannen, Tannin, Tansen, Tanson, Tannun, Tannyn

Tano (Ghanese) From the river
Tanu

Tao (Chinese) One who will have a long life

Taos (Spanish) From the city in New Mexico

Tapani (Hebrew) A victorious man
Tapanie, Tapany, Tapaney, Tapanee, Tapanea

Tapko (American) Resembling an antelope

Tappen (Welsh) From the top of the cliff
Tappan, Tappon, Tappin, Tappyn, Tappun

Taran (Gaelic) Of the thunder
Taren, Taron, Tarin, Taryn, Tarun

Taranga (Indian) Of the waves

Taregan (Native American) Resembling a crane
Taregen, Taregon, Taregin, Taregyn

Tarit (Indian) Resembling lightning
Tarite, Tareet, Tareete, Tareat, Tareate, Taryt, Taryte

Tarn (Norse) From the mountain pool

Tarquin (Latin) One who is impulsive
Tarquinn, Tarquinne, Tarquen, Tarquenn, Tarquenne, Tarquyn, Tarquynn, Tarquynne

Tarrant (American) One who upholds the law
Tarrent, Tarrint, Tarrynt, Tarront, Tarrunt

Tarun (Indian) A youthful man
Taroun, Taroon, Tarune, Taroune, Taroone

Tashi (Tibetan) One who is prosperous
Tashie, Tashy, Tashey, Tashee, Tashea

Tate (English) A cheerful man; one who brings happiness to others
Tayt, Tayte, Tait, Taite, Taet, Taete

Tausiq (Indian) One who provides strong backing
Tauseeq, Tauseaq, Tausik, Tauseek, Tauseak

Tavaris (American) Of misfortune; a hermit
Tavarius, Tavaress, Tavarious, Tavariss, Tavarous, Tevarus, Tavorian, Tavarian

Tavas (Hebrew) Resembling a peacock

Tavi (Aramaic) A good man
Tavie, Tavy, Tavey, Tavee, Tavea

Tavin (German) Form of Gustav, meaning "of the staff of the gods"
Tavyn, Taven, Tavan, Tavon, Tavun, Tava, Tave

Tawa (Native American) Born beneath the sun
Tawah

Tay (Scottish) From the river
Taye, Tae, Tai

Teagan (Gaelic) A handsome man
Teegan, Teygan, Tegan, Teigan

Tecumseh (Native American) A traveler; resembling a shooting star
Tekumseh, Tecumse, Tekumse

Ted (English) Form of Theodore, meaning "a gift from God"
Tedd, Teddy, Teddi, Teddie, Teddee, Teddea, Teddey, Tedric

Tedmund (English) A protector of the land
Tedmunde, Tedmond, Tedmonde, Tedman, Theomund, Theomond, Theomunde, Theomonde

Teetonka (Native American) One who talks too much
Teitonka, Tietonka, Teatonka, Teytonka

Tegene (African) My protector
Tegeen, Tegeene, Tegean, Tegeane

Teiji (Japanese) One who is righteous
Teijo

Teilo (Welsh) A saintly man

Teka (African) He has replaced

Tekeshi (Japanese) A formidable and brave man
Tekeshie, Tekeshy, Tekeshey, Tekeshee, Tekeshea

Telly (Greek) The wisest man
Telley, Tellee, Tellea, Telli, Tellie

Temman (Anglo-Saxon) One who has been tamed

Temple (Latin) From the sacred place
Tempel, Templar, Templer, Templo

Teneangopte (Native American) Resembling a high-flying bird

Tennant (English) One who rents
Tennent, Tenant, Tenent

Tennessee (Native American) From the state of Tennessee
Tenese, Tenesee, Tenessee, Tennese, Tennesee, Tennesse

Teon (Anglo-Saxon) One who harms others

Teris (Irish) The son of Terence
Terys, Teriss, Teryss, Terris, Terrys, Terriss, Terryss

^**Terrance** (Latin) From an ancient Roman clan
Tarrants, Tarrance, Tarrence, Tarrenz, Terencio, Terance, Terrence, Terrey, Terry

Terrian (American) One who is strong and ambitious
Terrien, Terriun, Terriyn

Terron (English) Form of Terence, meaning "from an ancient Roman clan"
Tarran, Tarren, Tarrin

Teshi (African) One who is full of laughter
Teshie, Teshy, Teshey, Teshee, Teshea

Tessema (African) One to whom people listen

Tet (Vietnamese) Born on New Year's

Teteny (Hungarian) A chieftain

Teva (Hebrew) A natural man
Tevah

Texas (Native American) One of many friends; from the state of Texas
Texus, Texis, Texes, Texos, Texys

Teyrnon (Celtic) A regal man
Teirnon, Tayrnon, Tairnon, Taernon, Tiarchnach, Tiarnach

Thabo (African) Filled with happiness

Thackary (English) Form of Zachary, meaning "the Lord remembers"
Thackery, Thakary, Thakery, Thackari, Thackarie, Thackarey, Thackaree, Thackarea

Thaddeus (Aramaic) Having heart
Tad, Tadd, Taddeo, Taddeusz, Thad, Thadd, Thaddaios, Thaddaos

Thandiwe (African) One who is dearly loved
Thandie, Thandi, Thandy, Thandey, Thandee, Thandea

Thang (Vietnamese) One who is victorious

Thanus (American) One who owns land

Thao (Vietnamese) One who is courteous

Thatcher (English) One who fixes roofs
Thacher, Thatch, Thatche, Thaxter, Thacker, Thaker, Thackere, Thakere

Thayer (Teutonic) Of the nation's army

Theodore (Greek) A gift from God
Ted, Teddy, Teddie, Theo, Theodor

Theron (Greek) A great hunter
Therron, Tharon, Theon, Tharron

Theseus (Greek) In mythology, hero who slew the Minotaur
Thesius, Thesyus

Thinh (Vietnamese) A prosperous man

*Thomas (Aramaic) One of twins
Tam, Tamas, Tamhas, Thom, Thomason, Thomson, Thompson, Tomas

Thor (Norse) In mythology, god of thunder
Thorian, Thorin, Thorsson, Thorvald, Tor, Tore, Turo, Thorrin

Thorburn (Norse) Thor's bear
Thorburne, Thorbern, Thorberne, Thorbjorn, Thorbjorne, Torbjorn, Torborg, Torben

Thormond (Norse) Protected by Thor
Thormonde, Thormund, Thormunde, Thurmond, Thurmonde, Thurmund, Thurmunde, Thormun

Thorne (English) From the thorn bush
Thorn

Thornycroft (English) From the field of thorn bushes
Thornicroft, Thorneycroft, Thorniecroft, Thorneecroft, Thorneacroft

Thuong (Vietnamese) One who loves tenderly

Thurston (English) From Thor's town; Thor's stone
Thorston, Thorstan, Thorstein, Thorsten, Thurstain, Thurstan, Thursten, Torsten

Thuy (Vietnamese) One who is kind

Tiassale (African) It has been forgotten

Tiberio (Italian) From the
Tiber river
*Tibero, Tyberio, Tybero,
Tiberius, Tiberios, Tyberius,
Tyberios*

Tibor (Slavic) From the sacred
place

Tiburon (Spanish) Resembling
a shark

Tiernan (Gaelic) Lord of the
manor
*Tiarnan, Tiarney, Tierney,
Tierny, Tiernee, Tiernea, Tierni,
Tiernie*

Tilian (Anglo-Saxon) One who
strives to better himself
Tilien, Tiliun, Tilion

Tilon (Hebrew) A generous
man
Tilen, Tilan, Tilun, Tilin, Tilyn

Tilton (English) From the
fertile estate
*Tillton, Tilten, Tillten, Tiltan,
Tilltan, Tiltin, Tilltin, Tiltun*

Timir (Indian) Born in the
darkness
Timirbaran

Timothy (Greek) One who
honors God
*Tim, Timmo, Timmy,
Timmothy, Timmy, Timo,
Timofei, Timofeo*

Tin (Vietnamese) A great
thinker

Tino (Italian) A man of small
stature
*Teeno, Tieno, Teino, Teano,
Tyno*

Tip (American) A form of
Thomas, meaning "one of
twins"
*Tipp, Tipper, Tippy, Tippee,
Tippea, Tippey, Tippi, Tippie*

Tisa (African) The ninth-born
child
Tisah, Tysa, Tysah

Titus (Greek / Latin) Of the
giants / a great defender
*Tito, Titos, Tytus, Tytos, Titan,
Tytan, Tyto*

Toa (Polynesian) A brave-
hearted woman

Toan (Vietnamese) One who
is safe
Toane

Tobias (Hebrew) The Lord is
good
Toby

Todd (English) Resembling a
fox
Tod

Todor (Bulgarian) A gift from
God
Todos, Todros

Tohon (Native American) One who loves the water

Tokala (Native American) Resembling a fox
Tokalo

Tomer (Hebrew) A man of tall stature
Tomar, Tomur, Tomir, Tomor, Tomyr

Tomi (Japanese / African) A wealthy man / of the people
Tomie, Tomee, Tomea, Tomy, Tomey

Tonauac (Aztec) One who possesses the light

Torger (Norse) The power of Thor's spear
Thorger, Torgar, Thorgar, Terje, Therje

Torht (Anglo-Saxon) A bright man
Torhte

Torin (Celtic) One who acts as chief
Toran, Torean, Toren, Torion, Torran, Torrian, Toryn

Tormaigh (Irish) Having the spirit of Thor
Tormey, Tormay, Tormaye, Tormai, Tormae

Torr (English) From the tower
Torre

Torrence (Gaelic) From the little hills
Torence, Torrance, Torrens, Torrans, Toran, Torran, Torrin, Torn, Torry

Torry (Norse / Gaelic) Refers to Thor / form of Torrence, meaning "from the little hills"
Torrey, Torree, Torrea, Torri, Torrie, Tory, Torey, Tori

Toshiro (Japanese) One who is talented and intelligent
Toshihiro

Tostig (English) A well-known earl
Tostyg

Toviel (Hebrew) The Lord is good
Toviell, Toviele, Tovielle, Tovi, Tovie, Tovee, Tovea, Tovy

Toyo (Japanese) A man of plenty

Tracy (Gaelic) One who is warlike
Tracey, Traci, Tracie, Tracee, Tracea, Treacy, Trace, Tracen

Travis (French) To cross over
Travys, Traver, Travers, Traviss, Trevis, Trevys, Travus, Traves

Treffen (German) One who socializes
Treffan, Treffin, Treffon, Treffyn, Treffun

Tremain (Celtic) From the town built of stone
Tramain, Tramaine, Tramayne, Tremaine, Tremayne, Tremaen, Tremaene, Tramaen

Tremont (French) From the three mountains
Tremonte, Tremount, Tremounte

Trenton (English) From the town near the rushing rapids
Trent, Trynt, Trenten, Trentyn

Trevin (English) From the fair town
Trevan, Treven, Trevian, Trevion, Trevon, Trevyn, Trevonn

Trevor (Welsh) From the large village
Trefor, Trevar, Trever, Treabhar, Treveur, Trevir, Trevur

Trey (English) The third-born child
Tre, Trai, Trae, Tray, Traye, Trayton, Treyton, Trayson

Trigg (Norse) One who is truthful
Trygg

Tripp (English) A traveler
Trip, Trypp, Tryp, Tripper, Trypper

Tripsy (American) One who enjoys dancing
Tripsey, Tripsee, Tripsea, Tripsi, Tripsie

*Tristan (Celtic) A sorrowful man; in Arthurian legend, a knight of the Round Table
Trystan, Tris, Tristam, Tristen, Tristian, Tristin, Triston, Tristram

Trocky (American) A manly man
Trockey, Trocki, Trockie, Trockee, Trockea

Trong (Vietnamese) One who is respected

Troy (Gaelic) Son of a foot-soldier
Troye, Troi

Trumbald (English) A bold man
Trumbold, Trumbalde, Trumbolde

Trygve (Norse) One who wins with bravery

Tse (Native American) As solid as a rock

Tsidhqiyah (Hebrew) The Lord is just
Tsidqiyah, Tsidhqiya, Tsdqiya

Tsubasa (Japanese) A winged being
Tsubasah, Tsubase, Tsubaseh

Tucker (English) One who makes garments
Tuker, Tuckerman, Tukerman, Tuck, Tuckman, Tukman, Tuckere, Toukere

Tuketu (Native American) Resembling a running bear
Tuketue, Tuketoo, Tuketou, Telutci, Telutcie, Telutcy, Telutcey, Telutcee

Tulsi (Indian) A holy man
Tulsie, Tulsy, Tulsey, Tulsee, Tulsea

Tumaini (African) An optimist
Tumainie, Tumainee, Tumainy, Tumainey, Tumayni, Tumaynie, Tumaynee, Tumayney

Tunde (African) One who returns
Tundi, Tundie, Tundee, Tundea, Tundy, Tundey

Tunleah (English) From the town near the meadow
Tunlea, Tunleigh, Tunly, Tunley, Tunlee, Tunli, Tunlie

Tupac (African) A messenger warrior
Tupack, Tupoc, Tupock

Turfeinar (Norse) In mythology, the son of Rognvald
Turfaynar, Turfaenar, Turfanar, Turfenar, Turfainar

Tushar (Indian) Of the snow
Tusharr, Tushare

Tusita (Chinese) One who is heaven-sent

Twrgadarn (Welsh) From the strong tower

Txanton (Basque) Form of Anthony, meaning "a flourishing man; of an ancient Roman family"
Txantony, Txantoney, Txantonee, Txantoni, Txantonie, Txantonea

Tybalt (Latin) He who sees the truth
Tybault, Tybalte, Tybaulte

Tye (English) From the fenced-in pasture
Tyg, Tyge, Tie, Tigh, Teyen

Tyfiell (English) Follower of the god Tyr
Tyfiel, Tyfielle, Tyfiele

*Tyler (English) A tiler of roofs
Tilar, Tylar, Tylor, Tiler, Tilor, Ty, Tye, Tylere

Typhoon (Chinese) Of the great wind
Tiphoon, Tyfoon, Tifoon, Typhoun, Tiphoun, Tyfoun, Tifoun

Tyrone (French) From Owen's land
Terone, Tiron, Tirone, Tyron, Ty, Kyrone

Tyson (French) One who is high-spirited; fiery
Thyssen, Tiesen, Tyce, Tycen, Tyeson, Tyssen, Tysen, Tysan

U

U (Korean) A kind and gentle man

Uaithne (Gaelic) One who is innocent; green
Uaithn, Uaythne, Uaythn, Uathne, Uathn, Uaethne, Uaethn

Ualan (Scottish) Form of Valentine, meaning "one who is strong and healthy"
Ualane, Ualayn, Ualayne, Ualen, Ualon

Uba (African) One who is wealthy; lord of the house
Ubah, Ubba, Ubbah

Uberto (Italian) Form of Hubert, meaning "having a shining intellect"
Ulberto, Umberto

Udath (Indian) One who is noble
Udathe

Uddam (Indian) An exceptional man

Uddhar (Indian) One who is free; an independent man
Uddharr, Udhar, Udharr

Udell (English) From the valley of yew trees
Udale, Udel, Udall, Udayle, Udayl, Udail, Udaile, Udele

Udi (Hebrew) One who carries a torch
Udie, Udy, Udey, Udee, Udea

Udup (Indian) Born beneath the moon's light
Udupp, Uddup, Uddupp

Udyan (Indian) Of the garden
Uddyan, Udyann, Uddyann

Ugo (Italian) A great thinker

Uland (English) From the noble country
Ulande, Ulland, Ullande, Ulandus, Ullandus

Ulhas (Indian) Filled with happiness
Ulhass, Ullhas, Ullhass

Ull (Norse) Having glory; in mythology, god of justice and patron of agriculture
Ulle, Ul, Ule

Ulmer (German) Having the fame of the wolf
Ullmer, Ullmar, Ulmarr, Ullmarr, Ulfmer, Ulfmar, Ulfmaer

Ultman (Indian) A godly man
Ultmann, Ultmane

Umrao (Indian) One who is noble

Unai (Basque) A shepherd
Unay, Unaye, Unae

Unathi (African) God is with us
Unathie, Unathy, Unathey, Unathee, Unathea

Uncas (Native American) Resembling a fox
Unkas, Unckas

Ungus (Irish) A vigorous man
Unguss

Unique (American) Unlike others; the only one
Unikue, Unik, Uniqui, Uniqi, Uniqe, Unikque, Unike, Unicke

Uolevi (Finnish) Form of Olaf, meaning "the remaining of the ancestors"
Uolevie, Uolevee, Uolevy, Uolevey, Uolevea

Upchurch (English) From the upper church
Upchurche

Uranus (Greek) In mythology, the father of the Titans
Urainus, Uraynus, Uranas, Uraynas, Urainas, Uranos, Uraynos, Urainos

Uri (Hebrew) Form of Uriah, meaning "the Lord is my light"
Urie, Ury, Urey, Uree, Urea

Uriah (Hebrew) The Lord is my light
Uri, Uria, Urias, Urija, Urijah, Uriyah, Urjasz, Uriya

Urjavaha (Hindu) Of the Nimi dynasty

Urtzi (Basque) From the sky
Urtzie, Urtzy, Urtzey, Urtzee, Urtzea

Usher (Latin) From the mouth of the river
Ushar, Ushir, Ussher, Usshar, Usshir

Ushi (Chinese) As strong as an ox
Ushie, Ushy, Ushey, Ushee, Ushea

Utah (Native American) People of the mountains; from the state of Utah

Utsav (Indian) Born during a celebration
Utsavi, Utsave, Utsava, Utsavie, Utsavy, Utsavey, Utsavee, Utsavea

Utt (Arabic) One who is kind and wise
Utte

Uzi (Hebrew) Having great power
Uzie, Uzy, Uzey, Uzee, Uzea, Uzzi, Uzzie, Uzzy

Uzima (African) One who is full of life
Uzimah, Uzimma, Uzimmah, Uzyma

Uzziah (Hebrew) The Lord is my strength
Uzzia, Uziah, Uzia, Uzzya, Uzzyah, Uzyah, Uzya, Uzziel

V

Vachel (French) Resembling a small cow
Vachele, Vachell

Vachlan (English) One who lives near water

Vadar (Dutch) A fatherly man
Vader, Vadyr

Vadhir (Spanish) Resembling a rose
Vadhyr, Vadheer

Vadim (Russian) A good-looking man
Vadime, Vadym, Vadyme, Vadeem, Vadeeme

Vaijnath (Hindi) Refers to Lord Shiva
Vaejnath, Vaijnathe, Vaejnathe

Valdemar (German) A well-known ruler
Valdemarr, Valdemare, Valto, Valdmar, Valdmarr, Valdimar, Valdimarr

Valentine (Latin) One who is strong and healthy
Val, Valentin, Valentino, Valentyne, Ualan

Valerian (Latin) One who is
strong and healthy
*Valerien, Valerio, Valerius,
Valery, Valeryan, Valere,
Valeri, Valerii*

Valin (Hindi) The monkey
king

Valle (French) From the glen
Vallejo

Valri (French) One who is
strong
Valrie, Valry, Valrey, Valree

Vance (English) From the
marshland
Vanse

Vanderveer (Dutch) From the
ferry
*Vandervere, Vandervir,
Vandervire, Vandervyr,
Vandervyre*

Vandy (Dutch) One who
travels; a wanderer
Vandey, Vandi, Vandie, Vandee

Vandyke (Danish) From the
dike
Vandike

Vanir (Norse) Of the ancient
gods

Varante (Arabic) From the
river

Vardon (French) From the
green hill
*Varden, Verdon, Verdun,
Verden, Vardun, Vardan,
Verddun, Varddun*

Varg (Norse) Resembling a
wolf

Varick (German) A protective
ruler
Varrick, Warick, Warrick

Varius (Latin) A versatile man
Varian, Varinius

Variya (Hindi) The excellent
one

Vasava (Hindi) Refers to Indra

Vashon (American) The Lord
is gracious
*Vashan, Vashawn, Vashaun,
Vashone, Vashane, Vashayn,
Vashayne*

Vasin (Indian) A great ruler
*Vasine, Vaseen, Vaseene,
Vasyn, Vasyne*

Vasuki (Hindi) In Hinduism, a
serpent king
*Vasukie, Vasuky, Vasukey,
Vasukee, Vasukea*

Vasuman (Indian) Son born
of fire

Vasyl (Slavic) A king
Vasil, Vassil, Wasyl

Vatsa (Indian) Our beloved son
Vathsa

Vatsal (Indian) One who is affectionate

Velimir (Croatian) One who wishes for great peace
Velimeer, Velimyr, Velimire, Velimeere, Velimyre

Velyo (Bulgarian) A great man
Velcho, Veliko, Velin, Velko

Vere (French) From the alder tree

Verge (Anglo-Saxon) One who owns four acres

Vernon (French) From the alder-tree grove
Vern, Vernal, Vernard, Verne, Vernee, Vernen, Verney, Vernin

Verrill (French) One who is faithful
Verill, Verrall, Verrell, Verroll, Veryl, Veryll, Verol, Verall

Vibol (Cambodian) A man of plenty
Viboll, Vibole, Vybol, Vyboll, Vybole

Victor (Latin) One who is victorious; the champion
Vic, Vick, Victoriano

Vidal (Spanish) A giver of life
Videl, Videlio, Videlo, Vidalo, Vidalio, Vidas

Vidar (Norse) Warrior of the forest; in mythology, a son of Odin
Vidarr

Vien (Vietnamese) One who is complete; satisfied

Vincent (Latin) One who prevails; the conquerer
Vicente, Vicenzio, Vicenzo, Vin, Vince, Vincens, Vincente, Vincentius

Viorel (Romanian) Resembling the bluebell
Viorell, Vyorel, Vyorell

Vipin (Indian) From the forest
Vippin, Vypin, Vypyn, Vyppin, Vyppyn, Vipyn, Vippyn

Vipul (Indian) A man of plenty
Vypul, Vipull, Vypull, Vipool, Vypool

Virag (Hungarian) Resembling a flower

Virgil (Latin) The staff-bearer
Verge, Vergil, Vergilio, Virgilio, Vergilo, Virgilo, Virgilijus

Virginius (Latin) One who is pure; chaste
Virginio, Virgino

Vitéz (Hungarian) A courageous warrior

Vito (Latin) One who gives life
*Vital, Vitale, Vitalis, Vitaly, Vitas,
Vitus, Vitali, Vitaliy, Vid*

Vitus (Latin) Giver of life
Wit

Vladimir (Slavic) A famous
prince
*Vladamir, Vladimeer,
Vladimyr, Vladimyre,
Vladamyr, Vladamyre,
Vladameer, Vladimer*

Vladislav (Slavic) One who
rules with glory

Volodymyr (Slavic) To rule
with peace
Wolodymyr

Vulcan (Latin) In mythology,
the god of fire
Vulkan, Vulckan

Vyacheslav (Russian) Form
of Wenceslas, meaning "one
who receives more glory"

W

Wade (English) To cross the
river ford
*Wayde, Waid, Waide, Waddell,
Wadell, Waydell, Waidell, Waed*

Wadley (English) From the
meadow near the ford
*Wadly, Wadlee, Wadli, Wadlie,
Wadleigh*

Wadsworth (English) From the
estate near the ford
*Waddsworth, Wadsworthe,
Waddsworthe*

Wafi (Arabic) One who is
trustworthy
*Wafie, Wafy, Wafey, Wafee,
Wafiy, Wafiyy*

Wahab (Indian) A big-hearted
man

Wainwright (English) One who
builds wagons
*Wainright, Wainewright,
Wayneright, Waynewright,
Waynwright*

Wakil (Arabic) A lawyer; a
trustee
*Wakill, Wakyl, Wakyle,
Wakeel, Wakeele*

Wakiza (Native American) A desperate fighter
Wakyza, Wakeza, Wakieza, Wakeiza

Walbridge (English) From the Welshman's bridge
Wallbridge, Walbrydge, Wallbrydge

Waljan (Welsh) The chosen one
Walljan, Waljen, Walljen, Waljon, Walljon

Walker (English) One who trods the cloth
Walkar, Walkir, Walkor

Wallace (Scottish) a Welshman, a man from the South
Wallach, Wallas, Wallie, Wallis, Wally, Wlash, Welch

Walter (German) The commander of the army
Walther, Walt, Walte, Walder, Wat, Wouter, Wolter, Woulter, Galtero, Quaid

Wamblee (Native American) Resembling an eagle
Wambli, Wamblie, Wambly, Wambley, Wambleigh, Wamblea

Wanikiy (Native American) A savior
Wanikiya, Wanikie, Wanikey, Waniki, Wanikee

Wanjala (African) Born during a famine
Wanjalla, Wanjal, Wanjall

Warford (English) From the ford near the weir
Warforde, Weirford, Weirforde, Weiford, Weiforde

Warley (English) From the meadow near the weir
Warly, Warleigh, Warlee, Warlea, Warleah, Warli, Warlie, Weirley

Warner (German) Of the defending army
Werner, Wernher, Warnher, Worner, Wornher

Warra (Aboriginal) Man of the water
Warrah, Wara, Warah

^**Warren** (English / German) From the fortress

Warrick (English) Form of Varick, meaning "a protective ruler"
Warrik, Warric, Warick, Warik, Waric, Warryck, Warryk, Warryc

Warrigal (Aboriginal) One who is wild
Warrigall, Warigall, Warigal, Warygal, Warygall

Warwick (English) From the farm near the weir
Warwik, Warwyck, Warwyk

Wasswa (African) The first-born of twins
Waswa, Wasswah, Waswah

Wasyl (Ukranian) Form of Vasyl, meaning "a king"
Wasyle, Wasil, Wasile

Watson (English) The son of Walter
Watsin, Watsen, Watsan, Watkins, Watckins, Watkin, Watckin, Wattekinson

^**Waylon** (English) From the roadside land

Wayne (English) One who builds wagons
Wain, Wanye, Wayn, Waynell, Waynne, Guwayne

Webster (English) A weaver
Weeb, Web, Webb, Webber, Weber, Webbestre, Webestre, Webbe

Wei (Chinese) A brilliant man; having great strength

Wenceslas (Polish) One who receives more glory
Wenceslaus, Wenzel, Vyacheslav

Wendell (German) One who travels; a wanderer
Wendel, Wendale, Wendall, Wendele, Wendal, Windell, Windel, Windal

Wesley (English) From the western meadow
Wes, Wesly, Wessley, Westleigh, Westley, Wesli, Weslie, Wesleigh

Westby (English) From the western farm
Westbey, Wesby, Wesbey, Westbi, Wesbi, Westbie, Wesbie, Westbee

^**Weston** (English) from the western town

Whit (English) A white-skinned man
White, Whitey, Whitt, Whitte, Whyt, Whytt, Whytte, Whytey

Whitby (English) From the white farm
Whitbey, Whitbi, Whitbie, Whitbee, Whytbey, Whytby, Whytbi, Whytbie

Whitfield (English) From the white field
Whitfeld, Whytfield, Whytfeld, Witfield, Witfeld, Wytfield, Wytfeld

Whitley (English) From the white meadow
Whitly, Whitli, Whitlie, Whitlee, Whitleigh, Whytley, Whytly, Whytli

Whitman (English) A white-haired man
Whitmann, Witman, Witmann, Whitmane, Witmane, Whytman, Whytmane, Wytman

Wildon (English) From the wooded hill
Willdon, Wilden, Willden

Wiley (English) One who is crafty; from the meadow by the water
Wily, Wileigh, Wili, Wilie, Wilee, Wylie, Wyly, Wyley

Wilford (English) From the willow ford
Willford, Wilferd, Willferd, Wilf, Wielford, Weilford, Wilingford, Wylingford

*ᵀWilliam (German) The determined protector
Wilek, Wileck, Wilhelm, Wilhelmus, Wilkes, Wilkie, Wilkinson, Will, Guillaume, Quilliam

Willow (English) Of the willow tree
Willowe, Willo, Willoe

Wilmer (German) A strong-willed and well-known man
Wilmar, Wilmore, Willmar, Willmer, Wylmer, Wylmar, Wyllmer, Wyllmar

Winston (English) Of the joy stone; from the friendly town
Win, Winn, Winsten, Winstonn, Wynstan, Wynsten, Wynston, Winstan

Winthrop (English) From the friendly village
Winthrope, Wynthrop, Wynthrope, Winthorp, Wynthorp

Winton (English) From the enclosed pastureland
Wintan, Wintin, Winten, Wynton, Wyntan, Wyntin, Wynten

Wirt (Anglo-Saxon) One who is worthy
Wirte, Wyrt, Wyrte, Wurt, Wurte

Wit (Polish) Form of Vitus, meaning "giver of life"
Witt

Wlodzimierz (Polish) To rule with peace
Wlodzimir, Wlodzimerz

Wolfric (German) A wolf ruler
Wolfrick, Wolfrik, Wulfric, Wulfrick, Wulfrik, Wolfryk, Wolfryck, Wolfryc

Wolodymyr (Ukranian) Form
of Volodymyr, meaning "to
rule with peace"
*Wolodimyr, Wolodimir,
Wolodymeer, Wolodimeer*

Woorak (Aboriginal) From the
plains
Woorack, Woorac

***Wyatt** (English) Having the
strength of a warrior
*Wyat, Wyatte, Wyate, Wiatt,
Wiatte, Wiat, Wiate, Wyeth*

Wyndham (English) From the
windy village
Windham

Xakery (American) Form of
Zachery, meaning "the Lord
remembers"
*Xaccary, Xaccery, Xach,
Xacharie, Xachery, Xack,
Xackarey, Xackary*

Xalvador (Spanish) Form of
Salvador, meaning "a savior"
*Xalvadore, Xalvadoro,
Xalvadorio, Xalbador,
Xalbadore, Xalbadorio,
Xalbadoro, Xabat*

Xannon (American) From an
ancient family
*Xanon, Xannen, Xanen,
Xannun, Xanun*

Xanthus (Greek) A blond-
haired man
Xanthos, Xanthe, Xanth

***Xavier** (Basque / Arabic)
Owner of a new house / one
who is bright
*Xaver, Xever, Xabier, Xaviere,
Xabiere, Xaviar, Xaviare,
Xavior*

Xenocrates (Greek) A foreign
ruler

Xesus (Galician) Form of
Jesus, meaning "God is my
salvation"

Xoan (Galician) Form of John,
meaning "God is gracious"
Xoane, Xohn, Xon

Xue (Chinese) A studious
young man

Yael (Israeli) Strength of God
Yaele

Yagil (Hebrew) One who rejoices, celebrates
Yagill, Yagyl, Yagylle

Yahto (Native American) Having blue eyes; refers to the color blue
Yahtoe, Yahtow, Yahtowe

Yahweh (Hebrew) Refers to God
Yahveh, Yaweh, Yaveh, Yehowah, Yehweh, Yehoveh

Yakiv (Ukranian) Form of Jacob, meaning "he who supplants"
Yakive, Yakeev, Yakeeve, Yackiv, Yackeev, Yakieve, Yakiev, Yakeive

Yakout (Arabian) As precious as a ruby

Yale (Welsh) From the fertile upland
Yayle, Yayl, Yail, Yaile

Yanai (Aramaic) God will answer
Yanae, Yana, Yani

Yankel (Hebrew) Form of Jacob, meaning "he who supplants"
Yankell, Yanckel, Yanckell, Yankle, Yanckle

Yaotl (Aztec) A great warrior
Yaotyl, Yaotle, Yaotel, Yaotyle

Yaphet (Hebrew) A handsome man
Yaphett, Yapheth, Yaphethe

Yaqub (Arabic) Form of Jacob, meaning "he who supplants"
Ya'qub, Yaqob, Yaqoub

Yardley (English) From the fenced-in meadow
Yardly, Yardleigh, Yardli, Yardlie, Yardlee, Yardlea, Yarley, Yarly

Yaromir (Russian) Form of Jaromir, meaning "from the famous spring"
Yaromire, Yaromeer, Yaromeere, Yaromyr, Yaromyre

Yas (Native American) Child of the snow

Yasahiro (Japanese) One who is peaceful and calm

Yasin (Arabic) A wealthy man
Yasine, Yaseen, Yaseene, Yasyn, Yasyne, Yasien, Yasiene, Yasein

Yasir (Arabic) One who is well-off financially
Yassir, Yasser, Yaseer, Yasr, Yasyr, Yassyr, Yasar, Yassar

Yegor (Russian) Form of George, meaning "one who works the earth; a farmer"
Yegore, Yegorr, Yegeor, Yeorges, Yeorge, Yeorgis

Yehonadov (Hebrew) A gift
from God
*Yehonadav, Yehonedov,
Yehonedav, Yehoash, Yehoashe,
Yeeshai, Yeeshae, Yishai*

Yenge (African) A hard-
working man
*Yengi, Yengie, Yengy, Yengey,
Yengee*

Yeoman (English) A man-
servant
Youman, Yoman

Yestin (Welsh) One who is just
and fair
Yestine, Yestyn, Yestyne

Yigil (Hebrew) He shall be
redeemed
*Yigile, Yigyl, Yigyle, Yigol,
Yigole, Yigit, Yigat*

Yishachar (Hebrew) He will be
rewarded
*Yishacharr, Yishachare,
Yissachar, Yissachare, Yisachar,
Yisachare*

Yiska (Native American) The
night has gone

Yngve (Scandinavian) Refers
to the god Ing

Yo (Cambodian) One who is
honest

Yoav (Hebrew) Form of Joab,
meaning "the Lord is my
father"
Yoave, Yoavo, Yoavio

Yochanan (Hebrew) Form
of John, meaning "God is
gracious"
*Yochan, Yohannan, Yohanan,
Yochannan*

Yohan (German) Form of
John, meaning "God is gra-
cious"
*Yohanan, Yohann, Yohannes,
Yohon, Yohonn, Yohonan*

Yonatan (Hebrew) Form of
Jonathan, meaning "a gift of
God"
*Yonaton, Yohnatan, Yohnaton,
Yonathan, Yonathon, Yoni,
Yonie, Yony*

Yong (Korean) One who is
courageous

York (English) From the yew
settlement
Yorck, Yorc, Yorke

Yosyp (Ukranian) Form of
Joseph, meaning "God will
add"
Yosip, Yosype, Yosipe

Yovanny (English) Form of Giovanni, meaning "God is gracious"
Yovanni, Yovannie, Yovannee, Yovany, Yovani, Yovanie, Yovanee

Yukon (English) From the settlement of gold
Youkon, Yucon, Youcon, Yuckon, Youckon

Yuliy (Russian) Form of Julius, meaning "one who is youthful"
Yuli, Yulie, Yulee, Yuleigh, Yuly, Yuley, Yulika, Yulian

Yuudai (Japanese) A great hero
Yudai, Yuudae, Yudae, Yuuday, Yuday

Yves (French) A young archer
Yve, Yvo, Yvon, Yvan, Yvet, Yvete

Z

Zabian (Arabic) One who worships celestial bodies
Zabion, Zabien, Zaabian

Zabulon (Hebrew) One who is exalted
Zabulun, Zabulen

Zacchaeus (Hebrew) Form of Zachariah, meaning "The Lord remembers"
Zachaeus, Zachaios, Zaccheus, Zackaeus, Zacheus, Zackaios, Zaccheo

Zachariah (Hebrew) The Lord remembers
Zacaria, Zacarias, Zaccaria, Zaccariah, Zachaios, Zacharia, Zacharias, Zacherish

*ᵀZachary (Hebrew) Form of Zachariah, meaning "The Lord remembers"
Zaccary, Zaccery, Zach, Zacharie, Zachery, Zack, Zackarey, Zackary, Thackary, Xakery

Zaci (African) In mythology, the god of fatherhood

Zaden (Dutch) A sower of seeds
Zadin, Zadan, Zadon, Zadun, Zede, Zeden, Zedan

Zadok (Hebrew) One who is righteous; just
Zadoc, Zaydok, Zadock, Zaydock, Zaydoc, Zaidok, Zaidock, Zaidoc

Zador (Hungarian) An ill-tempered man
Zador, Zadoro, Zadorio

Zafar (Arabic) The conquerer;
a victorious man
*Zafarr, Zaffar, Zhafar,
Zhaffar, Zafer, Zaffer*

Zahid (Arabic) A pious man
*Zahide, Zahyd, Zahyde,
Zaheed, Zaheede, Zaheide,
Zahiede, Zaheid*

Zahir (Arabic) A radiant and
flourishing man
*Zahire, Zahireh, Zahyr,
Zahyre, Zaheer, Zaheere,
Zaheir, Zahier*

Zahur (Arabic) Resembling a
flower
*Zahure, Zahureh, Zhahur,
Zaahur*

Zale (Greek) Having the
strength of the sea
*Zail, Zaile, Zayl, Zayle, Zael,
Zaele*

Zamir (Hebrew) Resembling a
songbird
*Zamire, Zameer, Zameere,
Zamyr, Zamyre, Zameir,
Zameire, Zamier*

Zander (Slavic) Form of
Alexander, meaning "a helper
and defender of mankind"
*Zandros, Zandro, Zandar,
Zandur, Zandre*

Zane (English) form of John,
meaning "God is gracious"
Zayne, Zayn, Zain, Zaine

Zareb (African) The protector;
guardian
*Zarebb, Zaareb, Zarebe,
Zarreb, Zareh, Zaareh*

Zared (Hebrew) One who has
been trapped
*Zarede, Zarad, Zarade,
Zaared, Zaarad*

Zasha (Russian) A defender of
the people
*Zashah, Zosha, Zoshah,
Zashiya, Zoshiya*

^**Zayden** (Arabic) Form of
Zayd, meaning "To become
greater, to grow"
Zaiden

Zeke (English) Form of
Ezekiel, meaning "strength-
ened by God"
Zekiel, Zeek, Zeeke, Zeeq

Zene (African) A handsome
man
Zeene, Zeen, Zein, Zeine

Zereen (Arabic) The golden
one
*Zereene, Zeryn, Zeryne, Zerein,
Zereine, Zerrin, Zerren, Zerran*

Zeroun (Armenian) One who is respected for his wisdom
Zeroune, Zeroon, Zeroone

Zeth (English) Form of Seth, meaning "one who has been appointed"
Zethe

Zion (Hebrew) From the citadel
Zionn, Zione, Zionne

Ziv (Hebrew) A radiant man
Zive, Ziiv, Zivi, Zivie, Zivee, Zivy, Zivey

Ziyad (Arabic) One who betters himself; growth
Ziad

Zlatan (Croatian) The golden son
Zlattan, Zlatane, Zlatann, Zlatain, Zlatayn, Zlaten, Zlaton, Zlatin

Zoltan (Hungarian) A kingly man; a sultan
Zoltann, Zoltane, Zoltanne, Zsolt, Zsoltan

Zorion (Basque) Filled with happiness
Zorian, Zorien

Zoticus (Greek) Full of life
Zoticos, Zoticas

Zsigmond (Hungarian) Form of Sigmund, meaning "the victorious protector"
Zsigmund, Zsigmonde, Zsigmunde, Zsig, Zsiga

Zubair (Arabic) One who is pure
Zubaire, Zubayr, Zubayre, Zubar, Zubarr, Zubare, Zubaer

Zuberi (African) Having great strength
Zuberie, Zubery, Zuberey, Zuberee, Zubari, Zubarie, Zubary, Zubarey

Zubin (English) One with a toothy grin
Zubine, Zuben, Zuban, Zubun, Zubbin

Zuzen (Basque) One who is just and fair
Zuzenn, Zuzan, Zuzin

Zvonimir (Croatian) The sound of peace
Zvonimirr, Zvonimeer

My Favorite Names

My Favorite Names

My Favorite Names

My Favorite Names

My Favorite Names

My Favorite Names

My Favorite Names

My Favorite Names

My Favorite Names

My Favorite Names